RIDING THE ROLLER COASTER

GREAT LAKES BOOKS

A complete listing of the books in this series can be found at the back of this volume.

PHILIP P. MASON, EDITOR
Department of History, Wayne State University

DR. CHARLES K. HYDE, ASSOCIATE EDITOR
Department of History, Wayne State University

a history of the

RIDING THE ROLLER COASTER

chrysler corporation

CHARLES K. HYDE

 WAYNE STATE UNIVERSITY PRESS DETROIT

Library of Congress Cataloging-in-Publication Data

Hyde, Charles K., 1945–
    Riding the roller coaster : a history of the Chrysler Corporation / Charles K. Hyde.
        p.   cm.
Includes bibliographical references and index.
    ISBN 0-8143-3091-6
    1. Chrysler Corporation.   2. DaimlerChrysler—History.   3. Daimler-Benz
Aktiengesellschaft.   4. Automobile industry and trade—Germany.   5. Automobile
industry and trade—United States.   6. Automobile industry and trade—Mergers.   I. Title.
    HD9710.U54   C467   2003
    338.7'6292'0973—dc21

2002008512

Published with the assistance of the UAW-DaimlerChrysler National Training Center

To the memory of Henry C. Hyde Sr. (1910–2001),
whose wonderful, well-worn 1957–60 Chrysler Imperials
were my introduction to the cars that Chrysler built.

CONTENTS

TABLES

The origins of this book go back to late 1980, when I took on the monumental task of documenting the sprawling Dodge Main factory complex in Hamtramck, Michigan, before its demolition. This was my first venture into Chrysler Corporation history, from which I quickly learned of the absence of any reliable business history of this important American corporation. I later documented Chrysler's Jefferson Avenue factory in Detroit and the company's headquarters and engineering complex in Highland Park, Michigan. Those projects gave me access to Chrysler's historical archives and a glimpse of the wealth of materials the company had saved. I later received permission from the Chrysler Corporation to use the corporate archives for this work, without restrictions, but this book is in no sense an "official" or "authorized" corporate history.

My research led me to write an 1,100-page (typescript) history of the Chrysler Corporation, filled with details that only the most avid automotive historian and Chrysler enthusiast would want to know. This book is a condensed version of that study, but with no major topic removed. Readers who would like to consult the unabridged history can find copies deposited at the DaimlerChrysler Historical Collection (Highland Park, Michigan), the Walter P. Chrysler Museum (Auburn Hills, Michigan), the National Automotive History Collection at the Detroit Public Library, and the Archives of Labor and Urban Affairs, Walter P. Reuther Library, Wayne State University.

The work of serious historical researchers depends greatly on the cooperation and assistance of archivist and librarians. I owe a great debt to Barbara M.

Fronczak, whose responsibilities as manager of the DaimlerChrysler Information Resource Center included the DaimlerChrysler Historical Collection. She not only arranged for access to this collection but constantly encouraged me to write "the definitive history of Chrysler." I am also grateful to Gene Weiss for his kind assistance and guidance over the four years or so I worked in the DaimlerChrysler Historical Collection. As a veteran of Chrysler and its archives, he knew where the "best stuff" could be found. I benefited greatly from the insight and good fellowship of other archives staffers, especially Rose Mary Lebryck, Marti Brown, Lou De Simone, and Charles Hanson. They made my days of research more enjoyable than I had imagined possible.

I am also grateful for the help and guidance of many other archivists. Mark Patrick of the National Automotive History Collection of the Detroit Public Library deserves special thanks. The late Dick Scharchburg of Kettering University in Flint, Michigan, helped me trace Walter Chrysler's days at Buick. I would also like to thank Dan Kirchner at the (now-defunct) American Automobile Manufacturers Association for allowing me access to its rich archives and library. Mike Smith at the Archives of Labor and Urban Affairs, Walter P. Reuther Library, Wayne State University, helped steer me through his institution's massive labor history collections, and Thomas Featherstone of the Reuther Library assisted me with the book's photographs.

The collections at a dozen additional archives were used in my research, but two were especially valuable. The Bentley Historical Library at the University of Michigan holds the Roy D. Chapin papers and other useful collections. The Hoover Institution Archives at Stanford University allowed me access to the unprocessed papers of B. E. Hutchinson, an important figure in the history of the Chrysler Corporation. I owe a special debt to Clifford L. Lockwood, who saved Chrysler's historical records and created the Chrysler Historical Collection in 1967.

Many friends and colleagues encouraged me to write this history, including Bob Casey, Mike Davis, Barry Dressel, and Tony Yanik. Arthur Evans, former director of the Wayne State University Press, strongly supported this project. I would especially like to thank Jane Hoehner, Wayne State University Press acquisitions editor, for pushing me and the book forward. Perhaps my greatest thanks goes to those who read draft versions this book, particularly Gene Weiss, Steve Babson, Jeff Godshall, Rudi Volti, and Larry Lankton. Any errors that remain are my responsibility alone.

The Chrysler Corporation, established in 1925, was the last of the "Big Three" American producers to enter the automobile industry, twenty-two years after the Ford Motor Company and seventeen years after the General Motors Corporation. Unlike Ford, which began as a cash-strapped newborn, or General Motors, which started off as a giant combination of dozens of automobile producers and suppliers, Chrysler was the reincarnation of the mid-sized Maxwell/Chalmers company. In its first three years as a separate entity, Chrysler enjoyed robust expansion, largely because of the energy and vision of Walter P. Chrysler.

Chrysler Corporation is an interesting case study of a relatively small latecomer into an industry dominated by General Motors and Ford. Chrysler became a major force in the American automobile industry in 1928, when it acquired Dodge Brothers and launched two entirely new car lines, Plymouth and DeSoto. Chrysler briefly became the second largest producer in North America in 1933, lost the spot to Ford in 1934–35, but then consistently held second place from 1936 through 1949. Chrysler slipped to third place in 1950, regained second in 1951 and 1952, but then permanently fell to third place in 1953. The company survived for much of its history on the strength of its automotive engineering. Chrysler can claim hundreds of significant "engineering firsts" in automobile design over the company's lifetime, as many as General Motors and Ford combined.

While the fortunes of all American car companies are sharply cyclical, the swings in Chrysler's economic fortunes were more frequent and more pronounced than those of its competitors. Under Walter P. Chrysler's disciplined and visionary direction, the company grew prodigiously in 1925–40 and was arguably the most successful American automaker of that era. Chrysler struggled to maintain its competitive position in 1941–50 while enjoying the artificial demands of wartime and the immediate postwar boom in auto sales.

Since 1950, Chrysler has remained in a perpetual cycle of serious economic crises followed by very sharp recoveries. The company has faced a major financial crisis every ten years, almost like clockwork, beginning in 1950. The long stretch extending from 1950 to 1978 was a period of chronic crisis and decline. From the arrival of Lee Iacocca in 1978 until the merger with Daimler-Benz in 1998, the Chrysler Corporation reinvented itself and achieved a good deal of success. The financial turmoil that began in 2000 at the Chrysler Group (division) of DaimlerChrysler is simply a repetition of a long-established pattern.

Chrysler's small size was one root cause of its roller-coaster history. The company always operated with a much smaller profit margin and with smaller cash reserves than its larger rivals. Mistakes in engineering or styling or in forecasting customers' preferences affected Chrysler much more than its competitors. Ford could overcome the disastrous Edsel and General Motors the equally costly Chevrolet Corvair fiasco, but faulty products such as the Dodge Aspen/Plymouth Volare line of cars nearly bankrupted Chrysler.

Chrysler made more mistakes than it could afford in part because it has lacked strong, experienced, and farsighted leadership for most of its history since the early 1950s. The company suffered from the lack of continuity in its top management from the 1950s on, particularly when contrasted with its principal rivals. At the Ford Motor Company, the continuing presence of a Ford family member either at the top executive level or directly offstage has brought a measure of management stability. At General Motors Corporation, Alfred P. Sloan Jr. established a management structure the early 1920s that produced a steady stream of competent executives experienced in the way the corporation operated.

Nearly every financial crisis at Chrysler brought new leadership and major changes in the company's products, market strategies, and policies, all reflecting the new boss's personality and preferences. The shifting interests, widely varying abilities, and distinctive visions of Chrysler's executives account for much of the company's turbulent past. A disastrous strike in 1950 helped bring Tex Colbert to power that year and he began a long-overdue upgrading of Chrysler's cars. A decade later, the departure of company president William Newberg amid a conflict of interest scandal catapulted Lynn Townsend to power and began another set of policy changes. A sales decline in 1968–70 brought Chrysler to the brink of bankruptcy, but Townsend survived. The company's virtual bankruptcy of 1978–80 brought Lee Iacocca and an all-new management team.

Chrysler was in the midst of another financial crisis when Iacocca finally retired in 1992 and Robert Eaton replaced him.

The company has also struggled for much of its history with the disruptive effects of mergers on managerial continuity. The Chrysler Corporation established in 1925 was initially nothing more than a renamed Maxwell Motor Corporation, itself a merger between companies producing Maxwell and Chalmers automobiles. In 1928, Chrysler took over Dodge Brothers, which had just merged with Graham Brothers, a truck manufacturer. Chrysler later took over the Briggs Manufacturing Company, a major independent body maker, in 1953. Finally, the Chrysler purchase of American Motors Corporation in 1987 was both disruptive and energizing. American Motors was itself the result of mergers of Nash-Kelvinator, Hudson, Kaiser Jeep, and other vehicle manufacturers. The recent combination of Chrysler and Daimler-Benz is simply the latest of many mergers that Chrysler has endured.

Chrysler Corporation developed a unique corporate personality and culture over its lifetime, distinct from those of General Motors and Ford. From the beginning, the company has produced innovative, "leading-edge" products, not always successfully. The 1924 Chrysler Six and the 1934 Chrysler/DeSoto Airflow are two early examples. In the 1950s and 1960s, Chrysler introduced production cars powered by Chrysler's Hemi engines and experimental cars with gas turbine engines. The so-called muscle cars of the 1970s and the innovative front-wheel drive vehicles of the 1970s and 1980s were also Chrysler firsts. More recently, minivans and the "cab-forward" sedans have continued this tradition.

Beginning with Walter P. Chrysler, the company has had innovative managers, engineers, and stylists who were willing to take risks. Chrysler Corporation historically has served as a haven for automotive malcontents, mavericks, and misfits, many coming over from rival companies. Chrysler's dashing, daring, risk-taking leaders achieved both monumental successes and colossal failures along the way. They helped produce the roller-coaster ride that best describes Chrysler's record—and that makes the company's history so intriguing.

BHL   Bentley Historical Library, University of Michigan, Ann Arbor, Michigan

DCHC   DaimlerChrysler Historical Collection, Detroit, Michigan

HFMGV   Research Center, Henry Ford Museum & Greenfield Village, Dearborn, Michigan

HIA   Hoover Institution Archives, Stanford University, Stanford, California

NAHC   National Automotive History Collection, Detroit Public Library, Detroit, Michigan

SA/KU   Scharchburg Archives, Kettering University, Flint, Michigan

WRL   Walter P. Reuther Library, Wayne State University, Detroit, Michigan

Chapter 1

FROM RAILROAD SHOP SWEEPER TO SECOND-IN-COMMAND AT GENERAL MOTORS

THE EARLY LIFE AND CAREER OF WALTER PERCY CHRYSLER

The fun I had experienced in making things as a boy was magnified a hundredfold when I began making things as a man. There is in manufacturing a creative joy that only poets are supposed to know. Some day I'd like to show a poet how it feels to design and build a railroad locomotive.

—Walter P. Chrysler

In December 1907, the Chicago Great Western Railroad named 33-year-old Walter P. Chrysler superintendent of motive power, with the responsibility of managing the railroad's locomotives and nearly 10,000 men. He was the youngest man ever to hold this position. Walter and his wife, Della Forker, enjoyed a comfortable life with their two children (Thelma and Bernice) in Oelwein, in the northeastern part of Iowa. His new job paid him a salary of $350 a month, respectable pay at a time when a skilled mechanic might earn $70 a month. He had come a long way from his first real job working as a railroad roundhouse sweeper earning $1 a day.

Early in the new year of 1908, Walter Chrysler made what turned out to be a momentous decision: he bought his first car. This was also a watershed year for the adolescent American automobile industry, marked by three events, both substantive and symbolic—William C. Durant's launch of the General Motors Company, Henry Ford's introduction of the Model T Ford, and the first American victory in the Vanderbilt Cup Race, won by a Locomobile. Walter Chrysler's purchase of his first automobile, also a Locomobile, was a defining moment in his life.

While visiting the 1908 Chicago Automobile Show, Chrysler admired a Locomobile touring car, white with a red leather interior. The price was $5,000 cash, but Chrysler had only $700 in family savings. Chrysler repeatedly asked an acquaintance, Ralph Van Vechten, vice president of the Continental National Bank of Chicago, for help in buying the Locomobile. The banker agreed to lend Chrysler the additional $4,300 only after Chrysler convinced William Causley,

1908 Locomobile Type I, seven-passenger touring car, the automobile that Walter P. Chrysler purchased in 1908. Courtesy of NAHC.

a Chicago Great Western official, to cosign the note. Because of the poor condition of the roads—and the fact that Chrysler did not know how to drive—he had the Locomobile shipped by rail to Oelwein and then hauled home by a team of horses.

Rather than drive his expensive toy, Walter Chrysler moved it into a barn behind his house. There he disassembled and reassembled the vehicle several times in order to understand the mechanical details of its design and operation. He read all the technical literature on automobile design that he could lay his hands on. Finally, three months after having the car delivered to Oelwein, he took it out for a spin, drove it off the road and into a neighbor's garden, and had to have it pulled out by a team of horses. The rest of the outing was more successful and by the end of the day, Walter Chrysler had learned to drive an automobile.[1]

RAILROAD MECHANIC AND LEADER OF MEN

Walter Chrysler's purchase of the Locomobile, much less his careful dissection of the automobile, would not have surprised anyone who knew about his early years in the railroad industry. The son of Henry (1850–1916) and Anna Marie Breymann Chrysler (1852–1926), he was born on 2 April 1875 in Wamego, Kansas, and grew up in Ellis, Kansas, where the Union Pacific Railroad operated substantial repair shops. His father worked for the Union Pacific as a locomotive engineer. Walter's first paid work as a youth involved selling calling cards, silverware, and milk from the family cows door-to-door. He worked as a delivery boy for a local grocery store one summer and again briefly after graduating from high school. Chrysler wanted to become an apprentice machinist with the railroad, but his father insisted that he to go to college instead. Defying the elder Chrysler, Walter worked as a sweeper for $1 a day at the Union Pacific shops in Ellis for six months before the master mechanic convinced his father to allow young Walter to enter the four-year apprentice program.[2]

As an apprentice, Chrysler fashioned his own tools, as was customary at the time. He began by making a set of calipers and a depth gauge. When only 18, Chrysler made a 28-inch operating model of the locomotive his father drove, complete with a tiny whistle. He built tracks in the yard of the family home and ran the locomotive for hours on end.[3]

During his apprenticeship in Ellis, Chrysler exhibited certain personality traits that would remain with him for the rest of his life. He was ambitious, adventuresome, and willing to take risks to advance in life. In his autobiography, *Life of an American Workman,* Chrysler conceded that he had a bad temper (a "short fuse") that got him into trouble as a youth and through middle age. He also developed a confidence in his own abilities that bordered on cockiness. He enjoyed the benefit of training with machinists who served as mentors, recognizing his intelligence and ambition. One such mentor was Arthur Darling, an old mechanic at the Ellis shops of the Union Pacific.

Darling taught Chrysler how to set the slide valve that controlled the intake and exhaust for each cylinder on a steam locomotive. Proper setting of the valve determined the power the locomotive would develop and was a prized skill. The locomotive manufacturer would set "port marks" on the valve gear showing the location of the piston at "top dead center," right at the end of the stroke of the (double-acting) piston. Because of wear and tear on the linkages between the piston and the valve gear, the manufacturer's port marks were always slightly off. Darling taught Walter Chrysler always to take—and trust—only his own port marks before setting valves. In his first effort as a journeyman machinist to set valves on a locomotive, he insisted on taking his own port marks, and successfully set the valves in record time. For the rest of his life, whenever Walter Chrysler heard a locomotive pulling a train, he could tell by the sound if the locomotive's valves were set properly.[4]

Chrysler had a lifelong intellectual curiosity about mechanical and scientific matters. While an apprentice, he wrote frequent letters to *Scientific American* requesting technical information on a variety of questions, including the chemical properties of acids. At work, he always tried to understand every operation and piece of machinery, even those not connected with his own job. He enrolled in dozens of correspondence courses, ranging from drafting to civil engineering, during his teens and twenties.[5]

At the end of his apprenticeship in 1897, Chrysler left Ellis at age 22 to work as a journeyman machinist for the Atchison, Topeka, and Santa Fe Railroad in Wellington, Kansas. He briefly returned to the Union Pacific shops in Ellis and then over the next three years held a series of short-lived jobs with more than a dozen western railroads.

Chrysler took a position in 1900 as a roundhouse machinist for the Denver & Rio Grande Western Railroad in Salt Lake City. A single incident there further boosted Chrysler's reputation and his self-confidence. In the fall of 1901, a locomotive returned to the roundhouse with a blown rear cylinder head, but the railroad needed the engine in only three hours for an important run to Denver. John Hickey, the master mechanic, asked Chrysler if he could complete the job in time and Chrysler responded, "If anybody can, I can." He handpicked two helpers and went to work before the fire was out of the locomotive's fire box. Replacing the cylinder head was normally a five-hour job, but Chrysler had the locomotive ready to run on time.

On 7 June 1901, Walter Chrysler married Della V. Forker (1877–1938), whom he had known from childhood. Although he enjoyed the challenges of life as an itinerant mechanic, Walter missed his family in Ellis and more important, his childhood sweetheart: "I knew the answer to my loneliness: Della Forker. We exchanged letters faithfully. She never wavered during that time when I was a wandering mechanic; she knew why I was roving, knew that she was completely interwoven with my ambitions."[6] Della Forker's role in understanding, tolerating, and supporting her husband through what must have been a maddening series of moves to new places and new jobs, sometimes with pay cuts, was critical to his career. How many women would understand a husband who would spend the entire family savings and borrow an additional $4,300 to buy a fancy Locomobile to tinker with?

Besides dedicating *Life of an American Workman* to Della Forker, Chrysler continually mentioned her unquestioned support of his ambition throughout the book. He would discuss any job move with her, but her typical response was, "Dad, if you think this is the place for us to go, don't worry about me. I'll be happy anywhere you think you ought to be to get ahead." Chrysler was specific in crediting Della with his own success: "Nothing in my life has given me more cause for pride and satisfaction than the way my wife had faith in me from the very first, through all those years when I was a grease-stained roundhouse mechanic."[7]

Chrysler's abilities as an all-around mechanic and his ambition brought him a series of quick promotions. In February 1902, at age 27, he became the roundhouse foreman at Denver & Rio Grande, the boss of 90 men.[8] He switched employers again in 1903 to become a general foreman for the Colorado & Southern Railroad shops in Trinidad, Colorado. Less than two years later, they promoted him to division master mechanic.[9]

This wandering railroad man was working as a master mechanic for the Fort Worth & Denver City Railroad in barren Childress, Texas, in 1906, when John E. Chisholm of the Chicago Great Western Railroad telegraphed him and offered him the job of master mechanic at the company's locomotive repair shops in Oelwein, Iowa.

Chrysler accepted the job offer from Chisholm in part because it paid $200 a month, some $40 a month more than he was earning in Texas. Beyond that, the modern state-of-the-art equipment in the Oelwein shops, reputedly the most advanced in the Midwest, were an attraction. Less than two years after Chrysler took control of the repair shops, he became superintendent of motive power for the entire Chicago Great Western system, which ran from Chicago to Oelwein and thence to Minneapolis. In December 1907, at age 32, he was in charge of 10,000 men, including engineers, firemen, and all the roundhouse and repair shop men. He was responsible for buying and maintaining millions of dollars' worth of equipment.[10]

Walter Chrysler's departure from the Chicago Great Western illustrates both his ambition and his hotheadedness. He recalled in his autobiography that he had concluded he had reached the limits of his career possibilities as superintendent of motive power. Of course, he could always take a similar position with higher pay at a larger railroad. However, the path to the top executive positions at the railroads was simply not open to men like him, coming from the mechanical or operational side of the business. Lawyers or finance men usually filled those positions.[11]

Matters came to a head in December 1909, when Samuel Morse Felton, the new president of the railroad, sent an urgent telegraph summoning Chrysler to his office in Chicago. Felton asked Chrysler to explain why one of the locomotives had developed a "hot box" and was three minutes late as a result. Enraged that Felton had questioned his competence, Chrysler quit on the spot, threw his railroad passes on the president's desk, and stomped out of the room.[12]

Chrysler telegraphed an old acquaintance, Waldo H. Marshall, the president of the American Locomotive Company (ALCO) and asked him for a job. Chrysler accepted a position as a general foreman at ALCO's Allegheny (Pittsburgh) shops, which manufactured locomotives. He took a pay cut, to $275 a month, which was a temporary setback, but the career switch opened better opportunities in the long run. Walter Chrysler was consistently a risk-taker throughout his life, willing to leave familiar jobs, sometimes taking pay cuts, to move into new arenas of opportunity. In a year and a half, Chrysler became the works manager at ALCO's Allegheny shops, and the operation turned a profit for the first time in three years. He was earning $8,000 a year, more than $650 a month, nearly double his peak railroad salary. In spring 1911, James J. Storrow, a director of American Locomotive, offered Chrysler an opportunity to work in the automobile industry.[13]

Storrow was the president of Lee, Higginson, and Company, one of the largest New York investment banks in the early twentieth century. By virtue of his firm's holdings, Storrow was a director of dozens of major American companies, including the General Motors Company. Chrysler's genius at organizing locomotive manufacturing efficiently and profitably had brought him to Storrow's attention. The investment banker called Chrysler to his New York office, where Storrow asked him if he might be interested in becoming the works manager for the Buick Motor Company in Flint, Michigan. Would Chrysler meet with Charles W. Nash, the president of Buick, in Pittsburgh? The railroad mechanic/locomotive manufacturer agreed to see Nash. He explained to Storrow that he had been thinking about automobile manufacturing for about five years, even before he bought the Locomobile. Chrysler saw automobile manufacturing as an up-and-coming industry because it provided personal transportation.

A week later, Chrysler and Nash met over lunch in Pittsburgh, and Chrysler agreed to come to Flint to view the Buick works. There he saw craftsmen hand-building automobiles much as they had hand-built fine wooden carriages. He saw an opportunity at Buick to immediately improve production and accepted the position. Nash asked him his current salary, which American Locomotive, in a last-minute bid to keep Chrysler, had just raised to $12,000 a year. The Buick president could offer a salary of only $6,000, which Chrysler promptly accepted, launching him into the industry where he would have a profound impact. Nash officially offered him the job on 30 November 1911, but Chrysler waited until January 1912 to move to Flint.[14]

CHRYSLER AT BUICK

Walter Chrysler enjoyed an extraordinarily successful initial stint in the automobile industry, first as Buick works manager (1912–16), then as general manager and president of Buick (general manager 1916–19 and president 1916–19), and finally, as executive vice president of General Motors (1919). He discovered right after arriving at Buick that not only was production still based on labor-intensive handicraft methods, but the plant management also had no system to determine the costs of production. His initial request for a copy of the schedule of piecework rates paid to workers produced a scribbled set of notes that would not permit serious cost analysis. Chrysler explained: "In the Allegheny works of American Locomotive, we had to bid $40,000 or so on a locomotive job; bidding low enough to get the job and still make a profit. The only way we could do that was to know to a penny what it was costing us to drill a hole and what it cost us to make an obscure little casting." In manufacturing locomotives, Chrysler also needed to know precisely how much time was needed for each job so he could coordinate the assembly of the final product. The absence of a cost accounting system at Buick simply appalled him.[15]

Much of the cost-cutting Chrysler achieved at Buick came from simple, commonsense rearranging of men's schedules and factory floor space. When he first arrived, Chrysler found teams of workers slowly and painstakingly assembling one car at a time on a fixed bench, with craftsmen painting the metal components in much the same way they had painted wooden carriage bodies decades earlier. Chrysler quickly reduced chassis assembly time from four days to two by eliminating unnecessary painting. In a later improvement, he cut the paint drying time in half by raising the temperature in the drying ovens. He greatly improved productivity at Buick's sheet metal plant by having the men who delivered raw materials and removed finished parts work during the lunch hour and for an extra hour at the end of the regular shift.

Buick's chassis assembly building, some 600 feet long, was a cluttered work space with a forest of timber posts no more than 20 feet apart supporting the roof. Walter Chrysler installed a superior roof truss that allowed him to eliminate most of the vertical posts. He also removed much of the clutter from the factory floor by simplifying the production process. At the same time Henry Ford was experimenting with an assembly line at his Highland Park factory, Walter Chrysler introduced a similar system at the Buick plant, pushing the unfinished chassis along tracks through the assembly area. Production immediately jumped from 45 cars a day to 75, and later reached 200 cars a day from the same factory space. Buick built 19,812 cars in 1912, but more than six times that many (124,834) in 1916, just four years after Chrysler took over.[16]

In 1915, some three years after coming to Buick, Walter Chrysler was still earning his initial $6,000 salary. He confronted Charles Nash and threatened to quit unless his pay was increased to $25,000. After consulting with James Storrow, Nash gave him the raise. Chrysler warned Nash that he would expect $50,000 the following year—given the profits he was generating for Buick, he would still be a bargain at that price. Besides, Buick was really the flagship division of General Motors through the 1910s and into the 1920s. Buick accounted for most of GM's profits and in some years was the only profitable division. Chevrolet did not become part of the giant automaker until 1916 and was not an instant success.[17]

Buick executives, November 1912. *Front row, from left to right,* purchasing agent Edward J. Copeland, consulting engineer Walter Marr, works manager Walter P. Chrysler, Buick president Charles W. Nash, sales manager Richard H. Collins, and Floyd A. Allen, assistant secretary and treasurer. Courtesy of SA/KU.

William C. Durant, the founder of General Motors, regained control of the company from the Storrow-led bankers in September 1915, but did not formally take the position of president from Charles Nash until 1 June 1916. In early 1916, Storrow tried to buy Packard Motor Car Company, with plans to have Nash and Chrysler operate it, but the effort failed. In June 1916, Storrow financed the purchase of the Jeffery Company in Kenosha, Wisconsin, so that Charles Nash could produce his own automobile. Chrysler had the opportunity to join the new Nash Motors Company.

Walter Chrysler and William C. Durant recalled quite different versions of Durant's efforts to keep him at Buick. According to Durant, Chrysler submitted a letter of resignation following Nash's departure as General Motors president in June 1916. Durant claimed that he immediately took the train to Flint from New York, appeared in Chrysler's office, and convinced him on the spot to stay at Buick. Chrysler claimed that he asked Durant for a 30-day delay so he could weigh his options.

Chrysler soon decided not to join Nash at Kenosha. This was a difficult decision for him; he felt indebted to Storrow and Nash for his position in the auto industry.[18] In the end he chose to remain at General Motors because the Nash operation was quite small and because Durant, who Chrysler said "could coax a bird out of a tree," appealed to his sense of loyalty to the men who had worked with him at Buick. Durant offered to pay him $500,000 a year for three years, with $10,000 a month in cash and the balance in cash or in General Motors stock, based on the current share price. The salary offer, some ten times what he was earning at the time, stunned Chrysler. He also found the stock options appealing and for the rest of his career at General Motors, Chrysler took stock instead of additional cash. One source claimed that Durant named him general manager of Buick on 29 June 1916, but Chrysler had to wait until 16 September to be officially named Buick president. He also served on the General Motors Board of Directors from 1916 on.[19]

Before accepting Durant's offer, Chrysler included one major condition, which Durant subsequently ignored: "I don't want interference. I don't want any other boss but you. If you feel that anything is going wrong, if you don't like some action of mine, you come to me; don't go to anybody else and don't split up my authority. Just have one channel from Flint to Detroit: from me to you. Full authority is what I want."[20]

Three months after Durant hired Chrysler as Buick president, the two men had their first of many run-ins. Durant promised an old friend the Buick sales branch in Detroit without consulting with Chrysler, who immediately confronted Durant in Detroit and forced him to rescind the commitment. The next year, Durant lured Buick's drop forge superintendent to run a plant in Detroit by offering him a 50 percent pay raise, but did this behind Chrysler's back. When Chrysler asked Durant to stick to a set of consistent company policies, Durant responded, "Walt, I believe in changing the policies just as often as my office door opens and closes."[21]

Much of what Chrysler accomplished at Buick was done despite Durant's chaotic management style and because of Chrysler's aggressive, "take-charge" approach. In the fall of 1917, Chrysler went to Durant's New York office to discuss possible war contracts, but upon seeing the office filled with hangers-on, he went instead directly to Washington, D.C., to the office of Colonel Edward Deeds, who managed aircraft production for the government. Within three hours, Chrysler had a contract to produce 3,000 Liberty aircraft engines. He returned to Flint with a roll of blueprints. He and his production staff, headed by K. T. Keller, the 30-year-old Buick master mechanic and later president of the Chrysler Corporation, worked around the clock for two weeks preparing blueprints for the tooling needed for this job. This is just one of many examples of the "can-do" attitude of automobile manufacturers when it came to making weapons in wartime.

Ford Motor Company was to supply Buick with cylinders for the Liberty engine but was slow in delivering the required quantities, in part because Ford was struggling to produce cylinder heads for the same motor. Buick was making cylinder heads efficiently, so Chrysler agreed to supply Ford with the heads if

Ford increased its deliveries of cylinders. Buick delivered the first Liberty engines for testing only two months after Chrysler made the trip to Washington.[22]

By the end of the war, Buick had built 1,338 Liberty engines—and 13,500 trucks. 11,000 sets of truck axles, 397,000 cartridge containers, 1.2 million three-inch mortar shells, 1.2 million mortar bases, and 1.05 million shell casings. Buick also manufactured ambulances and military tractors for the British government. The Buick engineering/manufacturing staff, led by Chrysler and Keller, showed how quickly an automobile company could convert to military production.[23]

Durant named Chrysler executive vice president of General Motors Company by the end of 1918, giving him broad responsibility for all operations of the giant corporation. Harry H. Bassett succeeded Chrysler as Buick general manager in 1919 and became president of Buick on 13 January 1920, ten weeks after Walter P. Chrysler's resignation.[24]

Little is known about Walter Chrysler's final years at General Motors because there are few surviving documents. Scattered letters and other materials offer only occasional glimpses of his work at the giant automaker. The few documents that exist show him struggling with day-to-day management and long-term planning for this sprawling enterprise. He spent much of his time simply trying to gain control over General Motors' enormous, far-flung operations. A new management structure put in place by Alfred Sloan Jr. in the early 1920s finally allowed for rational control and management of this huge enterprise, but by this time Chrysler had left the company.[25]

Chrysler also became involved in decisions that had little direct connection with managing automobile production. Because of severe housing shortages in Flint and Pontiac, General Motors got into the business of building affordable housing for its workers. On 1 February 1919, Chrysler announced in the *Flint Daily Journal* that GM had bought the property of the Civic Building Association and would build 1,000 houses on this site, known as Civic Park. In April 1919, GM created a subsidiary, the Modern Housing Corporation, to build houses in Flint and Pontiac. Initially capitalized at $3.5 million, Modern Housing eventually built 950 homes, mainly in the first two years of its existence.[26]

The inevitable break between Chrysler and Durant came in the summer of 1919. Chrysler was on the verge of signing a contract with the A. O. Smith Company of Milwaukee to supply Buick with frames, a contract that would save GM $1.75 million a year over five years. He had kept Durant fully informed of the negotiations as they moved forward. At a Flint Chamber of Commerce luncheon, J. Dallas Dort, an old business partner of Durant, read a telegraph from Durant announcing that Buick would build a $6 million frame plant in Flint. Chrysler then addressed the meeting and informed the chamber that General Motors would *not* build this plant as long as he was with the corporation.

At a General Motors Board of Directors' meeting in Detroit the following day, Chrysler openly and bitterly lambasted Durant for making such an unwise business decision and for doing so without consulting with him. He doubted Durant's cost estimate of $6 million to build the plant and argued that it would take GM at least three years to learn to run it effectively. Chrysler's judgment prevailed here, but it marked the end of his business relationship with Durant. He had previously vigorously disagreed with Durant's decisions to invest in a tractor company, the Janesville (Wisconsin) Machine Company, and to build the $20 million General Motors Building in Detroit.[27]

In the wake of these confrontations with Durant, Chrysler announced that he was quitting General Motors. Alfred P. Sloan Jr. and J. Amory Haskell tried to get him to reconsider, but Chrysler was adamant. In late summer 1919, Chrysler, along with most of GM's Executive Committee, traveled to Europe on the S.S. *France* to evaluate the properties of the French Citroën Company. (The group ultimately decided not to buy the French automaker because it had antiquated factories and the French government opposed the plan.) The committee invited Chrysler in part to induce him to reconsider his decision to leave GM. This pleasant overseas trip did not, however, change Chrysler's mind.[28]

Chrysler sent letters to many colleagues, including Charles F. Kettering, his longtime associate at Delco, on 28 October 1919 announcing his departure effective 31 October. Chrysler's letter to Kettering declared, "My association with you has been a source of pride as well as pleasure and I earnestly hope our friendship will continue and we may see each other frequently." Kettering responded a few days later: "There are just a few men in the world that I can stand on my head in the middle of the street for, and you are one of them."[29]

After leaving General Motors, Chrysler commuted daily from Flint to his office in Detroit, while telling his wife that he planned to retire. He entertained a steady stream of old friends and business acquaintances at his Flint home, driving Della Chrysler to exasperation. Sometime in late 1919, Chrysler's old banker friend, Ralph Van Vechten, who had helped finance his purchase of the Locomobile back in 1908, offered him a job. Van Vechten asked him to rescue the Willys-Overland Company from bankruptcy, and Chrysler agreed to take on this new challenge. He demanded a two-year contract at an annual salary of $1 million, the right to live in New York City and to manage Willys from its plant in Elizabeth, New Jersey, and the power to make any changes he thought necessary. The bankers agreed and announced Chrysler's appointment as executive vice president and general manager of Willys-Overland in early January 1920. John North Willys would remain as the titular head, but Walter Chrysler would have the authority to make all decisions.[30]

Flint's major business and professional clubs gave Chrysler a testimonial dinner on 22 January 1920 at the Flint County Club. With J. Dallas Dort serving as the toastmaster, industry leaders, including Charles Stewart Mott, representing General Motors, and John N. Willys, President of Willys-Overland Company, offered tributes. C. M. Greenway, representing the community, and Chrysler's close friend John J. Carton offered gushing praise. The honors included five songs expressing appreciation for Chrysler and his work.[31]

Perhaps even more telling was the tribute to Chrysler published in the *Flint Weekly Review*, the "Official Organ of the Flint Federation of Labor." The author was the Reverend J. Bradford Pengelly from St. Paul's Episcopal Church in Flint. He praised Chrysler for his fairness in dealing with all of his employees and for pushing General Motors to build houses for its employees: "He wanted these homes not only because of the theory that good homes increase the contentment of the men and therefore increases productivity, but because he was fond of the men and their families and actually wanted them to be comfortable and contented. This is his humanness. These men are his co-workers and his friends and that is why he wanted them to have good homes." In closing, the Reverend Pengelly said the following of Chrysler: "He is a big, honest, human-hearted man who has worked up from the ranks to the managership of one of the biggest factories in the U.S.A. He has never forgotten that he was once a private and has never put on airs of a general or grand mogul. He is as honest as the day is long, and as square as can be. I would take his word as quickly as his bond."[32]

Once Chrysler left General Motors, he was anxious to sell the stock he had accumulated during his three years as president of Buick. He drew a salary of $120,000 per year, but took $380,000 per year in stock, with a paper value of $1,140,000. General Motors stock prices, however, had risen sharply during Chrysler's tenure there. In early 1920, Durant offered to buy Chrysler's shares for his own account for $10 million in cash and Chrysler accepted, although the stock had a higher market value at the time. He was grateful to Durant for his past generosity. Durant paid Chrysler $2.5 million on the spot, with three equal payments of $2.5 million due at three, six, and nine months. The former shop sweeper walked away from General Motors at age 44 with $10 million in cash.[33]

Chrysler and Durant remained lifelong friends despite their often-contentious working relationship. Durant began writing an autobiography in 1939, but finished only a small part of it before his death in 1947. He sent a copy of the dedication page to Walter Chrysler and others in late 1939. "My Autobiography," as he called his book, was "Dedicated to Walter P. Chrysler, the best friend I ever had," and to seven others, including Alfred Sloan Jr. and Charles S. Mott. According to Walter Chrysler's secretary, F. A. Morrison, Chrysler cried when he read the dedication.[34]

January 1920 marked another period of transition for Walter Chrysler. His agreement with the bankers who controlled Willys-Overland allowed him to run the company from New York City. He lived in New York and commuted by train to a factory Willys-Overland had rebuilt at Elizabeth, New Jersey. In New York, he initially lived at the Biltmore Hotel, and then his family moved into an apartment in the Carlton House. Later, in 1923, he bought an estate (King's Point) at Great Neck on Long Island, where he lived until his death in 1940.[35]

Walter Chrysler had advanced in his working career from earning $1 a day sweeping floors in the Union Pacific shop in Ellis, Kansas, to becoming a "million-dollar-a year man" in 1920, a white knight capable of rescuing bankrupt automobile companies. As businessmen go, he was hardly an overnight success. Chrysler was 48 when the first car bearing his name appeared on the automobile market. His successes reflected his personality and character—his intelligence and intellectual curiosity, his appetite for learning, his ability to lead men and get the best from them, his desire to work hard and to "do the job right," and his willingness to take risks in order to create new opportunities for himself.

Chapter 2

ROOTS: WILLYS-OVERLAND, CHALMERS, AND MAXWELL

I believe that [Walter P.] Chrysler is conceded to be the best automobile manufacturer in the industry; at least, that is the reputation he bears everywhere.

—Hugh Chalmers

Chrysler Corporation descended from three pioneer automobile companies—Willys-Overland, Chalmers, and Maxwell—which struggled in a highly competitive industry and survived only because of Walter P. Chrysler's business genius. Their histories illustrate the difficulty of achieving long-term success in the adolescent Detroit automobile industry in the 1910s and 1920s. In 1908, 253 firms manufactured automobiles in the United States. Despite scores of new entrants into the industry after 1908, only 44 companies remained in operation in 1929. The Chrysler Corporation was one of the survivors and by 1929 had become the third largest American automobile company.[1]

The design, production, and sales of the first automobile to bear the Chrysler name took place before there was a business entity called the Chrysler Corporation. The first Chrysler car was indeed the child of Walter P. Chrysler, but the Maxwell Motor Corporation introduced the new model and manufactured it in a factory originally built by the Chalmers-Detroit Company. The tale is even more complicated because the Willys-Overland Company had earlier planned to produce the first car to bear the Chrysler nameplate at its factory at Elizabeth, New Jersey. One line of roots of the Chrysler family tree involved the Willys-Overland Company, established by John North Willys in 1908. A second set of roots extends back to the E. R. Thomas-Detroit Company (1906), later the Chalmers Motor Corporation. The third set goes back to the formation of the Maxwell-Briscoe Motor Company in 1904.

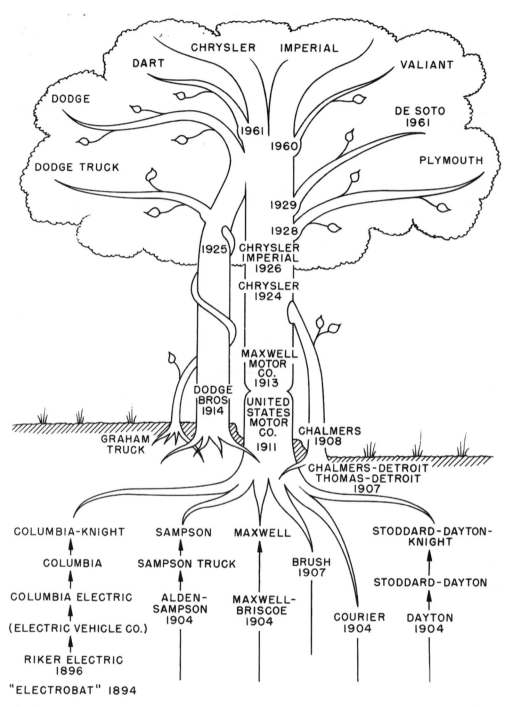

Chrysler Corporation family tree, 1961. Courtesy of DCHC.

WILLYS-OVERLAND

The origins of the Chrysler car extend back to Walter P. Chrysler's service as a "white knight" trying to rescue Willys-Overland starting in January 1920. Six months later, he convinced the engineering trio of Fred M. Zeder, Owen Skelton, and Carl Breer to leave the Studebaker Corporation and join him at Willys. Zeder had worked for Studebaker since 1912 and recruited Skelton and Breer to join him there in 1916. By late 1919, Zeder and his associates had a serious falling-out with Albert R. Erskine, president of the Studebaker Corporation. After promising Zeder ultimate authority over all engineering decisions, Erskine established a new department that passed judgment on the Zeder-Skelton-Breer decisions.[2]

According to Breer's reminiscences, a Detroit tailor named A. G. Brown, who knew all the top automobile executives because he made their suits, urged him to contact Chrysler. Donald S. Devour, the general manager of Willys-Overland, had known Zeder and Breer from his days at the Allis-Chalmers Company in Milwaukee and strongly recommended them to Walter Chrysler. The engineering trio visited Chrysler in New York and toured the new Elizabeth, New Jersey, factory before deciding to accept his offer.

Officially under contract with Willys-Overland on 14 July 1920, the Zeder-Skelton-Breer team moved to New Jersey, bringing twenty-eight men from Studebaker's engineering department. Walter Chrysler said of them: "Those three young automotive engineers were wizards. . . . You never would find, hunt high or low, three friends more harmoniously attuned, unless it might be those men of fiction, the Three Musketeers." The Zeder-Skelton-Breer (ZSB) partnership was the foundation for Chrysler's engineering leadership in the automobile industry for a quarter of a century.[3]

Walter Chrysler hired the ZSB team to create an engineering department at Willys's Elizabeth, New Jersey, plant and to bring into production the already-designed Willys Light Six, which was merely the Willys Four with a six-cylinder engine and a longer wheelbase. Testing of the new model, however, revealed fundamental design flaws that resulted in premature breaking of the car's springs, frame, and body. Chrysler decided to scrap that car entirely and have the ZSB team design a "hurried replacement car," to be manufactured at the Elizabeth factory by summer 1921. This Light Six featured a six-cylinder in-line engine, an updraft carburetor, and semielliptic front and rear springs, a far superior car than the existing Willys models.[4]

The new car would bear Walter Chrysler's name and would be produced by the Chrysler Motor Company, incorporated in Delaware in July 1920. Chrysler Motor was a division of the Willys Corporation, a holding company that included all of John North Willys's various enterprises, including Willys-Overland. The Willys Corporation announced in late October 1920 that the new model would be in production by spring of 1921. A rare photograph shows a large electric sign reading, "CHRYSLER—The Six Cylinder Motor Car," atop the roof of the Elizabeth factory. Engineering drawings for an automobile, prepared in October and November 1920, are also labeled, "Chrysler Motor Company, Division of Willys Corporation, Elizabeth, N.J."[5]

Willys-Overland went into receivership on 30 November 1921 without producing the Chrysler car. The receivers offered the Elizabeth plant and the ZSB blueprints for sale at an auction on 9 June 1922. Serious bidders included the Maxwell Motor Corporation and William C. (Billy) Durant's new enterprise, Durant Motors. Durant bought the plant and the plans for a new car with a bid of $5,525,000. He used the factory to produce the Star automobile and the ZSB design became the Flint automobile, manufactured in Flint, Michigan.[6]

One intriguing result of the sale of the Elizabeth factory and the plans for the ZSB car was a failed effort by Zeder to produce a car on his own. *Automobile Manufacturer* announced in March 1922 the formation of the Zeder Motor Company, which "plans to begin the manufacture of the Chrysler Motor Car at the plant of the Cleveland Tractor Co., Cleveland." A collection of sketches and drawings in the DaimlerChrysler Historical Collection suggest that the Zeder car was more than a fantasy of Fred Zeder. Several designers produced more than a dozen potential automobile emblems for Zeder, all featuring a stylized letter "Z" with a bolt of lightning passing through the middle. One version incorporated the names of White and Zeder into the letter. Rollin H. White, one of the White brothers of Cleveland, known for the White steam and gasoline cars, owned the Cleveland Tractor Company and planned to build the Zeder car.[7]

CHALMERS

One branch of the Chrysler root system was a series of car companies that evolved into the Chalmers Motor Corporation in 1916 and became a wholly-owned subsidiary of the Maxwell Motor Corporation in 1922. After Ransom Olds lost a battle with the majority stockholders of the Olds Motor Works in 1906 over the future car lines that Olds would manufacture, four of Olds's executives resigned from the firm—Howard E. Coffin (chief engineer), Roy D. Chapin (sales manager), Fred O. Bezner (purchasing agent), and James J. Brady (traffic manager). Chapin convinced Erwin R. Thomas, founder of the E. R. Thomas Motor Company (1902–12), based in Buffalo, New York, to finance a Detroit subsidiary to produce a lightweight, low-priced car that Thomas could sell as a companion to his luxury models. Thomas and the former Olds executives established the E. R. Thomas-Detroit Company on 2 May 1906, with

$300,000 of stock (half paid-in). Thomas invested $100,000, received two-thirds of the stock, and agreed to sell the car through his established dealer network. The four Detroit investors committed $50,000 and received the remaining third of the stock.[8]

Although Thomas-Detroit was successful in selling its first cars, Roy Chapin worried about the firm's dependence on the Thomas sales network. Chapin convinced Hugh Chalmers (1873–1932) to leave his position as vice president and general manager of the National Cash Register Company in Dayton, Ohio, to become president of Thomas-Detroit and to create an effective independent sales organization. Chalmers purchased half of E. R. Thomas's stock late in 1907 and agreed to take control of Thomas-Detroit. At a meeting of the company directors on 3 December 1907, E. R. Thomas resigned as president, and the directors elected Hugh Chalmers in his place. On 15 June 1908, the stockholders voted to rename the firm Chalmers-Detroit Motor Company, and on 26 January 1910, they changed the name to Chalmers Motor Company.[9]

Chalmers-Detroit enjoyed great success starting in 1908. For the year that ended 30 June 1909, sales of 3,047 cars yielded revenues of $4,754,929 and profits of $1,015,823 at a time when the paid-in capital stock was only $300,000. Two of Howard Coffin's coworkers from Olds, Roscoe Jackson and Howard Dunham, designed a new lightweight car, the Model 20, designed to sell for under $1,000, but Chapin and Coffin were unable to interest Hugh Chalmers in the project. In February 1909, the original Detroit investors (Chapin, Coffin, Bezner, and Brady) established the Hudson Motor Car Company as a subsidiary of Chalmers-Detroit to manufacture the new car. A key player was Roscoe Jackson, who was married to the niece of Detroit department store magnate Joseph L. Hudson, who invested $90,000 in the venture and gave his name to the company. The Chalmers and Hudson firms went their separate ways in December 1909.

Chapin's fears concerning the future of the Chalmers firm were well founded—over the decade that followed, the Hudson company prospered and the Chalmers company struggled. The design of the Chalmers Model 30 remained frozen from 1908 through 1913, while its price rose above $2,000. Still, Chalmers's sales of 6,350 cars in 1910 put the firm in ninth place among U.S. producers. The Chalmers Motor Company made 9,833 cars in 1915 and reorganized as the Chalmers Motor Car Corporation the following year.

Hugh Chalmers was a brilliant salesman who was not able to attract and keep competent, energetic engineers and production men after the defection of Roy Chapin and his partners to Hudson. Chalmers showed his 1916 models to his dealers in November 1915 and sold 13,000 cars worth $22 million in less than an hour. His friend Eugene Lewis wrote of him, "If Hugh had been as fine a manufacturer as he was a salesman, his car would probably be well-known

Chalmers Motor Corporation Jefferson Avenue plant, Detroit, 1920. Courtesy of NAHC.

today." By the end of 1915, the firm owned real estate and machinery worth more than $8 million and had between 7,000 and 8,000 employees. One newspaper reported that in 1915 Chalmers earned more than $1 million a year.[10]

The Chalmers Motor Company struggled to survive because it was a low-volume, high-cost producer. The firm assembled roughly 6,200 cars per year in 1910–14, then increased output to 9,833 units in 1915, and reached an all-time peak of 21,408 cars in 1916. In May 1916, Hugh Chalmers argued that the company should increase production to 60,000 cars per year and reduce prices, or alternatively, raise prices and reduce output. The actual results achieved in 1916 illustrate the problems the company faced. The Chalmers factory increased production in the first six months of the year and the sales department shipped cars to the dealers without regard to demand. Chalmers distributors in Dallas and Omaha had a year's supply of cars on hand. Hugh Chalmers was then forced to cut production from 15,659 units in the first half of 1916 to only 5,749 cars over the second half. From 1910 through 1917, Chalmers remained a struggling automobile manufacturer with excess factory capacity.[11]

The Maxwell Motor Company bailed out Chalmers by leasing its plants for five years beginning 1 September 1917. The Chalmers Motor Company issued $3.15 million in mortgage bonds and provided Maxwell with $3 million to use as working capital. Maxwell agreed to keep the Chalmers car in production and maintain its good name and reputation. Maxwell also agreed to pay the interest on the mortgage bonds and to pay the Chalmers company half of the net profits earned on all automobiles produced in the Chalmers plants. Walter E. Flanders, already president of the Maxwell Motor Company, became president of Chalmers, and Hugh Chalmers "moved upstairs" to become chairman of the board.

The Maxwell and Chalmers firms had the same managers from 1917 on but did not fully merge until 1922. Maxwell produced the Chalmers line of cars through 1923, but lost millions in the process.[12]

MAXWELL

Another major part of Chrysler's heritage extends back to 1904, when Jonathan Dixon Maxwell (1864–1928) and Benjamin Briscoe (1867–1945) founded the Maxwell-Briscoe Motor Company. Maxwell, a graduate of the Olds Motor Works, had designed a new automobile but lacked funds to start production. Briscoe, a successful manufacturer of sheet metal goods, turned to New York City and the J. P. Morgan banking interests to raise the $250,000 needed to get started.

The Maxwell was a well-built, popular model, with sales increasing from only 540 cars in 1904 to more than 8,000 in 1908, making Maxwell-Briscoe one of the largest producers in the industry. By 1910, the firm operated factories in Tarrytown, New York; Pawtucket, Rhode Island; Newcastle (later New Castle), Indiana; and Detroit (Highland Park).[13]

In February 1910, Benjamin Briscoe launched the United States Motor Company with $30 million in backing from several New York investment bankers. The new giant quickly bought nine firms that manufactured parts or assembled complete automobiles. These included Maxwell-Briscoe, Briscoe Manufacturing Company, Columbia Motor Car Company, Brush Runabout Company, Gray Motor Company, Grabowsky Motor Vehicle Company, and the Alden-Sampson Company. Few of the United States Motor Company's scores of models sold well and in September 1912, the firm went into receivership.[14]

Parts of the conglomerate, such as Columbia Motor Company, hung on briefly, but the Maxwell Motor Company, incorporated on 31 December 1912, was the only unit that survived for very long. The United States Motor Company creditors dumped Benjamin Briscoe and turned over control to Walter E. Flanders, a veteran automobile manufacturer who had worked for Ford, E-M-F, and Studebaker. Flanders then reorganized the remains of United States Motor Company as the Maxwell Motor Company.[15]

The new company enjoyed respectable sales and profits under Flanders's direction in 1914–18. Flanders introduced an entirely new four-cylinder Maxwell 25 in late 1913, priced at $750. This was an innovative design featuring a cone clutch and an engine with a removable head. Sales jumped from 17,000 in 1914 to 75,000 in 1917, when Maxwell also produced 25,000 trucks that used the same engine. Maxwell sales in 1919 stood at 50,000 cars, but production in 1920, initially planned for 80,000 cars, amounted to only 34,168. Sales suffered not only from the severe postwar recession of 1920–21 but also from a reputation of poor design. By the summer of 1920, the Maxwell Motor Company was $26 million in debt and on the brink of bankruptcy.[16]

Enter Walter Percy Chrysler, already hard at work trying to revive another gravely ill patient, the Willys-Overland Company. The same bankers who brought Chrysler to Willys also controlled Maxwell and convinced Chrysler to reorganize and save that ailing company. In August 1920, Walter Chrysler agreed to head a reorganization committee consisting of Maxwell's bankers and other creditors, but only if the stockholders of the reorganized company gave him an additional $15 million in working capital.

When Chrysler came on board at Maxwell, the company had unsold inventories of some 26,000 cars with damaged reputations because of poorly designed axles that frequently broke when driven on rough roads. He recalled the defective cars, strengthened their axles with braces, and then slashed prices to get rid of them. With these moves, Chrysler reduced inventories some $11 million and convinced Maxwell's banks to extend him another $12 million line of credit.[17]

Delays in the Maxwell takeover of Chalmers, which had begun in 1917, complicated Walter P. Chrysler's financial and managerial reorganization of Maxwell in 1920–22. It is hard to summarize the tangled tendrils of the Maxwell-Chalmers relationship. As Chalmers's fortunes declined after 1917 and Maxwell's performance improved, the original lease proved increasingly disadvantageous for Maxwell's owners. They were losing money on the Chalmers brand but sharing their profits on the more successful Maxwell car with the Chalmers stockholders. Stockholders from both firms agreed to modify the original lease and merge the two firms, but resistance from some Chalmers stockholders and threats of lawsuits delayed the merger.[18]

Walter Chrysler had the double burden of reviving Maxwell, which was sick, and Chalmers, which was even sicker. Chalmers's sales in 1920 (nearly 10,000 cars) were about one-third of Maxwell's sales of 34,000 cars, but in 1921, when Maxwell sales fell to 16,000, Chalmers sold only about 3,000 vehicles. Production of Chalmers cars in 1922 came to only 3,978 units, an especially anemic performance contrasted with Maxwell's strong sales of 48,883 cars. Maxwell had earned profits of $2,018,266 for the calendar year 1922, but Chalmers's losses for the year ($1,325,524) reduced Maxwell's net profit to only $700,000.

The long-running disagreements between the Chalmers and Maxwell stockholders finally ended with a U.S. District Court decree dated 3 November 1922 settling a lawsuit brought by the Fisk Rubber Company against Chalmers. The court placed the Chalmers company into receivership and ordered its property sold at an auction. The Maxwell Motor Corporation bought the Chalmers property on 7 December 1922 for $1,987,600, completing the takeover that had

Maxwell Motor Corporation, Oakland Avenue plant, Highland Park, Michigan, 1920.
Courtesy of NAHC.

begun in 1917. The Maxwell Motor Corporation produced its last Chalmers cars
in 1923 while preparing to launch the first Chrysler models.[19]

Walter Chrysler's greatest accomplishment at Maxwell before introducing the
Chrysler Six was the restoration of the Maxwell cars' reputation. For the 1921
model year, Walter Chrysler equipped the Maxwell cars with a new axle, dubbed
these "improved" models the Good Maxwell, and used the slogan in newspaper
and magazine advertising. In July 1922, a New Series Maxwell appeared in showrooms, sporting minor design changes. The revamped model had aluminum
pistons instead of cast-iron ones and featured a three-bearing crankshaft. Still,
it remained essentially the same Model 25 introduced in 1918, with a four-cylinder 21 horsepower (hp) engine and a 108-inch wheelbase.[20]

The sales performance of the Maxwell-Chalmers-Chrysler enterprise is not
well documented. The best available information is presented in table 2.1.

DESIGNING THE CHRYSLER SIX

Walter Chrysler's successful restoration of the Maxwell car's good name and the
profitability of the company was merely preparation for his more important
ambitions: taking control of the Maxwell Motor Corporation and manufacturing an innovative new car under his own name. This goal was the overriding
motive for most of Walter Chrysler's actions after June 1920.

25 Miles to the Gallon

58 Miles per Hour

5 to 25 Miles in 8 Seconds

Startling good news to tens of thousands—the first announcements of the new good Maxwell's amazing results. Never since the Chrysler took the country by storm has the automobile industry known such whole-hearted response—such a dramatic and decisive triumph.

Not content with designing into this car power and pick-up equaled only in the higher priced fields, Chrysler engineering genius and fine manufacturing facilities enable the new good Maxwell owner to enjoy these performance advantages with unparalleled economy.

In almost sensationally low cost of operation and maintenance —as in speed and acceleration—this great car has written a wholly new page in motor car achievement, and in the accomplishment of the great organization which builds the Maxwell.

Balloon tires, natural wood wheels, stop-light, transmission lock, Duco finish standard on all Maxwell models. Shrouded visor integral with roof, heater, standard on all closed models.

Touring Car, $895; Club Coupe, $995; Club Sedan, $1045; Standard Four-Door Sedan, $1095; Special Four-Door Sedan, $1245. All prices f. o. b. Detroit, Tax extra.

There are Maxwell dealers and superior Maxwell service everywhere. All dealers are in position to extend the convenience of time-payments. Ask about Maxwell's attractive plan.

The New Good MAXWELL

Advertisement for the "New Good Maxwell" cars, 1924. Courtesy of DCHC.

TABLE 2.1   Maxwell-Chalmers-Chrysler Unit Sales, 1920–25

	Maxwell	Chalmers	Chrysler	Total
1920	34,000	10,000	—	44,000
1921	16,000	3,000	—	19,000
1922	48,883	5,989	—	54,872
1923	74,000	9,000	—	83,000
1924	50,622	—	31,667	82,289
1925	30,811	—	106,857	137,668

Sources: Maxwell Motor Corporation and Chalmers Motor Corporation, consolidated balance sheets, 1921–25, box "Maxwell/Chalmers 1922–25," DCHC; W. A. P. John, "Walter P. Chrysler, Motor Car Manufacturer," *Motor;* September 1923, 112; and Chrysler Corporation, *Six Years' Progress of Chrysler Motors* (Detroit: Chrysler Corporation, 1929), 3.

The brilliant but frustrated engineering trio of Zeder, Skelton, and Breer left the Willys-Overland Company in December 1921, after Willys went into receivership. They immediately established an independent consulting firm, the Zeder, Skelton and Breer Engineering Company, and moved into rented space in Newark, New Jersey. The "Three Musketeers" sought work from several car companies, including Maxwell, but continued contract work for Durant. He hired ZSB Engineering to design a new and more powerful engine for the Flint car. The engineering trio also designed an engine for the Locomobile, Durant Motors' luxury car. ZSB Engineering rented the space they had previously occupied at the Elizabeth plant for $100 a month and used the dynamometers for their own projects, including the second car they designed for Walter P. Chrysler.[21]

This became the Chrysler Six, introduced in January 1924. Chrysler viewed the plans for this new car and signed a contract with ZSB Engineering on 11 November 1922, Armistice Day. ZSB Engineering agreed to refine the plans, build and test the engine, and have at least one prototype ready to test by 1 September 1923. Chrysler viewed the new engine on the Elizabeth dynamometer on 11 April 1923 and was so impressed that he wanted five prototypes instead.[22]

B. E. Hutchinson, the treasurer of the Maxwell Motor Corporation, recalled a meeting he had at the end of March 1923 with C. C. Jenks, chairman of the Maxwell Finance Committee. Jenks had discussed Walter Chrysler's Maxwell employment contract with James C. Brady, one of Maxwell's bankers. According to Hutchinson,

Jenks thinks Chrysler would like to have a car named after him. Brady on the other hand seems to be a little coy about going too far with W. P. unless and until Chrysler shows some disposition to put some of his own money into the venture. J. C. [Brady] remarked to Jenks that in talking the matter of contract over with W. P., he heard a good deal about options on stock, but none about the purchase of any at this time. This does not seem to sit very well with the New York contingent [of bankers].[23]

Walter Chrysler could move ahead with the new car only after receiving the full support of the Maxwell directors. On 1 June 1923, they signed an employment contract with him that allowed him to direct Maxwell for four years from New York City. They would pay him a salary of $15,000 a month for the rest of 1923 and then $100,000 per year for the remainder of the contract. More significantly, he would be paid 5 percent of the net profits of the corporation. This provision gave him an extra $205,800 in salary in 1924 and $856,300 in 1925. Chrysler also received stock options worth in excess of $2 million. The Maxwell Motor Corporation also agreed to pay Chrysler $100,000 for the ZSB design for a new car. On his part, Walter Chrysler agreed to purchase a $1 million life insurance policy payable to Maxwell.[24]

ZSB Engineering moved its staff to Detroit on 6 June 1923 and occupied space in the Chalmers factory on East Jefferson Avenue. It made sense for the design and prototyping work on the new model to be centered at the Chalmers plant, where the Chrysler Six was to supplant the Chalmers car. The ZSB team could also operate independently of the Maxwell engineering staff, which was located at the factory in Highland Park. They had the first operating prototypes, equipped with two-wheel mechanical brakes only, finished by 1 September. In mid-November, the ZSB test-driver, Allen B. (Tobe) Couture, along with Zeder and Skelton, drove the first Chrysler Six with four-wheel hydraulic brakes from Detroit to Washington, D.C., then to Newark and from there to Walter Chrysler's home on Long Island by Thanksgiving Day.[25]

Walter Chrysler faced the real possibility that the Maxwell Corporation would be bought by outside interests before he could bring his new car into production. James C. Brady, the major investor in Maxwell, fell ill in the fall of 1923 and tried to sell the firm, which was performing well under Chrysler's direction. In late November 1923, Brady came close to a deal with the Studebaker Corporation, led by Albert R. Erskine. Walter Chrysler and test-driver Tobe Couture took a group of five Studebaker executives on a series of secret nighttime test-drives of the Chrysler Six around Detroit.

Studebaker wanted the services of the ZSB Engineering team, along with the new six-cylinder car, and offered $27 million for Maxwell. Chrysler recognized that he would have to leave Maxwell if this were to happen, because "there would hardly be room for Erskine and Chrysler in one pasture lot." According to Couture, Fred Zeder vowed to have Carl Breer destroy all the Chrysler Six blueprints if the deal with Studebaker was approved. One source quoted Zeder railing at Walter Chrysler:

"Walter, if Erskine wants to pay twenty-seven million dollars for brick and mortar and machines, all right. But no automobile. Remember that. No automobile! I'm glad you remember that Zeder, Skelton, and Breer own the patents on the Chrysler engine. And, believe me when I tell you that I'll take a sledge hammer and personally smash the new models into bits before I'll let Erskine have them. I told you before and I'll tell you again, that I designed and built one car for Erskine. . . . He welched on his promises to me, and to my associates. He can't have two of my cars. Never!"

The proposed deal collapsed and Walter P. Chrysler moved ahead with manufacturing and marketing his new car.[26]

Chapter 3

WALTER CHRYSLER'S CAR AND HIS COMPANY, 1924–27

The important event in the operation of your Corporation during the fiscal year 1923 has been the development of the Chrysler car. The management has taken advantage of the opportunity afforded by the acquisition of the Chalmers property a little over a year ago to develop a new and outstanding line of cars for the manufacture of which that plant could be particularly well adapted. It has now been thoroughly overhauled and refitted and in it the Chrysler car can be manufactured competitively. It is now known as the Chrysler plant.

—Walter P. Chrysler

At the New York Automobile Show of January 1924, Walter Chrysler realized his long-delayed dream of introducing a new car of superior design bearing his name. The Chrysler Six, with a host of advanced features and a stylish look, was an instant success and propelled Chrysler onto the automobile industry's center stage. With Chrysler cars producing growing sales and profits, the Maxwell models disappeared—along with the Maxwell Motor Corporation, replaced by the Chrysler Corporation in June 1925.

Walter Chrysler's cars and his company enjoyed great success in 1924–27. Production and sales more than doubled, as the company developed new lines and redesigned its existing offerings. For the 1927 model year, Chrysler sold four distinct lines of cars, ranging from a four-cylinder model to the luxurious Chrysler Imperial. The company had become the fourth largest automaker in the United States and was ready for its fundamental transformation in 1928.

SELLING THE CHRYSLER SIX

The Chrysler Six was an instant success in the marketplace. In early December 1923, Walter Chrysler launched a media campaign to introduce the Chrysler Six before the car was even in production. The advertising blitz began with a drawn-out "tease" campaign that gradually revealed the car's features. Maxwell's advertising agency, MacManus Incorporated of Detroit, designed the campaign, probably with input from Walter Chrysler and Joseph E. Fields, Chrysler's sales manager. It included a series of weekly full-page ads in the *Saturday Evening Post* that began on 8 December 1923 and reached a climax on 5 January 1924.

The first three ads, which appeared on 7, 15, and 22 December, were entitled, "Walter P. Chrysler, Motor Car Manufacturer" and spoke of the man named Chrysler, not the car named Chrysler. They informed the reader that the name was "pronounced as though spelled, Cry-sler." The advertisement of 22 December finally revealed that Walter P. Chrysler was on the verge of introducing a new car. More important, this new car "represents the culmination of Mr. Chrysler's vast experience, and embodies qualities of design and performance so striking that they will constitute a ***profound sensation***." A week later, readers finally saw what the car looked like.[1]

Following on the heels of the advertising campaign, the new line had a spectacular introduction at the 24th Annual New York Automobile Show, held 5–12 January 1924 at the 256th Field Artillery Armory in the Bronx, a new venue. Reports of the show in the automotive press all mentioned the Chrysler cars as a major new introduction.[2]

But Chrysler's autobiography told a very different story, one that has little foundation in fact. Walter Chrysler claimed that he discovered late in December that the American Automobile Chamber of Commerce, which ran the automobile show, would not allow him to display the Chrysler Six because it was not yet a production car available to the public. According to Walter Chrysler, he quickly developed a stratagem—he would rent the lobby of the Commodore Hotel, where most of the manufacturers and salespeople stayed during the show, and exhibit the Chrysler Six there, all by itself. Joseph Fields made the arrangements and the new Chrysler car was the hit of the show, although it was not *in* the show.[3]

Despite Walter Chrysler's claims, the Chrysler Six went on display in the main exhibit hall of the show and at the Commodore Hotel. Chrysler placed an advertisement in the *New York Times* at the start of the show, announcing the Chrysler Six: "The most important new car of the year is on exhibition at the Commodore Hotel; and in Space 35 at the Automobile Show." *Motor Age* reported that the Chalmers space in the armory had only two Chalmers cars on display and three Chrysler models. Photographic evidence shows that the Maxwell Motor Corporation exhibited Chalmers, Maxwell, and Chrysler cars at both venues.[4]

Walter Chrysler displayed the Chrysler Six at the New York Automobile Show to generate sales, but more important, to find financing for the new car. Paying for the design, development, and initial production of the Chrysler Six was a daunting challenge to Walter Chrysler and the Maxwell Motor Corporation. The design alone cost Maxwell $100,000 and the experimental and development costs came to $248,751. The Maxwell directors estimated the cost of writing off the remaining stock of materials and tools associated with the Chalmers car at $650,555. These costs alone came to $1 million. Converting the Chalmers plant to produce the Chrysler Six would cost another $450,000. The total of roughly $1.5 million was the fixed capital cost only and did not include the required working capital, normally at least three times the fixed costs.[5]

The first Chrysler Six came off the production line at the (former) Chalmers plant on Jefferson Avenue in Detroit in late December 1923. Before Walter Chrysler could bring his new model into full production, the Maxwell Motor Corporation needed an influx of new capital. Once production was under way, Chrysler invited scores of dealers, parts suppliers, and bankers to come to Detroit to see the new model. According to Owen Skelton, Jules S. Bache, senior partner in the investment banking house of J. S. Bache & Company, was one of the first visitors to become enamored of the new car and to invest heavily in Maxwell as a result.[6]

Walter Chrysler went to New York Automobile Show in January 1924 to raise additional capital from the bankers who would be there. He wanted a bank to take $5 million in Maxwell Motor Corporation mortgage bonds, giving him the capital he needed to bring the new model into full production. An unnamed banker offered Chrysler only $70 per $100 face value on $5 million in mortgage bonds, which would give Maxwell only $3.5 million in cash. Walter Chrysler personally negotiated a deal with Edward R. Tinker of Chase Securities Corporation. Chrysler provided the details of dramatic, down-to-the-wire negotiations, in which he literally locked himself and Tinker inside a car displayed in the lobby of the Commodore Hotel until they came to an agreement. After several offers and counteroffers, Tinker agreed to take the bonds, which would bear interest of $5\frac{1}{2}$ percent, at a price of $94 per $100 face value, meaning that Maxwell would get $4.7 million in cash.[7]

The Chrysler Six was an immediate success in the automotive market. Its design was not radical or exotic, but it offered a combination of advanced standard features—a high-compression engine (4.7:1 compression ratio versus the standard 4:1 ratio), hydraulic four-wheel brakes, and balloon tires—in a mid-priced vehicle. Automotive trade magazines recognized that the Chrysler Six was a superior car in its price class, in part because it was an entirely new design. In December 1923, *Automotive Industries* devoted three pages to the new offering, and *Automobile Topics* gave it six pages. The latter publication's description reads like advertising copy—"Brand New Product Offered Those Who Want a Better Car—Is Remarkable Performer, Highly Developed." The article praised the Chrysler Six for its speed, power, riding stability, comfort, good looks, and reasonable price. The Chrysler Six embodied all the "best-practice" engineering of the time, with some innovative features thrown in as well.[8]

A *Fortune* article published in August 1935 made a perceptive observation concerning the Chrysler Six. Walter Chrysler and company had to overcome two perceptions of the auto buying public—that only large cars could be comfortable and fast, and that the price of a car should reflect its size. A Chrysler Six touring car, with a wheelbase of less than 113 inches, sold for roughly the same price as a seven-passenger Buick touring car with a wheelbase of 128 inches. Customers had to be convinced of the merits of a smaller, more maneuverable car. Only a car like the Chrysler Six, offering speed, style, and advanced features, could overcome buyers' prejudices.[9]

Two of the design innovations found in the Chrysler Six—balloon tires and four-wheel hydraulic brakes—were the talk of the New York Automobile Show of 1924. Balloon tires were available as options on only 60 models out of 297 exhibited at the show and standard equipment on only 14 of those. At the 1923 show, only two manufacturers, Duesenberg and Rickenbacker, had offered four-wheel brakes. A year later, 26 manufacturers offered them as either standard or optional equipment, while 45 manufacturers did not.[10]

Chrysler's leadership in braking systems was greater than the raw figures on four-wheel brake availability might suggest. Most of the four-wheel brake systems introduced in 1924 and in the years that followed were mechanical rather than hydraulic systems. Malcolm Loughheed (Lockheed) developed a four-wheel hydraulic braking system and received seven patents between December 1917 and July 1923. The Maxwell Motor Corporation was the second automaker to request a set of Lockheed brakes to test on its vehicles. (The Paige-Detroit Motor Car Company was the first.) In mid-October 1923, Maxwell began offering these brakes as an option on its Chalmers models for an additional $75 per vehicle.[11]

According to Carl Breer, the ZSB engineering team had to make improvements to the Lockheed design before using the braking system on the Chalmers cars. They discovered that the system's rawhide cups, which served as seals to prevent hydraulic fluid from leaking when the driver applied the brakes, quickly dried out and shrank when the system was under heavy usage, causing fluid leakage and brake failure. Working closely with the Manhattan Rubber Company, Zeder's engineers designed a more resilient rubber cup. Because the improvements were so substantial, Lockheed agreed to allow Maxwell the use of his system free of royalties provided that Lockheed could incorporate the improvements in his original design. Catalogues for the 1924 Chrysler Six refer to the brake system as "Chrysler Lockheed Hydraulic Four-Wheel Brakes," suggesting that Chrysler engineered the system.[12]

Advertisements for the Chrysler Six focused on its technical features such as the Lockheed hydraulic brake system, its speed and power, and its overall quality. A *Saturday Evening Post* advertisement in February 1924, entitled "Power without Precedent in the New Chrysler Six," promised customers an effortless

70 mph, with power to spare. In November 1924, Chrysler's ads emphasized the use of Fisher Body Company bodies exclusively in the Chrysler Six as additional proof of the high quality of the product.[13]

Manufacturers try to establish brand identity as one way to sell products. Chrysler adopted a round logo that resembled the blue ribbon prize awarded to produce or livestock at a county fair. It had the Chrysler name extending diagonally across the blue ribbon from roughly the eight o'clock position to the two o'clock position, with a lightning bolt above and below the name. This logo appeared with the first advertisements for the Chrysler Six in December 1923 and on the cover of the Maxwell Motor Corporation's "consolidated balance sheet" of 31 December 1923. Zeder had used lightning bolts in the mock-up emblems he had prepared in 1922 for the automobile that he never built. Since the 1924 Chrysler Six was Fred Zeder's design, it is likely that Walter Chrysler included the lightning bolts to recognize Zeder's contribution.

The new car came equipped with a decorative radiator cap topped with the wings of the Roman deity Mercury to indicate speed. Contemporary radiator caps, manufactured by the Moto-Meter Company, had a built-in column of mercury so the driver could see the running temperatures. The Chrysler Six designers instead installed a temperature gauge on the instrument panel, so they could use the wing motif with no clutter. The blue ribbon logo, which included the designation "SIX" under the Chrysler name, appeared on the front of the radiator, below the cap. By August 1924, designers combined the wings with the blue ribbon to produce a more elaborate corporate logo.[14]

The Chrysler Six received a good deal of free publicity from some early racing success, mainly in California. The Los Angeles Express offered a trophy for the fastest run up a steep, curvy gravel road leading to the summit of Mt. Wilson, home of the Mt. Wilson Observatory. Famed race car driver Ralph De Palma (1882–1957) won the trophy on 16 July 1924 in a stock Chrysler Six. De Palma completed the race in 25 minutes and 48.85 seconds, a full two minutes better than the nearest competitor. De Palma had to downshift into low gear only three times during his run because the Chrysler Six had so much power. He reached speeds up to 44 mph during the climb and the engine never overheated.[15]

De Palma continued setting speed records in California driving the Chrysler Six. The Los Angeles Times offered a trophy to the fastest stock car with a standard (factory) gear ratio (3.25:1) over a 1,000-mile distance. On 17 September 1924, De Palma drove a stock Chrysler Six the required distance at a speedway in Fresno in 16 hours 47 minutes, for an average speed of 59.54 mph. Less than four months later, on 5 January 1925, he averaged 76.32 mph at Culver City, California, using a stock Chrysler Six with a gear ratio of 3.75:1. These race results did nothing but enhance the Chrysler Six's reputation for speed.[16]

Walter P. Chrysler affixing inspection tag to a 1924 Chrysler roadster at the Jefferson Avenue factory in Detroit. Courtesy of NAHC.

The car also made a minor splash by entering and finishing the tough "24 Hours at Le Mans" race in 1925, one of the few American entrants in the early days of this endurance race. The team of Henry Stoffel and Lucien Desvaux drove a stock Chrysler Six and finished the race. Race officials disqualified them, however, because they completed only 117 laps, while their engine size (3.31 liters) required them to finish 119 laps.[17]

The popularity of the new Chrysler car was never in doubt. The greatest challenge faced by Walter Chrysler and his production managers was to turn out enough cars to satisfy the burgeoning demand.

MANUFACTURING THE CHRYSLER SIX

Gearing up to produce the Chrysler Six was complicated by the fact that the Maxwell-Chalmers enterprise operated multiple plants, all manufacturing and assembling a variety of products and all in a state of transition during the short span of eighteen months between December 1923 and June 1925. The Maxwell Motor Corporation stopped production of the Chalmers car by December 1923, and they retooled the entire Jefferson Avenue plant to produce the Chrysler Six. The larger Maxwell plant on Oakland Avenue in Highland Park continued to produce the Maxwell Model 25 until June 1925, when a modified version of the car emerged as the Chrysler Four. By the end of this transitional period, the Maxwell components plant at Newcastle, Indiana, produced axles and transmissions for the Maxwell and Chrysler cars.

Walter Chrysler's factory managers struggled to increase production of Chryslers, while Chrysler management was also deciding whether to build a redesigned Maxwell or simply drop the nameplate. Fortunately, detailed records created by George W. Mason, general works manager for Maxwell-Chalmers and Chrysler in 1922–26, have survived and offer insight into this crucial period. Mason had a long, distinguished career in the automobile industry. After working for the Studebaker Corporation (1913–14) and the Dodge Brothers Company (1914–15), he held jobs at auto supplier firms before becoming supervisor of production at the U.S. Army Ordnance Department's Rock Island Arsenal in 1917–18. Mason worked for the Irving National Bank in 1919–21 before joining Maxwell in October 1921 as an assistant to the vice president for manufacturing and became general works manager the following year.[18]

Mason was a production engineer who was allied to the growing corps of professional managers who comprised the "scientific management" movement in American industry. The "scientific" approach to factory management included time studies of work, experimentation in arranging the layout of machinery and the flow of production, and detailed cost analyses. Historians often simplistically label their work "Taylorism" after the most famous exponent of this approach, Frederick W. Taylor. Mason's files include lists of the cost of all parts used in Maxwell cars in 1918 and 1923 and detailed estimates of direct labor costs for manufacturing and assembling these cars. George Mason may not have been a disciple of Frederick W. Taylor, but he was a scientific manager.[19]

The automobile industry had long struggled with the production bottleneck caused by traditional methods of painting wooden bodies, practices inherited from the carriage industry. In the first decade of the twentieth century, body finishers applied as many as three dozen primer and finished coats of varnish, and with slow drying and sanding between coats, finishing times of three to eight weeks were common. The most important painting breakthrough came with the introduction of DuPont's new fast-drying "Duco" lacquer finishes in 1922. Duco was more durable than existing finishes, could be applied in less time with less labor, and was available in a variety of colors.[20]

The Maxwell Motor Corporation began to consider Duco in late July 1922, when George Mason sent his Highland Park paint superintendent, G. L. Paullis, to the Studebaker factory in South Bend, Indiana, where Duco was in use. Paullis reported that the materials costs for Studebaker were similar to other finishes Studebaker had used, but Duco saved two days of production time and a significant amount of labor. Following detailed time-and-motion studies in late July 1924, George Mason decided to use Duco blue lacquer on all the remaining Maxwell models and on the Chrysler Standard Sedan.[21]

The resounding sales success of the Chrysler Six put enormous pressure on Mason and his production staff to expand output. Sales for 1924 amounted to 31,429 units, probably very close to the numbers produced that year. They achieved roughly two-thirds of the production in the second half of 1924. A photograph dated 13 June 1924 has the caption "To George W. Mason upon the occasion of the building of the 10,000th Chrysler Car," and the signature of W. Ledyard Mitchell, vice president in charge of manufacturing.[22]

Walter Chrysler and the company bearing his name soon discontinued the Maxwell brand. The four-cylinder Maxwell Model 25, reworked in 1922 as the New Series Maxwell, had its engine revamped for the 1924 model year, probably by the Zeder-Skelton-Breer team. The new engine delivered 34 hp versus 30 hp from the engine it replaced. After launching the Chrysler Six, the ZSB engineering trio modified the four-cylinder Maxwell engine in early 1924 to power the Maxwell Model 25-C, introduced in September 1924 as the 1925 model. The reworked engine featured a three-bearing crankshaft, new intake and exhaust manifolds, forced feed lubrication, larger valves, and improved water jacket cooling, with output increased from 34 to 38 hp. The revamped model included balloon tires and an improved steering system. Chrysler's engineers designed a new Maxwell Model F, but when it went into production in June 1925, it carried the Chrysler Four nameplate. The Maxwell nameplate disappeared.[23]

The Formation of the Chrysler Corporation

During the critical time when the Chrysler Six went into production, Walter Chrysler had not decided the exact manner in which he would manufacture and sell the car. He kept the Maxwell car in production and the Maxwell Motor Corporation afloat while raising capital to pay for the launching of his new car. Once the Chrysler Six was a success, he eliminated the Maxwell nameplate and the Maxwell company name as well.

Chrysler Corporation was officially chartered as a Delaware corporation on 6 June 1925. The Maxwell Motor Corporation stockholders' meeting of 24 June 1925 agreed to transfer all the corporation's real estate and other assets to the Chrysler Corporation, provided that the latter assume all of Maxwell's debts

Walter P. Chrysler in the study of his home in Great Neck, Long Island, 1925. Courtesy of DCHC.

and liabilities. The stockholders also voted to dissolve the Maxwell Motor Corporation, marking the disappearance of the Maxwell name after twenty-one years. Nicholas Kelley, Walter Chrysler's attorney, served as president of the Chrysler Corporation from 8 June to 26 June 1925, shortly after Maxwell ceased to exist as a corporation. There was perhaps a legal restriction preventing Chrysler from holding both presidents' posts. Walter P. Chrysler replaced Kelly after only eighteen days in office.[24]

Because the Maxwell Motor Corporation and Chrysler Corporation relied heavily on bank loans to survive and grow, bankers served as directors of the Maxwell Motor Corporation starting in 1921 and of Chrysler Corporation from 1925 on. Jules S. Bache, senior partner in J. S. Bache & Company and one of the earlier financial backers of the Chrysler Six, was a director from 1925 to 1943. Edward R. Tinker from Chase Securities, who agreed to sell Maxwell's $5 million issue of mortgage bonds in January 1924, was a member of the Chrysler Board of Directors from 1925 to 1936. Finally, James C. Brady of Brady Security & Realty Corporation, who brought Walter Chrysler to Willys-Overland and then to Maxwell, served as a Chrysler director in 1925–26 and again from 1938 to 1966. All of these men insisted on a board seat so they could monitor their investments.[25]

The year 1928 marked a radical change in the position of the Chrysler Corporation in the American auto industry. Chrysler bought Dodge Brothers, a major producer in its own right, and successfully launched two new car lines—DeSoto and Plymouth. The company's remarkable success before 1928, however, should not be downplayed. Sales of Chrysler cars, which more than tripled from 31,429 in 1924 to 106,857 in 1925, then jumped sharply to 170,392 units in 1926 and to 192,083 the following year.

Walter Chrysler and his production staff struggled from 1924 to 1928 to increase manufacturing and assembly capacity to meet the growing demand for Chrysler cars. The trick was to avoid the delays and costs of building new facilities from scratch. Chrysler instantly increased its body manufacturing capabilities when it purchased the American Motor Body Company in September 1925. Chrysler gained a modern 700,000-square-foot body plant located directly across the street from the (former) Chalmers plant on Jefferson Avenue in Detroit. The new facility, soon known as the Chrysler Kercheval plant, supplied bodies to the Jefferson plant until February 1990, when both closed.[26]

Still, Chrysler, like most of the other automakers of this period, relied heavily on outside sources for bodies. The Fisher Body Company supplied most of Chrysler's bodies until 1926, when Fisher Body became a wholly owned subsidiary of General Motors. The giant automaker had bought a 60 percent controlling interest in Fisher Body in 1919, but had allowed the former carriage maker to continue to engage in outside business. After 1926, Fisher still provided

Chrysler with some bodies, but most of Chrysler's body business went to the Briggs Manufacturing Company, the Edward G. Budd Manufacturing Company, and the Murray Corporation of America. Starting in 1926, Chrysler also offered custom catalogue bodies for the Imperial models from three coach makers—LeBaron, Locke, and Dietrich. From the early 1930s on, Briggs supplied an ever-increasing share of Chrysler's bodies for all of its car lines.[27]

Chrysler enlarged its manufacturing facilities significantly in 1928. At the start of the year, Chrysler assembled its Models 52 and 62 at the Highland Park factory and the Model 72 and Imperial at Jefferson Avenue. Highland Park could produce about 1,000 cars per day. Major construction projects at Jefferson Avenue in 1928 included the Assembly Building ($503,105), Machine Shop ($360,574), Enameling Building ($118,746), and Shipping Dock ($122,002), all single-story steel-framed structures. A four-story reinforced concrete wing to one of the existing buildings was another major project, costing $146,326. These particular buildings, designed by the Detroit architectural firm of Smith, Hinchman & Grylls, cost $1.25 million in total. The building spurt of 1928 included a dozen additional "infill" structures. The new Assembly Building permitted Chrysler to move Model 65 production from Highland Park to Jefferson Avenue in August 1928, freeing space at Highland Park for the production of the Plymouth and the DeSoto.[28]

Construction of new facilities at the (former) Maxwell plant in Highland Park was also extensive in 1927–28. Two important new buildings were the Engineering Research Building (1928)and Building 243 (1928), a four-story structure that began its life as the "body and storage building," served as a general office building, and eventually became the K. T. Keller Building. The third was the Engineering Building (1928), a four-story structure that created nearly 1 million feet of floor space and cost $1 million. Chrysler added a fifth floor before the end of 1928. After the company added a sixth floor in 1936, Chrysler engineers simply called it "the six-story building." The firm of Smith, Hinchman & Grylls designed all the new buildings at Highland Park.[29]

By 1927, Chrysler Corporation stood fourth among American automobile companies in terms of sales, after Ford, General Motors, and Hudson. The fledgling automaker increased its sales by offering "new and improved" models every twelve months or so and by expanding the variety of cars it offered to the public. Chrysler produced four distinct car lines, with each line offering from four to nine body styles to customers. Effective advertising and continued success in racing helped generate sales as well.[30]

The original Chrysler Six, also called the "B-Series," was unchanged for the first eighteen months it was in production. This was the second automobile design done by ZSB Engineering for Walter Chrysler. Durant Motors had purchased the "A-Series" design, along with the Elizabeth, New Jersey, factory. The pioneer model was redesigned and introduced as the Chrysler 70 (Model G-70) in July 1925 and remained in production through September 1926. It featured a larger displacement engine and about 10 percent more power than the original Chrysler Six. Chrysler used numerical "badges" on their models to indicate the model's "effortless" cruising speed, thus the Chrysler 70 would cruise at 70 mph. These were conservative numbers, because the cars could easily reach top speeds of an additional 10 mph.[31]

The Chrysler Four, a Maxwell Model 25-C upgraded by the Zeder-Skelton-Breer team, went into production in July 1925. Renamed the Chrysler 58 in December 1925, it remained in production through June 1926. The initial sales brochures emphasized that this was a Chrysler-engineered car, implying quality and performance similar to the Chrysler Six. The potential customer was reminded: "The Chrysler organization is proud of the Chrysler Four. It presents this product of Chrysler genius as the most modern and soundest expression of the four-cylinder principle in the world, and with the conviction that the Chrysler combination of four-cylinder results is another phenomenal Chrysler achievement." The initial announcement of the Chrysler Four emphasized the fact that customers could have Lockheed four-wheel hydraulic brakes installed as an inexpensive option. A 1926 brochure for the Chrysler 58 declared that the model offered "[t]hree qualities combined in no other car—58 Miles per Hour, 5 to 25 Miles [per hour] in 8 seconds, 25 miles to the gallon." The 58 was the least expensive Chrysler line, with prices ranging from $845 (touring car) to $995 (sedan). In contrast, the Chrysler 70 ranged in price from $1,445 (coach) to $2,095 (crown sedan).[32]

Walter Chrysler also introduced a new luxury model in January 1926, the Imperial 80 (Model E-80), which Chrysler left unchanged until October 1927. The Imperial featured an engine with 288.6 cubic inches displacement (cid), developed 92 hp, and could do 80 mph. Available in eight body styles, the Imperial ranged in price from $2,494 to $3,695, still a modest price for a luxury automobile. Introduced at the New York Automobile Show in January 1926, the Imperial received rave reviews in the automotive press. *Automobile Topics* reported that "Chrysler was . . . the center of almost mob scenes. Viewed from the gallery, space A-2 appeared [to be] a lodestone drawing to itself a large percentage of the passers-by." The attraction was the Chrysler Imperial.[33]

The new luxury car also benefited from publicity coming from racing. A Chrysler Imperial 80 roadster served as the pace car at the 1926 Indianapolis 500 race, with famed racing driver Louis Chevrolet at the wheel. In June 1927, L. B. Miller and John E. Wieber drove a stock Imperial phaeton for seven straight days, completing the first transcontinental round trip, covering 6,720 miles. The endurance run went from San Francisco to New York City and then from

1926 Chrysler Imperial, the Indianapolis 500 pace car. Walter P. Chrysler (*right*) with Carl Wallerich. Courtesy of DCHC.

New York to Los Angeles. They finished the entire route in one minute less than seven days' elapsed time.[34]

The Chrysler Corporation offered three distinct car lines for the 1926 model year—the Chrysler 58, the Chrysler 70, and the Chrysler Imperial 80. A general advertisement for the 1926 Chrysler lineup proclaimed that these cars offered "Quality Beyond Comparison." Chrysler offered "Three Great Cars—Nineteen Body Styles" priced from $845 to $3,695 at the factory in Detroit.

Chrysler added a fourth line for the 1927 model year and changed the names of some of the existing lines as well. The Chrysler 50 (Model I-50) featured a four-cylinder engine developing 38 hp. The 50 came in three closed styles only (coupe, coach, and sedan), with bodies of all-steel construction by Budd. This was the first Chrysler line equipped with all-steel bodies. By early August 1926, with production still a month away, Chrysler already had 30,000 orders for the 50 on hand from distributors. Over the next three years, Chrysler Corporation reworked and rebadged the four car lines roughly every 12 months.[35]

Chrysler Corporation enjoyed fleeting international racing success in 1928.

Following the near success at the 24-hour race at Le Mans in 1925, no Chrysler cars entered the race in 1926 or 1927. Four Chrysler 72s (4.1-liter engines) entered the 1928 race and performed well. Two of these cars, driven by the teams of Zeno Zender/Jerome Ledur and Louis Chiron/Cyril de Vere, had to retire before completing the race. The car driven by the team of Henry Stoffel/Andre Rossignal finished third, and a second Chrysler 72, driven by the team of C. and G. Guica, finished fourth. Chrysler entered five cars in the Belgian Twenty-Four-Hour Grand Prix at Spa a few weeks later. An Imperial 80 finished second overall and two Chrysler 72s finished third and sixth.[36]

The network of dealerships selling the Chrysler brand quickly grew from 2,000 outlets in fall 1924 to 3,800 a year later, but despite its sales success, Chrysler Corporation struggled in the late 1920s to expand its dealer network. Chrysler placed advertisements in 1926–28 appealing to businessmen, especially those operating a franchise for other car companies, to consider becoming a Chrysler dealer, targeting *Automobile Topics, Automobile Trade Journal,* and *Motor World.* These efforts notwithstanding, growth was slow; by early 1928, 4,600 dealerships were selling Chryslers.[37]

The performance of the Maxwell Motor Corporation and Chrysler Corporation in 1924 to 1927 is summarized in table 3.1.

Chrysler also diversified in a small way when it introduced a new product in May 1927, a six-cylinder L-head marine engine that weighed only 835 pounds but developed 100 hp. The Chris Smith & Sons Company of Algonac, Michigan, not far from Detroit, adopted this engine as standard equipment for its new Chris-Craft Cadet model. This 22-foot speedboat could achieve a top speed of 35 mph with its powerful Chrysler engine.[38]

Chrysler Corporation was successful by any measure even before the watershed year of 1928 changed everything. The company had a widespread reputation for producing technically advanced, attractively styled cars that offered excellent performance. By 1928, Walter Chrysler had already fulfilled his dream of becoming a major independent automaker.

TABLE 3.1 Maxwell-Chrysler Performance, 1924–27

| | Unit Sales | | | Net Sales ($) | Exports as Share of Factory Output (%) | Net Earnings* | | |
	Maxwell	Chrysler	Total			Total	On Sales (%)	On Capital Invested (%)
1924	50,622	31,667	82,289	81,363,759	6.02	4,115,540	5.0	—
1925	30,811	106,857	137,668	137,301,904	8.40	17,126,136	12.5	24.4
1926	0	170,392	170,392	163,390,849	10.70	15,448,587	9.5	20.5
1927	0	192,083	192,083	172,343,952	15.76	19,484,880	11.3	22.8

Sources: Chrysler Corporation, *The Growth of Chrysler* (Detroit: Chrysler Corporation; 1928) and *Six Years' Progress of Chrysler Motors* (Detroit: Chrysler Corporation; 1930), 4–6; NAHC.
Corporation, 1929), 3–6; and Cram's Automotive Reports, *Analytical Report on Chrysler Corporation* (Detroit: 1930), 4–6; NAHC.

*After taxes

Chapter 4

THE DODGE BROTHERS AND THEIR COMPANY

The Dodge brothers are the two best mechanics in Michigan. There is no operation in their own shop from drop forging to machining, from tool-making to micrometic measurement, that they can't do with their own hands. . . . As a matter of fact, when the Dodge Bros. new car comes out, there is no question that it will be the best thing on the market for the money.

—Michigan Manufacturer and Financial Record

The lead article in *Automotive Industries* on 9 June 1928, "Dodge-Chrysler Merger Unites Two Great Properties," described the Chrysler purchase of Dodge as "one of the most startling developments in many years."[1] Chrysler Corporation, with assets of about $104 million at the close of 1927, had bought Dodge Brothers, with assets of nearly $132 million. Buying Dodge transformed Chrysler into the third of the Big Three automakers. Dodge Brothers, in addition to serving as a major supplier of parts and components to the Detroit automobile industry since 1901, had also been an important automobile manufacturer in its own right since 1914. Acquiring Dodge made Chrysler a better automaker and also a larger one. The Chrysler Corporation that emerged in the late 1920s was really a combined Chrysler-Dodge operation.

THE BROTHERS DODGE

Despite their distinct personalities, interests, and talents, John and Horace Dodge—partners in work, in play, and in life experiences—were a team. Even the corporate logo they adopted—the six-pointed star created with two intertwined triangles—embodied their utter dependence on each other. Ancient Hindu, Jewish, and Muslim cultures used this symbol, sometimes known as "Solomon's Seal," in part as a charm against evil. It stands for the mystical union of the body and the soul, of truth and beauty. For the Dodge brothers, the symbol represented the union of the two brothers into one. The intertwined D and B in the middle of the six-pointed star further emphasized the point.[2]

John Francis Dodge (1864–1920) and Horace Elgin Dodge (1868–1920) were two of the three children born to Maria Casto Dodge and Daniel Rugg Dodge, who ran a foundry and machine shop in Niles, Michigan, with two of his brothers. Both boys showed great personal initiative in their youth. John Dodge, boasting a three-year record of perfect attendance in grammar school, graduated from Niles High School in 1882, a major achievement in that era. Horace showed his mechanical talents early in life; at 13, with his brother's help, Horace Dodge built a working high-wheel bicycle from scrap materials.

After the deaths of his two brothers, Daniel Rugg Dodge moved his family to Port Huron in 1882, and started a machine shop that made internal combustion marine engines. In 1886, the Dodge family moved to Detroit, where John and Horace found work at the Murphy Boiler Works, which manufactured marine boilers. In 1894, the Dodge brothers took jobs as machinists for the Dominion Typograph Company in Windsor, Ontario. After Horace invented an improved bicycle ball bearing in 1895 and received a patent in September 1896, the brothers formed a partnership with Fred Evans. They leased the Dominion Typograph plant and manufactured the Evans and Dodge bicycle from mid-1897 to 1900. The brothers continued to live in Detroit, commuting across the Detroit River to Windsor every day.[3]

AUTOMOTIVE SUPPLIERS

The Dodge brothers dissolved their Canadian venture in 1900, receiving about $10,000 as their share of the enterprise. The next year, they started their own machine shop in rented space on the ground floor of the Boydell Building (Beaubien Street at Lafayette in Detroit) with twelve employees. A lengthy *Detroit Free Press* article in September 1901 praised the Dodge brothers and their machine shop to the skies. *Automobile Topics* argued in 1914 that the Dodge brothers "were the first to establish in Detroit a machine shop of the type where really close and accurate work could be done. They installed machine tools of a size and character that nobody else in Detroit had the courage to consider." (This statement is an exaggeration, given Henry M. Leland's highly successful Detroit machine shop.)

The Dodges became suppliers for the Detroit automobile industry when they built engines to power Ransom Olds's famous curved-dash Olds runabout (the Merry Oldsmobile). In June 1901, Olds gave them a contract for 2,000 engines and the next year, an additional contract for 3,000 transmissions, making the Dodge brothers the largest parts supplier to the automobile industry. In early

The Dodge brothers, John (*left*) and Horace (*right*), ca. 1914. Courtesy of DCHC.

1902, the Dodges moved into a new three-story machine shop at the corner of Monroe Avenue and Hastings Street in Detroit.[4]

The Dodge brothers' fortunes improved significantly and permanently in late 1902. Henry Ford, on the verge of launching the Ford Motor Company (his third company) and a new car, asked the Dodges to become his major parts supplier. Before they did any work for Ford, Horace Dodge examined the plans for Ford's new automobile and improved the design of the engine and rear axle.

On 28 February 1903, the Dodges agreed to supply Ford with sets of "running gear" (engine, transmission, and axles, mounted on a frame) at $250 each. The contract, personally guaranteed by Alexander T. Malcomson, the chief investor with Ford, provided for payments of $5,000 to the Dodge brothers on 15 March, 15 April, and with the first delivery of running gear on 15 May. The financially strapped Ford Motor Company was not prepared to receive the first sets of "running gear" until early July, when the Dodge brothers delivered these "machines" to Ford's rented assembly building on Mack Avenue in Detroit, conveying them on horse-drawn hayracks.

To begin production for Ford, the Dodge brothers spent more than $60,000 for retooling and raw materials before receiving any revenues. With the Ford Motor Company constantly short of cash and unable to pay them, the Dodges agreed in June 1903 to write off overdue payments of $7,000, extend Ford an additional $3,000 in credit (a note due in six months), and in return received 10 percent of the Ford Motor Company's stock. From that point until they introduced their own nameplate in 1914, the Dodges worked exclusively for Ford. They also remained major stockholders in the Ford Motor Company until 1919. The fortunes of the Dodges and Henry Ford remained intertwined for more than fifteen years.[5]

Fortunately for the Dodge brothers, most of the Ford models were successful in the marketplace. Ford moved into a large new factory at Piquette and Beaubien in Detroit in late 1904. There, Ford assembled his Models B, C, F, H, K, N, R and, starting in 1908, the Model T. He quickly increased Model T production to 10,607 cars in 1909 and the Dodge brothers' Monroe Avenue plant became woefully inadequate, although it was the largest and best-equipped machine shop in Detroit. The Dodges built a new manufacturing facility in rural Hamtramck Township in 1910, the same year Henry Ford opened his Highland Park factory not far away. Direct rail links connected the plants.

Albert Kahn designed the first segments of the Hamtramck factory complex, including a machine shop, forge shop, brass foundry, powerhouse, and office building, all completed in 1910–11. Kahn was the premier Detroit industrial architect at the time, having designed factories for Packard, Ford, Chalmers, and others. The Dodges broke ground for the new complex on 1 June 1910 and began moving into the new buildings in late November. Kahn designed two steel-framed buildings, a forge shop and a blacksmith shop, each 400 feet long; a steel-framed brick powerhouse; and a modest brick office building. Kahn's most important design was the machine shop, a four-story reinforced concrete building with flat-slab floors supported by reinforced concrete columns. This was a U-shaped building, with two wings, each 65 feet by 405 feet, joined at the northern end by a segment measuring 65 feet by 225 feet.[6]

The Dodges employed about 5,000 men at the Hamtramck plant by early

1914, when they were still manufacturing parts exclusively for Ford. The plant produced a quarter million transmissions, drive shafts, and rear axles annually for the Model T Ford, along with roughly 200,000 front axles, 200,000 crankshafts, and other parts. According to one estimate, between 1903 and 1913, the Dodge brothers manufactured 60 percent of the total value of the Ford cars, including the legendary Model T. They made every major component except bodies, wheels, and tires.[7]

The Dodge-Ford partnership was not without friction. Early in the contract, Ford complained about the poor quality of some components, but the problems were never serious enough to end their business relationship. In a detailed letter to the Dodge brothers in April 1906, James Couzens listed the most serious parts shortages Ford faced and asked for quick deliveries so that assembly could continue without further disruption. He listed eighteen different components needed for the Ford Models A, C, and F, including radiators, cylinders, connecting rods, crank cases, front springs, and gasoline tanks.[8]

Although Henry Ford never acknowledged their contribution, the Dodge brothers played a pivotal role in the success of his cars and his company. After some early hiccups, they provided Ford with a steady supply of high-quality, reasonably priced parts and components. The Dodges worried about their near total dependence on Ford, recognizing that he would eventually become self-sufficient. In its last contract with Dodge Brothers, the Ford Motor Company agreed to buy from Dodge at least 80 percent of its requirements of transmissions, rear axles and drive shaft assemblies, steering gear assemblies, bronze and brass castings, and drop forgings. Although nine years remained on their long-term contract with Ford, in July 1913 the Dodge brothers gave Ford the required one-year notice that they would stop making components for him.[9]

Manufacturing the Dodge Automobile

Even before they broke with Ford, the Dodges hired Frederick J. Haynes in June 1912 to manage their growing manufacturing facilities and to oversee production of the automobile they intended to build. As early as May 1912, the *Motor World* reported that the Dodge brothers planned their own automobile in the near future. The same trade magazine ran a story in late August 1912 claiming that the new Dodge car would appear soon and would definitely be a six-cylinder model; the new Dodge car, which went into production in November 1914, was a four-cylinder model.[10]

Frederick Haynes had considerable experience running manufacturing plants and was well known to John Dodge. Haynes had worked in the 1890s at the

Syracuse Bicycle Company and the Hunter Arms Company (bicycles) and managed factories for the E. C. Stearnes Company of Toronto (bicycles) and the Canadian Cycle & Motor Company. He joined the H. H. Franklin Company, a mid-sized automobile maker in Syracuse, New York, in 1904 as an assistant superintendent. John Dodge tried to get Haynes to supervise production for the Ford Motor Company, but he declined the offer. Haynes was willing to work for John Dodge, but did not trust Ford or his lieutenants.[11]

With Haynes managing their factory and with work on their own car under way, the Dodge brothers broke with Ford. John Dodge resigned as director and vice president of the Ford Motor Company in August 1913, but the Dodges kept their stock. When Henry Ford refused to pay substantial dividends on Ford Motor Company stock starting in 1915, the Dodges led a stockholders' lawsuit that forced Ford to resume payments. Finally, in July 1919, Ford bought the Dodges' 10 percent share in the Ford Motor Company for $25 million. The Dodges had earned $5.4 million in dividends from their Ford stock since 1903 and additional profits of nearly $2 million from their contracts with Ford. Their original investment of $10,000 in the Ford Motor Company in 1903 yielded a total return of more than $32 million.[12]

The Dodge brothers began production of their own nameplate in November 1914. They needed more than a year of preparation before the first car rolled off the line. Horace Dodge designed most of the new car as well as the machinery needed to produce it, doing much of the work in a cottage on John Dodge's Meadow Brook Estate in rural Rochester, Michigan. Legend has it that John Dodge tested several brands of automobile tires by dropping them off a four-story building and studied the crash-worthiness of one prototype car by driving it into a wall at 20 mph.[13]

The Dodges substantially enlarged the Hamtramck plant to manufacture the Dodge automobile. The major additions included a four-story reinforced concrete assembly building, steel body shop, carpenter shop, die shop, compressor building, test building, and a large addition to the office building. Total spending on buildings was more than $1 million in 1914–15, with the assembly building alone costing $500,000 and the body shop about $250,000. The expansion efforts increased factory work space from about 500,000 square feet to nearly 1.4 million square feet. The Dodge brothers spent an additional $500,000 on new machine tools and other equipment.[14]

Automobile manufacturers, parts suppliers, and car dealers all recognized the Dodge brothers as low-cost producers of top-quality parts and components. Their excellent reputation, largely spread by word of mouth, was so great that 21,181 individuals, including many Ford dealers, asked to become Dodge agents without seeing the new car.[15] The *Michigan Manufacturer and Financial Record* summarized the public's views: "[W]hen the Dodge Bros. new car comes out, there is no question that it will be the best thing on the market for the money."[16]

The Dodge brothers also used advertising effectively to promote their new automobile among the general buying public. A series of billboard advertisements had only the words *Dodge Brothers* for several weeks, then included *Motor Car* for several more weeks, and, finally, *Reliable, Dependable, Sound.* One early advertisement read, "Think of all the Ford owners who would like to own an automobile." They announced their new car in the *Saturday Evening Post* on 19 August 1914—"Dodge Brothers, Detroit, who have manufactured the vital parts for more than 500,000 motor cars, will this fall market a car bearing their own name." None of these advertisements included illustrations or specifications for the new nameplate. The Dodges deliberately and effectively created enormous public anticipation by revealing nothing about the new car.[17]

The first Dodge, later named Old Betsy, came off the line on 14 November 1914. John and Horace had a photographer record their important moment, posing in the backseat in front of John Dodge's mansion on Boston Boulevard in Detroit. The Dodge brothers held a luncheon for local newspaper reporters at the Hamtramck plant that same afternoon and gave their guests test rides in the new car. The *Detroit News* reciprocated by running a long, gushing article in its afternoon edition, complete with a photograph of the new model and the caption, "Dodge Bros. New Car Is a Model of Smartness, Grace and Power."[18] This was only the beginning of a continuing publicity campaign to promote the car.

Dodge offered only the touring car body during the first nine months of production and then an alternative roadster. In September 1915, Dodge Brothers also announced its "Winter Car" models, which were simply a standard touring car or roadster with a detachable solid "winter top" with removable glass windows. This option cost $165 and enabled owners to use the car year-round.

The Dodges also decided, much like Henry Ford, to "freeze" their car designs and thus avoid the costs of annual model changes. A Dodge sales brochure for the 1924 models used the slogan, "Constantly Improved—But No Yearly Models," showing a lineup of touring cars from 1914 through 1924, all looking essentially the same. The major advantages were the savings in engineering and tooling costs for the manufacturer and higher used-car values for the customer.[19]

One important feature of the new Dodge car often overlooked was its all-steel body. In 1914, most automakers used either wood or metal/wood composite bodies, reflecting the manufacturing heritage of the body companies. Automobile body manufacturers such as Fisher and Wilson were originally makers of horse-drawn carriage bodies. The Dodge brothers allied themselves with a Philadelphia manufacturer, Edward G. Budd (1870–1945), to make all-steel bodies

The first Dodge automobile, "Old Betsy," in front of John Dodge's house at 75 East Boston Boulevard in Detroit, 14 November 1914. Horace Dodge (*left rear*) and John Dodge (*right rear*). Courtesy of DCHC.

for all of their cars. Dodge Brothers enjoyed a long, if sometimes rocky, relationship with Budd.

They adopted the all-steel body in part because it was stronger and cheaper than its wooden or composite alternatives. The all-steel body had steel panels and a steel frame. The main advantage was in the painting process. On wooden or composite bodies, painting typically took 10 or 12 days, with as many as 20 slow-drying coats applied by brush, each hand rubbed before the next coat was added. Steel bodies permitted the use of baked enamel, which could be rapidly dried in ovens, where temperatures might reach 400 degrees. Finishing times typically dropped to five days.[20]

The Dodge brothers ordered 5,000 steel bodies in 1914 and followed with an order for 50,000 more in 1915. These were for open-car models, touring cars and roadsters. This was the first mass-produced car using an all-steel body. Because Budd was not able to estimate his costs accurately, the Dodges agreed to a contract with "flexible" prices to assure that Budd would make a modest profit but not an excessive one.[21]

Dodge production climbed steadily through 1920, as the figures in table 4.1 show.

TABLE 4.1 Dodge Brothers Factory Production, 1914–20

1914	231
1915	45,003
1916	70,799
1917	101,270
1918	85,459
1919	121,010
1920	145,139

Source: Memorandum, R. J. Kelley, Chrysler Public Relations Department, to Frank Wylie, Dodge Division Public Relations Department, 31 May 1968, DCHC.
Note: Kelley derived the figures from statistics gathered by the Automobile Manufacturers Association; they refer to all production, foreign and domestic. The figures include trucks and other light commercial vehicles manufactured by Dodge.

Dodge Brothers increased sales by introducing additional models over time. Dodge produced only a touring car and roadster during the 1915 model year and the winter car versions of both starting in September 1915. There were no significant changes in the lineup until the 1917 model year, when Dodge increased the wheelbase on all its models from 110 to 114 inches and added a coupe and (center-door) sedan to its offerings. In October 1917, Dodge introduced a "screen-side" delivery truck, the Commercial Car, as a 1918 model. A closed-panel delivery truck, the Business Car, followed in March 1918. The last significant addition to the model lineup before the deaths of the two Dodge brothers was a four-door sedan that debuted in February 1919, the first of its type in the industry. Over the entire period of 1914 to 1920, there were remarkably few styling changes to the Dodge models.[22]

Unusual customer endorsements helped spread the Dodge automobile's reputation for reliability. During the 1916 U.S. military expedition in Mexico, war correspondent A. H. E. Beckett reported in *Motor Age* on the use of three Dodge cars in a surprise raid against the headquarters of a bandit leader, Colonel Julio Cardenas, in Chihuahua. Efforts to capture these bandits with soldiers mounted on horses failed because the horses were too slow. On 14 May, a daring Lieutenant George S. Patton Jr. led a successful raid using three Dodge cars as "mounts" for his men. They sped over a mile-long approach and surprised the enemy. Patton explained, "We couldn't have done it with horses. The motor car is the modern war horse." The American commander, Brigadier General John H. "Black Jack" Pershing, liked the Dodge car so much that he requested 250 of them for his army and ordered his staff to use them exclusively. Pershing later used Dodge cars on the battlefields of France.[23]

The Dodge brothers took on an important ordnance contract during the

First World War that reaffirmed their reputation as innovative, energetic manufacturers. In the fall of 1917, the U.S. Secretary of War, Newton Baker, asked
the Dodge brothers to produce delicate recoil mechanisms for two French heavy
artillery pieces, the 155 mm Schneider Howitzer and the 155 mm Filloux rifle.
They agreed to build and equip the munitions plant and supply fifty of the
mechanisms per day, beginning four months later. On 27 October 1917, Baker
accepted the Dodges' offer. Dodge Brothers delivered the first mechanisms, all
perfectly finished, four months after signing the contract. The Dodges soon
produced thirty recoil mechanisms per day, not the promised fifty, but the
results were six times the French output.[24]

John and Horace Dodge's success as engineers, designers, and manufacturers
largely resulted from their complementary talents and their ability to work together. Throughout their careers as independent businessmen, the Dodge brothers made all of their important decisions together. They insisted that all mail to
them be addressed "Dodge Brothers." They would return unopened anything
addressed to one of them as an individual. The two had a basic division of
labor in their work and maintained separate offices at opposite ends of the
administration building at their Hamtramck factory. John Dodge negotiated
contracts with suppliers; managed the firm's finances; directed sales, advertising,
and public relations; and served as the general administrator for the company.[25]

Horace Dodge was a mechanical genius who designed the products Dodge
Brothers manufactured and many of the machines used in their operations. He
organized and managed production. The shop floor was Horace's domain. He
was responsible for the engineering and design of the Dodge automobile and
for the design of scores of machines needed to manufacture the French artillery
recoil mechanism during the First World War. In describing Horace's mechanical inclinations, one historian noted:

> His office was literally a museum of parts, past, present and prospective,
> for Dodge Brothers cars. He was constantly scheming improved details,
> new processes, new methods and always building new machinery. He
> never lost the touch of the craftsman, could never let machinery alone.
> The atmosphere of the shop, as he entered it, would cause a noticeable
> change in his bearing. Outside, in the offices, in the places where men
> gather, even at home, he was quiet, reticent, and could be termed shy. But
> within the four walls of the shop he was the taciturn yet unquestionable
> master of the business.[26]

In manufacturing automotive components and later, complete automobiles,
the Dodge brothers were extremely efficient large-scale producers of quality
products and were as innovative as the Ford Motor Company in developing and

using new machinery. To be sure, Ford revolutionized the assembly of automobiles by minutely dividing the work into simple tasks and by refining the moving assembly line to produce the Model T on an unprecedented scale. He also used thousands of specialized, single-purpose machines to manufacture Model T components. Historians, however, have exaggerated Henry Ford's accomplishments, reflecting Ford's success at self-promotion.[27]

The Dodge factory was already a well-equipped, highly efficient factory and the largest automobile parts plant in the United States before the Dodge brothers made their own automobile. A contemporary observer noted, "It takes efficient manufacturing to supply parts like crankshafts, connecting rods, steering gears, transmissions, differentials, and axles to the manufacturer of almost the cheapest car in the world, on which the manufacturer has made millions, and to make millions yourself in selling those parts. That's what Dodge Brothers have done."[28]

Much of the specialized machinery found at the Ford Highland Park plant in 1915 was also in the Dodge Brothers plant that same year. This is not to suggest that the two factories were identical. Photographs of the Dodge plant in the 1910s do not show machines packed close together as at the Ford Highland Park plant. Ford's production of the Model T consistently dwarfed Dodge Brothers' output after 1914. For example, Dodge clearly had achieved large-scale production in 1917, with an output of 101,270 automobiles. For the year ending 31 July 1917, Ford turned out 730,041 Model Ts at Highland Park.[29]

The pace of work and general working conditions also differed at the two plants. To be sure, the Dodge brothers were not producing a low-priced car with a low profit margin like the Model T Ford. Nor were they paying Henry Ford's rate of $5 a day. But descriptions of the Dodge factory often included comments about the reasonable pace of work at the plant, presumably in contrast to conditions at the Ford plant. One observer proclaimed that at the Dodge Brothers factory, "Human haste, sweat and anxiety have been reduced to a minimum by a combination of ripe experience, far-sighted planning, and bold expenditure of money, and whatever strain is involved in enormous production falls on the machinery, not on the men. Nobody in the whole Dodge plant seems under tension."[30] The Dodges even supplied their forge and foundry workers with cold beer and sandwiches on hot summer afternoons. Their labor practices stood in sharp contrast to those followed by the puritanical Henry Ford.[31]

Dodge Brothers was a highly profitable enterprise with John and Horace Dodge at the helm, as the figures in table 4.2 illustrate.

The Dodge brothers were immensely successful in Detroit's business, political, and social arenas in the 1910s, but they did not live long enough to enjoy

TABLE 4.2 Dodge Brothers Performance, 1914–20

Year Ended	Unit Sales	Net Sales ($)	Net Earnings before Taxes ($)	Net Earnings as Share of Sales (%)
30 June 1915	17,959	11,665,940	268,939	2.3
30 June 1916	60,390	39,621,171	6,833,351	17.2
30 June 1917	89,077	61,060,801	9,269,012	15.2
31 Dec. 1918*	135,336	112,477,214	10,824,141	9.6
31 Dec. 1919	121,010	120,970,810	24,196,836	20.0
31 Dec. 1920	145,389	161,002,512	18,190,310	11.3

Source: Dodge Brothers, prospectus for securities issues of 1925, submitted to the State of Michigan, Commerce Department, Securities Bureau, State of Michigan Archives, Lansing, Mich., accession 70–5-A, lot 15, box 135.

Note: The sales figures for the entire period from 1914 to 31 December 1920 are remarkably consistent with the figures for factory production presented in table 4.1. Total sales figures were 567,161 and total factory production was 568,911 units.

*Period of 18 months

fully the fruits of their success. In early January 1920, while attending the National Automobile Show in New York City, both contracted influenza. Horace slowly recovered, but John's condition worsened and he died on 14 January at the Ritz-Carlton Hotel, with Horace at his side. John Dodge was 55 years old. Public viewing of his body and the funeral took place at his Boston Boulevard home in Detroit, with burial at Woodlawn Cemetery in Detroit. Sixteen Dodge factory workers served as pall bearers. Neither Horace Dodge nor John's widow, Matilda, could attend the funeral because they were still too sick with the flu. The *Detroit Free Press* observed at the time of his death: "This community can ill afford to lose John Dodge. He was a citizen who counted. He was one of the big forces in the making of modern Detroit and there is every reason to believe that if he had lived, the next ten-year period would have been the time of his greatest accomplishment."[32]

Horace Dodge did not survive the year. Physically weakened by his battle with influenza and psychologically devastated by John's death, he lost his will to live. He spent most of 1920 in Palm Beach, Florida, hoping that the warmer climate would aid his recovery. He became melancholy and withdrawn and rarely visited the factory when he was in Detroit. Horace Dodge died in Florida on 10 December 1920 at age 52. His funeral at his Rose Terrace mansion featured the Detroit Symphony Orchestra playing a funeral dirge. The Reverend Forrer, the Presbyterian minister who delivered the eulogy, described Horace Dodge as

Test track and incline at the Dodge Brothers plant in Hamtramck, Michigan, 1915.
Courtesy of NAHC.

"a man with a passion for music . . . a mechanic with the soul of a poet." The
family buried Horace next to John in the Dodge Mausoleum at Woodlawn
Cemetery.[33]

Following Horace Dodge's death, the *Detroit News* ran a lengthy editorial
concerning the two brothers:

> And it was not the mere physical fact of brotherhood that welded these
> two, John and Horace Dodge, together. It was a bond that had in it some-
> thing of strange depth and purity and fineness—something that tran-
> scended the usual brother-bond of good fellowship by splendor hardly to
> be guessed by men who have known no such love, and became a thing
> richly spiritual and very beautiful. For the brothers loved each other as
> friends. They were friends.[34]

We can only speculate on what the Dodge brothers might have accomplished
had they lived another ten or fifteen years. One intriguing piece of evidence

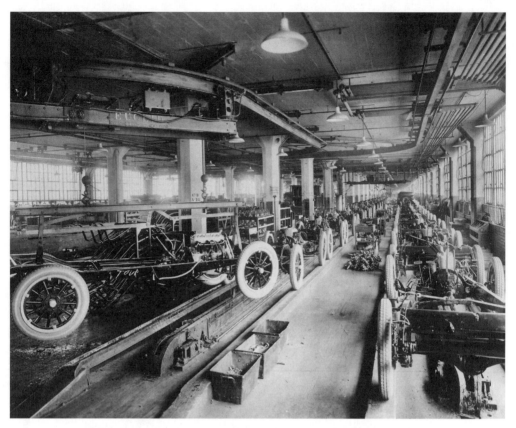

Dodge chassis assembly line, Dodge Brothers plant, Hamtramck, Michigan, 1915.
Courtesy of DCHC.

suggests that they were preparing to follow Henry Ford's lead in producing more of the raw materials needed for their automobiles. William G. Mather, president of the Cleveland-Cliffs Iron Company, a major Great Lakes iron ore producer, wrote to John Dodge in late December 1919, only three weeks before Dodge's death. H. A. Raymond, Cleveland-Cliffs's ore sales agent, had just returned from meeting with Dodge who had confirmed the Dodge brothers' plans to build blast furnaces and a steel mill somewhere on the Detroit River. Mather offered to supply them with iron ore for this new undertaking. The Dodge brothers were following Henry Ford's lead at his River Rouge site. Ford began building an iron works there in the fall of 1919 and the first blast furnace went into service on 17 May 1920. The untimely deaths of John and Horace Dodge in 1920 killed off their own plans.[35]

1919 Dodge four-door sedans, Dodge Brothers plant, Hamtramck, Michigan, 1919.
Courtesy of DCHC.

Chapter 5

DODGE BROTHERS IN THE 1920S

*Buying the Dodge [Brothers] was one of the soundest acts of my life. I say sincerely that nothing
we have done for the organization compares with that transaction. We had, before the merger,
an intensely sharp spearhead in the Chrysler Corporation, but when we put behind it all of
Dodge our spearhead had a weighty shaft and had become a potent thing.*

—Walter P. Chrysler

The Dodge brothers' company survived without its founders and continued to
produce cars and trucks profitably through the 1920s, but it struggled much of
the time. Frederick J. Haynes, groomed by the Dodges to run the company,
took control in 1920 and served as an effective leader until 1925. Dodge Brothers
enjoyed considerable success until the Dodge widows sold the firm to the investment banking firm of Dillon, Read, & Company in April 1925.

The Dillon, Read management, which lasted three years, brought a decline
in Dodge sales and profits, due largely to poor decisions made by executives who
had no experience in manufacturing or selling cars. Soured by its experience, the
investment bankers sold Dodge Brothers to Walter P. Chrysler in July 1928. The
Dodge nameplate survived and the Dodge enterprise became the core of a
greatly enlarged and prosperous Chrysler Corporation.

DODGE BROTHERS UNDER FREDERICK HAYNES, 1920–25

The death of John Dodge in January 1920 brought a realignment of the top
management positions at Dodge Brothers. Horace Dodge became president and
continued to serve as treasurer, Howard B. Bloomer became vice president and
Frederick J. Haynes, plant manager since 1912, became a director. At the end of
May 1920, the Dodge directors made Haynes a vice president and named him

general manager at a salary of $100,000 per year. The annual stockholders' meeting in mid-July 1920 confirmed these changes.[1]

By late November 1920, when Horace Dodge's continued poor health forced him to leave Detroit permanently for Florida, he set into motion a series of actions that would assure management continuity and the survival of the company bearing his family name. He wanted to be certain that his long-term associates, Howard Bloomer, Frederick Haynes, and John Ballantyne, "should be the controlling factors in the business." Ballantyne was a prominent Detroit banker and trustee for John Dodge's estate. Horace Dodge convinced his board to sign a five-year contract with Haynes to serve as president of Dodge Brothers after his death. In November 1920, the board extended Haynes's contract as general manager at a salary of $150,000 per year.[2]

Immediately after Horace Dodge's death, *Automotive Industries* predicted that New York financial interests would try to gain control of the firm and would probably succeed.[3] The Dodge brothers had rebuffed earlier offers by New York investment bankers, but the widows were more likely to sell. None of the children of John or Horace Dodge had any interest in running the business—or the ability to do so. The factory closed during the first three months of 1921 because of depressed sales, but then reopened in April with Haynes clearly in charge.

Dodge Brothers was in many respects controlled by the ghosts of the Dodge brothers until the property changed hands in 1925. The Dodge directors declared a special dividend of 120 percent ($12 million) at the end of 1921 to help the Dodge widows pay the heavy federal and state inheritance taxes that were due. They also agreed to buy lands to donate to the State of Michigan to create parks in memory of John and Horace Dodge. In fall of 1922, the company announced the donation of 11 park sites totaling 627 acres, all in Oakland County north of Detroit.[4]

Following the precepts laid down by John and Horace Dodge, Haynes promoted engineering improvements in the Dodge cars, rather than mere cosmetic changes. Dodge Brothers' introduction of the all-steel closed car in the 1923 model year was a good example of Haynes's willingness to innovate. The closed car was growing in popularity in the early 1920s. In the year starting in the fall of 1921, the share of closed cars in the Dodge production "mix" jumped from 13 percent to 35 percent. With the approval of the Dodge board of directors, Haynes and Edward G. Budd jointly developed the new models.[5]

The Dodge Business Coupe, introduced in summer 1922, was the first all-steel closed car in the automobile industry, although the Dodge brothers had developed an all-steel open car as early as 1914. An all-steel four-door sedan followed in fall 1922. The all-steel body used a steel frame and steel panels and was lighter and stronger than the composite wood and steel bodies of the time.

One great advantage of the steel body was that it allowed Dodge to use baked enamel finishes on its closed vehicles.[6]

Frederick Haynes's most important move during his tenure as president of Dodge Brothers was the alliance with Graham Brothers Company, a manufacturer of medium and heavy trucks, leading to the Dodge Brothers' outright purchase of the firm. The brothers Graham (Joseph B., Robert C., and Ray A.) began their industrial careers in glass manufacturing in Indiana in 1901. They sold the Graham Glass Company to the Libbey-Owens Sheet Glass Company in 1916 and the Grahams left the business. Libbey-Owens later merged in 1930 with the Edward B. Ford Glass Company to form giant Libbey-Owens-Ford. The Grahams also launched the Graham Brothers Company in 1916, with a factory in Evansville, Indiana, where they produced kits which converted automobile chassis into light-duty trucks. They reached an agreement with Haynes in 1921 to manufacture trucks in Detroit under their own name, but to use Dodge engines and transmissions and to sell their trucks exclusively through the Dodge dealer network.[7]

The Dodge–Graham Brothers relationship was useful for both parties. Graham could sell its trucks through the Dodge dealer network, which in 1924 boasted 3,500 outlets nationwide.[8] Graham gave Dodge customers a full line of truck options—Dodge commercial vehicles generally had a carrying capacity of three-quarters of a ton, while Graham Brothers produced trucks rated between one- and two-and-one-half-tons capacity. As table 5.1 shows, the volume of Graham Brothers trucks sold through Dodge grew substantially in the early 1920s. Graham Brothers was an informal affiliate of Dodge Brothers and kept its corporate independence until October 1925.

TABLE 5.1 Graham Brothers Truck Sales, 1921–26

1921	1,212
1922	3,403
1923	6,971
1924	10,744
1925	23,884
1926	37,463

Sources: Dodge Brothers, *Annual Report to the Stockholders For the Year Ended December 31, 1925,* 8 and *Annual Report to the Stockholders for the Year Ended December 31, 1926,* 8.

The Dodge Brothers directors decided in August 1924 to secure an option on 51 percent of the Graham Brothers Company stock and to work more closely with the firm. Graham became an operating division of Dodge Brothers, directly controlled by Dodge. More than a year passed before Dodge exercised its stock option on 1 October 1925. An appraisal of the Graham Brothers factories, dated 31 December 1925, included plants in Evansville Indiana; Stockton, California; Detroit; and Toronto. The "sound value" of all four was $2,328,452, with the Evansville plant accounting for $1,942,452 of the total.

In mid-December 1925, the three Graham brothers became directors of Dodge Brothers, and received important management positions—Ray became general manager, Joseph took over as vice president in charge of manufacturing, and Robert became vice president and general sales manager. Only four months later, in mid-April 1926, the Dodge directors bought the remaining 49 percent of the Graham Brothers stock, and the three Grahams severed all connections with Dodge. The Grahams bought the Paige-Detroit Motor Car Company in 1927, reorganized it as the Graham-Paige Motors Corporation, and produced cars for the next two decades.[9]

Dodge Brothers suffered through the recession of 1921 but then recovered quickly in 1922, as table 5.2 shows. After beginning as the number two producer behind Ford but well ahead of Chevrolet in 1920, Dodge slipped to third in 1921, behind Ford and Buick. Dodge fell to sixth place in 1923, but then rebounded to a strong number three position in 1924, only to slip back to fifth place in 1925. Dodge's last prosperous year as an independent automaker was 1926, when its production of 331,764 cars put it firmly back in third place behind Ford and Chevrolet.[10]

Despite Frederick Haynes's successful managerial record at Dodge Brothers and an apparently bright future for the company, the Dodge widows, Matilda Rausch Dodge and Anna Thomson Dodge, decided in early 1925 to sell the enterprise. Dodge Brothers' directors hired an outside firm, the Manufacturers' Appraisal Company, to put a dollar value on the physical assets. Manufacturers' report, issued on 31 March 1925, included the following commentary: "In all our appraisal experience we have never reviewed a more substantial group of buildings, they are not particularly elaborate or ornate in the common sense of the word but are constructed of the best materials obtainable applied in the best known art of the trade and are in keeping with the Dodge Brothers [insistence] on perfection." The "cost of reproduction" (replacement cost) for all the Dodge plants came to $54,687,352, but the "sound valuation" (depreciated value) was $40,823,601. The Dodge Main plant accounted for $37,175,024 of the later figure.[11]

The *New York Times* reported that when the Dodge widows informally put the company on the market in January 1925, more than a dozen offers came in. The Dodge widows accepted that from the New York banking house of Dillon, Read, & Company, for $146 million in cash. It included a $50 million valuation for "good will," which Dodge Brothers had always carried on its books valued at $1 only. A unanimous vote of the stockholders on 30 April 1925 ratified the sale. Each of the Dodge widows held or controlled 249,995 shares of stock (out

TABLE 5.2 Dodge Brothers Performance, 1920–27

Year Ended 31 Dec.	Car Sales	Truck Sales*	Total Unit Sales	Exports as Share of Sales (%)	Net Sales ($)	Net Earnings† ($)	Net Earnings as Share of Sales (%)	Dividends ($)
1920	—	—	145,389	—	161,002,512	12,798,127	7.9	—
1921	—	—	92,476	2.9	83,666,284	2,375,726	2.8	16,000,000
1922	142,041	21,996	164,037	6.9	130,625,774	16,874,722	12.9	46,000,000
1923	136,006	43,499	179,505	9.4	141,332,685	10,195,730	7.2	—
1924	194,341	27,894	222,235	10.2	191,652,446	17,520,221	9.1	7,000,000
1925	209,254	50,713	259,967	12.0	219,520,842	13,746,657	6.3	9,904,687
1926	264,471	67,293	331,764	—	252,997,484	21,591,920	8.5	21,591,919
1927	146,527	58,733	205,260	—	173,581,526	9,641,427	5.6	9,641,426

Sources: Dodge Brothers, prospectus for securities issues of 1925, submitted to the State of Michigan, Commerce Department, Securities Bureau, State of Michigan Archives, Lansing, Mich., accession 70–5-A, lot 15, box 135 and *Annual Report to the Stockholders for the Year Ended December 31, 1925; December 31, 1926; and December 31, 1927,* box "Dodge Brothers 7," DCHC. The unit sales figures for 1922–27 are the numbers submitted by Dodge Brothers to the National Automobile Chamber of Commerce, found in NAHC.

Note: Dividends for 1925, 1926, and 1927 are the totals paid on preference stock and on common stock.

*Sales of Graham Brothers trucks are included starting in 1926.

†Net of depreciation, interest, and taxes

Dodge Main plant, Hamtramck, Michigan, 1960. Courtesy of DCHC.

of 500,000), with five others holding two shares each. The deal was consummated on 30 April, when Clarence Dillon signed a certified check for $146 million, the purchase price. Business historians have claimed that this was the largest cash transaction in history up to that time.[12]

THE DILLON, READ YEARS, 1925–28

Immediately after buying Dodge Brothers, Dillon, Read, & Company created a new legal entity, Dodge Brothers, Inc. (chartered in Maryland), to take over the assets of Dodge Brothers, a Michigan corporation. Dillon, Read restructured Dodge's long-term finances in a way that left the banking houses firmly in control while making a quick profit. They offered $75 million in Dodge bonds and $85 million in Dodge nonvoting preferred stock (850,000 shares) to the public, which quickly snapped up the offerings. Dillon, Read thus received $160 million, turning a healthy profit of $14 million on their Dodge purchase.[13]

Dillon, Read substantially changed the Dodge managerial team after the Graham brothers left Dodge in April 1926. Edward G. Wilmer became president and Haynes was "bumped upstairs" to become chairman of the board. Dillon, Read paid Wilmer, who served as president until the sale of Dodge to Walter P. Chrysler, a regular salary of $250,000 annually, 1 percent of Dodge Brothers profits between $15 million and $20 million, and 2 percent of all profits above $20 million. The board of directors also gave him $50,000 to cover the expenses of moving his family from New York City to Detroit. In 1926, when Dodge Brothers had profits of nearly $27.8 million, Wilmer earned an additional $206,000 under his contract.[14]

Edward G. Wilmer became president of Dodge Brothers at age 39. Originally trained as a lawyer, he worked in several executive positions in the 1910s with the Milwaukee Coke and Gas Company, the Newport Mining Company, and the Steel & Tube Company of America. When Clarence Dillon refinanced and reorganized the troubled Goodyear Tire & Rubber Company in 1921, he asked Wilmer to direct the efforts. Wilmer led a dramatic financial turnaround at Goodyear, where he served as president from 1921 to 1923 and then as chairman of the board until 1926, when he took over the management at Dodge.[15]

By the end of 1926, Wilmer transferred the production of Dodge three-quarter-ton commercial vehicles to the Graham Brothers facilities in Detroit, and Dodge Brothers manufactured passenger cars exclusively. By then, Graham Brothers was wholly owned by Dodge, an operating division of the larger concern. In 1926, Graham produced chassis with capacities of one ton, one and one-half tons, and two tons, with a variety of bodies, all sold as Graham Brothers trucks. The 1926 Dodge lineup included a new Series Four commercial car, redesigned with a completely closed cab, and offered in the popular screen-side and panel body styles of the past.[16]

Dodge changed little in its 1927 lineup compared to 1926. However, the company did introduce a new four-cylinder engine with a five-bearing crankshaft, replacing the engine with a three-bearing crankshaft in use since 1914. Beginning in May 1927, Dodge Brothers announced an entirely new lineup of passenger cars for 1928, the first major shake-up of Dodge products since 1914. In addition to a new line of four-cylinder cars, the Fast Four, Dodge introduced three new lines of six-cylinder automobiles for the 1928 model year—the Senior Six, the Victory Six, and the Standard Six.[17]

The first new introduction, the Senior Six line, appeared in early May 1927 and was the most expensive new model, with prices ranging from $1,595 to $1,770. A completely reworked four-cylinder car, called the Fast Four (base price of $855) went into production in August 1927. Dodge Brothers produced 55,000 of these before the end of the calendar year. The mid-priced Victory Six debuted in January 1928, with a base price of $1,045, but with the price of some models as high as $1,295. Finally, in March 1928, Dodge announced the Standard Six (also known as the Light Six), priced at $875–$970, to replace the Fast Four, less than a year old.[18]

This last batch of new Dodge models of the pre-Chrysler era were solid, comfortable cars, but with few innovative features. They generally received good, solid reviews in the automotive press, but failed to sell well. Combined sales of cars and trucks fell sharply from 331,764 units in 1926 to 205,260 in 1927, a decline of 38 percent. Part of the downturn reflected the inherent production difficulties of simultaneously introducing all new lines of cars. The new models, markedly more expensive than the old Dodge four-cylinder cars, did not catch the public's eye. In going "upmarket," Dodge abandoned its longtime customers. By any standard, 1927 was a disaster for Dodge Brothers. Sales fell from nearly $253 million in 1926 to $173,581,526 in 1927, and net earnings dropped from $21,591,920 to only $9,641,427. In a single year, the company lost one-third of its sales revenues and more than half of its profits.

The financial value of Dodge Brothers as an asset also declined, and this alone probably convinced Dillon, Read to consider unloading it when the opportunity arose. From 1926 to 1927, profits per share of common stock fell from $6.46 to $1.43. The stock prices began to reflect the drop in earnings. Between 1 January 1927 and 1 January 1928, Dodge preferred stock fell from $82 a share to $74 a share, while common stock prices dropped from $25 to $23 per share. This decline was particularly striking in a year when the prices of automobile stocks increased approximately 50 percent for the shares of 23 major automakers.[19]

According to testimony given before the New York State Supreme Court in late June 1928, Edward Wilmer approached the Dillon, Read partners in April 1928 and practically begged them to find someone to buy Dodge Brothers. He conceded that after spending close to $15 million converting the Dodge plants for the new six-cylinder models, the company had introduced new models that it could not sell. These were the circumstances that first led Clarence Dillon to approach Walter Chrysler regarding the sale of Dodge. Fortunately, Walter Chrysler was more than simply amenable to this prospect—he was as desperate to buy Dodge as Wilmer was to sell it.[20]

MERGER OF CHRYSLER AND DODGE

Walter Chrysler wanted the Dodge property by early 1928. The Chrysler line of cars was popular and profitable, but the company was hard-pressed to increase production and reduce costs. It needed to do both in order to grow and survive in an increasingly competitive industry. Neither of the two major plants, the former Maxwell facility in Highland Park or the former Chalmers plant in Detroit, had significant casting or forging capacity. Dodge Brothers, however, had large, modern, and efficient foundries and forges.

Walter Chrysler also desperately needed more manufacturing capacity because of his well-advanced plans to expand his automobile offerings. Before the announcement of the Chrysler-Dodge merger on 1 June 1928, Chrysler had already started manufacturing two new models, the low-priced Plymouth and the mid-priced DeSoto. The official announcements of the new models came on 7 July and 4 August respectively, but both were already in production in

June. Walter Chrysler began planning for the DeSoto in 1926 and a separate DeSoto Division was already in place before Chrysler bought Dodge.

Before the Dodge merger, Walter Chrysler did his homework. He considered a merger with Willys-Overland and prepared an operating statement comparing the performance of Chrysler and Willys-Overland for 1927 and the first quarter of 1928. The "tale of the tape" reveals why Walter Chrysler shied away from Willys. Chrysler's sales in 1927 were slightly higher than Willys (192,083 versus 187,776), but Chrysler's net profits were more than three times those of Willys ($19,485,000 versus $5,529,000). Although Willys shipped 43 percent more cars in the first quarter of 1928 (74,578 versus 52,326 for Chrysler), its projected profits for the year were still less than half of Chrysler's.[21]

Someone in the Chrysler organization compiled comparative data for Dodge and Chrysler for 1927 and the first quarter of 1928. Although Dodge vehicle sales in 1927 were down substantially from 1926 (205,260 versus 331,764), Chrysler's forecaster projected them to rebound in 1928. Detailed comparisons of retail prices and sales volumes of the various Chrysler and Dodge models revealed that there was a good deal of overlap.[22]

Strategic thinking about the long-term future of the Chrysler Corporation led to the merger with Dodge, not the narrow calculations of likely sales and profit margins. A three-page summary of the advantages of the merger plan for Chrysler Corporation included a long list of the benefits the new entity would gain through larger size and sales volume. In brief, Chrysler could be more like General Motors—it could operate an export company to promote overseas sales and a finance company to finance dealers' inventories and consumer installment purchases, much like General Motors Acceptance Corporation. It could make a greater share of its own parts requirements, especially electrical equipment. Larger size would bring economies in research, engineering, and purchasing. Gaining a truck business was another significant benefit. The most significant overriding advantage was simple: "The combination will result in a strengthened company, better able to finance its requirements for development and expansion and better able to withstand the competition of the dominant factor in the motor industry, General Motors Corporation."[23] Long-term survival was at stake, and long-term success was not likely unless Chrysler Corporation became a lot bigger.

One feature of the Dodge business that appealed to Walter Chrysler was its large, efficient systems of dealers and distributors, generally viewed as one of the best in the industry. To produce the low-priced Plymouth and compete with Ford and Chevrolet without an extensive dealer system already in place would have been a daunting task. Automotive writer Walter Boynton estimated that Chrysler and Dodge each had about 4,600 dealers in 1928. Contemporary reports on the 1928 merger suggest a combined U.S. dealership network of about

9,000 outlets. By late 1929, after Plymouth and DeSoto were well established brands, the combined Chrysler dealer network had about 12,000 outlets in the United States, 2,600 in Canada, and 3,800 overseas.[24]

In reporting the merger, the *Automotive Daily News* offered the following analysis:

> Exactly what is the gain in the whole transaction? The Chrysler [sic], one of the strongest organizations in the industry, acquires an extremely efficient and well-located plant, capable of a higher production, even, than its past records prove it can give. The most important gain that Chrysler makes is unquestionably increased representation. It costs much time and money to build a dealer organization, and by this merger Chrysler is taking over a full-fledged and powerful merchandizing army.[25]

The story of how the Chrysler-Dodge merger took place is an often-repeated epochal tale based entirely on Walter Chrysler's version published in his autobiography. Clarence Dillon approached Chrysler in mid-April 1928 and initiated discussions. Dillon's move came fresh on the heels of Chrysler's announcement of the new DeSoto line of cars, priced to compete head-to-head with Dodge. Chrysler feigned a lack of interest, trying to depress the asking price. After more than a month of thrusts and counterthrusts, the two men rented adjoining suites at the Ritz in New York where, along with their financial experts and attorneys, they engaged in marathon negotiations for five days. They reached an agreement, which both men submitted to their respective boards of directors on 29 May for approval. Walter Chrysler also received a legal opinion that the proposed merger would not violate the Clayton (antitrust) Act.[26]

It was vital to Walter P. Chrysler that the merger involve no cash, because he had none to spend. Instead, the Chrysler Corporation issued new shares of common stock, with a market value of about $170 million, to exchange for the existing Dodge Brothers shares. Dodge stockholders would receive 1 share of Chrysler common stock in exchange for 1 share of Dodge Preference Stock, or 5 shares of Dodge Common Stock Class A (nonvoting), or 10 shares of Dodge Common Stock Class B (voting). A contemporary article in the *Magazine of Wall Street* examined the merger in terms of the financial interests of all categories of Dodge and Chrysler stockholders and concluded that the merger was a good deal for everyone.

The key precondition of this deal was a requirement that Dillon, Read get the owners of 90 percent of all three types of Dodge stock to agree to the merger by 1 July 1928. Walter Chrysler did not want to become embroiled with minority stockholders challenging the merger in court, as Chalmers stockholders had done in the early 1920s. Chrysler extended the deadline to 31 July and even then, Clarence Dillon barely produced the required amount of stock. Late that afternoon, Chrysler's executives took over the Dodge plants and posted signs that read, "Dodge Division, Chrysler Corporation."[27]

All of the contemporary reports of the merger recognized that Chrysler had emerged as a very large automaker, behind only General Motors and Ford in sales and manufacturing capacity and clearly well ahead of the remaining firms in the industry. With the successful introduction of the DeSoto and Plymouth lines of cars in 1928, production, sales, and profits soared at Chrysler. Following the merger announcement, the *Automotive Daily News* ran an editorial entitled simply "The Big Three"—thereby coining the expression. It noted: "With this merger completed, the automobile manufacturing field is now dominated by a 'big three,' composed of General Motors, Ford, and Chrysler-Dodge. On their present production schedules . . . these three companies will account for nearly 75 percent of the passenger car manufacturing in this country today."[28]

Chapter 6

SUCCESS AND STRUGGLE, 1928–33

Progress made by the Chrysler organization in the last six years constitutes an outstanding success among industrial corporations. No other company in the automobile industry exceeds Chrysler's record of accomplishment in this period. Few companies in other industries have attained a comparable position. In forward-looking motor car design and construction, in manufacturing skill, in financial stability, in marketing organization and in creating a continually enlarging public demand for its products, Chrysler Corporation has attained a commanding place in the American motor car industry.

—Six Years' Progress of Chrysler Motors

During the six years that began with the merger of Chrysler and Dodge Brothers in 1928, Chrysler Corporation experienced an intense roller-coaster ride of exhilarating successes in 1928 and 1929, followed by lost sales and profits from 1930 to 1933, the trough of the Great Depression. Still, its performance was nevertheless remarkably strong. Chrysler rebounded more rapidly than the other automakers, largely on the strength of the Plymouth brand. Overall sales in 1933 slightly surpassed the record for 1929, a remarkable turnaround.

CHRYSLER IN FULL BLOOM, 1928–29

One major task Walter Chrysler faced after taking over Dodge Brothers was the revival of Dodge sales. The actions of Chrysler Corporation in remaking the Dodge car lines was proof that the Dodge nameplate would survive. In September 1928, the Dodge Division introduced a new Senior Six line, with a longer wheelbase, a more powerful engine, more interior room, and a variety of additional mechanical improvements. Dodge had previously announced changes in its Victory Six line and was soon to disclose similar changes to the Standard Six line. These efforts stopped the sales slide and resulted in an increase of total Dodge car and truck sales from 205,260 units in 1927 to 231,384 in 1928, an impressive gain.[1]

In mid-September 1929, Walter P. Chrysler addressed the top Dodge managers, outlining his efforts to restore the prestige of the Dodge name, damaged during the years of Dillon, Read management. He planned to revive the "Dodge Brothers" emblem and nameplate on all the Dodge products, including trucks. The new Victory Six line, introduced in January 1929, was renamed the Dodge Brothers Six and was a great success. The eight-cylinder Dodge line introduced in 1930 was called the Dodge Brothers Eight, and as late as the 1932 models, both the Dodge Brothers name and the geometric Dodge symbol appeared as radiator emblems.

Chrysler first used the ram's head as a hood ornament on the 1931 model Dodge cars. Fred Zeder had decided to add a hood ornament that was "distinctive, attractive, and totally American." Since the Rocky Mountain big horn ram was an American species with the characteristics of strength and agility, it was a perfect symbol for Dodge. Not until 1938 did Chrysler Corporation entirely drop the old Dodge Brothers nomenclature and symbols.[2]

The Dodge purchase created some overlap with Chrysler's existing offerings of light trucks and commercial vehicles. In September 1928, Chrysler Corporation had announced a new Fargo line of commercial cars and light trucks. The basic Fargo vehicle design work had been completed in early 1928, and production of the Fargo line at the Highland Park plant was under way by June, well before the Dodge purchase. The line of trucks initially included a half-ton version, the Fargo Packet, and a three-quarter-ton truck, the Fargo Clipper. Each was sold in two versions—as a "commercial car" with removable seats and as a panel delivery truck.

The history of Fargo truck manufacturing is difficult to follow, for lack of records. Fargo produced only 1,063 Packet four-cylinder models from September 1928 through March 1929 and then two versions of the Packet Six from March 1929 through November 1930, for a grand total of 2,169 units. They manufactured 1,424 Clippers from August 1928 to March 1930 and a total of 5,014 Freighter models from June 1929 through October 1930, all in Detroit. Fargo also produced a line of 21-passenger buses starting in October 1930. By the late 1930s, Fargo Motor Company was a Chrysler division that handled all of the automaker's fleet sales and produced military vehicles for the U.S. Army. Fargo Motor continued to produce trucks for international sales at least through the 1974 model year.[3]

Chrysler Corporation's two new car lines introduced in mid-1928, sold as the 1928 Plymouth and the 1929 DeSoto, were closely intertwined in terms of design and components. Both enjoyed immediate success, but over the next decade, Plymouth became the mainstay of the Chrysler Corporation, enabling the company to survive the Depression of the 1930s and the Airflow disaster of 1934–37 (see chapter 7). Both car lines had an identical wheelbase and shared many parts and components, including body panels. The most significant difference was the engine—the Plymouth had a four-cylinder and the DeSoto a six-cylinder.

Walter Chrysler officially introduced the Plymouth to the public on 7 July 1928 and the DeSoto on 4 August. Although Plymouth predated DeSoto by about a month, this chapter will consider DeSoto first.

The origins of the DeSoto line are murky. In a 1958 interview, K. T. Keller claimed that Chrysler began developing the DeSoto as a mid-priced car right after he joined Chrysler in April 1926. Walter Chrysler planned to have this new line compete directly with the Dodge Brothers cars and hoped to convince Dodge dealers to carry both. He probably launched DeSoto to threaten Dillon, Read with such serious competition for Dodge that the banker would be forced to sell Dodge Brothers to him.[4]

One of Chrysler's challenges was to build a DeSoto dealer network from scratch. Once Chrysler announced the new line, 500 dealers took franchise options without seeing the product. They came to Detroit for a private showing of the DeSoto on 7 July 1928 and 95 percent immediately signed contracts. Chrysler placed a full-page advertisement signed by J. E. Fields in *Automobile Topics* in late July 1928 appealing to established dealers of other nameplates to take a DeSoto franchise. By January 1929, the DeSoto line had 1,500 dealers, and by late November 1929, more than 2,300, all carrying DeSoto exclusively.[5]

Chrysler named the new car line after Hernando DeSoto, the sixteenth-century Spanish explorer who conquered Florida, discovered the Mississippi River, and served as Spain's governor of Cuba. The courage, daring, and integrity of the man were to be embodied in the DeSoto automobile. The first set of advertisements for the new line emphasized that the DeSoto Six was a product of Walter P. Chrysler's commitment to engineering and manufacturing excellence. The maxim that accompanied the DeSoto crest, "Multum pro Parvo," meaning "much for little," proclaimed that this was a car of remarkable value.[6]

Automobile Topics gave the DeSoto rave reviews in early August 1928. This important industry trade publication noted that DeSoto had many features simply not found in other mid-priced cars, including a powerful Chrysler-designed engine with an unusually heavy-duty crankshaft. The reviewer noted, "The car has positively brilliant performance and handles with great ease." The DeSoto base prices ($845–$885) placed it clearly between Plymouth ($685–$735) and the Chrysler 65 ($1,040–$1,145), making the DeSoto a good value. More important, the buying public agreed with this evaluation of DeSoto. Early sales were impressive—34,518 cars shipped in calendar 1928, 81,065 units over the first twelve months, and more than 100,000 cars after only fourteen months of production. This was a first-year sales record that would not be topped until the 1960 introduction of the Ford Falcon.[7]

As successful as the DeSoto was, Walter Chrysler's low-priced model had far more significance to Chrysler. The first Plymouth car came off the assembly line in Highland Park on 11 June 1928, followed by the public introduction on 7

July. Advertisements informed potential buyers that the car was so named because it typified "the endurance and strength, the rugged honesty, the determination of achievement and freedom from old limitations of that Pilgrim band who were the first American colonists." The early product literature featured an illustration of the *Mayflower* dominating the covers. A few Chrysler dealers even dressed as Pilgrims, at least for the initial introduction.

Early print advertising and brochures called the new model the "Chrysler Plymouth" and emphasized that it was "Chrysler-designed" and "Chrysler-built." One of the earliest advertisements appeared in the *Saturday Evening Post* on 7 July 1928, announcing the Chrysler Plymouth as "a New Car . . . a New Style, a New Zenith of Low Priced Car—Luxury and Performance." The Chrysler name appeared 14 times, and readers learned Plymouth would be sold at dealerships selling the Chrysler nameplate. Plymouth was available in six body types, ranging in price from $670 for the coupe and roadster to $725 for the four-door sedan. The Plymouth was not yet priced to compete head-to-head with the other low-priced cars in the market. A comparable four-door Model A sedan sold for $600, while a Chevrolet sedan had a price of $675. In January 1929, the name "Chrysler" was removed from the radiator emblem.[8]

Initially, more than 4,000 Chrysler dealerships in North America sold Plymouths. Chrysler management, however, hoped to create a network of exclusive Plymouth dealerships as well. In the last six months of 1928, Chrysler Corporation placed advertisements in automobile trade magazines recruiting dealers to sell the new nameplate. The sales pitch offered "a new and special Plymouth franchise" and practically guaranteed high-volume sales.[9] However, there is no evidence that any significant number of exclusive Plymouth franchises were established.

The first Plymouth (Model Q) really was "Chrysler-designed," because it was a reworked version of the four-cylinder Chrysler 52, no longer produced after May 1928. Plymouth offered features not available from its low-priced competitors, Ford and Chevrolet. These included four-wheel hydraulic brakes, aluminum alloy pistons, full pressured lubrication for the engine (versus the "splash system" commonly used for low-priced models), and a separate hand brake. Plymouth production of 58,031 units for the 1929 model year was promising, but was still dwarfed by sales of 481,000 Fords and 767,000 Chevrolets. Production of Plymouth increased the following year to 93,613 units.[10]

Chrysler's major challenge of 1928 was to increase production of the Chrysler and Dodge lines while introducing the all-new Plymouth and DeSoto lines at the same time. Its strategy was to make the old plants more efficient and to build new facilities. K. T. Keller's manufacturing genius and organizational abilities freed up half the floor space at Dodge Main within ninety days after the Chrysler-Dodge merger. Keller rearranged component production to eliminate waste and create better production flow. He also increased output greatly in the existing departments at Dodge. Production from the foundry rose from 450,000 to 1,250,000 pounds per day, and the pressed steel plant capacity jumped from 600,000 to 1.5 million pounds per day, with no increase in floor space required.[11]

Chrysler Corporation brought an enormous plant to manufacture and assemble the Plymouth into full production in January 1929. Located at Lynch Road and Mt. Elliot Avenue in Detroit, near the Dodge Main plant, the factory was really an enlargement of the Dodge factory built for the Senior Six and completed in April 1927 at a cost of $4.5 million. The existing single-story building, measuring 250 feet by 1,950 feet, was enlarged to 375 feet by 2,490 feet. They broke ground on 10 October 1928, the first Plymouths rolled off the assembly line in late December, and the plant was finished by 15 January 1929.

Chrysler Corporation had changed radically in the course of 1928, especially in terms of the vehicle lines it produced. It was able to follow the successful marketing strategy pursued by General Motors under Alfred Sloan since the early 1920s—"variety marketing" using a hierarchy of models differentiated from each other by size, horsepower, and price. General Motors offered "a car for every purse" starting in 1921. By the late 1920s, the product lineup began with Chevrolet, then moved upward in price to Pontiac, Oldsmobile, Buick, La Salle, and finally Cadillac.[12] The same was true at Chrysler by the early 1930s, once DeSoto was permanently priced above Dodge. Chrysler Corporation could offer its customers a "stepladder" of cars, starting with Plymouth and then going upscale to Dodge, DeSoto, Chrysler, and Imperial.

At the end of 1928, Chrysler Motors adopted a new circular logo, a tree with branches and roots, with "Chrysler Motors" and "Standardized Quality" around the circumference. Under the logo was the statement, "All branches on the same tree; all growing out of the Chrysler root principle of standardized quality." A list of Chrysler Motors products followed: Chrysler Imperial; Chrysler 75; Chrysler 65; Dodge Brothers Senior; Dodge Brothers Six; DeSoto Six; Plymouth; Dodge Brothers trucks, buses, and motor coaches; Fargo trucks and commercial cars; and Chrysler marine engines.[13]

Chrysler Motors used the tree logo and the "Standardized Quality" theme in promoting the new Plymouth and DeSoto lines. In a two-page advertisement for the DeSoto Six in the *Saturday Evening Post*, one page was a specific ad for the DeSoto. The other was a brief essay, "The Real Genius of Chrysler," referring to Walter P. Chrysler. The meaning of "Chrysler Standardized Quality" also was spelled out. Engineering breakthroughs were first introduced on the highest-priced Chrysler products and then spread downward to the lowest-priced products, with no loss of quality. In summary, "It is this *applied* genius for giving greater value that is the real measure of Walter P. Chrysler and the inimitable means by which Chrysler Motors constantly seeks to achieve the greatest values in the motor world."[14]

Chrysler Corporation's early success was largely the result of its attractive automobile lines, which were technologically advanced in terms of design features, stylistically pleasing, and promoted well. Chrysler also produced its cars efficiently, with excellent quality control, reflecting the manufacturing background and interests of Walter P. Chrysler and his chief lieutenant, K. T. Keller. They achieved great efficiencies at their older factories as well as at the new plants like Plymouth Lynch Road.

By any measure, Chrysler Corporation enjoyed substantial success in 1928 and 1929 (see table 6.1). The number of vehicles sold and the dollar value of sales more than doubled from 1927 to 1929, reflecting the Dodge purchase and the launch of the Plymouth and DeSoto lines. The profit margins on sales fell by half from 1927 to 1929, reflecting the fact that all of the new car lines introduced in 1928—Dodge, DeSoto, and Plymouth—had lower prices and lower profit margins than the Chrysler line.

TABLE 6.1 Chrysler Corporation Performance, 1927–33

			Net Earnings*		
	Unit Sales	Net Sales $	Total ($)	On Sales (%)	On Capital Invested† (%)
1927	192,083	172,343,953	19,484,880	11.3	22.8
1928	360,399	315,304,817	29,949,800	9.5	24.8
1929	450,543	375,033,455	21,902,168	5.8	16.8
1930	269,899	207,789,338	234,155	0.0	0.0
1931	272,118	183,805,105	1,468,935	0.1	1.3
1932	222,512	136,546,522	(11,254,232)	(loss)	(loss)
1933	451,734	238,675,952	12,129,120	5.1	14.8

Sources: Chrysler Corporation annual reports, 1927–33, box "Annual Reports 1925–69," DCHC.
Note: Losses are indicated in parentheses.

*After taxes.
†Defined as stockholder equity and surpluses.

In late November 1929, Chrysler Corporation issued a 12-page booklet, *Six Years' Progress of Chrysler Motors,* touting its meteoric rise to prominence in the American auto industry. Chrysler had enjoyed vigorous growth in production and sales volumes every year since 1924, producing healthy profits and dividends. The corporation's working capital had grown from slightly over $28 million in 1925 to more than $88 million by 30 September 1929. Chrysler's plants had a combined capacity of 3,750 cars per day, and the corporation's dealer network included 12,000 domestic dealers, 2,600 Canadian outlets, and 3,800 dealerships abroad.

Using a hypothetical comparison, the booklet showed that shares of Chrysler stock had earned an excellent return on the investment. An investor who had spent $100 on the shares of the Maxwell Motor Corporation on 2 January 1923 would have earned more by 31 October 1929 than if that person had invested in other automobile stocks. The Maxwell shares would be worth $1,352.83, substantially better than the same investment in General Motors ($798.96), Nash ($773.33), Hudson ($374.78), or Studebaker ($184.36). Only Packard stock ($1,463.08) did better.[15]

DEPRESSION AND RECOVERY, 1930–33

Chrysler Corporation suffered the same sharp declines in sales and profits experienced by all the U.S. automakers starting in 1930. Chrysler's successful products, however, helped it survive even the worst part of the slump. Chrysler reinvented itself and by 1933 had regained its 1929 levels of production and earned respectable profits on a much lower dollar value of sales (see table 6.1 above). As a result of several strategic decisions made by Walter Chrysler, Plymouth became the flagship division of the corporation, accounting for more than half of all sales by 1932. Chrysler Corporation did well during the early 1930s, largely on the strength of Plymouth.[16]

Chrysler avoided outright losses until 1932 by cutting costs and reducing the workforce to reflect the lower demand for its products. In one apocryphal Depression story, Walter P. Chrysler met with his chief lieutenants in early 1930 and insisted that they reduce costs in their departments by 30 percent. Most of his executives, however, proposed spending increases instead. Engineering wanted budget increases to develop new products, the sales department argued that it needed additional resources, and K. T. Keller pleaded for funds to upgrade machinery and equipment. Annoyed by their responses, Chrysler asked B. E. Hutchinson, the treasurer, to bring him the company payroll book, which listed all of Chrysler's employees. Walter Chrysler then proposed, in a half-serious way, that they lay off everyone in the last one-third of the book. His lieutenants returned the next day with concrete proposals for the reductions Chrysler had demanded.[17]

Plymouth saved Chrysler in the early part of the Depression. The initial offering, the 1928 Series Q, remained in production only until January 1929, replaced by the Series U, manufactured through April 1930 and sold as a 1929 *and* a 1930 model. The Series U had a slightly larger engine (175.4 cid) than the earlier model. Plymouth introduced the "New Finer Plymouth," (Series 30-U) in April 1930 as the 1931 model and produced it until June 1931. The New Finer Plymouth had a much larger four-cylinder engine (196 cid) than its predecessors and other features not found in the competing low-priced cars, including all-steel bodies for the closed models, hydraulic shock absorbers, a mechanical fuel pump, and an electrical fuel gauge.[18]

The Chrysler Corporation began its serious challenge to Ford and Chevrolet for control of the low-priced market in March 1930 by reducing Plymouth prices by $65–$75 per car, resulting in base prices ranging from $535 (coupe) to $625 (four-door sedan). Walter Chrysler also announced in March 1930 that Dodge and DeSoto dealers would carry the Plymouth line in addition to their existing cars. This move added about 7,000 retail outlets for Plymouth, which before then had been sold exclusively by some 4,000 Chrysler dealers. A financial report on Chrysler compiled in September 1930 called this decision "one of the wisest moves that any automobile company could have made." One advertisement for the Plymouth that appeared in April 1931 emphasized the availability of the line in all three Chrysler Corporation dealerships. Combining Chrysler performance, Dodge dependability, and DeSoto "smartness," "Naturally . . . It's a Great Car with All This Greatness behind It."[19]

In early July 1931, Plymouth introduced the Model PA, which featured a radically new system for mounting the engine, dubbed "floating power" by its inventor, Fred Zeder. Standard practice in the industry was to bolt the engine directly to the car's steel frame at the four corners of the engine, which added torsional stiffness to the frame. When accelerating, the engine would "kick" sideways, transmitting vibrations and noise through the frame to the car's body.

Zeder devised a system whereby the engine rested on two rubber mounts, one located just under the water pump at the front of the engine and the other at the rear of the transmission. The center of gravity of the engine was midway between the mounts, allowing the engine to rotate around the axis line though the center of the engine, eliminating the "side-kick." To prevent the engine from turning excessively about its axis, Zeder introduced a five-leaf cantilever stabilizing spring attached to the transmission case at one end and to the right side of the frame at the other. This spring, which ran perpendicular to the axis of the engine, was encased in rubber where it connected to the frame. The net result is that nowhere in this mounting system was there metal-to-metal contact between the engine and the frame or body. The rubber mountings absorbed engine vibrations. The result was a car free of discernable engine vibration or noise.[20]

Model PA also featured "freewheeling," created by a clutch mechanism that automatically disengaged the drive shaft from the transmission when the drive shaft turned more rapidly than the crankshaft. By allowing the car to coast with the transmission no longer engaged, it provided significant fuel economies when going downhill. Freewheeling also reduced engine wear because the engine would not be working as a braking system under those conditions. However, the loss of engine braking made it more difficult to stop the car and produced more brake wear if the driver applied the brakes more often. The freewheeling mechanism could be disengaged at any time.

Chrysler spent about $2.5 million to launch the Model PA, when the combined earnings for 1930 and 1931 were only $1.7 million. When the model went into production in June 1931, Walter Chrysler took the third copy to come off the assembly line, and he, Zeder, Skelton, and Breer drove it to Dearborn to visit Henry Ford. After Ford gave them a tour of his laboratories, Chrysler proudly presented the car to Ford as a gift and took a taxi home. In the words of *Fortune* a few months later, "the gentleman with the tireless brown eyes [Walter Chrysler] certainly left the man with the snappy blue eyes [Henry Ford] something to think about."[21]

With base prices of different body styles ranging from $535 to $645, Plymouth was still slightly more expensive than Chevrolet ($475 to $635) and much more costly than Ford ($430 to $595), but it came equipped with floating power, freewheeling, and four-wheel hydraulic brakes as standard equipment. Ford and Chevrolet had none of those features. Plymouth used the slogan "smoothness of an eight, economy of a four" in advertising the "floating power" Plymouth in 1931.[22] The jump in sales enjoyed by Plymouth starting in 1931 can be seen in table 6.2.

TABLE 6.2 Plymouth's Share of Chrysler Corporation Unit Sales, 1928–33

	Total Chrysler Sales	Plymouth Sales	Plymouth Share of Chrysler (%)
1928	360,399	58,031	16.1
1929	450,543	93,613	20.7
1930	269,899	67,756	25.1
1931	272,118	106,319	39.1
1932	222,512	121,473	54.6
1933	451,734	255,566	56.6

Sources: Chrysler Corporation annual reports, box "Annual Reports 1925–69," DCHC; and Gary L. Blonston, *Plymouth, Its First 40 Years* (Detroit: Chrysler-Plymouth Division, 1968), 66.

For the 1932 model year, Chrysler applied floating power engine mounts to the DeSoto, Dodge, and Chrysler lines. The new system was recognized by other manufacturers, often grudgingly, as superior to existing engine mounting

THE SMOOTHNESS OF AN EIGHT · THE ECONOMY OF A FOUR

NEW PLYMOUTH

FLOATING POWER

and FREE WHEELING

Sedan (4-door 3-window) $635

$535
AND UP - F.O.B. FACTORY

A CHALLENGE

TO THE WORLD OF LOWEST-PRICED CARS

Advertisement for Plymouth "Floating Power," 1931. Courtesy of DCHC.

systems. In mid-April 1932, Europe's largest automobile manufacturer, André Citroën, signed a licensing agreement with the Chrysler Corporation to use floating power technology in his cars. Walter Chrysler allowed his friend John North Willys to use the floating power on his new Willys 77, which helped the Willys-Overland Company survive in 1933–36. (Willys hung on, eventually produced Jeeps, and was part of the American Motors Corporation acquired in 1987 by the Chrysler Corporation.)[23]

Racing continued to serve as cheap publicity for Chrysler products. In August 1931, race car driver Lou Miller established a nonstop transcontinental record in a Plymouth Model PA sedan. He drove from San Francisco to New York and back, a distance of 6,237 miles, in 132 hours, 9 minutes, at an average speed of 47.52 mph. Miller broke his own record, by nearly 36 hours, set in 1926 at the wheel of an Imperial. Chrysler Corporation used racing to emphasize the speed capabilities of its other models as well. On 13 February 1931, a Chrysler Imperial roadster and sedan each set six speed records at Daytona Beach, Florida, for a variety of distances from both standing and running starts. The Contest Board of the American Automobile Association certified all the records.[24]

Plymouth announced a new, improved floating power model, the PB Plymouth, on 2 April 1932. The PB chassis, at 112 inches, was 3 inches longer than the PA chassis. By using a double-drop, bridge-type frame with X-bracing, the passenger compartment could be lowered, as well as the roofline. The new 1932 model also had an engine producing 65 hp, versus 56 hp for the Model PA. Base prices ranged from $495 for the business roadster to $785 for a five-passenger convertible sedan.

An effective advertising campaign featuring Walter P. Chrysler made this the most successful Plymouth introduction yet.[25] In March 1932, a 31-year-old advertising executive, J. Sterling Getchell, went to a dealer preview of the floating power Plymouths. He had just won the DeSoto account for his firm the previous November, but found the proposed campaign for the new Plymouth too orthodox and dull. At Getchell's urging, DeSoto's general sales manager, Ray Peed, interrupted Walter Chrysler's dinner and convinced him to pose with the new Plymouth in the Chrysler Building in New York City. Chrysler stood with one foot on the front bumper, his right hand on the hood ornament. The combination of Chrysler's informal pose and the text created a classic advertisement. The headline read, "Look at All Three! But Don't Buy Any Low-Priced Car Until You've Driven the New Plymouth with Floating Power." A Chrysler quote appeared as a sidebar: "It is my opinion that any new car without Patented Floating Power is obsolete." Plymouth began its advertising campaign the first week of April, when Chevrolet and Ford both announced their new models. Droves of customers appeared at the Chrysler/Plymouth dealerships and sales soared.[26]

Walter Chrysler then pushed ahead with a six-cylinder Plymouth, the Model PC, introduced in the fall of 1932 as a 1933 model. The PC coupe sold for $495 and the sedan for $545, only $5 more than the comparable Ford and Chevrolet models. Chrysler Corporation spent $9 million retooling the Lynch Road assembly plant for the new Plymouth at a time when national economic conditions did not warrant much optimism about the future. A *Detroit News* editorial, "Chrysler Courageous," praised his optimism and more importantly his courage in "betting his company" on the future.[27]

The Plymouth Six was not very successful at first because it had a shorter wheelbase (107 inches) than the Model PB (112 inches), making it look short and stubby. By April of 1933, Plymouth had redesigned the car as the Model PD, with a wheelbase of 112 inches, marketed as the "Deluxe Plymouth Six," with far better results. Still, Plymouth's production and sales in 1932 were well above the levels of 1931, the only nameplate in the entire industry that could claim that feat.[28]

Chrysler also improved its market position versus both General Motors and Ford, as table 6.3 illustrates.

TABLE 6.3 Chrysler and Plymouth's Market Share among the "Big Three," 1928–33

	Chrysler* (%)	Plymouth† (%)
1928	10.6	2.3
1929	9.3	3.9
1930	8.6	3.7
1931	12.0	7.8
1932	17.4	16.1
1933	25.8	22.8

Sources: Chrysler Corporation annual reports, 1929–33, box "Annual Reports 1925–69," DCHC; and Plymouth Motor Corporation, *The Growth of Plymouth* (Detroit: Plymouth Motor Corporation, 1933), 7–9.

*As measured by new car registrations.
†Share of low-priced car market.

By the early 1930s, Plymouth was the third most popular nameplate in the U.S. market, with production of 255,566 units for calendar year 1933. Chevrolet was clearly the industry leader, with production of 481,134 cars, with Ford (334,969 units) a distant second. Chrysler Corporation's U.S. sales exceeded Ford's in 1933 and on that basis, Chrysler claimed to be the number two automaker. Chrysler, however, had only pulled dead even in worldwide production and sales. Still, this was a tremendous accomplishment, reflecting Chrysler's success—but also Ford's difficulties. What is perhaps more remarkable was Chrysler's return to its 1929 production volume in 1933, a feat not accomplished by General Motors until 1937 or by Ford until after the Second World War.[29]

This is not to suggest that Chrysler Corporation survived the years 1930–33 effortlessly, but Chrysler management ended the year 1933 feeling optimistic about the immediate future. Production and sales of all Chrysler models more than doubled from 1932 to 1933, with Plymouth leading the way. The overall national economic climate had improved dramatically in the course of 1933. Following the banking crisis of March 1933, Chrysler's production and sales curves moved steeply upward. The company's payroll in March stood at 26,976 workers, who averaged only 24 hours of work per week. By September 1933, the payroll had increased to 46,676 employees, who worked on average 38 to 40 hours per week. Chrysler also reported that it had added 1,482 new Chrysler/Plymouth dealers in 1933, bringing the total to 3,717. Chrysler Corporation would celebrate the tenth anniversary of the Chrysler Six at a time when it was gaining a larger share of the U.S. automobile market every year.[30]

Automobile Topics devoted its entire weekly issue of 30 December 1933 to a celebration of Chrysler's tenth anniversary as an automaker. The issue carried

New Chrysler sales office/showrooms in foreground, with the Chrysler Jefferson Avenue plant in the rear, Detroit, 1933. Courtesy of DCHC.

the title, "A Century of Progress in Ten Years: Celebrating the Tenth Anniversary of Chrysler Motors," a clear reference to the Century of Progress Exposition held in Chicago in 1933–34, which celebrated modern technology and the progress it brought to humankind. The special issue reveals a good deal about the industry's views of Chrysler's brief past, its current strengths, and its future.

Of the thirty-three articles in the special issue, six examined Chrysler's leaders and one discussed the general engineering staff. Ten articles (the most on any topic) covered Chrysler's automotive engineering, including pieces on individual engineers, general research programs, the Chrysler Engineering Institute, and various engineering breakthroughs—the Airflow car included.[31]

Chrysler and his lieutenants enjoyed the giddy successes of 1928 and 1929, followed by the difficult early years of the Great Depression. Chrysler survived the Depression and even prospered because the trio of Zeder-Skelton-Breer continued to produce important innovations in automotive design, with floating power leading the way. Chrysler's leaders practically "bet the company" on Plymouth and won the gamble. Plymouth emerged as a serious head-to-head competitor in the low-priced field, and Plymouth's success catapulted Chrysler ahead of Ford to the number two position in the industry, a remarkable achievement.

Chapter 7

CHRYSLER IN THE MID-1930S

Chrysler Corporation has pioneered many of the fundamental and lasting engineering advances in automobile design and construction in the last ten years. Its newest development, the Airflow design of 1934 Chrysler and DeSoto models, has already met with an enthusiastic public response.

—Ninth Annual Report of Chrysler Corporation, Year Ended December 31, 1933

Much of Chrysler's history in the mid-1930s centered around the serious miscalculation called Airflow, which could have sent Chrysler to its grave in 1934–37, even as the rest of the auto industry enjoyed economic recovery. The Chrysler Corporation introduced its revolutionary Airflow cars in 1934 in its Chrysler and DeSoto lines. Walter Chrysler, the "Three Musketeers," and other top company officials believed that Airflow would push Chrysler to leadership in the industry. Instead, the Airflow models were a great disappointment in sales and profits. After modifying Airflow's styling in 1934, 1935, 1936, and 1937, Chrysler ended the line.

The automaker survived Airflow and did well during this period on the strength of its other product lines, the company's operating efficiency, and its strong management team. Chrysler was able to earn profits on a smaller volume than Ford and General Motors because of its manufacturing prowess. The company was also renowned for innovations in automotive design, and had a long list of automotive engineering "firsts" to its credit. With the exception of Airflow, the auto buying public embraced Chrysler's cars and trucks during the mid-1930s.

SURVIVING THE AIRFLOW, 1934–37

One late August afternoon in 1927, engineer Carl Breer was driving his family north from Detroit to Port Huron, where they planned to enjoy a sandy beach on Lake Huron. Off in the distance, Breer spotted what he thought was a flock of geese flying low to the ground, but discovered was a squadron of fighter aircraft returning to nearby Selfridge Field. He noted that the planes' stream-lined design imitated that of geese, allowing the planes to remain aloft at low speeds. Breer began thinking about how the airflow around an automobile might affect its performance. He then set in motion a series of experiments and investigations that eventually led to the introduction of the Chrysler Airflow line in 1934.

Breer asked William Earnshaw, a Dayton, Ohio–based engineer who had just joined Chrysler's staff, to investigate the effect of automobile body design on the movement of the car through the air. In Dayton, Earnshaw consulted with Orville Wright about measuring wind resistance, and Wright suggested that Earnshaw build a small wind tunnel to test various shapes, using wooden models. Breer authorized Earnshaw to go ahead, and he finished a wind tunnel at Dayton in November 1927. A 35 hp electric motor powered propellers that created the wind, which passed over the models through a throat. With woodworking machinery to build models, Earnshaw had created an aerodynamic laboratory.[1]

The Dayton wind tunnel operated from November 1927 to late October 1928, experimenting on fundamental shapes, existing Chrysler cars, and modified car bodies. Using a mixture of oil and lamp black, the engineers were able to trace the patterns of wind currents over different shapes. When a new wind tunnel went into service at Highland Park in late 1928, the Dayton operations moved there. The move made sense because almost all of Chrysler's engineering and design personnel were at Highland Park. A summary of the wind tunnel tests shows that about fifty scale models underwent testing between September 1928 and April 1930. The tests showed that the front-end treatment of the car was the overwhelming factor in determining wind resistance. Wind tunnel tests also showed that running conventional cars backward reduced wind resistance by 30 percent.[2]

Breer and his staff decided that a smooth, streamlined auto body with a rounded hood and a tapered rear end would minimize drag. Eliminating the traditional square back end meant that the rear seats had to be moved forward to give rear passengers sufficient headroom. This in turn required that all the other chassis components be moved forward as well. In doing so, Breer and company broke all the conventions of automobile design and produced a car with unique handling qualities. Before Airflow, conventional American passenger cars were "rear-heavy," that is, with a full load of passengers, the rear tires bore 60 percent of the total weight. In conventional cars, the front springs would oscillate at roughly 120–130 cycles per minute, producing passenger fatigue. The rear seat was located directly over the rear axle in conventional cars, giving rear passengers a bumpy, bouncy ride.

Breer's engineers moved the chassis elements forward. The rear seat moved 20 inches forward of its old position, so rear passengers rode in front of the rear axle. The trunk and gasoline tank were located behind the passenger compartment. The engineers also moved the engine forward so it was over the front axle instead of behind it and tilted the engine and transmission slightly downward, which lowered the drive shaft and allowed a lower floor. The center of gravity of the car was lowered and moved forward about 18 inches. With six passengers on board, about 54 percent of the total load was carried by the front tires.

The Airflow therefore was "front-heavy" and of necessity, Breer introduced longer and stronger front leaf springs to take the heavier loads, but these produced oscillations of only 90–100 cycles per minute, much like a natural walking gait. The result was a more stable, comfortable ride. Vertical bouncing was greatly reduced, side-sway was nearly eliminated, and the car remained stable while cornering.[3] Airflow was Chrysler's first "cab-forward" passenger car, well in advance of its much-touted "cab-forward" LH cars of 1993.

At some point before Airflow went on sale, Chrysler's test-driver Tobe Couture invited Ross Roy, the head of the advertising agency that handled most of Chrysler's promotions, to ride in an Airflow prototype. First, Ross Roy and two of his employees rode in the back seat of a Buick Roadmaster that Couture drove along a rough road. This was a big, heavy car known for its comfortable ride, but the passengers hit the back of their heads on the roof. Couture then drove them along the same road at the same speed in the back seat of an Airflow, and they enjoyed a smooth ride, with no bouncing whatsoever. This test-ride convinced Ross Roy of the superior design of Airflow.[4]

Finally, the Airflow incorporated a radically different frame and body structure. Conventional American cars had a heavy steel chassis frame, which supported the engine, drive train, and the body. Automobile bodies, merely bolted to the chassis frame, usually consisted of metal panels framed in wood. The body did not add strength or rigidity to the car. Airflow instead used a unit body/frame design, in which the body is integrated with the frame. Chrysler called the Airflow structure the "bridge truss" body/frame. A series of horizontal and vertical steel truss members welded together created a ribbed cage structure that encased the passengers. The result was a strong, rigid frame resistant to vibration and largely free of rattles. The doors, fenders, and hood lid were attached to the frame with hinges, while the body panels were electrically welded to the frame.[5]

Carl Breer and his engineering staff developed this innovative, thoroughly "modern" car only after years of building large-scale models and road-test prototypes. The earliest known prototype of the Airflow was completed in September 1932 and road tested in late 1932 and early 1933. Chrysler Corporation

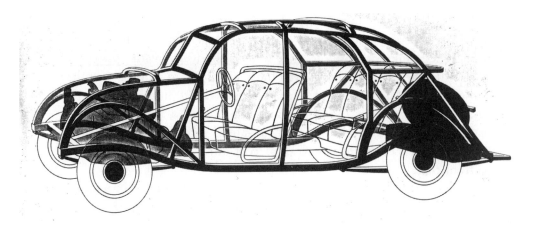

Chrysler Airflow integrated body/frame construction, 1934. Courtesy of NAHC.

dubbed this vehicle the "Trifon Special" and registered the car in the name of Demitrion Trifon, a mechanic/driver working in the Chrysler road-test garage. For security reasons, the Chrysler name appeared nowhere on any of the paper-work.[6]

Notes that have survived from an anonymous Chrysler engineer refer to the development of an early design, possibly the Trifon. Following "conception" in July 1929 came the first "blackboard drawing" a year later on 1 August 1930, with final drawings completed in January 1932. The first "running job" was listed as "Spring, 1932." This was almost certainly the Trifon Special.[7]

The Chrysler engineers took the Trifon Special by van to a secret location in northern lower Michigan in September 1932 for road testing. They arranged to rent garage space and living quarters on the Strubble family farm north of Gray-ling and ran the prototype on the rural roads of this isolated area, arousing some attention from the locals but creating no publicity. Road testing for the Trifon and other prototypes continued through 1933. Walter Chrysler went to the northern woods for test-drives in the fall of 1933 and gave his final approval for the Breer team to proceed with production.[8]

Chrysler Corporation introduced the Airflow cars at the New York Automo-bile Show on 6 January 1934, expecting to repeat the enormous success achieved a decade earlier with the Chrysler Six. The Airflow was to be a celebration of Chrysler's ten-year anniversary. Chrysler Corporation struck a bronze medal, one side portraying the 1924 Chrysler Six and the inscription "10th Anniversary of the Chrysler Car," and the other side a view of the 1934 Chrysler Airflow and the inscription "A Century of Progress in a Decade."[9]

Carl Breer and company went to New York in January 1934 with Airflow show models to exhibit, but quantity production was still months away. Why the rush to market? According to William Jeanes, Walter P. Chrysler pushed

Walter P. Chrysler proudly showing off a scale model of his 1934 Chrysler Airflow.
Courtesy of DCHC.

Airflow's debut after receiving reports that General Motors was on the verge of
introducing its own streamlined models. Chrysler's men had secretly photo-
graphed a partially streamlined prototype called the Albanita on a General Motors test track in mid-1933. The specter of competing with a streamlined GM
car may have forced Chrysler's hand.

By all reports, Airflow *was* the hit of the automobile show and Chrysler's salespeople took thousands of orders on the spot. Buckminster Fuller's three-wheeled streamlined Dymaxion car was scheduled to occupy the featured spot at the auto show, but Chrysler convinced auto show officials to move the Dymaxion elsewhere. In a report to the stockholders for the year 1933, Chrysler management reported that "its newest development, the Airflow design of 1934 Chrysler and DeSoto models, has already met with an enthusiastic public response." They had decided to bring out the Airflow in the higher-priced DeSoto and Chrysler lines "in the belief that buyers in this price class would be receptive, and that belief has since been justified." Carl Breer claimed that customers ordered more Airflows at the auto show than had been the case for any new car previously exhibited there and there is no reason to dispute his claim.[10]

Chrysler Corporation began its promotion campaign for Airflow well before the car appeared in January 1934, emphasizing the car's superior design. A series of two-page spreads in *Automobile Topics* starting in December 1933 had the following enthusiastic headlines: "A New Kind of Car That Literally Bores a Hole through the Air"; "Read a Newspaper at 80 Miles an Hour on a Dirt Road!"; "History Repeats Itself—Again Chrysler Revolutionizes the Motor Car"; and "Good-Bye 'Horseless Carriage.' . . . Here's the New Airflow DeSoto." Chrysler ran the same ads in the *Automobile Trade Journal* in January 1934. Slightly toned-down ads appeared in *American Automobile, Fortune,* and elsewhere during the early months of 1934.[11]

According to a Chrysler Sales Corporation "confidential bulletin" no. 909 issued 1 June 1934, the automaker spent enormous sums on its media blitz to promote Airflow:

> Beginning with our smoke-up campaign in December, and continuing up until the first of June, we have pounded the Airflow story in all the important weeklies, the best monthlies, the women's magazines, the important class magazines, technical magazines, a boys' magazine and the trade papers. We had a job to do and we spent liberally to insure the success of this job. With the scarcity of cars in the field due to our early production problems, we must give our advertising credit for the popularization of the Airflow design.

With no national advertising budget remaining, the best Chrysler Sales could offer its distributors was to contribute half the cost of any local newspaper advertising they wanted to do.[12]

Chrysler Airflows were sold in a variety of body styles under the Chrysler nameplate, along with the more traditionally styled, lower-priced Chrysler models. Airflows equipped with six-cylinder engines were the only DeSoto models offered in 1934. Customers could buy Airflow models in either four-door sedan

1934 Chrysler Airflow. Courtesy of DCHC.

or town sedan versions. In addition, the Chrysler Airflow Eight (Model CU) was available as a six-passenger coupe and as a two-door sedan, and the Airflow Imperial (Model CV) had a six-passenger coupe version. Two Custom Imperials (Model CW and Model CX) offered an eight-passenger limousine sedan as well. The DeSoto Airflow (Model SE), which had a six-cylinder engine, was available as a coupe and four-door sedan only.[13]

Sales in 1934 for all Airflows were a major disappointment—bordering on a disaster—for Chrysler Corporation. Chrysler's quarterly financial reports for the first half of 1934 painted a rosy picture, but it was false. Chrysler reported that as of the end of March, it had 15,580 unfilled domestic orders for Airflow and then claimed that it would ship about 25,000 Airflows by the end of July. Production figures for the year, however, tell the real story. Chrysler manufactured 11,292 Chrysler Airflows and 13,940 DeSoto Airflows in 1934, a total for the year of only 25,232 cars. The sales performance was particularly disastrous for DeSoto, which had produced 20,186 cars the previous year.

Carl Breer, the "father" of the Airflow, offered several explanations for Airflow's disappointing sales, but mainly blamed production delays. Introducing

Airflow at the New York Auto Show in January 1934, when Chrysler Corporation was not ready to deliver the cars to dealers, was a major mistake. Assembling Airflows was more complicated and costly than was the case for conventional models because the body required a lot of welding. Airflows did not start coming off the production line in substantial numbers until April 1934. The long delays killed customer enthusiasm and created doubts about the new car. Breer suggests that competitors started rumors that Airflows were not available because the car was flawed and Chrysler Corporation was desperately trying to fix a host of problems. Breer also admitted that DeSoto Airflow sales were depressed because the new models were more expensive than the DeSotos they replaced.[14]

The long production delays were serious. In mid-January 1934, *Iron Age* remarked, "It is scarcely a secret that neither a DeSoto nor a Chrysler has come off the assembly line at the Jefferson Avenue plant in Detroit." Chrysler struggled to get Airflow into production in early 1934 because the unit body/frame design required an entirely different assembly process. The front-end and rear-end parts of the body were assembled in two different plants, welded together to form a single body, and only then were welded to the bridge-type frame. In describing the welding needed to assemble Airflow bodies, Joseph Geschelin noted the unprecedented variety of equipment and skills required:

> Practically every trick in the master welder's repertory has been adopted in the fabrication of Chrysler and DeSoto Airflow bodies, particularly on the unique front section. That this is no idle boast is evidenced by the fact that we find in this operation a variety of processes including electric arc welding, oxy-acetylene welding, spot welding with both fixed and portable equipment, indirect welding, flash welding, and the Chrysler method of hydromatic welding.

The Airflow body department was equipped with 12 hydromatic welders, 12 gas welders, 38 arc welders, 31 fixed spot welders, 28 portable spot welders, and 12 indirect welders. The hydromatic welders, which did multiple welds at once, completed 313 spot welds on each Airflow body.[15]

A Chrysler announcement to its dealers in June 1934 claimed that the delays were "due to the die makers strike." In fact, a strike of tool and die makers in September and October 1933, led by the Mechanics Educational Society of America (MESA), held up the introduction of the 1934 models at several Detroit automakers. The strike slowed or stopped production of dies for the major automakers, independent body manufacturers, and the independent job shops. Because of the late delivery of dies, most of the Detroit automakers had no 1934 cars to sell in late December 1933. According to *Iron Age,* "Because there were no important changes in design of the new V-Eight car, Ford was not affected by the recent strike of tool and die makers." Chrysler, however, faced a multitude of production problems.[16]

Chrysler's factory records show how serious these bottlenecks were. The combined production of the Chrysler and DeSoto Airflows, both assembled at Jefferson Avenue in Detroit, was only 60 units for the entire month of December 1933 and 50 units in January 1934. Combined production then climbed steadily in February (1,269 units), March (3,754), and April (4,662), before reaching a monthly peak of 6,212 units in May. Chrysler then reduced production to 2,253 units in June, 1,162 cars in July, and then to fewer than 1,000 units in August and September, the end of the model run. Even the peak output in May (3,340 Chryslers and 2,872 DeSotos) was barely enough to provide each Chrysler and DeSoto dealership with one Airflow car.[17]

Breer had reason to suggest that the competition was denouncing Chrysler's new Airflows. Indeed, General Motors launched an anti-Airflow advertising campaign. In the first six months of 1934, General Motors ran five ads in the *Saturday Evening Post* extolling the advantages of General Motors cars as a whole, as opposed to promoting individual nameplates, which they did as well. A common slogan appears in all the ads: "An Eye to the Future—An Ear to the Ground," which described GM's policy "by which the public is given what it wants in better cars year after year, and yet is protected against ill-timed or dubious experiments." General Motors claimed it tested public buying preferences by sending out a million questionnaires each year to the auto-buying public. General Motors had streamlined cars too, but its streamlined vehicles "did not leap full-born into being; they are the product of deliberate growth, rather than abrupt inspiration." General Motors developed streamlining "in styles that say beauty as well as speed." Informed readers would have recognized that General Motors was attacking the Airflow cars.[18]

But much more damaging, the General Motors campaign against Airflow had some foundation in fact. Airflow cars were not only rumored to be flawed—they were. Carl Breer's son Fred reported that the early Airflows had serious mechanical problems, which quickly disillusioned the buying public. According to Fred Breer,

When they finally came down the line in April, because of the unique production problems, the first two or three thousand had a lot of problems. All the letters that came back from dealers and customers came to my father and I can remember him bringing them home and reading them to me. Some of the problems were unbelievable, like engines breaking loose at 80 mph. The workmen just didn't know how to build the car

Chrysler showroom, Jefferson Avenue, Detroit, with 1934 Chrysler Airflow cars.
Courtesy of DCHC.

properly, and by that time the public—and the dealers particularly—had
become disillusioned with the Airflow.[19]

Chrysler Corporation tirelessly promoted Airflow for the remainder of 1934,
but without success. The company distributed free filmstrips to movie theaters
showing Airflow's handling abilities, the strength of its all-steel unit body/frame,
and its safety features. The car completed several stunts at the Century of Progress Exhibition in Chicago, including making skid-free stops on wet pavement
and taking sharp corners without rolling over. When the driver finally coaxed
the Airflow to roll over, the steel frame held strong. Doors and windows could
then be opened and closed with ease. Chrysler also drove an Airflow (without
driver) over a 110-foot cliff in Ligommer, Pennsylvania. It fell end over end,
landing on its wheels, but the driver started it and drove it away under its own
power, apparently unaffected.[20]

Chrysler also returned to the old standby promotional tool of racing. Driver
Harry Hartz set 72 new AAA stock car records in mid-August 1934 at the Bonne-
ville Flats course in Utah with a stock Imperial Airflow coupe. At the end of the

month, Hartz drove the same car from Los Angeles to New York City and set an economy record of 18.1 miles per gallon (mpg) for the run. One reporter noted that Hartz did not need to add water to his Imperial at any time during these races. An Airflow DeSoto made the same run, with an even better record of 21.4 mpg.[21]

Despite the debilitating problems of delayed production, the rumor campaign, and the Airflow's mechanical flaws, there is a broad consensus among automotive historians that car buyers shunned Airflow largely because they did not like the car's looks, especially the look of the front end. The stubby hood, the "waterfall" grille, headlights, and fenders were all squashed together into a massive anonymous lump. Airflow was ugly, pure and simple. Styling historian Paul Wilson put it more brutally: "Airflow had some of the same grotesque anonymity as a human face covered by a nylon stocking. The Airflow had a lumbering, stupid look, a rhinoceros ugliness."[22]

Chrysler made cosmetic changes to the Airflow grille, the focus of customer complaints, in the middle of the 1934 model year and for the 1935, 1936, and 1937 models as well. The original Airflow body styling was the work of Carl Breer and Oliver H. Clark, Chrysler's chief body engineer. To fix the Airflow grille, Chrysler hired Norman Bel Geddes, an independent industrial designer. Bel Geddes replaced the original compound-curve waterfall grille with its very thin bars with a heavier-looking design with fewer, thicker, and straighter bars. Walter Chrysler had brought stylist Ray Dietrich, formerly with LeBaron, into the Chrysler Art and Colour Department in 1932, but Dietrich had no staff and little influence for several years. Dietrich took over Art and Colour in 1935 and redesigned the grilles for the 1935, 1936, and 1937 Airflows. The later grilles had a more conventional, prow-like appearance. In reviewing the 1935 Airflow, *Automotive Industries* described the revamped grill as "V-shaped and sloping from top to bottom, rather than rounded, . . . materially improving the appearance of these cars."[23]

The cosmetic changes did not end Airflow's weak performance in the market. The combined sales of Airflow fell from 25,232 in 1934 to 14,548 in 1935 and further to 11,272 units in 1936. Chrysler Corporation discontinued the DeSoto Airflow after 1936, but produced a Chrysler version for 1937, selling a disappointing 4,600 cars. The number of distinct models (combinations of makes, engines, and body styles) offered fell from fifteen in 1934 to ten the following year and to only two by 1937, the last year of production. Chrysler never earned profits on Airflow, but Chrysler survived this debacle on the strength of its other offerings.[24]

Walter Chrysler gambled on Airflow and lost. Given the economic uncertainties of the early 1930s, why would he "bet his company" on an automobile that was radically different from conventional cars in both design and appearance?

Airflow ran counter to everything he had done in the car business starting with the Chrysler Six. Before Airflow, Walter Chrysler sold mechanically advanced cars that had a stylistic flair, but they were conventional-looking. The shape of Airflow may have been ideal from an engineering or streamlining point of view—but the auto buying public judged it unacceptably ugly.[25]

Unfortunately, Walter Chrysler never revealed his thinking in going ahead with this unconventional-looking car. Airflow is not mentioned in *Life of an American Workman.* An August 1935 *Fortune* article on Chrysler Corporation offered one plausible explanation—Walter Chrysler and his lieutenants decided that "comfort sells," and that the public would gladly pay an extra $1,000 for cars noticeably more comfortable than the competition. This was the way to spur sales of medium- and high-priced cars in a depressed market.[26] Whatever Walter Chrysler's reasoning, it was a rare error in judgment.

One outgrowth of the Airflow design was a limited-production Dodge Airflow truck, equipped with a standard chassis and cab, but with customized bodies for individual customers. They served as gasoline tanker trucks for Texaco, Standard Oil, Mobilgas, Shell, and other oil companies. Production began in December 1934 (1935 model) and continued through February 1940 (1940 model), with combined output of only 266 units. Dodge rated all of them as four-ton capacity trucks. Few of these handsome trucks have survived.[27]

Chrysler Corporation introduced the popular Chrysler Airstream and DeSoto Airstream models for 1935. Airstream was the work of Phil Wright, a stylist with the Briggs Manufacturing Company, Chrysler's main source of bodies. These were moderately priced, modern-looking, attractive, but not streamlined. They benefited from rave reviews in the automotive press, which praised their mechanical features and their styling. Airstream was especially critical in the revival of the DeSoto Division, which sold 20,784 Airstreams in 1935, but only 6,797 Airflows. The DeSoto recovery continued through 1937, when the division built more than 82,000 cars. Similarly, the Chrysler Division rebounded, despite keeping Airflow in production through 1937. Chrysler introduced two entirely new models for the 1936 model year, the Chrysler Six and the Chrysler Deluxe Eight. Both received enthusiastic reviews in the automotive press.[28]

Despite Airflow, Chrysler Corporation did more than merely survive in the mid-1930s, largely because of its ability to cut costs while increasing sales volume—the latter based mainly on the success of Plymouth. Table 7.1 shows the overall performance.

Chrysler's strong earnings in 1935–37 did not go unnoticed in the automotive and financial press. *Barron's* gushed with enthusiasm over Chrysler's reported earnings for the first two quarters of 1936.[29] Plymouth remained the cornerstone

TABLE 7.1 Chrysler Corporation Performance, 1933–37

| | | | Net Earnings* | | |
	Unit Sales	Net Sales ($)	Total ($)	On Sales (%)	On Capital Invested† (%)
1933	451,734	238,675,952	12,129,120	5.1	14.8
1934	597,756	362,254,000	9,534,837	2.6	11.1
1935	843,599	516,830,000	34,975,819	6.7	31.2
1936	1,066,229	667,138,391	62,110,543	9.3	50.4
1937	1,158,518	769,807,839	50,729,211	6.6	39.2

Sources: Chrysler Corporation annual reports, 1933–37, box "Annual Reports 1925–69," DCHC.

*After taxes.
†Defined as stockholders' equity and surpluses.

of Chrysler's ability to earn profits with high-volume production and low overall costs. The importance of Plymouth is illustrated in table 7.2.

TABLE 7.2 Plymouth's Share of Chrysler Corporation Unit Sales, 1933–37

	Total Chrysler Sales	Plymouth Sales	Plymouth Share of Chrysler (%)
1933	451,734	255,566	56.6
1934	497,756	351,113	70.5
1935	843,599	442,281	52.4
1936	1,066,229	527,177	49.4
1937	1,158,518	514,061	44.4

Sources: Chrysler Corporation annual reports, box "Annual Reports 1925–69," DCHC; and Gary L. Blonston, *Plymouth, Its First Forty Years* (Detroit: Chrysler-Plymouth Division, 1968), 68.

By 1937, the Plymouth Lynch Road assembly plant ran three parallel assembly lines, each producing a car per minute, giving the plant the capacity of 180 cars per hour, or 2,880 cars per 16-hour day. Chrysler was unique in the industry in that all of its popular Plymouth assembly was done at a single plant.[30]

An analysis of the Plymouth Division that appeared in *Fortune* in December 1940 revealed Chrysler's remarkable achievement. In 1937, for example, Chrysler received average revenues of $573 per Plymouth, while GM took in $556 for every Chevrolet sold. However, Chrysler's total costs per car, including sales

The One-Millionth Plymouth, built in 1934 at the Plymouth Lynch Road assembly plant in Detroit. Walter P. Chrysler is behind the wheel with treasurer B. E. Hutchinson at his side. Courtesy of DCHC.

and administrative costs, were slightly lower for Plymouth than were GM's costs for Chevrolets ($524 versus $527). Chrysler earned nearly as much profit from Plymouth as General Motors did from Chevrolet ($22.5 million versus $26.3 million), with only half the volume (458,518 versus 905,928).[31]

Chrysler also remained actively involved in the production of marine engines and general-purpose industrial engines through the 1930s. The firm introduced a new Regal model marine engine featuring rubber-cushioned mountings in 1931. Production of specialized engines for nonautomotive use seems like a logical side business for a car company. Marine and industrial engines endure much harder "duty" than automobile engines in that they typically run under heavy loads for many hours or even days at a time. Chrysler Engineering's experience in designing high-quality engines with excellent valve cooling served the corporation well in these specialized markets.[32] But Chrysler's foray into the manufacture of air-conditioning equipment starting in 1934 took the automaker far afield from its normal expertise.

Walter Chrysler became interested in air conditioning when he became dissatisfied with the equipment used to air condition the Chrysler Building in New York City. He discovered that the current technology was both expensive and bulky, so he hired Charles R. Neeson to develop better equipment, with the aid of the Chrysler Corporation engineering staff. They developed a high-speed lightweight radial compressor that was vastly superior to existing equipment. In mid-1934, Walter Chrysler announced that his company had developed the "Airtemp Conditioner," already adopted as a trademark, and would manufacture the equipment and sell it through the Temperature Corporation of New York. Chrysler formed the Airtemp Corporation on 22 October 1934 and began manufacturing in the (former) stamping plant on Conant in Detroit.[33]

In its annual report for 1934, Chrysler announced its new air-conditioning equipment operations: "It is believed that air conditioning of homes, as well as of office, factory, and other buildings, offers a great potential field for further development." In August 1935, Chrysler established Airtemp, Inc., a subsidiary of the Chrysler Corporation, renamed the Airtemp Division in September 1938. Airtemp engineers developed capacity regulators (1937), which helped their systems adjust to varying loads, and the first self-contained air-conditioning units, which Airtemp patented in 1938. Manufacturing moved in June 1936 into the former Maxwell plant in Dayton, Ohio.[34]

The survival and likely future success of the Chrysler Corporation was a certainty by 1937, at least in the eyes of Walter P. Chrysler and most industry observers. He could look back with pride over the remarkable success of the Chrysler Corporation since the appearance of the first Chrysler cars in January 1924.

THE ANATOMY OF SUCCESS

Observers of the Chrysler Corporation in the 1930s noted the automaker's phenomenal success. *Automobile Topics,* one of the premier auto industry trade journals, produced a special issue on Chrysler in December 1933 and *American Machinist* did likewise in May 1936. *Fortune* ran lengthy articles on Chrysler in August 1935 and December 1940, both focusing on Chrysler's remarkable performance in the 1930s. All of these analyses emphasize two major themes—the competence and dedication of Walter Chrysler's chief lieutenants, and the critical importance of Chrysler Corporation's engineering innovations.

In describing the Chrysler Corporation in a 1935 article, *Fortune* argued that there were only two significant "personalities" in the auto industry—Henry Ford and the Chrysler Corporation. Industry insiders said of the Chrysler Corporation that "it was vigorous, it was tough, and it was no respecter of the established opposition. Those attributes it owed and still owes in general to seventeen men and in particular to four." The 17 were the members of the Operation Committee. The 4 were Walter P. Chrysler; K. T. Keller, general manager in charge of production; B. E. Hutchinson, vice president and treasurer; and Fred M. Zeder, chief engineer. In describing Chrysler's leaders five years later, *Fortune* remarked that Keller, Hutchinson, and Zeder "probably make a combination that under present conditions is hard to surpass." The three were "a first-rate production man, first-rate financial man, and first-rate engineer."[35]

Some general observations should be made about Keller, Hutchinson, and Zeder. Walter Chrysler's lieutenants, sometimes referred to as "the princes," served Walter Chrysler and his company well during the first quarter-century of the firm's existence. Hutchinson was the first to join Walter Chrysler, as treasurer for the Maxwell Motor Corporation in 1921. Zeder arrived in June 1923, along with Owen Skelton and Carl Breer. Keller was the last to join the management team, hired by Chrysler in April 1926. All three remained at Chrysler until the early 1950s. If Walter P. Chrysler was the king, he chose gifted and hardworking men to serve as his "princes," and had the wisdom to grant them wide-ranging power and responsibility.

The contrast with the management style and structure at both Ford and General Motors is striking. Henry Ford's autocratic and idiosyncratic management style meant that his company faced constant turnover of its executives, engineers, and designers. The ruthless struggle for power within Ford Motor Company, encouraged by Henry Ford, brought managerial and planning chaos. Starting in the mid-1920s, Henry Ford became increasingly dependent on Harry Bennett and the Ford Service Department to run his company. In contrast, Alfred Sloan created a decentralized and impersonal organizational structure at General Motors in the early 1920s that produced a competent, efficient management team.[36] Given Walter Chrysler's good judgment and charismatic personality, the Chrysler management structure, combining strong leadership with individual freedom, was ideal.

Walter P. Chrysler took much of his own pay from the corporation in the form of profit sharing and stock options and believed this was an appropriate incentive system for his executives as well. Chrysler's employment contract with Maxwell, which ran for four years starting on 1 June 1923, included profit sharing and stock options. His new contract with Chrysler Corporation, beginning 1 June 1927, was similar. For the first six months, Chrysler was paid a salary of $96,400 a year and 5 percent of the net profits of the company. Then his salary increased to $150,000 and 10 percent of the net profits. The corporation also agreed to pay the expenses of maintaining an office in New York City. His profit-sharing payments were $907,211 in 1927; $2,466,941 in 1928; $1,550,000 in 1929; and no additional payments until 1933, when he collected $370,000. In his last employment contract, which ran from 1 October 1933 until his death, Chrysler agreed to an annual salary of $200,000, but with no profit sharing.[37]

Chrysler's top managers were also well paid in salaries and "management bonuses," normally in the form of stock. In 1937, when Chairman Walter P.

Chrysler drew a salary of $200,700, President K. T. Keller earned $100,500, Vice President B. E. Hutchinson was paid $90,600, and Fred M. Zeder drew a salary of $80,616. Chrysler Corporation, much like many other industrial firms, also paid substantial bonuses to its managers in the form of cash and stock. The firm paid out $980,000 in bonuses to its salaried workers in 1928, with $650,000 of the total paid in cash and stock to about fifty top executives.[38]

Of the three "princes" serving the Chrysler Corporation during Walter Chrysler's life and beyond, Kaufman Thuma (always "K. T.") Keller (1885–1966), had a set of life experiences closest to those of Chrysler himself. Born on a farm in Mt. Joy, Pennsylvania, east of Harrisburg, Keller worked in a hardware factory while in high school. After graduating first in his class at age 16, he attended Wade Business College in nearby Lancaster starting in 1901. As secretary to a Baptist preacher, he toured England in 1904–6.[39]

Keller began his adult working life at Westinghouse Machine Company (later Westinghouse Electric) in East Pittsburgh, starting off as a clerk in the manager's office at $75 a month. After about a year, Keller transferred to the machine shop as an apprentice, starting at only 20¢ an hour. He remained at Westinghouse from 1906 to 1910; in 1908, he became assistant superintendent in the automobile engine department, which made engines for the Chalmers-Detroit Motor Company.

Keller moved to Detroit in 1910 and worked for various auto companies, including Metzger, Hudson, and Maxwell. In November 1911, he joined General Motors. He was general master mechanic for the Buick Motor Company (1917–1920), vice president for manufacturing for the Chevrolet Motor Company (1921–24), and general manager of Canadian Operations for General Motors (1924–26). Walter P. Chrysler hired him in April 1926.

Walter Chrysler believed that Keller was the right choice to manage Chrysler Corporation's rapidly expanding manufacturing operations. Keller remained vice president in charge of manufacturing until 1928, when he became general manager of the newly formed Dodge Division of Chrysler. Keller served as president of the Dodge Division from 1929 until 22 July 1935, when he succeeded Chrysler as president of the Chrysler Corporation. Walter Chrysler was chairman of the board from 1935 until his death in 1940, when the corporation temporarily eliminated the position. K. T. Keller continued as president until 1950 and then became chairman of the board, a position created specifically for him.[40]

Keller, much like Walter Chrysler, was a self-made man who was more a doer than a thinker. Keller was forceful, hard-working, ambitious, and a risk-taker. Long after he had achieved great success, Keller continued to say, "I am a machinist by trade." *Fortune* described him in 1935 as "heavy, hearty, two-fisted, go-getting." Keller spent his working hours touring the plants or the engineering laboratories. His work was his life and his life was his work. In an 11-year span ending in 1939, Keller took a total of three vacations, to fish.[41]

Bernard Edwin Hutchinson (1888–1961) also spent much of his early life in manufacturing before he came to Maxwell Motor Company as its treasurer in 1921. Hutchinson graduated from Hyde Park High School in Chicago at age 16 and attended the Massachusetts Institute of Technology. Asked to leave MIT after two years, because he was more interested in working as a reporter for the *Boston Globe* than in his studies, he returned to Chicago, where he worked as a "cinder snapper" in his father's open-hearth furnace plant. At age 24, Hutchinson became chief engineer for the Blair Open Hearth Furnace Company of London, England, which manufactured and installed open-hearth furnaces.

Hutchinson joined the staff of Ernst & Ernst, certified public accountants, in 1918. The accounting firm put him in charge of the financial reorganization of the American Writing Paper Company of Holyoke, Massachusetts, and he then served as the paper company's treasurer. Hutchinson was at American Writing Paper until he came to Detroit in August 1921 as treasurer for the Maxwell Motor Corporation.

Walter Chrysler had Hutchinson appointed to the Maxwell board of directors in 1922 and made him a vice president, a position he held until 1952, when he retired. Hutchinson was the key player in the financial reorganization of Maxwell starting in 1921: he arranged loans in January 1924 that allowed the production of the Chrysler Six to move ahead, put together the financing for the Chrysler merger with Dodge Brothers in 1928, and eliminated Chrysler's long-term debt in the middle of the Depression.[42]

Hutchinson was a highly skilled financial analyst whose work with Chrysler went well beyond that of a treasurer or accountant. He had the best "people skills" of any of Chrysler's lieutenants: he was easygoing, genial, articulate, witty, and smart. He was a credible negotiator because he could be honest and frank without offending the other party. He could be very stubborn and unyielding as well. Hutchinson often referred to himself as "a bookkeeper," with a false modesty that belied his contributions to Chrysler's success.[43]

The single characteristic of the Chrysler Corporation that has set it apart from the other contemporary automakers was its strength in automotive engineering, as opposed to automotive styling. From the first Chrysler Six of 1924 until well into the 1960s, Chrysler vehicles incorporated the most advanced automotive engineering in the industry. Chrysler Corporation introduced 45 significant new engineering features on its products in the period 1924–41 alone. The original Chrysler Six of 1924 itself had seven "firsts" on American cars (high compression engine, four-wheel hydraulic brakes, oil filter, air cleaner, independent hand brake, temperature gauge on the dash, and electric fuel gauge on the dash).[44]

Space does not permit a thorough discussion of even the first fifteen years of Chrysler "firsts," much less the entire record. In his history of Chrysler engineering, Carl Breer has an entire section entitled, "Reminiscences of Early Product Developments at Chrysler Corporation." Breer included in his list the chilled cast-iron valve tappet, the aluminum piston, bronze bushings for engine bearings, cellular-type radiators, the automatic choke, the rubber steering wheel, the valve seat insert, "Oilite" powdered metal bearings, the helical gear transmission, "Keller" overdrive, "Fluid Drive," the sealed-beam headlight, Amola steel, the fresh air heater, and a dozen "minor" improvements.[45]

Walter Chrysler laid the foundation for Chrysler's engineering excellence in June 1923, when he convinced the Zeder, Skelton, Breer Engineering Company to come to Detroit to complete design work on the Chrysler Six car for the Maxwell Motor Corporation. The ZSB team at that time had a total of 24 men—a decade later, 18 of them were still employed by Chrysler. Zeder recalled that only 35 people worked on the design and testing of the first Chrysler Six. By 1928, more than 300 worked in Chrysler Engineering.[46]

Zeder, Skelton, and Breer were each distinct in skills, interests, and personalities, yet they made a highly effective team. Frederick Morrell Zeder (1886–1951) grew up in Bay City, Michigan. While still in high school, Zeder worked as a machinist apprentice at the Bay City Industrial Works, a manufacturer of heavy-duty cranes for railroads. After graduating, he worked at the Industrial Works for about a year before joining the Michigan Central Railroad as a machinist in the Motive Power Division. Zeder entered the University of Michigan's College of Engineering in 1905 and earned a bachelor of science degree in mechanical engineering in 1909. He then entered the apprentice program at the Allis-Chalmers Company in Milwaukee with fellow apprentice Carl Breer. Zeder was named erecting engineer at Allis-Chalmers in 1910, but left the firm to join the E-M-F (Everitt-Metzger-Flanders) Company, a Detroit-based automaker, to manage its engineering labs.

The Studebaker Corporation, which acquired E-M-F in 1912, named Zeder consulting engineer the following year and chief engineer in 1914. In an effort to improve Studebaker's products, Zeder hired Owen Skelton and Carl Breer in 1916, bringing together the members of the soon-to-be-famous Zeder-Skelton-Breer triumvirate. In July 1920, Walter Chrysler convinced the Zeder-led team to join him at Willys-Overland. Fred Zeder severed his relationship with the Willys company in December 1921 and established an independent consulting firm, Zeder, Skelton, and Breer Engineering Company. Walter Chrysler hired Zeder's team to design what became the Chrysler Six, and they officially went to work for the Maxwell Motor Corporation in early June 1923.

Fred Zeder became the head of engineering at Maxwell, and following the establishment of the Chrysler Corporation in June 1925, he was vice president in charge of engineering. He managed the merger of the Dodge Brothers engineering operations into Chrysler following the 1928 takeover. Fred Zeder was responsible for all the engineering activities of the Chrysler Corporation from 1925 until his death in 1951. Along with Keller and Hutchinson, Zeder was one of Chrysler's "princes," a major force within the corporation for more than a quarter-century.[47]

Owen R. Skelton (1886–1969) is the least-famous member of the "Three Musketeers." Born in Edgerton, Ohio, in the northwest corner of the state, Skelton began working as an apprentice in his father's harness and saddle shop before earning a degree in mechanical engineering from the Ohio State University. From 1905 to 1907, he worked for the Pope-Toledo Company, a Toledo automaker, where he became an expert on transmissions and axles. Skelton joined the Packard Motor Car Company in Detroit in 1907, working in the design drafting department. In 1916, he went to work for Zeder at Studebaker, with the job of redesigning Studebaker's drive trains, transmissions, and rear axles. When Skelton came to Maxwell in June 1923, he was named executive engineer, a title he retained at Chrysler. Skelton retired in 1951, but remained on the board of directors through 1954, when he moved to Palm Beach, Florida.[48]

The third member of the "Three Musketeers" was Carl Breer (1883–1970). He grew up in Los Angeles and worked as a youngster in his father's blacksmith and carriage shop. Breer attended the Throop Polytechnic Institute (later California Institute of Technology) in Pasadena for one year (1904), which qualified him to enter Stanford University's engineering program in the fall of 1905. After graduation in 1909, Breer entered the apprentice program at Allis-Chalmers in Milwaukee with Fred Zeder. He then worked for a variety of automobile companies until 1916, when Zeder lured him to Studebaker. At Chrysler, Breer held the title of research director from 1925 until his retirement in 1949, and continued to consult for Chrysler for another four years.[49]

Chrysler Engineering flourished because Walter Chrysler was willing to support it with buildings, equipment, staff, and funds. The completion of the Engineering Building at the (former) Maxwell plant in Highland Park in 1928 symbolized that commitment. The four-story building cost $1 million and provided 960,000 square feet of space for laboratories, showrooms, and offices. The building had modern laboratories and test facilities, including a "cold room," which maintained below-zero temperatures, and a "chassis roll," (also called a "Belgian roll"), a machine that subjected the car chassis, frame, and body to stress and strain.[50]

Chrysler Corporation went on to construct a large complex of laboratory,

The "Three Musketeers" in 1934: *left to right,* Owen Skelton, Fred Zeder, and Carl Breer.
Courtesy of DCHC.

design, and testing facilities at the Highland Park site. The Engineering Building received a fifth floor in 1929 and a sixth in 1936. Later construction included
the Dynamometer Building (1939) and North Laboratory Building (1940, 1942).
Chrysler published *New Worlds in Engineering* to mark the opening of the new
laboratories in 1940. Nearly half of this colorful, glossy 96-page book was devoted to Chrysler's manufacturing and assembly operations.[51]

Chrysler established its own "college of engineering" in 1931, when it
launched the Chrysler Institute of Engineering. The corporation employed hundreds of qualified engineers, but needed to train new men, whether fresh out of
college or with prior work experience, in the "Chrysler way" of doing things.
John J. Caton, the former head of the automotive engineering department at the
University of Detroit, served as director of the institute. Caton studied existing
programs at Westinghouse, General Electric, Allis-Chalmers, Bell Telephone,
and General Motors before establishing Chrysler's curriculum.[52]

The institute began as a two-year postgraduate program combining academics with "hands-on" practical experience. Chrysler paid the students, all recent college graduates, a starting engineer's salary while they attended classes and worked in various departments within Chrysler Engineering—eight three-month assignments in total. With the assistance of Dean Paul Anderson of the University of Kentucky and Dean Mortimer Cooley from the University of Michigan, the institute received a charter from the Michigan Department of State that allowed it to grant degrees; successful completion of the course earned a master's degree in mechanical engineering. Caton and his admissions committee accepted 15 applicants (11 came) for fall 1931 and another 5 in January 1932. The second class, admitted in August 1932, had 9 students, selected from over 500 applicants.[53]

The institute's educational offerings immediately grew beyond its graduate program. Starting in September 1931, the institute began offering evening classes, taught by the graduate students, to engineering employees who wanted additional training in technical subjects, including drafting. Fifty employees enrolled at the start. In the fall of 1933, Chrysler opened the evening courses to all Chrysler employees at no cost. The undergraduate school soon offered courses in mechanical drawing, body drafting, higher mathematics, mechanical engineering, and business administration. Enrollments jumped from 354 in 1933 to over 1,000 the following year. This program granted a diploma, but not a degree.[54]

At the first commencement exercises, held on 11 July 1933, the Chrysler Institute of Engineering awarded 14 graduate degrees and 21 undergraduate diplomas. The institute also granted Walter P. Chrysler an honorary doctor of engineering degree. A year later, the institute awarded 10 graduate degrees and 36 diplomas, plus honorary degrees of master of engineering to Carl Breer and Owen R. Skelton. The ceremonies began with the singing of the "Chrysler Institute March," dedicated to Walter P. Chrysler. At the fifth graduation, held in June 1938, the institute granted 30 master's degrees and 131 diplomas.[55]

Among the 1938 graduates earning a master's degree was M.(Mary) Virginia Sink (1913–86), admitted in 1936 as the first woman in the program. She had earned a degree in 1936 in chemical engineering at the University of Colorado. Sink also appeared in Chrysler Institute of Engineering yearbooks for 1937 and 1938 as a member of the teaching staff. Upon graduation, she managed Chrysler's chemical radiography and spectrographic department. During the Second World War, she served as personnel director of women and supervised 500 laboratory employees. Starting in 1950, Sink worked on various emissions measurement and control projects for Chrysler and in 1962, she helped develop Chrysler's "Clean Air Package." When Sink retired in 1979, she was manager of Chrysler's vehicle emissions certification program.[56]

This educational enterprise had modest beginnings, but became a major source of trained staff for Chrysler. In January 1940, the institute allowed messenger boys from the drafting room to study drafting; women were admitted in March 1942. Disabled veterans were given the same opportunity in November 1942. During its first ten years, the institute held classes all over the Highland Park plant and at Highland Park High School. A new Chrysler Institute Building opened on 1 October 1942, with 20 classrooms, 6 drafting rooms, 6 laboratories, and an auditorium. The Chrysler Institute of Engineering had come of age. Over its first two decades, ending with the class of 1953, a total of 545 students had earned masters' degrees. The vast majority of institute graduates stayed with Chrysler and in time held executive positions throughout the corporation.[57]

Chrysler Corporation's survival and success in the 1930s and later was no accident. Walter Chrysler surrounded himself with competent, energetic, farseeing men beginning in his days with Maxwell, while emphasizing innovative engineering of automobiles and other products. Walter Chrysler could not have predicted the events of the late 1930s, including labor strife and economic recession, but he left the company that bore his name well prepared to deal with the turbulent years to come.

Chapter 8

CHRYSLER IN THE LATE 1930S

Walter Chrysler was the last great individual constructive force in the automobile industry; offhand, one cannot think of a contemporary in any industry who can be compared with him.
—E. D. Kennedy

The Chrysler Corporation faced serious and ever-changing challenges during the brief period from 1937 through the end of 1940. For the first time, the corporation had to contend with a well-organized, militant, and increasingly entrenched labor union representing its production workers. After enjoying substantial economic recovery through 1937, Chrysler and the rest of the auto industry faced another depression in sales in 1938 and 1939. This period also marked the retirement and death of Walter P. Chrysler, the company's founder, leader, and visionary. After giving up the presidency in 1935, Chrysler remained active in company affairs until suffering a stroke in 1938. His death in 1940 marked the end of the founding period of the corporation. The Chrysler Corporation of 1940 was vastly different from the corporation of just five years earlier.

ORGANIZED LABOR

At precisely 1:30 P.M. on Monday, 8 March 1937, thousands of factory workers at nine Chrysler plants in the Detroit area simultaneously walked out of their workplaces or sat down in the factories. The well-planned sit-down strike continued until 25 March, when the workers evacuated the plants. Chrysler operations remained shut down until two weeks later, when the Chrysler Corporation signed an agreement with the United Automobile Workers of America-CIO (UAW). Chrysler and the UAW engaged in many more struggles in the late 1930s, during the Second World War, and later, but the UAW has remained a permanent fixture in Chrysler's industrial relations since March 1937. From that point forward, Chrysler could no longer operate in an "open shop" or nonunion environment, with a free hand to change wages, hours, production standards, and other working conditions at its whim.

Walter P. Chrysler, K. T. Keller, B. E. Hutchinson, and the rest of the corporation's executives probably felt certain at least through 1935 that they would never have to deal with a strong labor union representing their blue-collar workers. Detroit was a bastion of the "open shop" until the early 1930s. Detroit manufacturers had kept organized labor out of their plants until the 1930s through a wide range of methods, including "welfare" programs, spies, and company unions. The Detroit automobile industry epitomized the success of the open shop movement through the 1920s and beyond.[1]

In mid-1929, Chrysler established the Chrysler Industrial Association (CIA), an employee organization with the goal of stabilizing workers' lives. Initially, the CIA offered three major programs. First, Chrysler workers could buy inexpensive life insurance and sickness/accident insurance as a single policy through the Aetna Life Insurance Company. The second program was the "Good Cheer Fund," which made gifts or loans to workers unable to pay medical expenses or with unusual medical needs; provided special Christmas packages of food, clothing, and gifts for the impoverished; and offered loans to employees with temporary financial emergencies. Finally, the CIA supported athletic and recreational activities for Chrysler employees.[2]

The Chrysler Industrial Association expanded its activities until the beginnings of labor agitation at the Chrysler plants in late 1936 and 1937. Starting in June 1935, the CIA produced *Chrysler Motors Magazine,* a professionally designed glossy monthly that carried news of employee activities. The number and range of programs eventually supported by the CIA were impressive, including group health insurance, emergency loans, home nursing service, assistance with naturalization, girls' clubs, "Fresh Air" camps, the Chrysler Boys' Tours, the Chrysler Male Choir, *Chrysler Motors Magazine,* the Chrysler Gardeners' Club, picnics and special excursions, various plant bands and orchestras, and the Chrysler Apprentice School, which offered "earning while learning." Finally, the CIA sponsored athletic activities including summer baseball and softball leagues; girls' softball teams; and other sports including bowling, soccer, golf, boxing, and horseback riding.

In addition to using these "welfare" programs to discourage unions, Chrysler and other large employers used spies to identify disgruntled employees so the companies could dismiss them. The larger firms either hired undercover agents provided by outside detective agencies or, in the case of the Ford Motor Company Service Department, developed their own intelligence-gathering system. Chrysler hired the Corporations Auxiliary Company of New York to gather intelligence. Thirty-eight of their operatives worked in Chrysler plants in 1933, at a cost of $61,627.48, 45 in 1934 ($76,411.81), and 38 in 1935 ($72,611.89). The spies would enter the plants as ordinary workers and then submit written reports to Corporations Auxiliary, identifying themselves only by number, and the detective agency would then pass the reports on to Chrysler. Corporations Auxiliary paid one operative (L-392) $40 a month for his work and then billed Chrysler $9 a day for his time.[3]

Chrysler and other large manufacturers also promoted company-dominated unions as an alternative to independent unions. These company unions typically took the form of an "employee representation plan," which would provide for joint meetings of labor and management ("works councils") to discuss problems and grievances, with the goal of achieving labor peace. The company union first emerged in large American manufacturing firms during the First World War and remained in many industries into the 1930s. Chrysler's company union fits nicely into this pattern.[4]

Walter Chrysler proposed an employee representation plan in October 1933 and gave the employees the opportunity to vote on it. He said,

> As a former shop worker I have long looked forward to the time when the employes [*sic*] and the management of the Chrysler Corporation would sit down around a table to discuss and decide matters of mutual interest to all of us. I have always believed that if we could do this in a spirit of friendly understanding and confidence in each other, we would accomplish a great step.
>
>   It is inevitable in a large organization such as this that from time to time questions should arise. The aim should be to provide a mutually satisfactory method of dealing with these matters, of jointly establishing what the facts are and then, jointly, in a friendly, co-operative way, decide what we are going to do about them. I have enough confidence in the fairness of men to believe that when they know the facts and have an equal voice in deciding matters that concern them, they will come to decisions that are fair and reasonable.

The plan provided for joint shop councils in all the plants, with representatives chosen by secret ballot. Each council would have an equal number of employee and management representatives, but a two-thirds vote was required for any action. Even if all the employee representatives could agree on some issue, which was unlikely, they would then need to get at least one-third of the management representatives to vote with them before they could take any action. The shop employees at Chrysler were allowed to vote on this plan and 86 percent of the 33,000 employees who participated approved.[5]

The Chrysler Employees' Representation Plan was unusual in that the employees had a chance to vote for it. Other automobile companies simply presented their plan to the workers as an accomplished fact. The Chrysler Industrial Association ran the election for the plan and the first elections for the joint shop councils. Once in place, the joint councils conducted the elections. The lopsided vote at Chrysler, however, should not be interpreted as strong rank-and-file support for the plan. Workers believed that the voting was not secret to begin with and that voting against the plan was seen by management as a sign of labor union sympathies. When Chrysler workers registered their union preferences a few months later in independent elections supervised by the Automobile Labor Board, only 96 out of 41,029 who voted chose the company union.[6]

The organization of blue-collar workers in the American auto industry was a difficult and complicated struggle that involved several rival unions, false starts, and temporary reversals. The effort began in earnest in 1933, but was not substantially completed until the unionization of Ford Motor Company by the UAW in 1941. Ironically, at Chrysler, the company union put in place in 1933 to prevent "real" labor unions from taking hold became the platform union activists used to organize Chrysler's workforce.

Despite the competition from company-controlled unions and the other weapons used by employers against them, automobile workers in the Detroit area established legitimate independent unions starting in 1933. The Mechanics Educational Society of America (MESA) was initially an organization of skilled tool and die makers who struck against the auto industry as early as September 1933. After a six-week struggle that achieved modest gains, MESA recruited semiskilled metal workers and by January 1935, claimed about 35,000 members, mostly in Michigan.[7]

One group of highly skilled metal body workers known as "dingmen" established the Dingmen's Welfare Club, a labor union. We know little about them until 30 April 1935, when 260 dingmen at Chrysler and Briggs walked off their jobs, complaining that Chrysler was deliberately replacing them with less-skilled metal finishers. The club ordered its members to return to work after six weeks with few gains except an understanding that Chrysler would not discriminate against them. An article in *Fortune* in August 1935 described their action as

> a short-lived strike of special body finishers which brought to the delighted attention of the world the existence of a curious phenomenon known as a dingman. That car bodies just off the line have to have their dents and bumps pounded out was interesting in itself. But that these blemishes were pounded out by a restricted priesthood known as dingmen and that

dingmen could strike and had struck for higher pay was something to remember in one's sleep.[8]

The dingmen's strike was part of a rising tide of autoworker militancy in the Detroit auto plants.

The legal and organizational terrain of labor-management relations changed substantially after President Roosevelt signed the National Labor Relations Act, more commonly known as the Wagner Act, in early July 1935. The Wagner Act established machinery to run certification elections and to process "unfair labor practice" charges brought against employers, including evidence that they used spies. The Wagner Act, however, was not fully tested by the U.S. Supreme Court for constitutionality until April 1937 and had little direct influence on automobile industry labor relations until 1939. It did, however, encourage automobile workers to establish unions.[9]

The successful efforts to organize workers at Dodge Main and the other Chrysler plants in Detroit eventually led to the companywide sit-down strike that began on 8 March 1937. The road to successful organization at Chrysler was a long and winding one, with numerous twists and turns, detours, and dead ends. The key developments took place at Dodge Main and then spread to other plants.

Labor activists like John Zaremba and Richard Frankensteen, who were committed to independent unionism but who also served on the Dodge Works Council, soon recognized that Chrysler management was unwilling to engage in genuine collective bargaining. They created instead an "in-plant" union structure, complete with shop stewards, which became affiliated after July 1936 with the UAW-CIO. The activists became more confrontational with Chrysler management through the works council and achieved some gains. On 11 November 1936, for example, Chrysler agreed to pay time and a half for overtime work, the first automaker to do so. In the last corporationwide election to the works councils, held on 28 January 1937, candidates who openly ran as UAW supporters won 103 of the 120 seats. When Walter Chrysler launched his employee representation plan in October 1933, he could not have imagined this outcome.[10]

The UAW had staged a successful 44-day sit-down strike against General Motors in January and February 1937.[11] On 24 February 1937, the UAW's Richard Frankensteen asked the Chrysler Corporation for a national conference to negotiate a single contract covering all Chrysler employees. On 3 March, 103 works council representatives resigned in favor of the UAW and Frankensteen renewed his demand. Chrysler officially informed him of its refusal to deal with the UAW as the sole bargaining agent on 8 March, immediately touching off the sit-down strike at the Chrysler plants in the Detroit area.

In the early days of the strike, the UAW allowed Chrysler executives into their offices and permitted mail and telephone service to continue, while Chrysler agreed not to resume operations during negotiations. On 10 March, Chrysler asked the courts for an injunction forcing the union out of the plants and in retaliation, the UAW occupied the offices at the Highland Park headquarters and in the plants. On 15 March, circuit judge Allan Campbell ordered the workers out of the plants by 9:00 A.M. on 17 March. After the workers refused to leave, the court on 19 March issued a meaningless order to the county sheriff to arrest the sit-down strikers. With only two dozen deputies, the sheriff was not able to force thousands of workers from the plant.

On 23 March 1937, Governor Frank Murphy stepped in to end the impasse by inviting Walter P. Chrysler and John L. Lewis, the leader of the Committee for Industrial Organization, to meet with him in Lansing to settle the dispute. Chrysler and Lewis came to Lansing on 24 March, each with a staff of lieutenants and advisors. Murphy immediately crafted an agreement by which the strikers would leave the plants, which the governor would guarantee would remain closed during negotiations. The UAW evacuated the Chrysler plants the next day, ending seventeen days of occupation.[12]

Negotiations in Lansing produced an agreement on 6 April. The Chrysler negotiating team included Walter Chrysler; K. T. Keller; B. E. Hutchinson; T. J. Ross, a public relations advisor; Herman L. Weckler, Chrysler's vice president for industrial relations; Lester L. Colbert, Chrysler's Detroit attorney; and Nicholas Kelley, Chrysler's general counsel. Lewis referred to Chrysler's retinue as "Chrysler's House of Lords." The union negotiators were Lewis; UAW president Homer Martin; Richard Frankensteen, representing the Chrysler workers; and Lee Pressman, counsel to Lewis. John L. Lewis and Walter Chrysler conducted most of the negotiations one-on-one.

The agreement Murphy announced late on 6 April was a compromise that allowed both sides to claim victory. Chrysler did *not* agree to a union shop, but agreed that it would not discriminate against union members and more important, would not promote, finance, or sign agreements with other labor organizations. For its part, the union would not recruit members on company property or intimidate workers into joining. Further, the UAW would return to work and agree not to strike through 31 March 1938, the duration of the contract. Chrysler and the UAW reached a supplemental agreement on 14 April 1937, covering grievance procedures, layoffs, transfers of employees, and seniority rules.[13]

After enjoying expanding sales and profits in 1937, Chrysler and the other automakers faced a severe slump in 1938. For Chrysler, sales fell by more than 50 percent, from 1,159,000 units in 1937 to only 571,000 the following year. The sales decline of 1938 made Chrysler unwilling to grant further concessions to the

UAW sit-down strikers leaving the Dodge Main plant in Hamtramck, Michigan, on 25 March 1937 after seventeen days of occupation. Courtesy of WRL.

UAW and increasingly aggressive in seeking wage cuts. The initial contract between Chrysler and the UAW ran for a year and the parties renewed it for an additional year on 31 March 1938. The UAW had hoped to get a commitment from Chrysler for no wage cuts during the extension, but finally gave up the effort.[14]

After March 1939, month-by-month extensions continued the contract through 30 September 1939. By the summer of 1939, the national economy and the auto industry were enjoying a sharp recovery from the recession of 1938. When production began on the 1940 models in mid-August 1939, both sides were ready for a long struggle for a new contract. The confrontation began around 23 August 1939, when the UAW began "slowdown" strikes in select departments of Dodge Main and other Chrysler plants. Unable to maintain production, Chrysler closed the Dodge Main plant on 11 October and a week later, the UAW launched a conventional strike.

The strike came on the heels of the National Labor Relations Board (NLRB)

Settlement of the sit-down strikes at Chrysler, 6 April 1937, Lansing, Michigan. *Seated, left to right,* CIO president John L. Lewis, Michigan governor Frank Murphy, and Walter P. Chrysler. *Standing, left to right,* Richard T. Frankensteen, UAW organizational director; Lee Pressman, CIO legal counsel; Herman L. Weckler, Chrysler vice president; and K. T. Keller, Chrysler president. Courtesy of WRL.

certification elections held in all of Chrysler's plants on 27 September 1939. The elections offered workers three choices—the UAW-CIO, the UAW-AFL, and "neither." Workers at 11 of the 14 plants chose the UAW-CIO as their bargaining agent, giving the union an overwhelming victory and strongly supporting its claim to be the sole representative of Chrysler employees. In Chrysler's plants as a whole, 49,713 (out of roughly 54,000 eligible workers) voted, with the UAW-CIO getting 40,564 votes (81.6 percent), the UAW-AFL only 4,673 votes (9.4 percent), and the "no union" option a mere 4,476 votes (9.0 percent). Only in the three plants in Indiana (Kokomo, Evansville, and New Castle) did the UAW-CIO not win a majority.[15]

The UAW held a strike vote on 15 October 1939, with a 90 percent majority of a very large turnout authorizing a strike. The company viewed 6 October as the start of the strike because that was the point at which the slowdowns began to cause shutdowns, but the union "officially" went on strike on 18 October and stayed out for 45 days.[16]

Contract negotiations accompanied by bitter public accusations issued by both sides went slowly during the six weeks of the strike. Philip Murray, vice president of the CIO, entered the negotiations on 27 November. The next day, K. T. Keller offered a general pay raise of 3¢ an hour, plus wage adjustments in particular classifications. The last stumbling block removed, the two parties agreed to a new contract at 6:30 A.M. on 29 November. The locals ratified the agreement later that same day and most of the Chrysler plants reopened on the 30th and 31st.

Assessing the results of the slowdown and strike that followed is difficult. Chrysler recognized the UAW as the sole bargaining agency in its plants, but it would have been morally, if not legally, obligated to do so anyway because of the NLRB certification elections. The UAW did not get a union shop or paid vacations. While the company still established rates of production, the rates were now subject to a stronger grievance process. Chrysler recognized the shop steward system and agreed to pay stewards while they did their contractual duties, including settling grievances.

The union won time-and-a-half pay for overtime, double-time for holiday work, and a minimum of two hours' pay for employees sent home after reporting for work, all significant economic gains. The across-the-board pay raise of 3¢ went to workers who earned, on average, $1 an hour. None of the financial issues were "deal-busters," and the settlement had little effect on Chrysler's profits. The company estimated that the contract would increase its labor costs about $5 million a year, which turned out to be less than 1 percent of its 1940 sales of $775 million. Even with the increased labor costs, Chrysler enjoyed profits of nearly $38 million that year.[17] The 1939 strike was a test of strength for the UAW and a test of resolve for Chrysler. Both passed.

THE LATE 1930S: THE END OF AN ERA

At the end of the 1930s, the automobile market returned to the instability of the early Depression years. Table 8.1 illustrates the wild fluctuations in sales from 1937 to 1940 and the resulting swings in profits. The more than 50 percent drop in 1938 sales from 1937 levels was a sharper dip than Chrysler had experienced between 1929 and 1930. Sales rebounded in 1939 and went over the 1 million mark in 1940 and 1941, but Chrysler still was not able to reach its 1937 sales and earnings records.

Chrysler's products during the 1938–42 model years were for the most part

TABLE 8.1 Chrysler Corporation Performance, 1937–45

| | | | Net Earnings* | | |
| | | | Total ($) | On Sales (%) | On Capital Invested† (%) |
	Unit Sales	Net Sales ($)			
1937	1,158,518	769,807,839	50,729,211	6.6	39.2
1938	570,852	413,250,000	18,798,294	4.5	13.4
1939	778,781	549,800,000	36,879,829	6.7	23.7
1940	1,044,290	744,561,239	37,802,279	5.1	23.1
1941	1,028,130	888,366,410	40,114,419	4.5	22.6
1942	52,351	623,655,208	15,529,000	2.5	8.7
1943	—	886,467,702	23,322,566	2.6	12.4
1944	—	1,098,023,025	24,819,489	2.3	12.4
1945	39,361	994,545,000	37,464,624	3.8	15.0

Sources: Chrysler Corporation annual reports, 1937–45, box "Annual Reports 1925–69," DCHC; and *The American Car since 1775* (Kunztown, Pa.: Automobile Quarterly, 1971); 141 (sales for 1942).

*After taxes.
†Defined as stockholders' equity and surpluses.

conservatively styled and well engineered. Engineering continued to dominate Chrysler's small Art & Colour Department, which had the tasks of developing interiors and decorative exterior trim only. The body engineers controlled the shape of the sheet metal. A talented stylist like Ray Dietrich, who worked for Chrysler from 1932 to 1940, had little influence on the overall look of the cars. He redesigned the Airflow grilles in 1935–37 and made minor changes to the popular Airstream designs of 1937–38, but never worked well with the body engineers. Four days after the death of Walter Chrysler, his patron, the company fired him.[18]

Chrysler exhibited at least moderately daring styling changes in several of its 1940–42 models, before the needs of war abruptly ended civilian car production for four years. For the 1941 model year, Chrysler stylist Buzz Grisinger developed the first model of what became the classic Chrysler Town & Country line. He combined a Chrysler seven-passenger sedan roof with windshield, cowl, and fenders from a Chrysler Windsor to create a station wagon, then clothed it in light and dark woodwork.

More remarkable were two eye-catching "show cars" or "dream machines" built by Chrysler in 1941. The Thunderbolt was a convertible with retractable headlights and metal roof raised electrically and stored in the trunk. The other show car, the Chrysler Newport, was a classic dual-cowl phaeton with soft lines and a futuristic look. The custom coach maker LeBaron designed and built the Newport bodies. The automaker made six copies of each of these cars. One of the Newports served as the pace car for the 1941 Indianapolis 500 race.[19]

Another Chrysler engineering first of this period was Fluid Drive. Chrysler adopted a hydraulic torque converter, which eliminated most manual shifting of gears. Instead of manually shifting (and declutching) between four forward gears, the driver would have a choice of two gear lever positions: "low," which controlled first and second gear, and "high," which controlled third and fourth. Chrysler introduced Fluid Drive on the Imperial for 1939, all other Chryslers in 1940, and then as an extra-cost option on the DeSoto and Dodge the following year. However, by this time, General Motors already had a fully automatic transmission in some of its car lines.[20]

For all the problems Chrysler faced in the 1930s, along with the other automakers, its success and size brought advantages. Chrysler went well past the 500,000 sales mark in 1934 and enjoyed sales of more than 1 million vehicles in 1936, 1937, 1940, and 1941. One of the economies of large size involved advertising, where companies could spread their fixed advertising costs, such as a full-page advertisement in a national magazine, over a larger and larger volume of sales.[21]

Chrysler turned to commercial network radio in the 1930s as a cost-effective way to reach an affluent national audience. Late in 1935, the *Major Bowes Amateur Hour* first appeared on the National Broadcasting Company (NBC) radio network and was a runaway success. The show's host, Edward Bowes, would welcome his amateur guests of all ages, but then "gong" those who were inept, right in the middle of their performance. William S. Paley, the president of the Columbia Broadcasting System (CBS), lured Major Bowes to his struggling network in mid-1936, along with the program's new sponsor, the Chrysler Corporation.[22]

The *Major Bowes Amateur Hour* aired every Thursday evening from 9:00 to 10:00 P.M. on the CBS radio network. Telecast live from the CBS Radio Theater in New York City, the program allowed people to vote for their favorite amateur by telephone from the New York City area and from one "honor city" selected each week. Listeners from other parts of the country could vote by telegraph or letter. Winners then had a chance to tour with one of the Major Bowes shows that traveled the country. A broadcast program from June 1937 claimed a national radio audience upwards of 20 million, and promotional materials from October–November 1941 boasted an audience of 27 million.

The ties between Major Bowes and Chrysler went beyond simple sponsorship. Walter Chrysler and Major Bowes became close friends; early in their commercial relationship, Chrysler had a 1936 Chrysler Imperial Airflow specially made for Major Bowes. It featured a body modified by LeBaron and a custom interior with a special console between the driver and passenger compartment. After Chrysler's death in August 1940, Major Bowes broadcast a personal eulogy: "On Sunday last, Walter Chrysler was called home to his eternal rest. For many years he was close to my heart—I loved him as a brother. My personal loss seems irreparable."[23] Major Bowes was not alone in mourning this man's passing.

WALTER P. CHRYSLER (1875–1940): A RETROSPECTIVE

Although Walter Chrysler turned over the presidency of the Chrysler Corporation to K. T. Keller in 1935, he kept the post of chairman of the board and remained active in the company's affairs, at least selectively. For example, he led the negotiations that ended the March 1937 sit-down strike. Walter Chrysler was never able to enjoy a long, happy retirement from business. But on 26 May 1938, he suffered a serious stroke that left him incapacitated.

A little more than two months after Walter Chrysler's first stroke, on 8 August 1938, his wife, Della Forker Chrysler, had a fatal stroke. She was 66. She and Walter had married on 2 June 1901 in Ellis, Kansas. In addition to raising their four children, she had been a constant source of support and encouragement for Walter Chrysler through his long and sometimes tortuous career. Her death and his own incapacitation must have been devastating to his normally optimistic outlook. A second stroke on 18 August 1940 killed him at age 65. His funeral service was held on 21 August 1940 at St. Bartholomew's Church in New York City.[24]

More than a decade before his passing, Walter Chrysler was already enshrined as an American folk hero, a twentieth-century Horatio Alger figure. Chrysler consciously fostered this view through frequent interviews with the financial and popular press. His *Life of an American Workman,* published serially in 1937 in the *Saturday Evening Post,* was the story of his life achievements made against great adversity. That he would present his life story in a way that guaranteed mass readership says much about his ego. (The work was published in book form in 1950.) The story emphasized his youth and early career, with only 28 pages of its 203 pages devoted to his success in the auto industry after he took charge of Maxwell in 1921.

Chrysler's status as a folk hero dates from 1928, when *Time* selected him as "Man of the Year"—he was only the second man so honored (the first was Charles Lindbergh the year before). His face appeared on the cover of the magazine and the article within recounted his remarkable accomplishments in 1928—

Walter P. and Della Chrysler in Palm Beach, Florida, 17 February 1937. Courtesy of SA/KU.

the merger with Dodge and the introduction of the Plymouth and DeSoto lines. *Forbes Magazine* published a lengthy article on Chrysler in January 1929, based on an interview he granted B. C. Forbes, the publisher. Forbes uncritically accepted everything Chrysler told him, including the mythic tale about the 1924 New York Automobile Show and Chrysler's preposterous claim that he had spent $3 million of his own money developing the Chrysler car while employed by Willys-Overland in New Jersey.[25]

The Chrysler story appeared in less elite publications as well. A five-page article in *Popular Mechanics* in 1932, entitled "The Man Who Bet on His Dreams," repeats the myths, but without the exaggeration of some earlier versions. On the heels of the article, *Popular Mechanics* sent a special offer to attract new subscribers through a mass mailing of 1 million letters. New subscribers could receive seven issues for only $1 instead of the usual $1.75. Half of the two-page letter was a summary of Walter Chrysler's life and career as a self-made man. The message was clear—if you want to be like Walter P. Chrysler, subscribe to our magazine.[26]

Walter Chrysler also appeared in the comics. In late April 1934, *Ben Webster's Page,* a comic strip written by Edwin Alger, recounted Chrysler's boyhood days in "The Boy Mechanic." His entire life and career were later summarized in a full-page comic strip (1949) written by E. and I. Geller and drawn by Max Rasmussen. This was one of a series "Sponsored by Firms Built by Free Enterprise" that recounted modern American business success stories, presumably to educate the public about the advantages of the free enterprise system. The Chrysler Corporation was one of the sponsors of this series. This Chrysler biographical comic strip closely followed *Life of an American Workman.*[27]

In the days following Walter P. Chrysler's death, the expected public statements flowed from Chrysler officials, from other automobile industry leaders, and from the editorial columns of Detroit's three daily newspapers. For the most part, these statements repeated the same common themes—Walter Chrysler had risen from rags to riches through hard work; he had remained in many respects a common workman despite his great wealth and always felt at home on the factory floor; he had always treated others with respect, whatever their social position.

There is at least anecdotal evidence of Walter Chrysler's genuine humility. Ray Ayer, who began working at Chrysler when Walter Chrysler was still active in day-to-day management, recalled that Chrysler punched a time card just like the other workers in his office building. Despite his wealth, he wore only one piece of jewelry, a ring on the small finger of his right hand. He would always buy three suits at once, in brown, blue, and gray. Walter Chrysler remained a popular figure among his workers, despite unpleasant labor relations in the late 1930s. According to Nicholas Kelley, a UAW delegation picketed the Lansing hotel where Governor Murphy, John L. Lewis, and Chrysler held their negotiations in March 1937. When Chrysler appeared on the balcony above the demonstrators, they cheered.[28]

In his oral reminiscences recorded in March 1953, long after Chrysler's death, Nicholas Kelley, a Chrysler confidant for two decades, offered his assessment of the man:

> Chrysler was a rough tough man. He was a driver. He was an engaging man, but I still think it is fair to say he was rough and tough. He had two other qualities, so it was a wonderful mixture, and made an outstanding man. He had an exceedingly active mind, just as fine and delicate and accurate as the finest Swiss watch, or the finest piece of machinery. Besides that, he had what I call intuition, very delicate intuition, like that of a woman's. . . . You hear people say that Walter Chrysler was a great man. He was a great man because he combined all these things.[29]

Historian E. D. Kennedy assessed Walter Chrysler's career right after his death. He pointed out that Chrysler spent his career struggling against the prevailing trends in the automobile industry, making his success even more remarkable. He organized the Chrysler Corporation very late in the evolution of the American automobile industry and sold an expensive car when that part of the market was stagnant. Most contemporaries viewed his purchase of Dodge as a major mistake. He introduced the Plymouth into an already-crowded field of low-priced cars, coming head-to-head with Ford and Chevrolet. Kennedy offered the following perspective: "If automobile history were divided into two parts, a pre-1920 section and a post-1920 section, Chrysler's name would be as noteworthy in the second half of the auto story as Ford's was in the first."[30]

Despite the high praises of automobile industry historians and others for Walter P. Chrysler, he has generally not been honored in the usual public ways. To be sure, his boyhood home in Ellis, Kansas, is restored as a museum. I have found only two schools named after him—the Walter P. Chrysler Memorial High School in New Castle, Indiana, and the Chrysler Elementary School in Detroit. The segment of Interstate 75 passing through Detroit was named the "Walter P. Chrysler Expressway" when construction began in 1959. The "ribbon cutting" for the first section of 2.7 miles, which opened in June 1964, was in fact a ribbon "chiseling." Chrysler Corporation vice president John Leary used a hammer and chisel from Walter P. Chrysler's toolbox to cut the ribbon. In time, the Chrysler Expressway ran next to the corporation's (former) headquarters in Highland Park, Michigan, and now extends past the new Chrysler Technology Center in Auburn Hills, Michigan.[31]

Chapter 9

CHRYSLER IN THE SECOND WORLD WAR

When the new job called for equipment Chrysler didn't have on hand, tool engineers simply remade the old equipment. They even turned drills into lapping machines, a press into a broach, a turret lathe into a boring mill, to get production fast.

—American Machinist

Well before the United States officially entered the Second World War as a combatant, Chrysler Corporation began to manufacture a variety of military hardware and equipment. By early 1942, the automaker converted to making war goods exclusively. Wartime production profoundly affected Chrysler. Manufacturing entirely new products created enormous problems for Chrysler's engineers, managers, and production workers. Chrysler's managers and engineers cooperated with government procurement officials, military planners, and with outside firms in ways that would have been inconceivable during peacetime. They did much of the work in government-owned factories. Chrysler's labor force changed significantly as well, including for the first time many women and African Americans.

THE STRUGGLE TO CONVERT TO WAR WORK

The American automakers, including Chrysler, faced disruptions to their "normal" operations starting in 1941, which proved drastically different from the experience of the First World War. For the car companies, the production of war goods in 1917–18 was a "side business" that only mildly affected automobile production. Dodge Brothers, for example, built a new munitions plant to produce 155 mm recoil mechanisms and did not change production in the rest of its plants. In the Second World War, Chrysler and the other auto companies entirely converted their existing manufacturing facilities to war work and stopped producing cars for the civilian market.

Chrysler and the other automakers were understandably reluctant in 1939–41 to give up the familiar and lucrative automobile business to accept government contracts to produce unfamiliar war goods, knowing that war contracts would bring government controls and reduced profits. This is not to say that all of the auto industry leaders opposed war production. William S. Knudsen, the president of General Motors, resigned his position in May 1940 to serve as chair of the National Defense Advisory Council. In January 1941, Knudsen became the codirector of the Office of Production Management (OPM), which managed all war production. Still, the U.S. auto industry as a whole strongly resisted government efforts to force them to reduce civilian car production and convert to war work.[1]

In December 1940, Walter P. Reuther proposed an ambitious plan to convert part of the auto industry's resources to produce airplane engines, fuselages, and wings, and to help the aircraft industry in assembling them. Reuther, who was the director of the General Motors Department of the UAW at the time, believed that the industry could produce 500 planes a day within six months by using excess capacity in the industry. Production of cars would continue at 5 million per annum. The most radical element of the Reuther plan was a nine-member board to control production of war goods *and* cars for the civilian market. Auto industry leaders and military procurement officials rejected this program out of hand. It became moot following Pearl Harbor, when the government simply ordered the end of civilian car production.[2]

The defense work the automakers reluctantly accepted was limited to work that did not force them to convert vehicle assembly lines. They would accept contracts to design war goods or to engage in defense work in government-owned plants. Many of the most substantial successes in war production at Chrysler and throughout the auto industry came in government-owned–company-operated (GOCO) plants. To minimize the manufacturer's risk, the Defense Plant Corporation would build and equip war plants and then lease the plants to companies like Chrysler for a nominal fee. The government would own the plants and all the machinery, drastically reducing risks to the manufacturer.

Through most of 1941, Knudsen protected the auto industry from demands by Roosevelt's administration that it convert quickly to war work. He announced in mid-April 1941 that the industry would reduce production by only 20 percent and would not start the cutback until August. As late as November 1941, the automakers had not substantially cut civilian production. Even with the Pearl Harbor disaster, Knudsen permitted civilian production to continue until 31 January 1942, with some exceptions that extended production through

1942 DeSoto, the last model manufactured before the conversion to war production. Courtesy of DCHC.

15 February. Chrysler finally ended car production on 31 January, but received permission to continue civilian light truck assembly until 10 February. President Roosevelt created the War Production Board in January 1942 to manage all war production and named Donald M. Nelson its head, ending what had been a cozy relationship between the automakers and Knudsen.[3]

Despite their apparent reluctance to take on military contacts, the auto companies did so well before the start of the war. Chrysler and other manufacturers initially learned to make war goods at little risk through "educational orders" from the military well before the start of hostilities. The Educational Order Act of 1938 permitted the federal government to grant select companies contracts to produce small volumes of products as a learning exercise. The government supplied the machinery and guaranteed a modest profit on the contract.[4]

Starting in December 1939, Chrysler submitted proposals for "educational contracts" for more than a dozen products. Chrysler at first refused to bid on a contract for 500,000 75 mm cartridge cases, claiming it had no experience in making them. Chrysler finally received an "educational order" for 5,000 75 mm cartridge cases on 4 March 1940, followed by a second order for 10,000 cartridge cases on 3 May 1940, and a third for 878,000 cases in late September 1940. As part of this system, Chrysler shared its expertise on cartridge case manufacturing with the Motor Products Company of Detroit.[5]

In the early years of rearmament, Chrysler, along with other automobile companies, turned down several contracts. In late May 1940, Secretary of the Treasury Henry Morgenthau Jr. met with Keller and Hutchinson to convince them
to take on production of Rolls-Royce aircraft engines for the British government. After Chrysler's engineers and production managers examined the engine
carefully, Keller rejected this job, largely because of the trouble he foresaw in
converting the engine to U.S. specifications and standards. In June 1940, Henry
Ford refused to produce Rolls-Royce aircraft engines when he discovered they
were going into English airplanes, which his isolationist politics would not tolerate. Packard Motor Car Company, however, agreed to make the engines a
month later.[6]

The government did not accept all the proposals coming from the automakers, either. Between October 1941 and 15 April 1942, the Ordnance Department
rejected Chrysler proposals to manufacture at least 11 different products ranging
from 37 mm projectile forgings to canteen covers. The department also rejected
a proposal to make incendiary bombs because Chrysler had not subcontracted
at least 60 percent of the value of the work, one of the general rules for war
contracts.[7]

WAR PRODUCTION

By mid-1941, Chrysler had already begun equipping its plants to produce several
of its most important war products. Chrysler and the U.S. Army signed an
agreement in August 1940 by which the automaker would manufacture medium
tanks at a tank arsenal the government would build in Warren, Michigan. Full
assembly-line production was under way in less than a year. The experience
with tanks will be considered in more detail below. In mid-June 1941, Chrysler
began buying machinery and equipment to produce three important war goods:
aluminum forgings at its Dodge Forge plant in Detroit; the nose and center
fuselage sections of the Martin B-26 "Marauder" bomber at the Warren Avenue
DeSoto plant in Detroit; and the Bofors 40 mm anti-aircraft gun, which it
would manufacture at several of its Detroit factories.[8]

With the exception of trucks and possibly tanks, which are vaguely automotive, war contracts sent Chrysler far from familiar ground. Aircraft fuselages, for
example, are not at all like steel automobile bodies. Chrysler's engineers first
examined the Swedish-designed Bofors gun on 4 January 1941, and the navy
gave the automaker a contract to redesign the gun for mass production. Chrysler
had to convert the original specifications from meters to inches and from European to American metallurgical standards. By making the gun parts interchangeable, Chrysler's engineers reduced the assembly time from about 450 hours
under the European hand-filing and fitting methods to fewer than 14 hours with

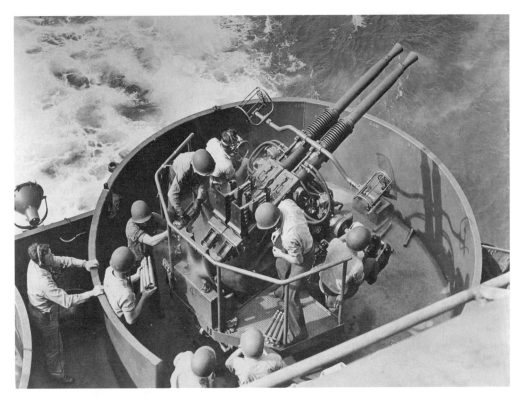

Bofors anti-aircraft gun, U.S. Navy version. Courtesy of DCHC.

the modern assembly system. The company designed a twin-mounted version for the navy and a single-mounted version for the army. On 5 February 1942, the first mass-produced Bofors guns came off the assembly line.[9]

Summarizing Chrysler Corporation's war production is at best a daunting task. The corporation produced several lists of its principal war products and identified about fifty major products or significant components manufactured for other firms. Chrysler's war production can be broken down into a few broad categories: trucks and tanks; aircraft parts and components; guns, ammunition, rockets, and bombs; a variety of goods that were not weapons per se, but were still a vital part of military operations; and war materials that enhanced war production, but were not used on or near the field of battle.[10]

The Dodge truck plant in Warren, Michigan, assembled 403,515 military trucks. A three-quarter-ton 4 X 4 model accounted for 255,193 of the total, but Dodge also produced 5 other models. The Chrysler tank arsenal produced a total of 22,235 tanks in 4 separate models but with several different engines, resulting in a total of 8 distinct tanks. Chrysler also completed major modifications to an additional 3,272 tanks and manufactured 18 pilot and experimental models.

Chrysler's production of aircraft parts and components for various aircraft involved about half of all of its factories. The most important aircraft work was the manufacturing and assembly of the Wright "Cyclone" engine used in the Boeing B-29. Chrysler mass-produced nose sections, engine cowlings, and leading wing edges for the B-29; some 5,669 center wing sections for the Curtiss-Wright "Helldiver," a Navy dive bomber; nearly 1,600 nose and center wing sections and 1,895 sets of wing flaps for the B-26 Martin "Marauder" bomber; 4,100 cockpit enclosures for the Douglas B-17 "Flying Fortress" bomber; cockpit flight stations for the Lockheed PV-2 Ventura bomber; more than 10,000 sets of landing gear and arrester mechanisms for the Chance-Vought "Corsair," a carrier-based Navy fighter plane; and 163,290 ski pedestals for amphibious aircraft.[11]

This summary does not give a true indication of the size and complexity of the aircraft component work. Chrysler did the final assembly of the center wing section for the Curtiss-Wright Helldiver, which incorporated more than 10,000 parts. The center wing section included the retractable landing gear and the hydraulic controls to retract the gear, the bomb bay doors and their hydraulic equipment, fittings for bombs, extra fuel tanks, and miles of hydraulic tubing and electrical wires. Five Chrysler plants completed aluminum forgings and stampings for this job or did machining on parts, while 464 subcontractors provided various components.[12]

The Bofors antiaircraft gun was one of Chrysler's major contributions to the war effort. By the end of the war, the company had produced 30,095 single guns and 14,442 pairs, all assembled at the Plymouth Lynch Road plant in Detroit, and more than 120,000 Bofors gun barrels. Twelve Chrysler plants were involved in the Bofors project, along with more than 2,000 subcontractors. In the category of "things that blow up," Chrysler made 101,232 incendiary bombs, and Chrysler-powered B-29s dropped many of these on Japanese targets; 4.5-inch rockets, 328,327 in total; 20 mm practice shells (3 million); 20 mm projectile balls (19,933,000), 20 mm armor-piercing shot (1,989,801), and armor-piercing cores for .50-caliber machine gun cartridges (222 million).

Chrysler's Evansville, Indiana, factory literally produced "bullets by the billions," including 485,463,000 cartridges for .30-caliber carbines and 2,768,688,000 cartridges for .45-caliber carbines. Remarkably, just as Chrysler prepared for production at its Evansville plant in July 1942, the Ordnance Department ordered the automaker to substitute steel for brass for the cartridges cases to conserve brass. Although this last-minute change required Chrysler's engineers to complete a quick analysis of the steel they would need and to retool much of the plant, full-scale production began in October.[13]

The company also produced a wide range of war goods that were not weapons in the usual sense, but were nevertheless a vital part of the war effort. The Dodge Main plant made two products that were perhaps the furthest from the automaker's "normal" production. The first was the Sperry Gyroscope Company gyrocompass. The U.S. Bureau of Ships asked Chrysler on 5 February 1942 to consider manufacturing the delicate, complicated mechanism. In about a week, after examining a sample and the blueprints, Chrysler agreed to make the device. It delivered the first compass on 11 September 1942 and by the end of the contract (February 1945) had produced 5,500 compasses, three times more than Sperry thought possible.[14]

The second exotic product was an antenna mount for mobile short-range radar units. Chrysler did this work as a subcontractor for General Electric under an agreement signed on 22 September 1942. The company completed the first production unit in February 1943, but did not achieve quantity production until May. When the contract ended a year later, in May 1944, the Dodge Main plant had turned out 2,098 sets of radar equipment. The basic radar "antenna mount" included the radar "dish," the intricate gearing mechanisms used to both elevate and turn the dish, and the pedestal supports. Chrysler also designed a special semitrailer to house the mobile radar unit, but because Dodge's truck plant was already overcommitted, Fruehauf built it.[15]

The Chrysler Jefferson Avenue plant in Detroit produced a remarkable mix of new products for the war effort. The plant manufactured 9,002 steel pontoons and a curious and useful hybrid marine vehicle, the marine tractor, more commonly known as the "sea mule." By modifying one or more pontoons and equipping them with an engine and steering equipment, Chrysler produced an extremely reliable and inexpensive tugboat. Chrysler assembled them on-site and launched them into the Detroit River at the back of the factory. The Jefferson plant had assembled 8,229 sea mules by the end of the war, in 15 different types, with engines producing up to 560 hp.[16]

Jefferson Avenue also manufactured 253 sets of equipment that artificially generated smoke screens used to conceal ships and amphibious troops from the enemy; 20,404 heavy-duty fire pumps, powered by Chrysler industrial engines; 352 air raid sirens; 1,994 special submarine nets; and 1,550 searchlight reflectors. Chrysler designed lightweight submarine netting that would allow enemy submarines to penetrate it, but would release flares to pinpoint the submarine's position. Chrysler used its "superfinishing" process to create parabolic reflectors for searchlights that gave them a range of more than 30 miles.[17]

Finally, Chrysler played an important role in the development of the atomic bomb. In April 1943, the U.S. Army asked Chrysler to manufacture large metal diffusers used in the gaseous diffusion process to separate U-235, the raw material for one type of atomic bomb, from uranium. The diffusers had to be made of nickel, the only metal able to resist the hexaflouride gas produced in the diffusion process. Rather than make the equipment of solid nickel, which would have exhausted the existing national supply, Chrysler instead carefully nickel-plated the diffusers, each with hundreds of thousands of precisely drilled holes. The manufacturing operation took place at the Plymouth Lynch Road plant in Detroit. Chrysler made four types of diffusers, which it shipped to the Oak Ridge, Tennessee, U-235 plant by rail. To ship these fragile tanks safely, Chrysler designed a new railroad flatcar suspension system.[18]

Chrysler's rapid conversion to war production starting in 1942 included the modification of existing machinery and floor space for war work, the construction of additional factory space by the Defense Plant Corporation (DPC), and the purchase of new machinery by the government. In early May 1942, Chrysler was already using a grand total of 20 million square feet of space in 19 plants for war work, 78 percent of its machine tools, and 40,000 employees for defense work.[19]

By mid-November 1943, some 18 months later, Chrysler's defense operation had expanded enormously. The automaker was using 17 million square feet of its own space, 1.5 million square feet of leased space, and 11.5 million square feet of space in government-owned plants, or 30 million square feet in total, for war work. Chrysler used 17,909 of its own machine tools (of a total stock of 20,665) and 19,277 machine tools owned by the government for war production.[20]

The statistics on the sales of war products in table 9.1 illustrate the rapid shift to war work.

TABLE 9.1 Chrysler Corporation Military Sales, 1941–45

	Military Sales ($)	As Share of Total Sales (%)
1941	116,693,068	13.1
1942	547,995,311	87.9
1943	886,467,702	100.0
1944	1,098,073,025	100.0
1945	869,000,000	86.9

Sources: Chrysler Corporation annual reports, 1941–45, box "Annual Reports 1925–69," DCHC.

Two of Chrysler's wartime operations deserve a closer examination—the tank arsenal in Warren, Michigan and the Dodge–Chicago plant, where Chrysler built Wright "Cyclone" engines for the B-29. Both cases involved new plants built and owned by the federal government. These were newly engineered products that were still under development when Chrysler agreed to make them. Because of its engineering and manufacturing experience, Chrysler quickly moved up the learning curve and exceeded the government's expectations in making both products. It is worth noting that of the combined value of Chrysler's war contracts, some $3,518,229,000, the contracts for tanks, tank modifications, and spare parts came to $1,731,301,542, nearly half the total. The B-29

Cyclone engine contract amounted to $872,129,295, so the two combined accounted for nearly three-quarters of the dollar value of the company's war contracts.[21]

The "mix" of Chrysler's war work was distinct from the rest of the automobile industry, which contributed about one-fifth of all war production nationally. Tanks accounted for only 13.1 percent of auto industry war contracts as a whole, but nearly half of Chrysler's contracts. Military vehicles other than tanks represented 29.7 percent of the dollar value of military contracts for the auto industry as a whole, but less than 10 percent for Chrysler. The automobile industry concentrated production heavily in aircraft and aircraft parts manufacture, which accounted for 38.7 percent of military contract dollars. The combination of Chrysler's Cyclone engine contracts and the other work it did on aircraft wings and fuselages was roughly one-third of its wartime contract work.[22]

The Tank Business

William S. Knudsen, codirector of the federal Office of Production Management, first contacted K. T. Keller by telephone on 7 June 1940 to discuss a possible tank contract. Knudsen came to Detroit two days later to confer with Keller, who agreed in principle that Chrysler would produce a tank, but only in a government-owned plant. The army shipped a complete set of blueprints, weighing 186 pounds, to Chrysler in Detroit. Once the plans arrived on 17 June, a team of 197 men worked for four and a half weeks to estimate the cost of producing the tank, designated as Model M2A1. The estimators worked seven days a week, from 8:30 A.M. to 11:00 P.M. during the week and from 8:30 A.M. to 5:00 P.M. on Saturdays and Sundays. Chrysler also had its pattern shops produce a full-scale mock-up of the M2A1 tank in wood and shellacked each part to check on the "fit" of the components.

On 19 July 1940, Chrysler presented the army with a contract proposal—it would produce either 1,000 tanks at $33,500 each or 2,000 at $31,500 over the next two years. The army agreed to the lower quantity and on 15 August 1940 awarded Chrysler a contract to build the tank plant at a cost of about $200 million. Chrysler had already selected a 113-acre site in Warren Township, roughly seventeen miles from downtown Detroit.[23]

On 28 August 1940, just as Chrysler was starting to collect the needed machinery and tooling for the M2A1 tank, the army dropped that design, declaring it obsolete, and proceeded to develop an entirely new model, the 28-ton M3 tank, subsequently named the General Grant. The army was to modify the original contract once the design was complete and Chrysler could generate new cost figures. Chrysler moved ahead on tank plant construction, with ground-breaking on 9 September, not knowing exactly what it was going to build there. By 4 October, the army had finished the design of the new M3 tank and Chrysler had already ordered more than half the required machinery and tools.[24]

Plant construction and "tooling up" for production moved ahead at a feverish pace. Despite a cold Detroit winter, steel erection for the plant, which began on 19 November 1940, was finished on 28 January 1941. At that point, Chrysler partitioned off the part of the main building with windows, about one-third of the total, and operated a steam locomotive inside the building to provide heat. This allowed the installation of machinery before the permanent powerhouse went into service. The contractor finished all glass installation by 1 March 1941 and the concrete floors shortly after that. The main assembly building, a single-story steel-framed building encased in glass, measured 500 feet by 1,380 feet and enclosed 690,000 square feet. Detroit's Albert Kahn was the architect. The facility included a one-mile figure-eight test track.[25]

Even after the army had settled on the final design, getting all the necessary tools and equipment in place in the tank plant was no easy task. Final blueprints for all the parts and a final parts list were not completed until early February 1941. Chrysler had already ordered a majority of its machine tools by mid-October 1940, but orders and deliveries were two different matters. The first production castings arrived at the plant on 12 February 1941, and machinery installation continued throughout March. The plant completed the first "pilot" tank on 12 April, and after nearly two weeks of performance tests, Chrysler delivered the first M3 tank to the government on 24 April 1941. The tank plant employed only 230 hourly workers in mid-April 1941, with full-scale production not planned until late summer.[26]

The tank arsenal went into full-scale production gradually, completing only seven tanks in July 1941. The tank plant workforce, already 2,107 strong on 24 July 1941, shot up to over 5,000 a month later. The plant turned out 192 tanks in November, 237 in December, and a total of 729 for the first six months of operations, well above the original targets.[27]

Production of the M3 tank was barely under way when the army deemed it obsolete. The General Grant had two major design flaws—a riveted body and a main gun (75 mm) mounted into the right side of the hull, giving it a limited field of fire. Its replacement was the 32-ton M4 General Sherman tank, the first U.S. tank with an all-welded body and with its main gun, a 75 mm cannon, mounted on a turret that rotated a full 360 degrees. The M3's second large gun, a 37 mm cannon, disappeared in the M4. In early October 1941, the Aberdeen Proving Ground sent the drawings for the M4 to Chrysler. By mid-November 1941, Chrysler had agreed in principle to make the M4 tank and to expand production at the tank arsenal to 750 tanks per month.[28]

In late March 1942, Chrysler signed supplemental agreements with the army for the production of 1,000 M4 tanks per month. The army authorized Chrysler to buy another forty acres of land at the tank arsenal and built an additional 500,000 square feet of floor space. The total cost of the new plant, including dies, jigs, tools, and machinery, was roughly $23 million. Chrysler completed the first handmade copy of the M4 on 27 June 1942 and the first production version on 22 July. The tank plant finished the last M3 on 3 August, having produced 3,352 of them during the plant's first year of operation.[29]

Before putting the M4 Sherman tanks into production, Chrysler also designed a new engine for the model. A modified nine-cylinder Wright radial aircraft engine made by Continental Motors had powered the M3 General Grant tanks. These Wright engines were needed for aircraft production, so the army asked Chrysler to develop a new engine for the M4. Rather than try to design an engine from scratch, Chrysler's engineers developed an innovative design using existing automobile engines. They took five 200 hp six-cylinder Chrysler engines, installed an engine drive gear at the end of each crankshaft, and then meshed the gears together with a single large gear that turned the tank's drive shaft. The result was a "multibank" engine that eventually powered 7,500 General Sherman tanks.

Army personnel sarcastically called this unusual engine "the Egg Beater" and "the Dionne Quints," after the identical female quintuplets born in Canada in 1934, but it proved to be reliable and durable. In a 4,000-mile endurance test (11 October 1943 to 10 February 1944) against 12 tanks equipped with other engines, 3 of the 4 Chrysler tanks finished the course, while only 1 of the 12 competitors finished. The Army Ordnance Department saw one disadvantage to Chrysler's multibank engine—it was longer and higher than other motors installed in tanks, leaving less space for ammunition and supplies. In October 1942 and again in December 1942, the Ordnance Department ordered Chrysler to switch back to Continental engines, but rescinded the order because those engines were in short supply.[30]

American military and civilian leaders alike quickly recognized Chrysler's achievements at the tank arsenal. The army awarded the plant the Army-Navy "E" Pennant for production excellence on 10 August 1942, the first awarded to a defense plant. In September 1942, President Franklin Roosevelt made a secret twelve-day cross-country tour of defense plants, with no information about the tour released until after he had returned safely to Washington. The first stop on the tour was the tank arsenal, which Roosevelt visited on 18 September. The presidential train pulled into the arsenal complex at 1:30 P.M., and Roosevelt got into a seven-passenger Chrysler parade car for a drive through the plant and then to the nearby test track. Roosevelt observed gear cutting, an engine and transmission being dropped into a tank, and about fifty tanks running through their paces at the test track. Roosevelt's train left after an hour or so and continued on to the Willow Run bomber plant near Ypsilanti, Michigan, the next stop in this secret tour.[31]

After clamoring for 1,000 tanks a month from the plant, in September 1942, the army cut tank production scheduled for the rest of the year by 40 percent because of steel shortages. The cutback in orders was moot, because the War Production Board never supplied Chrysler with enough machine tools to produce the larger volume. Still, the tank arsenal delivered 896 tanks in December 1942, its highest monthly output during the war and three times the number produced in January 1942.

Chrysler increased output at the tank arsenal by shifting most parts manufacturing to other plants, thereby converting the tank plant into an assembly operation. By June of 1944, Chrysler ran five parallel tank assembly lines at the plant. Peak employment there was 6,212 in 1942, and for the rest of the war ranged between 4,500 and 5,500 workers. The automaker's work on tank production went well beyond the tank arsenal. In June 1944, Chrysler devoted 3.2 million square feet of space at 12 plants to tank production, with only 1.3 million square feet of the total at the tank arsenal. About 14,000 employees worked on tank production in these other facilities, where Chrysler used more than 5,000 machine tools.[32]

Over the course of the war, the Chrysler tank arsenal assembled a grand total of 22,235 tanks. The M3 (General Grant) accounted for only 3,352 of the total. The vast majority, a total of 17,948, were six different versions of the M4 (General Sherman) tank, differentiated either by the engine or by the size of the main gun. Chrysler's tank production was nearly half of the auto industry's tank output of 49,058 units and more than one-quarter of combined U.S. production of 86,000 tanks from all sources.

The largest runs of tanks were the Shermans equipped with a 75 mm gun and the Chrysler multibank engine (7,500 produced) and Shermans powered by Ford engines (7,050). At the very end of the war, the arsenal produced the 45-ton General Pershing tank, with 90 mm guns (500) and 105 mm howitzers (185). Chrysler also built two tanks that never saw battle—the T-23, equipped a Ford V-8 engine that powered an electric drive system developed by General Electric and a model powered by a Caterpillar radial diesel engine. Additionally, Chrysler designed and built another dozen pilot and experimental models that never went into production.[33]

The end of the war brought an instant cancellation of the tank contracts and a quick end to work at the tank arsenal. The war work was already winding down well before the end of the war. The last Sherman tanks came off the line on 7 June 1945, but production of the General Pershing tank continued into

K. T. Keller with grandson on General Sherman tank, Family Day at the Chrysler tank arsenal, 1944. Courtesy of DCHC.

Assembly of General Pershing tanks, Warren tank arsenal, 1945. Many women and African Americans can be seen in this view. Courtesy of DCHC.

late September. Employment at the tank plant, some 5,074 workers on 1 June 1945, dropped to 3,446 a month later, slid further to 1,999 by 19 September, and by 19 October 1945, was down to a mere 520. Finally, on 26 October 1945, Chrysler Corporation officially turned the tank arsenal over to the Detroit Ordnance District.[34]

Engines For the B-29

Chrysler's second major wartime project was the manufacture of the Wright Cyclone engine for the B-29 Superfortress. This was an air-cooled 3,350-cid engine that developed 2,200 hp and had 18 cylinders arranged in a radial configuration. The Wright Aeronautical Corporation and the Aircraft Production Branch of the War Production Board approached Chrysler at the end of December 1941 about a contract. The U.S. government first proposed that Chrysler take over existing factory space near Milwaukee or Chicago, but by 20 January

1942, the War Production Board approved a new plant and Chicago became the only location considered. After some wrangling, the government agreed to Chrysler's choice, a site at 75th Street and Cicero, near Chicago's southwest border.[35]

The initial supply contract of 27 February 1942 was for 10,000 engines. Deliveries would start in March 1943 and continue through August 1944, with production reaching 1,000 engines per month in January 1944. The contract included an estimated price of $253,146,200 for the engines plus $43,034,854 for spare parts, or a total of $296,181,054. The air force changed the initial contract in early April by increasing the peak production from 1,000 to 1,500 engines a month, so that Chrysler could produce a 2,220 hp *and* a 2,300 hp version of the engine. The total cost of the original supply contract increased by $57,130,426 to reflect the larger production figure. The Defense Plant Corporation would acquire an additional 120 acres of land and increase the total floor space to 5,551,744 square feet. Given the enormity of this project, Keller and company created an independent Dodge–Chicago Plant Division of Chrysler Corporation, mainly for administrative purposes, with L. L. Colbert named general manager.[36]

The general contractor, the George Fuller Company of Chicago, broke ground for the tool shop on 4 June 1942 and by mid-August, a dozen buildings were under construction and Fuller had 7,000 men working two shifts. A month later, the labor force had grown to 12,000 and by November, more than 16,000 construction workers were on the job, working around the clock. Designed by Albert Kahn, this was a monumental plant by any standard. The major structure, the machining and assembly building, measured 2,340 feet by 1,520 feet, enclosing 3,556,800 square feet (nearly 82 acres) under one roof. The complex also included fifteen additional major buildings, which Fuller completed by April 1943. However, at that date, Chrysler was still nine months away from beginning quantity production of the Cyclone engine.[37]

Building the massive Dodge–Chicago plant turned out to be the easiest part of the effort to produce airplane engines. Chrysler had to contend with two daunting problems—an unfinished engine design and long delays in getting the machine tools needed to start production. In early March 1942, Chrysler's management complained that Wright Aeronautical Corporation was not cooperating in transmitting the blueprints, specifications, parts lists, tool lists, and other information.

Chrysler quickly discovered that Wright had not even finished the design for the engine, much less produced any of them. Carl Breer reported that Chrysler took apart several Wright engines and discovered that the parts were not interchangeable. Further, the engines they examined did not follow the drawings with respect to dimensions. These were in effect handmade engines, unsuitable for mass production. Even the drawings were problematic. When Chrysler's engineers carefully studied the drawings to assure proper fit of the components, they discovered over 200 "interferences" that required changes in design tolerances. With decades of experience in mass-producing automobiles, Chrysler was ready to mass-produce the Wright engine, but the Wright Aeronautical Corporation was not. In time, the Wright and Chrysler engineering staffs worked together to improve the engine design and get it into production.[38]

Long delays in getting machine tools moved the start of production back from March 1943 to January 1944. Chrysler had initially intended to have its production "pilot line" operating by December 1942, but this was postponed a full year. Chrysler had ordered the machinery needed for full-scale production, more than 7,000 machines tools in total, and these trickled in slowly. In early April 1943, the Dodge–Chicago plant had only one-third of the machines it needed. Given the severe shortages of machine tools needed for the defense industry in 1942 and 1943, plus the fact that the design of the engine and of the B-29 airplane were still undergoing revision through 1942, the War Production Board simply diverted machinery to other war plants.[39]

The pilot line began operating on 1 December 1943 and the main assembly operations started up in January 1944, when the plant produced 15 engines. Once Dodge–Chicago began to produce engines in quantity (507 in July 1944), the army air force raised its production targets considerably. The plant was initially set up to make 750 engines a month, but by February 1944, the air force already planned for production to reach 1,600 engines a month by May 1945 and 2,200 a month later in the year. Actual Dodge–Chicago production was 1,327 engines in January 1945 and then reached a peak of 1,697 engines in July 1945, the all-time record for the war period.[40]

Once Dodge–Chicago went into full production, plant operations expanded dramatically. Employment climbed quickly from 10,104 in late August 1943 to 19,245 in December 1943. A year later, 31,828 worked at the complex, and employment peaked at Dodge–Chicago at 33,245 in February 1945. Although the plant could draw from the Chicago labor market, maintaining a workforce was difficult, despite extensive use of female and African American workers. In late July 1944, when 27,251 worked at the plant, women (7,575) made up over one-quarter of the total. During the eight months ending 30 June 1944, Dodge–Chicago hired 23,404 new employees, but 10,483 left for military service or for other jobs.[41]

Managing production of the Wright Cyclone engine at the Dodge–Chicago plant was the most frustrating experience Chrysler faced during the war. The organization had to incorporate 6,274 design changes to the engine, usually involving dozens of parts, resulting in 48,500 change notices from the engineering division to planning and production. Chrysler was originally supposed to

L. L. (Tex) Colbert (*left*) with U.S. officials and a B-29 equipped with a Chrysler-built engine. Courtesy of DCHC.

manufacture 110 of the engine's parts, but because of problems finding reliable suppliers ended up making 160 components.[42]

The end of the war brought the cancellation of the engine contract on 15 August 1945, but some final assembly continued into September, when the plant delivered 64 engines to the army air force. The Dodge–Chicago workforce, some 28,543 on 15 August, fell slowly to 22,594 on 5 September, but then fell precipitously to only 5,949 the following day. The plant still had 2,660 employees in early December, but 1,042 of these were salaried workers and virtually all of the rest were what Chrysler called "hourly non-productive" workers, mainly guards and maintenance staff.[43]

With the last engine assembled on 7 September 1945, Chrysler's Dodge–Chicago plant had achieved an impressive production record. This single plant manufactured 18,413 Wright Cyclone engines, or 60 percent of the total made during the war. Production included 16,427 carburetor engines and 1,986 fuel-injected engines. The engine contract amounted to $872,129,295, including Chrysler's fixed fee (profit) of $37,724,176. While the engine contracts were only half the value of the tank contracts, the B-29 engines were easily Chrysler's second-largest war project. The U.S. government declared the Dodge–Chicago plant surplus after the war, but Chrysler had no interest in buying it.[44] Instead, Preston Tucker leased part of it in 1947 to produce his ill-fated automobile.

LABOR IN THE WAR

With the onset of the war, Chrysler's labor force grew considerably, despite the loss of nearly one-third of its prewar workforce to military service. In December 1941, Chrysler employed 71,600, down from its peak peacetime level of 82,243. With the end of civilian production in January 1942 and the dismantling of existing Chrysler plants, employment fell to only 50,700 in March 1942. By November 1943, the workforce more than doubled to 106,600 and finally peaked at 125,481 in January 1945. The layoffs of experienced workers during the first half of 1942 and the loss of 23,431 men to military service made this quick expansion of the labor force even more remarkable.

The enlarged labor force was the result of tremendous growth in a few plants. The Chrysler plant at Evansville, Indiana, which made ammunition, saw its workforce jump from 650 in 1941 to 12,560 in September 1943. The tank arsenal employed only 5,500 for much of the war, but tank contracts involved 20,000 workers, counting all the factories. The Dodge–Chicago plant reached its maximum employment of 33,245 in February 1945, but Chrysler hired more than 70,000 to work there during the course of the war. For all of its operations, Chrysler hired 60,000 new workers in 1944 alone.

To meet its labor needs, Chrysler, like the other automakers, turned to two large untapped sources of labor—women and African Americans. Chrysler's female workforce jumped from 6,160 (7.5 percent of the total) before the war to 35,223 in March 1945, more than 29 percent. Before the war, women primarily did office work, wiring assembly and installation, sewing in the seating and trim departments, and inspection work. During the war, they worked in most factory operations outside of the foundries. Of the 11,500 new workers Chrysler trained to assemble bomber airframes, 70 percent were women. Chrysler's engineering division, historically an all-male bastion, hired hundreds of women as laboratory technicians or as draftspersons in the blueprint department. M. Virginia Sink, Chrysler's first female engineer, supervised these employees and taught evening courses in technical subjects for female students.[45]

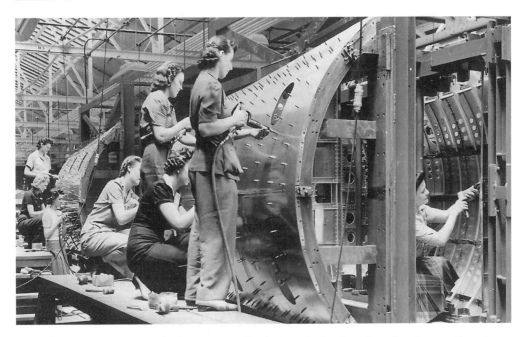

Women workers assembling fuselage sections for the Martin B-26 medium bomber in a Detroit Chrysler plant. Courtesy of DCHC.

Similarly, Chrysler employed only 1,978 African American men (2.4 percent of the total) before the war, primarily as foundry workers and janitors. Their numbers grew to 18,148 by March 1945 (15 percent of the workforce) and included 5,160 African American women. The vast majority worked in Detroit-area plants and at Dodge–Chicago, but African American workers could be found in almost all of Chrysler's plants. A report on the Evansville, Indiana, ordnance plant indicated that women made up 60 percent of the workforce of 12,000 and African Americans, mostly women, roughly 6 percent.[46]

The onset of the war did not end labor unrest, including strikes. To be sure, ten days after Pearl Harbor, representatives from labor and industry met in Washington and agreed to a "no-strike, no-lockout" policy for the duration of the war. Many industries were largely strike-free during the war, but the automobile, rubber, aircraft, and coal-mining industries had hundreds of strikes. Labor unions, including the UAW, feared that wartime controls on wages, their limited ability to strike, and the influx of thousands of inexperienced workers would weaken their organizations and their ability to protect their members. The UAW held the War Emergency Conference, a special UAW convention in effect, in early April 1942 to clarify union policies during the war. The UAW reaffirmed the "no-strike" pledge and agreed to eliminate premium pay rates for weekend and holiday work. Chrysler would pay overtime rates only for work beyond 8 hours per day and 40 hours per week. These concessions were part of the UAW's larger "Victory through Equality of Sacrifice" program, which included rigid limits on profits and executive salaries. The auto companies, including Chrysler, took advantage of the "no-strike pledge" to limit negotiations with the UAW on a wide ranges of grievances and standards.[47]

The underlying tensions in several Chrysler plants, especially Dodge Main and Jefferson Avenue, bubbled to the surface in May 1943 in the form of a corporation-wide strike. During the war, management stalled grievances in the bargaining machinery because management did not fear strikes and would use wildcat strikes to embarrass the UAW. The union wanted an impartial arbitrator to settle all remaining disputes, but Chrysler adamantly opposed the idea.

Workers at Dodge Main and other Detroit-area Chrysler plants walked off their jobs on 20 May 1943 after the Dodge Main manager hired 6 outside workers for well-paying jobs without first offering the work to other Dodge workers. The walkout of 27,100 workers lasted four days, ending only after the National War Labor Board (NWLB) promised fast action in reforming the grievance procedure at Chrysler. On 27 August 1943, the NWLB ordered Chrysler to add an impartial arbitrator at the final- appeal stage for grievances.[48]

The last corporation-wide strike during the war also started at Dodge Main after management unilaterally introduced new work standards for gear cutters on 7 February 1945. The entire gear-cutting workforce of 1,100 men struck for three days, touching off a plantwide strike on 21 February. When the truck drivers who moved parts and materials between Chrysler's Detroit plants also struck, more than 24,000 workers were idled.

The Dodge strikers finally returned to work after eleven days, but only after the NWLB agreed to set up a special inquiry into the production standards and to allow the UAW to use its own time-study experts to examine the job. Chrysler won its higher production standard, but the UAW won the concession that management could not unilaterally impose new standards. By the end of the war, there was little hope that relations between the company and the union would be any less confrontational and bitter than before.[49]

CHRYSLER'S WAR RECORD

Chrysler Corporation's leaders, particularly Keller and Hutchinson, were justifiably proud of the company's record in war production. Starting in January 1942, *Chrysler Motors Magazine* changed its name to *Chrysler War Work Magazine*. This monthly in-house magazine for all Chrysler employees ran articles highlighting the war goods Chrysler manufactured, the various war bond drives held in the plants, and sadly, the former Chrysler workers who died in the war. The automaker published two glossy paperback booklets during the war,

Peacetime Enterprise Put to War Work (1942), a 64-page publication dominated by photographs and drawings, and *Chrysler Division at War* (1943).[50]

Following the war, Chrysler commissioned the author Wesley W. Stout to write a series of seven books celebrating its accomplishments. K. T. Keller wrote forewords to all seven. The first of these, *A War Job "Thought Impossible"* (1945) considered the production of the Sperry gyrocompass. Three volumes appeared in 1946: *The Great Detective,* dealing with mobile radar units; *Bullets by the Billion* (the Evansville arsenal); and *"TANKS Are Mighty Fine Things,"* covering the tank arsenal. Chrysler published the next two volumes of the series in 1947: *Great Engines and Great Planes,* which was the second-longest book in the series (133 pages) and considered all of Chrysler's aircraft manufacturing work, and *Secret,* which outlined Chrysler's work on U-235 gaseous diffusion equipment for U-235 separation. The second of these books had to clear the U.S. Army Corps of Engineers censors before publication. The longest book in the series, *Mobilized* (216 pages), published in 1949, covered the work of Chrysler Engineering in the war and the significant war production not covered in the other volumes.

Shortly after the war, Chrysler commissioned 16 artists who had battlefield experience to paint battlefield episodes or other war scenes that they had personally witnessed. Chrysler hired Lieutenant Colonel Charles Baskerville to select the artists and direct the entire project. The oil paintings, all completed in 1947, decorated the walls of the executive level of Chrysler's main office building in Highland Park until the automaker donated them to the City of Detroit for the Veteran's Memorial Building. They later transferred 14 of the 16 to the Detroit Historical Museum in 1986. Chrysler also reproduced the paintings in a booklet. All 16 paintings show at least one Chrysler war product in the battle scene.[51]

Chrysler's leaders entered the postwar era with a sense of pride in the accomplishments of the previous four years. The company had quickly converted to war production in 1942. Chrysler faced the reconversion back to civilian vehicle production with valid concerns over how long and costly the reconversion might be. In many respects, returning to civilian production proved more difficult than converting to war production in 1942.

Chapter 10

POSTWAR RECOVERY AND CRISIS, 1945–50

During a stormy thirteen-year bargaining history, Chrysler and the union have somehow managed to retain a deep ignorance of each other's operations and a spectacular suspicion of each other's motives.

—Fortune

Chrysler Corporation's successes of the late 1930s and during the Second World War gave way to a series of chronic problems that plagued the automaker for more than a decade after the end of the war: lingering difficulties in returning to civilian production; unimaginative, unappealing new products until the appearance of the "Forward Look" cars for the 1955 model year; an aging management and an outdated corporate structure; and continuing adversarial and destructive labor relations. Sales suffered and Chrysler lost a substantial part of market share; after 1953, the company slipped back to a distant third place among the Big Three.

Chrysler emerged from the Second World War with a strong sense of pride in past accomplishments and confidence in the future. It was, after all, the second largest car company in the United States, with more than one-quarter of the market. It had enjoyed a long history of engineering leadership in the auto industry, and its post-Airflow products had been successful. But in the brief time between the end of the Second World War and Keller's retirement as president in November 1950, the company suffered a serious reversal of fortune.

RECONVERSION TO CIVILIAN PRODUCTION

Chrysler's conversion in 1941–42 from civilian production to the manufacture of military products was difficult and frustrating for the company. The reconversion back to civilian production was equally troublesome—and in many respects more costly. To be sure, Chrysler's sales of just over 1 million vehicles in

1947 and 1948 regained the levels of 1940 and 1941, but still did not equal the 1937 sales of 1,158,518 units. Chrysler did not achieve "full production" until 1949, when it sold 1,330,938 vehicles.

The end of the war brought abrupt reductions in Chrysler's operations. Saturday work stopped in late August 1945 and the work week fell from 48 to 40 hours. Chrysler's government orders on hand fell from $922 million on 14 August 1945 to $6 million by 24 October. Peak employment had reached 125,481 in January 1945, but fell off precipitously in the month following Japan's surrender. Chrysler had only 72,671 employees on 10 September and 62,610 a week later. Average employment on 31 December 1945 (59,245) was only half the 120,835 employees of 31 December 1944.

In the six months after the end of the war, government controls over materials, prices, and wages virtually disappeared. Serious shortages developed for a variety of materials, but steel shortages plagued the auto industry generally and Chrysler in particular through 1947. The automaker produced only 39,361 vehicles in 1945 and faced shortages of components from suppliers, which were hit with material shortages and strikes. Production rose to nearly 712,000 units in 1946 and then to over 1 million the following year. Chrysler management complained that the firm operated at only two-thirds capacity in 1947 because of shortages of raw materials, especially steel. Rising prices of raw materials, components, and labor forced the automaker to raise prices as well. In July 1948, K. T. Keller argued that Chrysler still priced its cars too low and shortages were the natural result. Chrysler's customers faced delays of between 23 and 27 months between ordering a car and taking delivery.[1]

The postwar material shortages did eventually end, as did the seller's market for automobiles once the industry increased production enough to satisfy the pent-up demand for cars. No new cars had come from Detroit for the four years of war, while existing cars wore out and a new group of drivers came on the scene. In some respects the industry was more competitive in the early 1950s than it had been in the late 1930s. A revitalized Ford Motor Company, led by Henry Ford II and his young management team, the "Whiz Kids," suddenly became an efficient producer with attractive products. The 1949 model Ford, its first new postwar model, was an enormous sales success. Ford leaped over Chrysler back into the number two position in sales briefly in 1950 and permanently in 1953 and has not relinquished that spot since. Chrysler lost to Ford in 1950 in large part because of a bitter 100-day strike that cost Chrysler about 500,000 vehicles.

DARK CLOUDS ON THE HORIZON

By the late 1940s, the more perceptive observers of the automobile industry did not see a very bright future for Chrysler. In October 1948, the authors of a

lengthy article in *Fortune* on the Chrysler Corporation predicted serious problems on the horizon. They suspected that the all-new 1949 models were likely
to be dull and stodgy, based in part on K. T. Keller's comment that the interiors
would allow ladies or gentlemen to comfortably wear hats anywhere in the car.
Fortune guessed that "the '49 Chryslers, Plymouths, DeSotos and Dodges may
or may not knock your eye out when you look at them, but they will certainly
not knock your hat off." The company seemed in good shape, however, with
efficient manufacturing operations and excellent engineering. *Fortune* wondered
if "Chrysler is playing to its operational strength to such as degree that the
creative qualities that made its success are in danger of becoming atrophied."[2]

The analysis, however, noted that *this* Chrysler Corporation was not the firm
that Walter P. Chrysler had directed. Its leaders had aged and lacked the vision
and flair of the founder. *Fortune* labeled the photographs of Keller, Hutchinson,
and Zeder, all in their sixties, "Twenty-Four Years Later: the Mechanic, the
Bookkeeper, and the Engineer." In a lecture delivered at Stanford University
in July 1948, Keller emphasized that Chrysler was not attempting to develop
"revolutionary vehicles and power plants." This was clearly not the mentality
that had dominated the Chrysler Corporation in the 1920s and 1930s. *Fortune*
remarked that the automaker's memorable innovations seemed to have ended
with the retirement of Walter P. Chrysler: "It is realized that K. T. [Keller] is
Walter[Chrysler]'s legitimate heir in toughness, drive, and shopside skill, but
some like to think that if Walter were around today, he'd want to come up with
some headlining development, just for the hell of it."[3] These observations and
concerns became all too true for Chrysler Corporation in the years ahead.

Chrysler began the postwar era by simply reintroducing the 1942 models, as
did the other automakers. Given the pent-up demand following the war and
the materials shortages Chrysler faced, there was no urgent need to redesign
these models. The independent American car companies led the way with the
all-new Frazer, Kaiser, and Studebaker for 1947 and the new Hudson and Packard
for 1948. The Big Three did not introduce all-new cars until the 1949 model year.

General Motors and Ford introduced cars that were longer and lower (and
more sleek) than their prewar designs, but Chrysler's new offerings were four to
five inches shorter and two inches taller than the models they replaced. Chrysler's 1949 models remained essentially unchanged through the 1952 model year,
in part because of the effects of the Korean conflict on the auto industry. Chrysler's redesigned new line for 1953 kept this square, boxy shape, but nevertheless
sold well, largely because demand was strong for all American cars. But with an
ample supply of competitive cars available in 1954, the boxy design finally led to
a sales disaster for Chrysler.[4]

Why did Chrysler continue so long with this conservative styling? K. T.

Keller's strongly held views on car design and customers' preferences, plus his dominating managerial style, largely explain this. The company did not have a styling department with any influence until the early 1950s. Body design was simply carried out by the body engineers under a highly centralized corporate engineering department headed by the legendary trio of Zeder, Skelton, and Breer. They all remembered that Chrysler's single departure from middle-of-the-road styling, the Airflow, was a disaster.

Keller stated his views on automobile design in a speech he delivered at Stanford University on 22 July 1948. While conceding that a car owner is interested in the car's appearance, Keller pointedly added, "But he bought the car to ride in, and for his wife, and children, and friends to ride in." Chrysler's president then made his famous statement about headroom: "Many of you Californians may have outgrown the habit, but there are parts of the country, containing millions of people where both the men and the ladies are in the habit of getting behind the wheel, or in the back seat, wearing hats. If the last word in millinery is knocked off the little woman's head, and a superb hairdo is disarranged, the standing of the car that does this is impaired."

Keller unashamedly admitted that Chrysler designed the 1949 models with the main focus on driver and passenger comfort and on the mechanical performance of the cars, rather than on body styling. He estimated that Chrysler would spend about $75 million on tools, dies, and machinery for the new model. It actually spent about $90 million. Before the war, a similar program would have cost under $20 million. It is a Detroit legend that at the press preview for the 1949 models, a reporter asked Keller why the Chrysler models were noticeably taller than the new Ford and General Motors models. He allegedly replied, "Chrysler builds cars to sit in, not piss over."[5]

Dodge advertising that ran in magazines in April through June 1950 emphasized the practical advantages of the design. The Dodge was touted as "Bigger Three Ways: LONGER on the inside . . . SHORTER outside! WIDER on the inside . . . NARROWER outside! HIGHER on the inside . . . LOWER outside!" An advertisement that ran in August explained, "Yes, Dodge is longer, wider, higher on the *inside* for extra leg room, shoulder room, head room. Yet on the *outside,* Dodge is shorter, narrower for easier handling and parking . . . lower for road hugging stability."[6]

LABOR RELATIONS

Chrysler's general approach to labor relations after the war was shared by the other automobile manufacturers. They responded to the growth of union power in the late 1930s and especially during the war by launching a counteroffensive

K. T. Keller in his office at the time of his retirement in 1950, with a model of one of his boxy cars. Courtesy of DCHC.

aimed at weakening unions and eliminating the worst of what they considered to be union abuses. Managers specifically objected to wildcat strikes, violence against nonstrikers and those who did not join unions, and undemocratic union governance. With the end of government wartime controls, companies like Chrysler tried to regain much of the power it had given up since the 1937 sit-down strikes.[7]

Chrysler's top management members became even more militantly antiunion after the war than their counterparts at General Motors and Ford, resulting in more bitter labor relations at Chrysler. The top managers at General Motors and Ford were more pragmatic in dealing with labor, while Chrysler's leaders were more ideological and rigid. K. T. Keller was by no means sympathetic to labor, but B. E. Hutchinson was the principal source of Chrysler's intransigence.

Chrysler Corporation and the UAW signed a new contract on 26 January 1946 providing a general pay increase of 18½¢ an hour, the same increases negotiated with the other auto companies. A second postwar agreement, signed 26 April 1947, provided for six paid holidays. Both of these contracts were achieved without a strike. However, in May 1948, the UAW struck Chrysler for seventeen days before reaching a settlement. In many respects, this was a "normal" strike over financial issues. The UAW initially demanded a 30¢ an hour pay increase, Chrysler offered 6¢, and they settled on 13¢. The increase comprised a 10¢ "flat rate" cost-of-living allowance (COLA) plus a 3¢ an hour general raise. The UAW signed a contract with General Motors that gave workers an across-the-board raise of 11¢ and a cost-of-living allowance on top of it.[8]

The 100-day strike of 1950 was a prime example of the dysfunctional relationship between Chrysler and the UAW. The major disagreements centered around a pension plan for Chrysler employees. In an eleven-page summary of contract negotiations pieced together by Chrysler in February 1950, the automaker claimed that under a contract extension of 28 May 1948, the two parties had agreed that each had the right to renegotiate wage rates only, and that only one time before the contract expired on 1 August 1950. As the company interpreted this agreement, no other issues could be discussed.

In June 1949, however, the UAW asked for an increase of 38¢ an hour, with much of it earmarked for pensions and hospital-medical insurance. Chrysler contended that these matters were not subject to the wage renegotiating clause, but still agreed to discuss pensions with the union. The UAW took a strike vote in late September 1949, but did not call a strike until 25 January 1950, when it presented 182 additional demands.[9]

During the strike, both sides issued a constant stream of propaganda aimed at Chrysler workers and the public. The harsh words underlined how far apart the two sides were on a wide range of issues, particularly pensions. The company agreed to provide pensions that would, combined with Social Security payments, total $100 a month. Chrysler's obligations would decline if government benefits increased. The UAW wanted a fixed $100 benefit in addition to Social Security. More critical was Chrysler's unwillingness to create a separate pension fund that would guarantee the safety of the pensions, regardless of the automaker's financial condition.[10]

Once the strike began, both sides dug in and there was no movement until late March, when Chrysler began to abandon its position that pensions did not need to be funded. A settlement first appeared possible on 16 April, the eighty-second day of the strike, when Chrysler agreed to put $30 million into a separate pension trust fund to cover past and future pension obligations. The company also agreed to pay half the costs of a health insurance program. The strike dragged on until 3 May, when the two sides settled all remaining issues relating to the powers of shop stewards, grievance procedures, promotions, and other matters.[11]

Chrysler and the UAW fought much of this struggle away from the negotiating table, each making accusatory public statements about the motives and integrity of the other side. Chrysler mailed twenty letters to every Chrysler employee and most of these were reprinted as full-page advertisements in the Detroit newspapers and elsewhere. Even Chrysler's announcement of the settlement (4 May) included yet another attack on the UAW, arguing that the strike was totally unnecessary, that Chrysler would have made the same agreement through negotiations only.[12]

This was also a costly, damaging strike for the UAW, which had to produce its own propaganda to counteract Chrysler's and to keep up its members' morale. The union's position on the strike is summed up by the title of its full-page newspaper advertisements when the strike ended—"Workers' Courage and Solidarity Win Victory over Chrysler Corporation's Blind Selfishness." The advertisement included a detailed "Calendar of Gains Won during Strike" in an effort to show its members the major gains won through this 100-day struggle. In some respects, the 1950 strike set the tone for Chrysler's labor relations for the rest of the decade. At the public announcement of the settlement, Walter Reuther refused to pose for the traditional handshake with the officials of Chrysler Corporation.[13]

A *Fortune* feature story on the issues involved in the struggle, entitled "Chrysler's 100 Days," also discussed the general climate of labor relations between Chrysler and the UAW. The article claimed that the automaker's labor relations policies were largely determined by Nicholas Kelley, Chrysler's attorney, rather than by the top management in Detroit. The *Fortune* writer observed: "During a stormy thirteen-year bargaining history, Chrysler and the union have somehow managed to retain a deep ignorance of each other's operations and a spectacular suspicion of each other's motives."[14]

The same magazine ran a story in the next month's issue dealing with the innovative labor agreement just reached by General Motors and the UAW, in contrast to the Chrysler outcome. *Fortune* called this contract "The Treaty of Detroit," and praised both sides, but especially General Motors for its foresight. The two sides had agreed to a five-year contract with no provision for reopening any part of it. In early June 1950, within a week of the start of negotiations between the UAW and General Motors on a new contract, GM granted the UAW all that it had gained at Chrysler with such difficulty and acrimony—and more. General Motors workers would get an automatic pay raise of 4¢ an hour based on expected productivity improvements plus COLA, thus guaranteeing "real" and significant pay raises. GM agreed to make pension payments to workers on top of whatever federal benefits they received, starting off with a total of $117 a month versus the $100 at Chrysler.(Ford quickly agreed to essentially the same package, including the "annual improvement" increase of 4¢ an hour and COLA adjustments, and endured no work stoppage.) The contract cost GM an additional $1.6 billion a year in labor costs, but it bought the automaker five years of labor peace. Chrysler's 100-day struggle with the UAW, in contrast, cost the company sales of about 500,000 vehicles in a very robust automobile market.[15] The intransigence of Keller, Hutchinson, and company was counterproductive.

When L. L. Colbert took over as Chrysler president in early November 1950, he reopened negotiations with the UAW, recognizing that Chrysler needed to adopt the same contract provisions as its rivals or face continued labor turmoil. Chrysler and the UAW amended the contract of 4 May on 11 December 1950 to bring it into compliance with the agreements at Ford and General Motors. This marked the beginning of the "pattern bargaining" in which the UAW's negotiated contract with one of the Big Three would also apply to the other two companies. Pattern bargaining was not altered until 1978, when Chrysler nearly went bankrupt.[16]

WALTER'S AGING LIEUTENANTS

During his days at Maxwell and in the early years of the Chrysler Corporation, Walter P. Chrysler had surrounded himself with executives who in many respects were responsible for the success of Chrysler—the man and the corporation. These men—whether we label them Chrysler's "lieutenants" or his "princes"—were intelligent, innovative, hard-working, and loyal to Walter

Chrysler almost to a fault. He gave them considerable independence; he rewarded them with status, power, and money; but he nevertheless molded them into a smooth-running team. Walter Chrysler had the ability to hitch this team of independent horses to a single wagon and get them to pull in harmony. It was a management system that depended on Walter Chrysler's charisma to work well. It stood in marked contrast to Henry Ford's style with his lieutenants (management by terror) and the General Motors management system, which was decentralized but relied on centralized financial controls to bring coherence to the operations.[17]

Chrysler Corporation's management worked well while Walter P. Chrysler was at the helm, but less so after his retirement in 1935. The presidents who followed simply did not have the dynamic personality of the founder, much less his broad understanding of automotive engineering, manufacturing, and marketing. Walter P. Chrysler was a bold, risk-taking visionary. His lieutenants were not.

The contrast between Chrysler and the Ford Motor Company in the postwar period is striking. Within a few months of taking control of Ford in September 1945, Henry Ford II hired a new management team of 10 young army air force officers, the so-called "Whiz Kids," to update and restructure Ford's management system to resemble that of General Motors. The new Ford managers were very young—the oldest (Tex Thornton) was 36 and six of the remaining nine were 30 or younger. Within a year, the old management system and the old managers were gone.[18]

The longevity of service of Walter Chrysler's lieutenants allowed them to occupy entrenched positions of power within the Chrysler Corporation. As a result, the automaker suffered from a kind of hardening of management arteries in the immediate postwar years. By 1950, Keller was 65, Hutchinson 62, and Zeder was 72 years old.

The key to understanding Chrysler's relatively poor performance after the Second World War is K. T. Keller. Reginald Stuart offered a brutal and simplistic assessment: "Keller presided over the Chrysler Corporation's transition from an aggressive and innovative corporation under Walter Chrysler, to a company fiscally conservative and slow to update its cars. Chrysler followed trends rather than set them."[19] Keller remained a "production man" all his life. This was what he knew and loved. When he said, "I am a machinist by trade," he was not being falsely modest—he meant it.[20] He remained deeply rooted in the factory and never developed the broader knowledge and interests of a Walter P. Chrysler in engineering, styling, and sales.

This machinist-turned-corporate leader seemed most comfortable and content producing defense products during the Second World War. He did not have to worry about style, customers' preferences, sales campaigns, costs, or the competition. The military gave him the specifications and he could go ahead and organize production. This was what Keller did best and he did it well. He was the recipient of several honors from the military and the government, including the Medal of Merit from Secretary of War Robert P. Patterson (October 1946): "K. T. Keller, for distinguished and exceptionally meritorious conduct in the performance of outstanding services to our country at war since June 1942, in a position of great importance as a voluntary and unremunerated advisor to the chief of ordnance, Army Service Forces, on problems of management, production, and supply." Even Hollywood paid tribute to Keller's war work. Following the end of the conflict, Metro-Goldwyn-Mayer released a film on the development of the atomic bomb, entitled, "The Beginning of the End," which included the character of K. T. Keller, played by the actor John Litel.[21]

Critics of Keller have emphasized his habits of maintaining centralized control, micromanaging operations he took an interest in, and interfering with the work of others. Stuart claimed that Keller insisted that company directories and office nameplates include only the first initials of the officeholder. Keller occasionally would personally supervise (and interfere with) the installation of new machinery in Chrysler factories, driving his staff crazy. Once expensive new machinery was left unused for nine months because Keller had told the plant manager that he wanted personally to supervise its installation and layout. He often interfered with the work of Chrysler's body engineers/stylists by ordering changes in the new models' appearance. Keller supposedly ordered that an extra inch and one-half height be added to the 1949 lineup of Chrysler Corporation cars.[22]

In his reminiscences, Carl Breer was particularly critical of Keller's management style, which Breer believed cost Chrysler Corporation dearly. In a section covering the postwar years, "Dominating Policy Overriding Engineering Department Judgement," Breer noted that after the war "we could sense that the dominant directive atmosphere had changed. There was less open discussion. There seemed to be more running interference and selfish decisions by the so-called headquarters outside of engineering. There seemed to be more of a deliberate 'do it my way' policy." Breer complained about Keller's management style: "He came from General Motors Canadian Division, new to us and being of a different personality of that of our leader [Chrysler], could not have the same understanding as the man we were so closely and so successfully associated with. These differences in leadership undoubtedly accounts for a lot of what happened in the motor car business after the war."[23]

A *Forbes Magazine* article published in 1948 named Keller one of "America's 50 Foremost Business Leaders," but noted no innovations in production methods or automotive design associated with him. The *Forbes* article noted that Keller personally designed the conference room, including the furniture, where he regularly met with his vice presidents.[24] It is difficult to imagine how the president of the number two automaker could grasp the "big picture" of Chrysler's operations when he spent time on such trivia.

B. E. Hutchinson's fiscal and social conservatism also negatively affected Chrysler Corporation operations. He told *Fortune* in a 1948 article: "The fundamental policy of Chrysler is to engineer good products, provide good facilities with which to make them, pay off our debts, and divide what is left with our stockholders, giving them as much of it as you can." Except for the years 1928–35, when Chrysler carried the Dodge debts it had inherited, Hutchinson kept the company debt-free until his retirement in 1953. He reduced the funds available for investment by paying out most of the profits to the shareholders. Chrysler dividends in the period 1950–54 ($1.62 per share) were nearly double those paid in 1946–49 ($0.82 per share), when profits and market shares were higher. Chrysler's production facilities remained underfunded, outdated, and inefficient as long as Hutchinson controlled the purse strings.[25]

K. T. Keller left the office of president of Chrysler Corporation on 3 November 1950, at the mandatory retirement age of 65. He had served as president for fifteen years and three months, five years longer than anyone else, and then held the post of chairman of the board for an additional five years and five months. With Keller's retirement, Chrysler named Lester Lum (Tex) Colbert (pronounced "Cahlbert") as his replacement. This former Texan cotton speculator with a Harvard law degree must have seemed at first glance to be a peculiar choice to walk in the shoes of Walter P. Chrysler.

Chapter 11

THE TEX COLBERT ERA, 1950–61

When we speak of the Forward Look we are talking about more than the design and styling of our cars. We are talking about the spirit of our organization. We are talking about our belief that this company's place is out front—setting the pace for the industry in building new beauty, new style, new quality, new performance in automobiles. We are talking about the growth of our business—and the growth of the people associated with it in all of its phases. We are expressing our faith in the Chrysler future—which is going to be even greater than the Chrysler past.

—L. L. Colbert

The Chrysler Corporation remade itself in many respects during the Tex Colbert era, but with mixed results. The transition to a new management team and a new management structure was painfully slow and difficult. Chrysler Corporation also diversified in significant ways during the 1950s—it again became a significant defense contractor, making tanks, trucks, and missile systems. The company did not do well in the 1950s because its core automobile business did not fare well. Overall, the company slipped badly. Its market share, normally 21–22 percent from 1947 to 1952, fell to roughly 11–14 percent from 1958 to 1961. Chrysler's decline in the 1950s is illustrated by the figures in table 11.1.

The business press throughout 1954 offered gloomy predictions of Chrysler's fate and blamed poorly styled cars for the company's troubles. In a *Fortune* article in April 1954, William B. Harris discussed Chrysler's styling blunders at some length. Its 1954 models were made shorter at the same time that the buying public was choosing longer, lower cars. The cars were so unpopular that Chrysler dealers were discounting them eight weeks into the new model year, at a time when overall demand for new cars was robust. Harris concluded that 1954 was a lost cause and that the 1955 models would determine Chrysler's fate. A *Forbes Magazine* article in December made the same diagnosis. "Chrysler at the Crossroads," which appeared in *Colliers* in December, pointed out that in 1954, Plymouth's sales had fallen from third to fifth, behind Buick and Oldsmobile.[1]

Chrysler's recovery, based on the "Forward Look" cars of 1955–57, was only temporary. The 1957 models suffered from serious quality problems due to poor

TABLE 11.1 Chrysler Corporation Performance, 1946–61

	Unit Sales	Market Share* (%)	Net Earnings†		
			Total ($)	On Sales (%)	On Capital Invested‡ (%)
1946	711,859	27.7	26,899,407	3.09	9.5
1947	1,005,566	21.8	67,181,221	4.93	20.7
1948	1,064,759	21.5	89,187,240	5.69	23.2
1949	1,330,938	21.4	132,170,096	6.34	28.0
1950	1,313,239	17.6	127,876,791	5.84	24.8
1951	1,395,833	21.8	71,973,469	2.68	13.8
1952	1,114,228	21.3	78,696,774	3.03	14.4
1953	1,344,583	20.3	74,788,617	2.23	13.1
1954	883,769	12.9	18,516,770	0.89	3.1
1955	1,579,215	16.8	100,063,330	2.89	15.3
1956	1,077,877	15.5	19,952,969	0.75	3.1
1957	1,381,951	18.3	119,952,406	3.36	16.4
1958	704,099	13.9	(33,824,565)	(loss)	—
1959	917,364	11.3	(5,431,024)	(loss)	—
1960	1,183,311	14.0	32,154,393	1.14	4.6
1961	802,003	10.8	11,138,436	0.52	1.6

Sources: Chrysler Corporation annual reports, 1946–61, box "Annual Reports 1925–69," DCHC; and "Financial and General Fact Book," June 1973, DCHC.
Note: Losses are indicated in parentheses.

*As measured by new car and truck registrations
†After taxes.
‡Defined as stockholders' equity and surpluses

design and shoddy assembly. Chrysler was more badly hit than the other automakers by the 1958–59 recession and lost a substantial part of market share. A *Business Week* article of April 1960, entitled "A Rebuilt Chrysler Corp. Gets Back in the Fight," put an optimistic spin on Chrysler's chances for a full recovery.[2] But with the brief exception of the "Forward Look" cars of 1955–57, the company's products failed to appeal to the auto-buying public.

This is not to suggest that Chrysler either stood still during this decade or became grotesquely inefficient. The corporation greatly improved its manufacturing capacity by building more efficient plants. In most respects, the relative

L. L. (Tex) Colbert showing off the new "Control-Tower" windshield available on many 1958 Chrysler products. Courtesy of NAHC.

decline was the result of poor decisions with regard to the design, styling, and marketing of Chrysler's cars and trucks. This period ended with William C. Newberg, Chrysler's new president, resigning on 30 June 1960 after only two months in office in the midst of a serious corruption scandal. Lester L. Colbert returned to the presidency but lasted only a year, forced out by a stockholders' revolt.

REMAKING THE CHRYSLER CORPORATION

Late in 1950, Chrysler had a new president named Tex. Lester Lum Colbert (1905–95) was born in Oakwood, Texas, the son of Lum Herbert Colbert, a prosperous cotton farmer and cotton trader in this small (population 759) East Texas town. ("Lum" is a common southern contraction of the name Columbus.) His father taught him how to trade cotton at age 13, and by trading in cotton every summer and fall from 1922 through 1929, Colbert earned enough money to pay for his education at the University of Texas and Harvard Law School. His father made him a partner in his firm, changing the name to "L. H. Colbert & Son."

Colbert went to law school mainly to please his father and not from any love or respect for the law; when he graduated in 1929, his dean refused to write him a letter of recommendation because he had not taken his studies seriously enough. Colbert applied for jobs at six top New York City law firms and one of these—Kelley, Drye, Newhall and Maginnes—hired him as a law clerk. Partner Nicholas Kelley was a longtime legal advisor to Walter P. Chrysler and the Chrysler Corporation. When Walter P. Chrysler asked Kelley to assign an attorney from his firm to work for Chrysler Corporation in Detroit in 1933, he named Colbert.[3]

As Chrysler's resident attorney in Detroit, Colbert served on the company's Operations Committee. He impressed K. T. Keller, who named him vice president of the Dodge Division in 1935, at age 30, while he continued to serve as Chrysler's resident legal counsel. In 1935, Keller also appointed Colbert vice president of the Chrysler Export Corporation and Fargo Motor Corporation, giving him wide experience in Chrysler's many operations.

Tex Colbert spent the late 1930s learning all aspects of the Dodge operation, including engineering, production, inventory control, and sales. For three nights a week over a two-year stretch, Colbert studied drafting and machining techniques to broaden his knowledge of design and production. When the Dodge Division took on the assignment of building 18-cylinder engines for the B-29 in a massive new plant in Chicago in early 1942, Keller appointed Colbert operating manager (second in command). Colbert became general manager of the

Dodge–Chicago plant on 22 March 1943 after general manager William O'Neil took ill. Under extremely challenging circumstances, Colbert made the Dodge–Chicago plant a success.[4]

At the end of the Second World War, Colbert returned to Detroit, and Keller named him president of the Dodge Division in December 1945. This was the second most important position within Chrysler Corporation because the Dodge Division employed one-third of all of Chrysler's workers, had half the assets, and manufactured most of the parts and components for the other divisions. Colbert became a director and vice president of Chrysler in November 1949 and only a year later, on 3 November 1950, became Chrysler president when Keller retired.[5]

During the sales crisis of 1954, Colbert hired outside management consultants McKinsey & Company to conduct a thorough study of Chrysler's operations, including its management structure. McKinsey took two years to produce its report, which was a scathing criticism of the way Chrysler was managed. Along with scores of minor recommendations, the report suggested six major changes that, taken together, would have meant a revolution in the way the company operated. McKinsey called for the decentralization of Chrysler's management; modernization of its financial reporting system; greater integration of parts manufacturing, including increased interchangeability of components across division lines; decentralization of automobile assembly away from Detroit; the dispersal of most of Central Engineering's functions; and the development of an international presence to expand sales and to increase Chrysler's prestige.[6]

Under Colbert, Chrysler began to implement many of these recommendations before the McKinsey report was even completed, including greater vertical integration of manufacturing, decentralizing automobile assembly, and more component interchangeability. Chrysler later established a significant presence in Europe with the purchase of an interest in Simca in 1958. However, the rest of the McKinsey recommendations were not implemented.

Chrysler upgraded its manufacturing facilities after the war. The company bought existing factories for expansion, built new ones, and modernized its existing facilities. Between January 1946 and January 1954, Chrysler more than doubled its useable floor space at its various plants from slightly more than 18 million square feet to nearly 38 million square feet, investing more than $500 million on new plant and equipment. Although some of the new facilities were located in southeastern Michigan, most of the investment was not, with much of it outside of the Midwest.[7]

In late 1953, Chrysler Corporation became self-sufficient in automobile bodies by purchasing Briggs Manufacturing Company. Walter Owen Briggs, who had worked for an automobile trimming and painting company since 1901, had established Briggs Manufacturing in 1909 and immediately won a contract to

Change in signage at a Briggs Manufacturing Company plant in late 1954, after Chrysler bought the body manufacturer. Courtesy of DCHC.

make bodies for Ford Motor Company. Following a bitter strike at Briggs in 1933 that disrupted the supply of bodies to Ford, the automaker canceled its contract with the body maker. Briggs rebounded by producing more bodies for Chrysler, eventually making all of the bodies for the Plymouth line as well as for some Chrysler and DeSoto convertibles.

Chrysler officially acquired Briggs Manufacturing Company on 29 December 1953, paying $35 million for the plants and equipment, and an additional $27.5 million on 29 March 1954 for the inventories and dies.[8] Chrysler received ten Detroit-area plants, a stamping plant in Youngstown, Ohio, and a body assembly plant in Evansville, Indiana, expanding its manufacturing floor space by 6,650,000 square feet and adding another 40,000 employees to its workforce of about 125,000. The body plant on Mack Avenue in Detroit was the largest facility (2.2 million square feet) acquired in this deal.[9]

Chrysler Corporation also made a major investment in a modern automobile proving grounds near Chelsea, Michigan, some 50 miles west of Detroit. The Chrysler Corporation Engineering Proving Grounds, dedicated on 16 June 1954, included a 60-foot wide concrete oval test track (4.7 miles long); two concrete straightaway tracks (1.6 miles and 2.2 miles long); a gravel endurance road (8.4 miles); three inclined tracks with grades of 7, 15, and 31 percent; and several obstacle courses for testing cars in water, mud, sand, and on rough pavement.

The high-speed oval test track was designed to allow for 140 mph speeds on the turns without side thrust. Early on opening day, a 1954 Chrysler New Yorker with a stock 235 hp V-8 engine set a new 24-hour speed and endurance record by covering more than 2,800 miles at an average speed of 118.184 mph. Two weeks later, driver Sam Hanks set yet another new record (182.554 mph) on the track with a race car equipped with a special 447 hp Chrysler racing engine.[10]

Chrysler again served as a defense contractor in the 1950s. The cold war brought the beginnings of American rearmament and the Korean conflict, which began on 25 June 1950, quickly accelerated government demand for weapons. A month after the outbreak of war, Keller and Hutchinson discussed over the phone the wording of a statement concerning Chrysler and military production. This was to be part of a Keller letter to the stockholders in the company's semiannual financial statement. A recording of that conversation has survived and it reveals, among other things, Keller's concern over the precise language of this statement. The letter served to reaffirm Chrysler's patriotism, but also to alert stockholders of the possible impact of military contracts on automobile production:

> The Corporation is currently engaged in a number of production studies, research projects and other special activities for the armed services. . . . The magnitude and timing of the impact of the military demands upon the availability of steel and certain other materials used in automotive production is, for the moment, unpredictable. . . . Now, as in World War II, Chrysler Corporation stands ready to serve to any extent called for in the country's mobilization program.[11]

Patriotism and K. T. Keller's mind-set were probably more prominent factors in Chrysler's return to defense work than financial considerations. Defense sales of $76 million in 1951 comprised only 3 percent of the company's total sales, leaping to $360 million (14 percent) in 1952, $660 million (20 percent) in 1953, and declining again to $290 million (14 percent) in 1954. Defense work fell sharply in 1955–57, but then jumped to $325 million in 1958, some 15 percent of total sales in a depressed automobile market.[12]

The spurt of war contracts brought on by the Korean conflict was not limited to familiar products such as trucks and tanks. Part of Chrysler's Evansville, Indiana, Plymouth assembly plant assembled hulls for the Grumman Albatross air-sea rescue plane. Shipment of completed hulls to Grumman had commenced in November 1951. Chrysler shipped the hulls, some 60 feet long, 13 feet high, and 8 feet wide, by truck from Evansville to the Grumman plant in Bethpage, Long Island, some 600 miles distant.[13]

The company completed an 880,000–square foot addition to its Los Angeles assembly plant, where it planned to build wing sections, tail sections, and center wing flap assemblies for the Douglas C-124 Globemaster II transport plane. Production was under way by January 1953 and employed an additional 1,000 employees. Chrysler was to produce Hamilton Standard propellers for various military aircraft in a 750,000–square foot addition to its San Leandro, California plant. Recognizing the automaker's burgeoning defense business, *Chrysler Motors Magazine* devoted an entire issue in 1952 to the company's defense work.[14]

In December 1950, the U.S. Army awarded Chrysler a contract to build engines for the new M-48 Patton (medium) tank. The engine was an 810 hp, air-cooled V-12 engine jointly developed by Continental Motor Company and the army. The contract specified that Chrysler would produce the engines at the army's Michaud Ordnance Plant in New Orleans. Initially, Chrysler used 1.2 million square feet at Michaud, but by early 1952, the army had turned over the entire plant of 1.6 million square feet, with plans to expand to 2 million square feet. Chrysler equipped the plant with 2,300 machine tools and hired 2,200 workers. In March 1952, Michaud delivered its first tank engine.[15]

Chrysler was not the exclusive supplier of the M-48 Patton tank, despite having designed it jointly with the Army Ordnance Corps. The Fisher Body Division of General Motors and the Ford Motor Company also received contracts. Construction on Chrysler's Newark (Delaware) tank plant began in January 1951, with the buildings completed by fall. Chrysler finished the first hand-built pilot model on 14 December 1951 and delivered the first two production models of the M-48 on 11 April 1952.

The Delaware plant simultaneously produced the T-43 heavy tank, also designed in part by Chrysler. This behemoth weighed more than 60 tons and carried a 120 mm gun, versus the M-48 Patton's 90 mm gun. The T-43 evolved into the M-103 heavy tank after modifications carried out by Chrysler. On 20 July 1952, the company also took over the management of the Detroit tank arsenal, which produced the M-47 or Patton II medium tank. On 29 September 1954, Chrysler won a $160 million contract from the Department of the Army to manufacture 1,800 Patton M-48 tanks, beating proposals submitted by Ford and General Motors.[16]

Defense contracts fell off to only 5 percent of Chrysler sales in 1955–57, but rebounded to $315 million (15 percent of total sales) in 1958, slipped to $213 million (7 percent of sales) in 1960, but then recovered in the early 1960s. The continuing contracts included production of updated versions of the M-48 and M-103 tanks, the fire control system for the M-48, and spare parts for all models. Chrysler also designed and manufactured guided and ballistic missile systems, an entirely new endeavor for the company.[17]

Chrysler Corporation became indirectly involved in the U.S. missile program in the early 1950s, years before the firm had any formal contracts with the government. On President Truman's recommendation, Secretary of Defense

George C. Marshall named K. T. Keller director of the U.S. guided missile program on 25 October 1950. Keller's job was to coordinate missile research and development to accelerate production and deployment. Chrysler Corporation released Keller to serve in this post at no pay. Keller worked part-time directing the new Office of Guided Missiles.[18]

Keller served in this position through December 1953, for some 37 months in total. Given the top-secret nature of the missile program and Keller's unwillingness to discuss his role in it, we have only scattered information about his accomplishments. He was able to bring several missiles from a state of experimentation into production. Keller pushed the deployment of the Nike antiaircraft missile and promoted the development of the Army Redstone, a ballistic missile with a range of about 500 miles. Coincidentally, one of Chrysler Corporation's first substantial missile contracts was for the Redstone.[19]

In October 1952, the U.S. Army chose Chrysler to work with Wernher von Braun's team of 120 German rocket engineers, which was developing the Redstone. Chrysler Engineering sent 26 of its top research scientists to work at the Army Redstone arsenal in Huntsville, Alabama. Following successful flight tests of the Redstone in August 1953, the army awarded Chrysler a contract in August 1954 to manufacture five Redstones, and the company delivered the first copy to the Army in November 1955. A second contract in 1956 provided for 13 additional Redstones.[20]

The Defense Department also awarded Chrysler a contract in February 1956 to develop what became the Jupiter missile, a common army-navy liquid fuel intermediate-range ballistic missile that used a modified Redstone as the booster rocket. In late 1957, the company received a contract from NASA for seven Jupiter/Redstone boosters for the Explorer (satellite) program and a $52 million contract in January 1958 for Redstone and Jupiter missiles for the army. Chrysler produced Redstone and Jupiter rockets through June 1961 and then turned to related work, including the Saturn booster rocket.[21] The design and manufacture of missiles certainly seemed modern and progressive, pointing Chrysler toward high technology and new products. However, Chrysler Corporation was not always as "forward-looking" when it came to its core products—passenger cars and trucks.

AUTOMOTIVE PRODUCTS

Keller's conservatism influenced Chrysler's designs until the introduction of the Forward Look for 1955. According to Carl Breer, Keller vetoed the adoption of one-piece curved windshields, first proposed by Owen Skelton in the early 1950s. Keller argued that curved windshields would not sell more cars and were

Scale models of Chrysler-built Redstone and Jupiter rockets on display
at an exhibition in the late 1950s.
Courtesy of DCHC.

too expensive to replace. Ironically, Chrysler had pioneered the use of the single-
piece curved windshield on its 1934 Chrysler Custom Imperial Airflow and again
on the Chrysler Crown Imperial of 1941–42. Keller finally permitted the use of
these newfangled windshields in the 1953 models.[22]

Chrysler Engineering made several significant mechanical improvements during the 1950s. The most important was the new V-8 engine featuring a hemispherical head, introduced on the 1951 models. The "hemi-head" engine design
increased the compression ratio, used larger bore pistons and a shorter stroke
than other V-8s. This V-8 engine, Chrysler's first, weighed less than the in-line
engine it replaced, but offered one-third more power and better fuel economy.
The Chrysler line was the first to get the new engine, dubbed the Chrysler
FirePower V-8. With a displacement of 331.06 cubic inches, it developed 180
hp, well above the 160 hp produced by the largest Cadillac engine.[23]

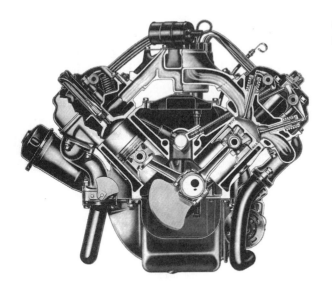

Chrysler V-8 Hemi engine, 1951.
Courtesy of DCHC.

Chrysler developed unique "Hemi" engines for each division, requiring costly tooling for each. The DeSoto Division received its version of the V-8 Hemi engine in February 1952, a year after the Chrysler Division. Called the FireDome V-8, it had a displacement of only 276 cubic inches and produced 160 hp. Dodge was the last division to have the Hemi, with the introduction of the 1953 models in October 1952. The Dodge Red Ram V-8 developed only 140 hp from an engine of 241.4 cubic inches displacement. Plymouth did not have a Hemi engine until 1964, but offered its first V-8 in 1955.[24]

The advanced, innovative Hemi engine, for all the power, speed, and fuel economy it delivered, did little to help Chrysler's sales. In reviewing the 1952 DeSoto, with its Hemi engine, *Motor Trend* began by praising the horsepower the engine delivered, given its relatively modest displacement. DeSoto's Fluid Drive semiautomatic transmission produced gear shifting that was slow and jerky. The testers disliked the car's styling, both inside and out: "There are many more of yesterday's ideas in the DeSoto body than there are of tomorrow's; witness the lines themselves, the twist-type door handles." The Hemi engine was not sufficient to overcome the other inadequacies of the car: "The '52 DeSoto is a car of many contradictions: It has one of the world's best and most modern engines; its transmission keeps that engine from doing its best work; the engine that sets the pace for tomorrow propels a body that's tied to the past."[25]

By the summer of 1953, Chrysler executives, particularly president Lester L. Colbert, had concluded that the corporation's car styling had to be drastically improved and fast if the automaker were going to survive. Before Chrysler could change the looks of its cars, the corporation needed to give its stylists rather than its body engineers the power to determine the shape of the products. The company turned to Virgil Max Exner for help.

Despite his own rigid notions of automobile styling, K. T. Keller had decided in 1949 that Chrysler needed an advanced styling studio and had hired Exner (1909–73) from Studebaker to establish one.[26] Exner had enjoyed a distinguished automotive styling career and in many respects, his initial job at Chrysler was a demotion. Exner went to work at General Motors Art and Colour Section in 1934 and served as the Pontiac studio design chief in 1936–38. Industrial designer Raymond Loewy hired him in 1938 to work on Loewy's Studebaker projects and to run his South Bend, Indiana, studio. Exner broke with Loewy in 1944, when Studebaker's chief engineer, Roy E. Cole, encouraged Exner to establish a rival studio at Studebaker. Exner was responsible for the 1947 Studebaker Champion, a striking and popular car. He became, in effect, Studebaker's chief stylist. When Cole was ready to retire in 1949, he arranged for Exner to meet K. T. Keller in August 1949 and Exner came to Chrysler shortly thereafter.[27]

Exner spent his first four years at Chrysler in a small advanced styling studio isolated from the mainstream styling operations for production cars. Exner called his studio "solitary confinement" and he reported only to Keller, not to the engineers. Keller assigned Exner three design tasks: a dual-cowl Chrysler Imperial parade car; a series of what Exner called "idea cars," to be featured at automobile shows; and advanced styling concepts that might be used in production cars of the future.

Exner designed the 1952 Chrysler Imperial 8–passenger phaeton for parade use and enlisted two Italian custom coach makers, Carrozzeria Ghia and Pinin Farina, to help develop a dozen "idea cars." With fewer than a half-dozen assistants, Exner produced these one-of-a-kind expensive automobiles combining Italian bodies with Chrysler chassis. One of the more notable of these "idea cars" was the Chrysler K-310 (1951), a two-door sports coupe. Named after Keller, the "310" referred to the engine horsepower (although one wag claimed it referred to Keller's weight). The Chrysler C-200 (1952) was a dramatic-looking convertible. Exner's team designed the Falcon (1955), a sport roadster, using production-car components extensively, with the notion that this might end up in showrooms. Chrysler never produced the Falcon, which would have competed head-to-head with Ford Thunderbird and Chevrolet Corvette.[28]

Virgil M. Exner Jr. claimed that in late 1952, K. T. Keller showed his father the renderings of the 1955 models. The stylist shook his head and predicted that these cars would be a sales disaster. Keller then gave Exner the task of redesigning the 1955 lineup in its entirety, a job that had to be completed in eighteen months. The 1955 models, which went on sale in October 1954, would be in production by July 1954. However, according to Vance Johnson, Chrysler president Lester L. Colbert, not Keller, ordered the redesign. Exner began with the Chrysler Imperial and then turned to the other brands in the corporate lineup. After Colbert named Exner director of styling early in 1953, Exner enlarged and upgraded the styling staff, a mere seventeen people when he took control. By April 1956, his staff stood at 268, including 107 clay modelers and seventeen body layout draftsmen.[29]

Exner's task of redesigning the 1955 models only eighteen months before they were to hit the showrooms was difficult by itself, but he also had to reduce the influence of Chrysler's managers on design. Exner ignored all the efforts by Colbert to interfere and went ahead creating styles that he believed would work. Gradually, Colbert and even Keller came to appreciate Exner's efforts. In an article explaining the styling of the 1955 models written for Chrysler's employee magazine, Exner listed seven styling features ("style notes") of the Forward Look line that were borrowed from the earlier "idea cars." He cited the K-310 and the C-200 as especially significant.[30]

Colbert and the Chrysler management team understood the critical importance of the 1955 line to the automaker's future. At the press preview of 17 November 1954 announcing the Forward Look models, Colbert noted: "The cars you are going to see and drive this afternoon display what we call the Forward Look. . . . We are expressing our faith in the Chrysler future—which is going to be even greater than the Chrysler past." Colbert claimed that Chrysler had spent more than $250 million to complete the design and tooling for the new lines. The automaker's short-term goal was to capture 20 percent of the market, but had plans for an even larger share over the longer run.[31]

The first ads for the 1955 Chrysler brand referred to the models as cars with "the 100 Million Dollar Look," which offered "the 100 Million Dollar Drive" to their owners. By May 1955, advertising for all of the Chrysler Corporation lines used the slogan, "the Forward Look" and a distinctive logo, both developed by the advertising agency of McCann-Erickson. The Forward Look label appeared through the 1957 model year in advertising, and the logo remained in use through 1961, when the familiar Pentastar replaced it.[32]

As the advertising promised, the 1955 models *were* strikingly different from the previous offerings. Some 3 inches lower and 16 inches longer than the 1954 models, they were sleeker looking than the competition. Part of this new look was the extensive use of color. As early as the 1950 models, customers could buy two-tone paint jobs, but choices were limited. Starting in 1955, Chrysler used body side inserts called "color sweeps" to allow for more color combinations. In the 1955 models, customers had the choice of 56 solid colors, 173 two-tone

1954 Dodge, the last of the boxy cars of the early 1950s, serving as the Indianapolis 500 pace car. Courtesy of DCHC.

combinations, and even some three-tone mixtures. With the 1957 models, buyers could pick from 462 two-tone color combinations. The public response was as enthusiastic as any Chrysler had enjoyed in decades. Sales in calendar year 1955 nearly doubled from 1954 (1,579,215 units versus 883,769) and market share rebounded from 12.9 percent to 16.8 percent.[33]

Chrysler's 1956 line included cosmetic changes to sheet metal, but Exner added fins to all of Chrysler's offerings, a first in the auto industry. Fins created a wedge-shaped side view of the vehicle, suggesting motion. The 1956 models came with Powerflite automatic transmissions with pushbuttons on the dashboard, improved power steering, and better heaters. Sales in 1956 dropped by a third from calendar year 1955, but were still above one million. To be sure, sales for the entire U.S. auto industry suffered in 1956, but Chrysler's market share declined (16.8 percent in 1955 to 15.5 percent in 1956) as well.[34]

Exner designed a complete remake of all the Chrysler lines for 1957, complete with tall, undercut fins. Exner insisted that engineering find a way to make the hardtop coupes a full 5 inches lower than the 1956 models. Chrysler's engineers

Chrysler's 1956 Forward Look models, with jet fighter aircraft. Courtesy of DCHC.

in time devised a series of innovations that allowed the lower-slung car—torsion-bar front suspension systems, the use of 14-inch wheels, and drop-over air cleaners. With the 1957 models, all of the Chrysler Corporation car lines, except Imperial, shared the same common bodies. Chrysler was the industry leader in this cost-cutting move, but General Motors introduced common bodies for its 1959 car lines.

The 1957 models represented the Forward Look in its purest form and made Chrysler the industry styling leader. After a group of General Motors stylists led by Bill Mitchell secretly viewed 1957 model Chryslers in a storage lot in Detroit, Mitchell concluded that the 1959 models GM had on the drawing boards could never compete with Chrysler's products. He led a revolt against Harley Earl, the GM styling chief, and completely redid GM's 1959 lines.[35]

The 1957 lineup won Chrysler the 1957 Gold Medal Award of the Industrial Designers' Institute. *Motor Trend* gave the cars its Award for Superior Handling and Roadability for the Torsion-Aire suspension system. Colbert rewarded Exner for his work by promoting him to the new position of vice president for styling in 1957 as well. More important from Chrysler's viewpoint was the sales "bump" it enjoyed in 1957, with total sales 1,381,951 and a 18.3 percent market share. Plymouth, with more than 600,000 sales, regained third place from Buick.[36]

Following on the heels of the 1957 sales revival was the worst single-year slump in sales that Chrysler had ever experienced, a near 50 percent drop to only 704,099 vehicles in 1958. This was a year of nationwide recession, but

Chrysler suffered deeper losses than its competitors and saw its market share fall from 18.3 percent to 13.9 percent in one year. Jeffrey Godshall and others have argued that this sharp decline of popularity was due to massive quality problems that plagued the 1957 models—faulty seals around doors and windows produced wet seats and floors, parts fell off, bodies rusted through in less than a year's time, and torsion bars broke. Godshall summed up the most vexing defect of the 1957 models: "A new sound was heard throughout the land—the sharp retort of a breaking torsion bar, followed by the settling of one side of the car."

This and other problems were the result of producing a car requiring numerous new parts without Chrysler's engineering or manufacturing departments having enough time to get it right. The 1957 models were originally supposed to be slightly reskinned versions of the 1956 cars; the radically different new models were supposed to wait until 1958. Colbert, however, pushed the production of the new cars ahead to 1957 and the result was a poor-quality product that would haunt Chrysler for years to come.[37]

In February 1955, when Virgil Exner's first generation of production cars enjoyed success across all of Chrysler Corporation's lines, the Chrysler Division introduced a high-powered, limited production model called the Chrysler C300. So named because the 331–cubic inch displacement Hemi engine developed 300 hp, this was the first of a long series of fast, powerful production cars offered by Chrysler. The 1956 model, the Chrysler 300-B, came equipped with a 354–cubic inch Hemi engine that developed 340 hp. Chrysler offered these so-called "letter cars" through the 1965 Chrysler 300-L. Enthusiasts altered the factory car to squeeze more even horsepower and speed from the "beautiful brute," as the press dubbed these machines. DaimlerChrysler recently revived the 300 series, or at least the nameplate, with the 300-M (1999).[38]

The 300 series grew directly out of the early racing successes of Briggs Cunningham and others with Hemi-equipped cars. Chrysler's customers sent the company a mountain of letters asking for a "performance car." Chrysler Division's chief engineer, Bob Rodger, and Cliff Voss, the head of the Chrysler/Imperial design studios, created a car that combined a Chrysler Windsor body with an Imperial grille. Adding a second four-barrel carburetor to an existing FirePower Hemi V-8 increased its output from 245 to 300 hp. They built a prototype in October 1954 and began production of the first Chrysler 300s in January 1955 at the Jefferson Avenue plant in Detroit.[39]

Chrysler then enjoyed a bit of good fortune. Carl Kiekhaefer, the manufacturer of Mercury outboard motors for boats, decided to promote his outboard motors through stock car racing. Kiekhaefer was so excited about the Chrysler 300s that he immediately equipped his Mercury Outboard Team with these performance cars. It is ironic that Chrysler racing cars promoted the product of a direct competitor of Chrysler's Marine Division. For the rest of the 1950s,

Chrysler 300s dominated the major racing circuits. They won the NASCAR National Speed Trial Championships in 1955 and 1956. In the latter year, 300s won *both* NASCAR and AAA National Stock Car Championships. Through the rest of the 1950s, Chrysler 300s often won the first five or six places in major stock car races.[40]

Virgil Exner and Chrysler Corporation were unable to repeat the successes of the 1955–57 models. Exner remained at Chrysler as vice president of styling until November 1961, when new Chrysler president Lynn Townsend hired Elwood P. Engel from Ford to replace him. But a combination of circumstances had already reduced Exner's power and effectiveness at Chrysler. In July 1956, at age 47, Exner suffered a massive heart attack, which he barely survived. As a result Colbert hired William M. Schmidt, former design vice president at Studebaker-Packard, in February 1957 to serve as executive stylist. For more than a year, Exner and Schmidt fought for control of the studios and the designs. Late in 1957, Colbert fired Schmidt, leaving Exner in control again, after a two-year period of conflict and confusion.[41]

Exner's influence waned in part because the magic touch that had produced the 1955, 1956, and 1957 models eluded him in his last years at Chrysler. The 1958 models were virtually unchanged from 1957, while the styling changes introduced for 1959 did not appeal to car buyers. Chrysler's sales slumped in 1958–59, recovered in 1960, but then dropped some 380,000 units in 1961. Sales also suffered in 1962 because Chrysler management foolishly "downsized" it entire line. The last Chrysler cars strongly influenced by Exner were the 1963 models, which sold extremely well. He worked for Chrysler Corporation as a consultant until 1964, when he turned 55 and was eligible for a Chrysler pension, but he had no significant impact on the company's car styles in those later years.[42]

With the exception of the 1955–57 models, Chrysler's product lines from 1949 to 1961 were largely unappealing to the average American car buyer. Chrysler's cars were dull, dated, stodgy, and otherwise out of step with what consumers wanted from 1949 to 1954. The Forward Look cars of 1955–58 led the industry in styling, but the 1959–61 models were seen by potential customers as bizarre. Except for Hemi engines and torsion bar suspension systems, Chrysler vehicles seldom incorporated "leading-edge" engineering as they had in the 1920s and 1930s. More frequently, they were poorly engineered or lacked the most modern features, such as fully automatic transmissions. (Although initially behind the times, Chrysler became the industry leader with its Torque-Flite automatic transmission, introduced in 1956.) Much of Chrysler's weak product performance can be attributed to the company's "old guard" managers, who had been with the automaker since the Maxwell days, and the highly centralized management system that was a legacy of Walter P. Chrysler.

LABOR RELATIONS

Chrysler's labor relations history after 1945 was substantially different from that of General Motors or Ford. Chrysler suffered more official, authorized strikes by the UAW than either of its major competitors. Beyond that, unofficial or wildcat strikes seemed to be a way of life at Chrysler. In the period 1946–56, there were 1,434 unauthorized strikes, well over 100 a year. Wildcat strikes took place at Chrysler 13 times more often than at General Motors from 1945 to 1954 and 35 times more frequently from 1955 to 1959. Part of this distinctive history was the legacy of the strong shop steward system at Dodge Main colliding with an authoritarian management that tried to turn back the clock of labor relations to pre–New Deal conditions.[43]

Labor unrest continued in various Chrysler plants, but particularly at the Dodge Main plant in Hamtramck, until the late 1950s. Wildcat strikes remained common and generally involved disputes over production standards. A strike at Dodge Main in the Trim Department (Dept. 99) in mid-July 1954 was typical. Dodge unilaterally introduced what it called a "simplified method" for installing door garnish moldings, which would allow management to reduce the garnish molding crew from 26 to 18 men. When several workers refused to work in the new way and Dodge management fired them, 97 workers from the trim line did not return to work after lunch. The Dodge local union then called a plant-wide strike, which in a few days caused 35,600 layoffs companywide. The UAW International Executive Board ordered the workers to return to their jobs and Chrysler then bargained with the union on production standards.[44]

Labor relations at Chrysler changed dramatically in 1958. Chrysler Corporation used the circumstances of the severe auto recession of 1958 to extract concessions from Walter Reuther regarding the handling of production standards, grievances, and bargaining on working conditions and other issues at the plant or department level. Dodge Main workers struck Chrysler on 2 December 1958 for 18 days, primarily over working conditions, and shut down much of Chrysler's operations.

An agreement ending the strike granted management the exclusive right to determine rates of production, thus eliminating the role of the shop steward in resolving future disputes. In place of stewards, the UAW introduced a more formal grievance procedure that concentrated power in the hands of the International Union officials. The new arrangements brought a drastic drop in wildcat strikes. Chrysler Corporation had slightly more than 500 wildcat strikes in its plants in 1957 and 1958, only 42 in 1959, and a mere 17 in 1960. The number three automaker had fewer strikes from 1960 to 1965 than General Motors.[45]

THE LATE 1950S: EXIT DESOTO, ENTER VALIANT

An integral part of Chrysler's survival strategy in the late 1950s and early 1960s was the restructuring of the company's product lines. In an effort to rebuild its market share and to tap into the apparent rising demand for smaller cars, Chrysler introduced the compact Valiant in October 1959. A year later, Chrysler discontinued the DeSoto line of cars. These two developments illustrate the problems Chrysler faced during this difficult period and some of the solutions it developed to revitalize itself.

With a terse announcement on 18 November 1960, Chrysler Corporation discontinued the DeSoto line, a key component in the company's emergence in 1928 as the third largest automaker in the United States. A year earlier, DeSoto had celebrated its thirtieth birthday and the production of over 2 million cars. This unhappy announcement came thirteen months after Chrysler introduced its new Valiant line of compact cars in October 1959.

DeSoto was one of many Detroit mid-priced car lines to suffer severe sales slumps in the mid- and late 1950s. The arrangement of car lines first established by Alfred P. Sloan Jr. at General Motors in the 1920s and imitated by Ford and Chrysler, was based on the notion that price and size would differentiate each car line from the others. Each line of GM cars (Chevrolet-Pontiac-Oldsmobile-Buick-Cadillac) was larger and more expensive than the car line below and came equipped with a more powerful engine. This traditional marketing hierarchy dissolved in the 1950s when Chevrolet, Ford, and Plymouth models became larger, with bigger powerplants. One comparison illustrates this trend—the 1928 Cadillac was five feet longer than Ford and more than four feet longer than Chevrolet and Plymouth, but by 1958, it was only 18 inches longer.[46]

This change in strategy for selling low-priced cars directly threatened the mid-priced models, which became distinct from their lower-priced relatives in price only. In explaining its decision to discontinue DeSoto, Chrysler management pointed out that DeSoto's sales decline of 64 percent between 1955 and 1959 was only slightly better than Buick's drop of 66 percent. Over the same period, Oldsmobile sales fell 49 percent, Dodge by 41 percent, Mercury by 38 percent, and Pontiac by a more modest 28 percent. DeSoto's sales losses were more important because of its relatively small volume, roughly one-third the sales of competing brands like Mercury and only one-fifth those of Pontiac and Oldsmobile. The decline in DeSoto sales to only 42,000 in 1959 was bad enough, but in the first nine months of 1960, customers bought only 19,000 DeSotos, including 2,600 of the 1961 models. The market had decided DeSoto's fate by summer 1960 and Chrysler Corporation was left to announce the end of the brand.[47]

Chrysler Corporation first tried to prevent the demise of DeSoto, attempting to promote the 1960 line and at the same time create the strong impression that DeSoto would be around forever. An undated list, "Ideas Designed to Build Confidence in DeSoto's Future," created before the introduction of the 1960 line, had 51 promotional ideas, including the "planting" of various stories with the automotive and general press.[48] But once the decision was made by late summer 1960 to discontinue DeSoto, Chrysler Corporation officials turned their attention to managing the costs and negative publicity of discontinuing the line.

A report dated 2 November 1960 to H. E. Chesebrough, head of the Plymouth-DeSoto Division, laid out the general strategy for handling DeSoto's demise. The decision would be kept secret until it was announced at the DeSoto Factory-Dealer Council meeting on 18 November in Detroit. Letters of explanation would be sent to all owners of 1957 through 1961 model DeSotos. Chrysler, hoping to calm angry customers now stuck with an "orphan car," would offer DeSoto owners a $300 rebate, which they could use toward the purchase of any 1961 or 1962 Chrysler product by 1 January 1963. Unfortunately, this offer did little to satisfy them.[49]

Chrysler estimated the direct costs of discontinuing DeSoto at $2,205,500, with much of this spent on the dealerships. Chrysler gave its DeSoto dealers a $300 rebate on every 1960 and 1961 model DeSoto they had in stock at the time of the announcement, for a total cost of $932,700. The next largest single expense was for changing signs at dealerships, which the company estimated would cost $897,000. The company estimated that only 836 customers would take advantage of the $300 rebate offer, costing Chrysler only $250,800 in rebates.[50] Chrysler could have used the demise of DeSoto as an opportunity to create a Plymouth-only dealer network, but failed to do so. With the discontinuation of DeSoto, the Plymouth-DeSoto-Valiant Division became simply the Plymouth Division, but did not get exclusive dealerships.

The long-term cost to Chrysler Corporation, particularly in terms of customer loyalty, is impossible to measure. E. C. Quinn, Chrysler's vice president for sales, sent a letter to all DeSoto owners a day after the "death notice" in which he reassured them that they could have their DeSoto properly serviced at any authorized Chrysler dealership. Quinn also urged them to consider trading in their DeSoto for the purchase of any of Chrysler's other lines, assuring them they would be offered "an outstanding allowance" on their DeSoto. Three dozen surviving letters from DeSoto owners show nothing but hostility toward Chrysler for its decision to drop the brand and for the "settlement" it offered them.[51]

It was not only DeSoto customers that were unhappy with the demise of the model line—several dealers were as well. By May 1963 a group of eleven New

Jersey DeSoto dealers were suing Chrysler over the discontinuance. Eventually, thirty-five DeSoto dealers sued Chrysler for damages and some of the lawsuits were still being fought in the early 1970s. Aside from whatever legal fees and money settlements Chrysler paid as a result of the demise of DeSoto or any permanent loss of customers, dropping an entire line of cars involved a serious loss of prestige and credibility in the marketplace. Ford suffered similar problems in the aftermath of the Edsel fiasco.[52]

Chrysler and the other American automakers also faced a shift in consumer preferences in the second half of the 1950s, away from the increasingly large, overpowered offerings from Detroit toward smaller compact cars, mainly from Europe. Imports increased fourfold from 1955 to 1959, when they surpassed 500,000 units and accounted for 10 percent of the U.S. market. American Motors Corporation enjoyed a spectacular increase in the registrations of its compact Rambler, from 42,196 units in 1958 to 120,603 in 1960. Even Studebaker's compact Lark sold 133,000 units in 1959. In the late 1950s, compact cars, both foreign and domestic, made significant inroads into the U.S. car market. By 1959, the compacts had captured 15 percent of the market.[53]

In spring of 1957, Chrysler Corporation established a special product planning committee to develop a compact car for the American market. The 1960 model Valiant was the result. Chrysler's Small Car Study Program emerged in the first five months of 1958 through a series of nine product planning meetings chaired by H. E. Chesebrough. The planners grappled with the major questions that needed to be answered before a small car could become a reality. An overriding assumption in these early discussions was that the earliest Chrysler Corporation could design and produce an all-new small car would be for the 1962 model year. Competitive realities quickly changed these assumptions, as Chrysler learned that both Ford and General Motors planned to launch new compact cars in late 1959.[54]

Members of this product planning group had disagreements about some of the design dimensions and features of the small car they were developing, but they began with some general assumptions. Chrysler would not try to make a Volkswagen-sized car (wheelbase of 94 inches), nor try to approach Volkswagen's fuel economy of 40 mpg, nor opt for a rear-engine design. They were all thinking in terms of a car that would carry four adults comfortably. J. A. Lawson, director of market analysis, argued that the car should deliver at least 25 mpg "tank mileage" (overall mileage) and 30 mpg at cruising speeds, it should retail for no more than $1,850, should match the performance of a standard Plymouth Six, and should have a distinctive appearance.[55]

Chesebrough's group presented the small car program to the Chrysler Administrative Committee on 8 July 1958. They showed three clay models, two for a 106-inch wheelbase car and the other for a 103-inch wheelbase version. Already, many of the "economy" characteristics of this car had changed. Vehicle weight had grown to 2,700 pounds, some 400 pounds more than originally proposed, and "tank mileage" had fallen from 25 to 22 mpg. At some point in the planning process, the seating capacity was increased from four to six adults. The version with a 106-inch wheelbase became the only viable choice. The administrative committee approved the new line and in only thirteen months, a special engineering group finished the work needed to bring the all-new compact car into production.[56]

The new car, the Valiant, became known as "the Secret of Midland Avenue" because a special task force of over 200 engineers who worked in secret at a plant at 403 Midland Avenue in Detroit completed the design work. Security was so tight that most people within Chrysler not directly involved with the project thought the work was a special defense contract. This early example of a "platform team" began its efforts in July 1958 and finished in August 1959. The first Valiants rolled off the production line in September and were in the dealerships by late October.[57]

Naming the new compact car became an interesting challenge as well. Virgil Exner had designed a sporty "idea car" named Falcon in 1955 and Chrysler was considering the name for its new compact car. Ford Motor Company was planning its own compact car, and Henry Ford II asked Tex Colbert to refrain from using the Falcon name so that Ford Motor Company could use it. Colbert agreed. Chrysler conducted extensive polling of potential customers to come up with a brand-new name for its brand-new car. Company officials reduced a list of 2,000 suggestions down to five and then did an in-depth consumer survey. "Valiant" was the hands-down favorite.[58]

The automotive and enthusiasts' press reacted favorably to Valiant's engineering innovations, overall size, and "peppy" performance. The "tilted" or "Slant-Six" engine, which was mounted on the chassis on a 30-degree angle, provided a low center of gravity for Valiant, but more important, allowed for a low hood line. The Slant Six engine proved to be so durable that engineers and customers alike called it "bulletproof." The introduction of an A.C. alternator in place of the conventional D.C. generator improved the output of the electrical system and reduced battery drainage while idling. The unitized body construction eliminated the conventional frame.[59]

Valiant was a success, selling 180,000 units during the initial model year, but finished well behind the Ford Falcon, which sold 417,000 units. The Valiant easily fared the worst of the three compacts introduced by the Big Three as 1960 models. Comparing combined sales for calendar years 1959, 1960, and 1961, Falcon led the pack with 1,094,000 units, Chevrolet Corvair was second with 655,000 units, and Valiant a distant third at 374,000 cars sold. Valiant had clear

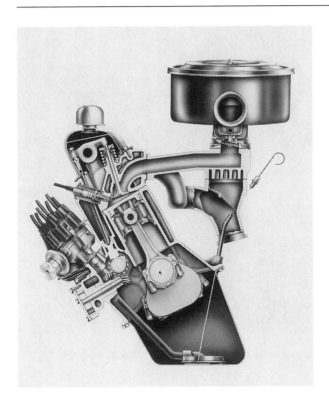

The radical new Slant Six engine designed for the 1960 Plymouth Valiant. Courtesy of DCHC.

disadvantages in the "economy car" market—it weighed 300–400 pounds more than its competitors and delivered 2–3 mpg less in fuel economy.[60]

THE END OF THE COLBERT ERA

The management duo of Tex Colbert and William C. Newberg became a symbol of Chrysler's internal management ills in the late 1950s. Colbert named Newberg his successor as president of Chrysler Corporation on 28 April 1960, but Newberg held the post for only two months before being forced to resign on 30 June. Newberg had worked for Chrysler his entire adult life and seemed well prepared to succeed Colbert. Born on 17 December 1910 in Seattle, Washington, Newberg earned a degree in mechanical engineering from the University of Washington in 1933. He received a master's in automotive engineering from the Chrysler Institute of Engineering in 1935 and worked for Chrysler starting in 1937. After serving as chief engineer at the Dodge–Chicago plant from 1942 to 1945 under Colbert, Newberg held various positions in central engineering in 1945–47.

Newberg moved quickly into the higher ranks of Chrysler management, becoming president of the Dodge Division in September 1951. Colbert promoted

Mamie Eisenhower, former first lady, taking delivery on a 1962 Plymouth Valiant.
Courtesy of DCHC.

Newberg to the post of group vice president for automotive operations on 16 July 1956 and executive vice president on 24 April 1958. Only two years later, Newberg became president and chief operating officer of Chrysler Corporation, with Colbert moving "upstairs" to become chairman of the board and chief executive officer.[61]

The new administration came to a quick end on 30 June 1960, when the Chrysler Board of Directors announced Newberg's resignation as president, effective immediately. Colbert would resume the presidency and remain as chairman of the board. The terse announcement of the change at the top issued by Chrysler's press information service simply stated, "His resignation was due to differences of opinion on certain corporation policies." The automobile and general press were shocked by the news and speculated about the "real reason" for Newberg's sudden departure.[62]

Stunning details about Newberg's resignation surfaced on 21 July 1960, when Chrysler issued the following statement: "Chrysler Corporation and William C. Newberg have entered into an agreement under which Chrysler will receive from Mr. Newberg profits in excess of $450,000 made by him from interests in vendor companies. Chrysler recently learned of such interests as a result of an investigation instituted by L. L. Colbert as Chairman of the Board and conducted by Chrysler's General Counsel and independent auditors, in which Mr. Newberg cooperated." Newberg agreed to pay Chrysler a total of $455,000 to settle claims made against him and his wife, Dorothy B. Newberg, because of their financial interest in two companies that were Chrysler vendors.[63]

The scandal got much uglier after the start of the new year. Newberg filed a lawsuit in mid-January 1961 naming L. L. Colbert as defendant, in which he sought to overturn his agreement of the previous 21 July and collect $5,250,000 in personal damages. Newberg claimed that he was falsely promised the position of chairman of the board at Studebaker-Packard if he signed the restitution agreement, but was threatened with criminal prosecution by Chrysler and financial ruin if he did not. Newberg argued that he was made a scapegoat for Colbert's years of corruption and mismanagement. Newberg's lawsuit was still in the courts three years later.[64]

The conflict-of-interest charges and counterchanges were the opening battles of a broader attack on Chrysler's top leaders by Detroit attorney Sol A. Dann, a Chrysler stockholder and corporate gadfly. In August 1960, stockholders Sol Dann, Karl Horvath, and Samuel Schwartzberg asked a Wilmington, Delaware, court to place Chrysler Corporation into receivership and named a total of 23 companies and 43 persons as defendants. By early February 1961, the scandal had produced at least 11 lawsuits, including 8 against Chrysler and 3 initiated by Chrysler against some of its suppliers.[65]

The revolt of Chrysler's stockholders peaked at the Chrysler stockholders' meeting of April 1961. Although William Newberg was not present, he issued the following statement—"It is my conviction that we cannot ever again have a strong Chrysler—the great company of old—under the czarist rule of Mr. Colbert." Dann and others sponsored six resolutions, mainly aimed at reducing the number of full-time managers on the board. They all failed, but received from 12 to 16 percent of the votes, clear evidence of widespread stockholder discontent. The high (or low) point of the meeting was Dann's 79-minute harangue against Colbert.[66]

Tex Colbert's reputation was tainted by these scandals. Columnist Drew Pearson revealed that Daisy Gorman Colbert, Tex's wife, owned shares in the Dura Corporation, a Chrysler supplier, which she conveniently sold right before Tex purged Newberg. Far more intriguing was the revelation that Colbert kept $200,000 in negotiable U.S. bonds in his office safe at Highland Park. Pearson's associate, Jack Anderson, pressed Colbert for an explanation. Colbert offered none, except to say that this money was his life savings. Pearson insinuated in his column that these were Colbert's "kickbacks" from suppliers.[67]

Colbert survived until 27 July 1961, when he resigned as Chrysler's president and chairman of the board. He went off quietly to serve as chairman of Chrysler of Canada until 1965, when he was eligible for an executive pension and retired from Chrysler.

Assessing Colbert's presidency is at best difficult. In many respects, he was a transitional figure between the founding fathers of Chrysler Corporation—Chrysler, Hutchinson, Zeder, and Keller—and the generation of "modern" businessmen—Lynn Townsend, John Riccardo, and Eugene Cafiero—that led Chrysler in the 1960s and 1970s. The relative decline in fortunes that began under Keller in the late 1940s continued under Colbert, with few interruptions. Problems with poor-quality vehicles, unpopular styling, and internal scandals all hurt Chrysler in the marketplace. The final responsibility must rest with the man in charge, Tex Colbert.

Chapter 12

THE LYNN TOWNSEND ERA

THE FAT YEARS, 1961–68

Connoisseurs of American corporate life may never again relish the likes of Chrysler Corporation as Chrysler was in all its years leading up to 1962. For years their superb display of non-conformity was a spectator's bonanza. All of Chrysler's capers, serious or otherwise, coalesced to create the most vivid corporate personality since Henry Ford. Chrysler was the last fortress of unfettered, buccaneering, industrial individualism. Management's peculiar instinct for failure was linked to a certain genius for recovery, a combination which gave the company both a roller-coaster history and a striking idiosyncratic quality. In an industry where vacillation is commonplace, Chrysler was outstandingly capricious.

—Ward's Quarterly

Lynn A. Townsend became president of Chrysler Corporation on 27 July 1961, at age 42, following the resignation of L. L. Colbert as president and chairman of the board. Two months later, on 21 September 1961, George H. Love filled the position of chairman of the board. This was both a symbolic and a substantive changing of the guard at Chrysler. Colbert was the last president to have worked with Walter P. Chrysler and to come to power with the support of Chrysler's lieutenants Keller and Hutchinson. Lynn Townsend had worked for Chrysler for only four years, beginning in 1957 as comptroller, and George H. Love had run the Consolidation Coal Company of Pittsburgh since 1946. To have such men as the chief executives of an automobile company was unprecedented. For Chrysler, however, the early 1960s were unique times that required unique measures.

Lynn A. Townsend served as president of Chrysler through 31 December 1966 and then as chairman of the board until 30 September 1975. His protégé, John J. Riccardo, followed him as president and then as chairman in 1975–79, so Townsend's impact on Chrysler extended for nearly two decades. He wrought substantial changes in Chrysler's product focus, organizational structure, and corporate identity. Chrysler's roller-coaster performance during the Townsend-Riccardo era came despite serious efforts to revive the company and return it to its earlier successes. The company's continued weak position in the late 1970s contributed to the economic crisis that nearly resulted in bankruptcy in 1979.

Townsend enacted a series of short-term "fixes" for Chrysler's problems during the first three years of his presidency, including improved styling, enlarging the force of salespeople and dealers, and giving the corporation a more positive image. He also reformed Chrysler's management structure, improved product planning, and expanded into overseas markets. Chrysler Corporation, at least through 1968, seemed ready for permanent prosperity.

REFORMS, RECOVERY, AND RACING

Lynn Alfred Townsend (1919–2000) seemed like an even less likely person to become president of Chrysler Corporation than Tex Colbert. Townsend was the son of a Flint, Michigan, auto mechanic—the only Flint native to head a major U.S. automobile company. His family moved to Beverly Hills, California, when Lynn was in grade school, largely to give his asthmatic mother a more healthy climate. Lynn's mother died in 1929 and his father in 1934, leaving him an orphan at age 14. He returned to the Midwest to live with an uncle, North I. Townsend, who was the comptroller of a company in Evansville, Indiana.

After graduating from high school, Lynn Townsend worked as a teller in a local bank in 1935–36 to earn money for college. He earned a bachelor of arts degree from the University of Michigan in June 1940 and a master's in business administration a year later. While in college, he landed a part-time position with an Ann Arbor accounting firm. Townsend worked as an accountant for much of his early career, beginning with a stint at the Detroit accounting firm of Ernst & Ernst from June 1941 to June 1944. He then served in the U.S. Navy from June 1944 until April 1946, with the job of disbursing officer on the aircraft carrier *Hornet*.[1]

Townsend returned to Ernst & Ernst in April 1946 for a year before joining the firm of George Bailey & Company (later Touche, Ross, Bailey, & Smart) in Detroit as a supervising accountant. In 1952, he became a partner in the firm, which was Chrysler Corporation's national accounting firm. Townsend worked on the Chrysler books and also handled the accounts of American Motors Corporation, so he developed an understanding of how a small and "lean" auto company operated. Chrysler Corporation appointed Townsend comptroller in April 1957, and he then moved rapidly up the corporate ladder. Chrysler named him group vice president for international operations in October 1958 and a director in January 1959. Less than two years later, on 1 December 1960, Tex Colbert named Townsend administrative vice president. Newspaper stories about the promotion identified Townsend as Colbert's likely successor.[2] Eight months later, at age 42, Townsend assumed the presidency of the Chrysler Corporation.

A special committee of Chrysler directors chaired by George Love chose Townsend as president on 27 July 1961. George Love was another man who followed a peculiar path to leadership in the auto company. He had built a career restoring financially troubled coal companies to prosperity. In 1946, Love took control of the newly merged Consolidation Coal Company and Pittsburgh Coal Company, both money losers for more than a decade, and immediately turned a profit. Tex Colbert invited Love to serve on the Chrysler Corporation board of directors in 1958 and he accepted the offer.

Love's committee picked Townsend to lead Chrysler after they had unsuccessfully courted two GM vice presidents, Edward N. Cole and James E. Goodman, and also Ford vice presidents James O. Wright and Irving A. Duffy. Other candidates who chose not to come to Chrysler included Ernest Breech, former chairman of Ford Motor Company; George Romney, president of American Motors Corporation; and Richard M. Nixon, the just-defeated presidential candidate.

Although he was clearly not their first choice, Love and the other directors were impressed by Townsend's accomplishments. In the eight months he had served as administrative vice president, Townsend had initiated the severe cost-cutting measures Chrysler needed to return to profitability. He naturally had the mentality of the cost accountant because that was his training. *Automotive Industries* summed up his approach: "An idea of the way Mr. Townsend operates is given by a close friend who said [that] balance sheets, profit statements, statistics, percentages, and charts carry a great deal of weight in his decisions. This tends to insulate him from action based on [the] personal opinions of his associates." Townsend quickly laid off 7,000 white-collar workers, closed and sold off excess plants and office buildings, and merged the Chrysler-Imperial Division with the Plymouth Division. He reduced costs by $50 million through the layoffs and saved another $60 million through inventory reductions, allowing Chrysler to earn a tiny profit of $11 million in 1961 on sales of $2.13 billion and a volume of only 800,000 vehicles.[3]

George Love hired Townsend to run Chrysler, but agreed to serve as chairman of the board, a position he held from 21 September 1961 to 31 December 1966. The Chrysler directors had agreed to hire the young and inexperienced Townsend as president only if Love would agree to supervise and advise him. Love seldom second-guessed Townsend's decisions, but the two men consulted frequently on important issues. In an interview with *Fortune*, Love commented on his working relationship with Townsend—"I wouldn't expect him to consult with me on anything unless it was going to the board; and I wouldn't take anything to the board without consulting him." When *Ward's Quarterly* interviewed Townsend in 1965, he pointed to his own chair and said: "The final responsibility for running the business rests here. George Love and I have a beautiful working relationship. I always know where he is. I talk to him often.

But we're running the company here in Detroit with this administrative committee."[4] George Love's work was hardly a labor of love. Chrysler Corporation paid him $301,500 in salary and bonus in 1963 alone.

The fundamental problem Chrysler faced in the early 1960s was shrinking sales. An article in *Fortune* emphasized the grim facts. Chrysler's market share had declined from 20.4 percent in 1953 to only 9.4 percent in 1962. The bottom point of the decline came in February 1962, when its share of new car sales was only 8.3 percent. Chrysler's share of cars on the road fell from 22 to 16 percent in ten years, while Ford remained at 25 percent and General Motors' share increased from 43 percent to 47 percent. With its customer base shrinking, Chrysler's stated goal of regaining a 20 percent share of the market would require a monumental effort.[5]

Chrysler's dealers had several obstacles to overcome in selling the company's products in the early 1960s, including continued poor quality, unpopular styles, the wrong "mix" of models, and confusion over brand and model identity. In describing the poor quality of "fit and finish" of the 1961 and earlier models, a Chicago Chrysler dealer noted, "when the cars came in here from Detroit, the doors didn't fit, the moldings didn't jibe, and the upholstery wasn't straight."[6]

The 1962 models, hurriedly restyled in late 1959 over Virgil Exner's objections, were a disaster for Chrysler. William Newberg, Chrysler's executive vice president, overheard a casual comment made by Edward Cole, Chevrolet's general manager, at a garden party that Chevrolet was going to introduce a smaller car in 1962, and Newberg mistakenly thought that GM was going to downsize *all* of its models. Cole was referring to the introduction of the Chevy II compact and nothing else. A panicky Newberg ordered all of Chrysler's 1962 models immediately downsized to "meet the competition." The result was a series of ungainly, ugly cars that few customers wanted.[7]

Chrysler Corporation's penchant for changing model designations in rapid order often left customers confused about brand and model identities. Under the Chrysler nameplate, for example, the pricy Saratoga disappeared in 1961 and Chrysler introduced the Newport, priced in the DeSoto range. The company offered two indistinguishable compacts for 1962—the Plymouth Valiant and the Dodge Lancer. Townsend summed up the problem in a *Time* interview in December 1962: "There are very few people who don't know what the Olds '88 is. It has always been in the same position and in the same price class. But at Chrysler we have had so much interruption in continuity of size, name and styles that customers didn't know what the Dodge 440 was or what the Plymouth Fury was—and they couldn't be assured that they would still be there next year." Finally, Chrysler's 1962 lineup featured compact and intermediate-sized cars, while offering little in the way of standard-sized models, which were popular that year.[8]

All of these failures relating to Chrysler's products produced a shrinking and demoralized dealer body and sales force. Since 1953, when Chrysler had 10,300 dealers, the automaker had had only two outstanding sales years—1955 and 1957. The total number of Chrysler Corporation franchises in North America had fallen to only 5,600 in 1962, the low point for the 1960s. In contrast, in 1962 Ford had 7,900 dealers and General Motors some 13,800. To make matters worse, in the early 1960s Chrysler had few dealers in the burgeoning suburbs and in the fast-growing Sunbelt states. Townsend estimated that the company lost 150,000 sales a year because it did not have enough outlets and another 150,000 units because the existing franchises were not very effective.[9]

During his first two or three years in office, Lynn Townsend introduced a series of temporary "fixes" that quickly reversed Chrysler's sales slump. In November 1961, Townsend replaced Virgil Exner as vice president for styling with Elwood Engel from Ford Motor Company. Engel, who was responsible for the highly acclaimed 1961 Lincoln Continental, was the director of Ford's advanced styling studio. The new Chrysler president, displeased with Exner's recent designs, was looking for a new head of styling. He and Engel met and discussed design ideas, salary, stock options, and the like. As part of the employment arrangement, Townsend agreed to have Engel report directly to him.[10]

Engel was able to make only minor cosmetic changes to the exterior look of the 1963 model cars, which were Exner's last designs for Chrysler. He did, however, make substantial changes to the all-new 1963 Valiant and designed Chrysler's 1963 turbine car. More important, Engel introduced a philosophy of styling that would give each car "continuity" and "identity." Styling changes from year to year would be gradual, so that customers would still recognize the model. At the same time, each model would be sufficiently distinctive in its appearance to establish its identity. Engel also reorganized the Chrysler styling operations. He replaced design studios that worked on a single body size across all the divisions (A-body, B-body, and so on) with independent Chrysler-Imperial, Dodge-Dart, and Plymouth-Valiant studios.[11]

By distinguishing the car lines from each other by size and price and by adding new models, Chrysler greatly improved its coverage of the market. For the 1962 model year, right after Townsend became president, Chrysler had no full-sized cars in its lineup and covered only about 60 percent of the potential market. By the 1965 model year, Chrysler calculated that its offerings covered 94 percent of the U.S. car market.[12]

To strengthen Chrysler's sales efforts and its dealerships, Townsend hired Virgil Edward Boyd (1912–)as vice president and general sales manager in February 1962. Boyd took a job in 1954 with the American Motors Corporation (AMC) as an assistant to the president. Appointed general sales manager for the Hudson Division in March 1956, Boyd became director of sales operations for

Lynn A. Townsend (*right*) and Phillip Buckminster (*left*), general manager of the Chrysler-Plymouth Division, with a 1965 Plymouth Fury. Courtesy of NAHC.

AMC in April 1960 and vice president of automotive sales in November 1961. He had barely settled into his new job when Townsend convinced him to work for Chrysler. Virgil E. Boyd later served in a variety of executive positions at Chrysler, concluding in 1967–70 with a stint as president.[13]

One of Boyd's goals was to build new dealerships in underrepresented locations and areas of population growth. He launched the Dealer Enterprise Program, by which Chrysler would advance up to 75 percent of the cost of opening a new franchise, but dealers would buy back the corporation's interest over time. Following this strategy, Chrysler expanded its coverage of two high-growth markets, Miami and Houston, spending $2 million in Miami alone. By the end of 1965, Chrysler had 6,507 dealers, a substantial improvement over the 5,600 dealers three years earlier.[14]

In a striking move to improve customer confidence, Townsend announced in August 1962 an extended warranty on Chrysler's 1963 model passenger cars. From 1931 through the 1960 models, Chrysler had offered customers what was the industry's standard coverage of the entire vehicle—90 days or 4,000 miles. Chrysler, Ford, and General Motors all increased the length of their warranties to 12 months/12,000 miles for the entire vehicle for the 1961 and 1962 models. Townsend offered Chrysler customers a five-year or 50,000-mile coverage on the power train (the engine, transmission, drive shaft, rear axle, differential, and

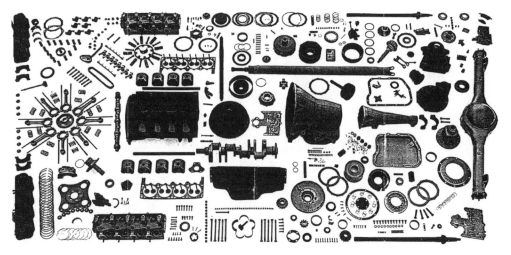

CHRYSLER CORPORATION WARRANTS EVERY PART YOU SEE HERE FOR 5 YEARS OR 50,000 MILES

Chrysler Corporation's quality engineering makes possible this new warranty*, by your authorized Chrysler Motors Corporation Dealer, covering all major parts of the engine, transmission, torque converter, drive shaft, universal joints, rear axle, differential, and rear wheel bearings.

It pays for labor as well as parts. It lasts for 5 years or 50,000 miles, protects your investment, and makes your car more valuable at trade-in time. It comes with our 1963 Plymouth, Valiant, Dodge, Dart, Chrysler and Imperial cars, and Dodge trucks.

It can be transferred to the new owner if you should sell your car. The only thing asked is that you have your car serviced at reasonable intervals. (You'd probably do that anyway.) It's another great automotive "first" from Chrysler

Corporation—another result of establishing and maintaining the highest engineering and production standards.

Advertisement for the Chrysler Corporation power train warranty for five years/50,000 miles, 1963 models. Courtesy of DCHC.

rear wheel bearings), while keeping the existing 12 months/12,000 miles warranty on the rest of the vehicle. Chrysler played to its greatest strength—its leadership in power train engineering.

A crucial element in Townsend's efforts to improve Chrysler's sales was a corporate identity program developed by a New York design and marketing consultant, Lippincott & Margulies (L&M). One of their goals was the creation of a new corporate symbol or logo. The Forward Look logo, which Chrysler had used since 1955, was closely tied with the Forward Look cars and especially with their fins. The new logo would represent all of Chrysler's products and services, not just passenger cars.[15]

Robert D. Stanley, who served as L&M's Chrysler account executive, developed the new corporate logo for Chrysler. His instructions were to develop a design that was simple, strong, easily recognized, and unique. Stanley considered more than 700 designs before settling on the Pentastar, a pentagon surrounding a five-pointed star. It had a unique, "engineered" appearance that Townsend found appealing.[16]

Chrysler introduced the Pentastar in fall 1962 on advertisements, product literature, and dealers' signs. From the beginning, the Pentastar was made part of a distinct motif using a newly-formulated color dubbed "Chrysler blue" and white. Chrysler/Plymouth Dealers used the blue and white scheme, while

Dodge dealers had the more daring red and white motif. The Pentastar, however, was only one part of the corporate identity campaign. Townsend created a separate corporate identity office in September 1962 and named Francis E. Cogsdill as its director.[17]

Chrysler Corporation also became heavily involved in automobile racing in the 1960s and early 1970s, using it as a promotional device. Robert Anderson, vice president for product planning, explained corporate policy toward professional racing at a meeting of automotive and mechanical engineers in Pittsburgh in February 1964:

> Automobile men can argue by the hour about the value of competitive racing in terms of its effect on sales of conventional cars. And no one has ever come up with a definitive measure of that value. We do feel sure at Chrysler, however, that for a company with our tradition of emphasis upon engineering and our long record of automotive innovation and product leadership, it is definitely to our advantage to make a respectable showing in competitive events.[18]

Chrysler's Hemi V-8 engines powered Carl Kiekhaefer's Mercury (outboard motor) racing team to many NASCAR (National Association for Stock Car Auto Racing) victories starting in 1955. Lee Petty (father of Richard Petty) was also a force on the NASCAR circuit in the 1950s, winning championships in 1954 and 1959 with his own Hemi-equipped Chrysler and Dodge cars.

Chrysler had a long relationship with the Petty family through Petty Engineering of Randleman, North Carolina. Lee Petty drove a Plymouth to his third NASCAR title in 1959, but following an accident at Daytona in 1961, son Richard replaced him behind the wheel. Richard Petty began racing on the NASCAR convertible circuit in July 1958 and won his first race a year later in a 1959 Plymouth. From 1960 through the end of 1967, Richard Petty started 360 races, won 76 of these, and finished in the top five in 206. He drove his famous Number 43 Plymouths in all of his victories over this stretch. Richard Petty won the NASCAR Grand National Title in 1964, 1967, and 1971, while finishing high in the rankings in the years he did not win.[19]

Richard Petty shocked the racing world by leaving Chrysler for the 1969 season and racing for Ford. He cited Plymouth's lack of a competitive car as his reason for the change. He returned to Plymouth in 1970, racing its new streamlined winged Superbird. Chrysler's relationship with Petty Engineering (Petty Enterprises by 1970) continued into the late 1970s. Richard Petty raced a Plymouth Hemi Roadrunner in 1971 and 1972 and a series of Dodge Chargers from 1972 to 1977. Petty Enterprises suddenly ended its relationship with Chrysler in late July 1978 and started racing Pontiacs and other General Motors cars.[20]

Driver Richard Petty with his famous Number 43 Plymouth race car meets President Richard M. Nixon at the White House, 1971. Courtesy of DCHC.

The combined effect of Townsend's short-term moves to bolster sales and a strong market for new cars brought a quick recovery for Chrysler, as table 12.1 illustrates.

Early in his tenure, Townsend made two strategic decisions that greatly benefited Chrysler by the mid-1960s. He created a modern, centralized, and computer-based system for reporting sales, orders, and costs. His corporate information processing center in Highland Park had five mainframe computers and a staff of 100. The system brought improved financial control over the automaker's far-flung operations and permitted more meaningful market forecasts. In late 1963, when Chrysler's sales were within 300,000 units of its manufacturing capability, Townsend opted for an aggressive capital spending program to increase capacity. By investing $400 million in 1964 and another $500 million in 1965, he increased capacity by the end of 1966 by 200,000 units.[21]

Much of what Townsend accomplished happened through the sheer force of his energy, determination, and intelligence, shown in his blunt, aggressive management style. He had a quick, analytic mind, and before his brief term as administrative vice president was done, he understood all of the automaker's key operations. One Chrysler executive, in describing Townsend, said: "He pushes hard. He's a driver. He doesn't like memos. He handles things on a man-to-man basis, drops in your office and says, 'How about this?' He's very

TABLE 12.1 Chrysler Corporation Performance, North American Market, 1960–69

	Unit Production	Market Share* (%)	Net Earnings†		
			Total ($)	On Sales (%)	On Capital Invested‡
1960	1,136,963	14.0	32,154,393	1.1	4.6
1961	772,633	10.8	11,138,436	0.5	1.6
1962	873,488	9.6	65,433,936	2.8	8.5
1963	1,254,688	12.4	161,595,098	4.6	17.5
1964	1,481,040	13.8	213,770,302	5.0	19.1
1965	1,763,302	14.7	233,377,308	4.4	14.7
1966	1,766,734	15.4	189,227,700	3.4	11.1
1967	1,723,111	16.1	200,434,400	3.2	10.9
1968	1,972,871	16.3	290,728,807	3.9	14.1
1969	1,771,480	15.1	88,771,222	1.2	4.2

Sources: Chrysler Corporation annual reports, 1960–69, box "Annual Reports 1925–69," DCHC; and "Financial and General Fact Book," June 1973, DCHC.

*As measured by new car and truck registrations.
†After taxes.
‡Defined as stockholders' equity and surpluses.

direct and keeps the pressure on all the time. Lynn doesn't hide behind committees. He doesn't need a committee for self-defense."[22] In meetings, he expected people to speak bluntly and would respond likewise, sometimes appearing rude. His executives often said things in public that you would never hear from top officials at GM or Ford. When Chrysler was actively promoting stock car racing in the early 1960s at Daytona Beach and elsewhere, Paul Ackerman, vice president for engineering, publically spoke against Chrysler's involvement. In describing Townsend's style, Robert Anderson, Chrysler vice president for manufacturing, noted, "Lynn has a nice, friendly, damned long needle which he administers with a cheery smile."[23]

Above all else, Townsend was careful, cautious, and deliberate in making decisions. Describing his approach, Townsend said, "I am methodical, not flamboyant, in my thinking, and I tried to touch all the bases." He believed in the overriding importance of planning. He once explained: "I'm not interested in having one particular hot car; I'm interested in having each one go in accordance with our plans." Townsend's personality and management style brought to Chrysler exactly what it needed in the early 1960s—a cold, objective evaluation of everything the company was doing.[24]

By any measure, Lynn Townsend's initial four and one-half years as Chrysler's president were successful. Vehicle production in 1964 was higher than any other year since 1955, and in 1965 production reached an all-time high. Townsend achieved this turnaround through cost-cutting, a return to middle-of-the-road styling, and by reviving the sales force and dealer network. In the early 1960s, he also set into motion several long-range initiatives—some bearing fruit in the late 1960s and beyond, others proving disappointing. Four deserve a detailed examination—the globalization of Chrysler Corporation, the expansion and modernization of facilities in North America, continued involvement in the defense and space business, and the experimental turbine car.

CHRYSLER INTERNATIONAL

Lynn Townsend's greatest single achievement at Chrysler was changing the company into a multinational automobile producer. With the exception of Chrysler of Canada, established in 1925, the corporation had at best a minor international presence until Townsend took the post of group vice president for international operations in 1958. The other members of the Big Three, however, had long-established manufacturing operations overseas, particularly in Europe. Ford established the Ford Motor Company (England) in March 1911. Ford's strategy was to manufacture cars in Great Britain and thence ship them to the rest of Europe. General Motors came to Europe a bit later, buying Britain's Vauxhall Motors in 1925 and an 80 percent interest in Germany's Adam Opel A.G. in 1929. As early as 1925, General Motors controlled six automobile assembly plants in Europe, one in South Africa, and another in Australia.[25]

Chrysler's presence in Canada changed substantially during the Townsend years. By manufacturing vehicles in Canada, part of the British Empire and (later) Commonwealth, Chrysler could ship its cars throughout the "Sterling Block" free of duties, allowing access to the United Kingdom, Australia, New Zealand, and South Africa. The Canada–United States Automotive Trade Agreement (Autopact) signed in early 1965 allowed duty-free trade in vehicles and parts in both directions, provided that the value of imports and exports were equal. Before this agreement, American auto companies had to produce almost all the cars and trucks for the Canadian market in Canada, resulting in low production runs and higher costs. With the Autopact, American companies could reduce the number of models they assembled in Canada while increasing the volumes of the models they assembled there.[26]

Chrysler and its predecessor companies were successful in exporting a goodly number of cars to foreign markets during the 1920s. Exports virtually ended in the 1930s and 1940s and when they revived in the 1950s, Chrysler sold what were called "Completely Knock-Down Sets" or CKDSs. These were kits of components that were assembled in their destination country. In Argentina, for example, Fevre & Basset became the Dodge distributor for that country in 1916 and the Chrysler distributor in 1931. In Mexico, local investors launched Fabricas Automex in October 1938 and assembled 1,200 cars in the following year. By the mid-1960s, Automex assembled 25,000 Chrysler cars annually.[27]

Tex Colbert and Lynn Townsend made several unsuccessful efforts to gain instant entry into the global automobile industry. In the late 1950s, Colbert tried to buy Rolls-Royce and Volkswagen, but both rebuffed him. In the early 1960s, Chrysler approached the Quandt brothers of Munich, owners of the Bavarian Motor Works (BMW), but they were not interested in selling. In a move that today seems ironic, Chrysler made a bid to purchase Daimler-Benz, mainly to get its heavy-duty truck business. The Flick family, which controlled the company, was not interested in selling outright, proposing instead an exchange of shares, which would have made them the largest stockholder in Chrysler Corporation. The American company rejected that offer.[28]

Chrysler's second major move to expand into international car markets was the 1958 purchase (for $28.1 million) of 25 percent of the stock of Simca. This was the largest privately owned automobile company in France and the second largest in terms of production. Established in 1934, Simca (Société Industrielle de Mécanique et Carrosserie) initially manufactured Fiats for the French market. Ford Motor Company had sold its French operations to Simca in November 1954 for 15.2 percent of the French automaker's stock. Chrysler simply bought up Ford's shares and an additional 9.8 percent from other sources. By investing another $97 million in 1963, Chrysler acquired an additional 38 percent stock ownership in Simca Automobiles, giving it a controlling interest of 63 percent. The French company became the Société des Automobiles Simca at the end of 1965. With further investments of $17 million in 1965 and $19 million in 1966, Chrysler increased its Simca holdings to 77 percent.[29]

With the Simca purchase, Chrysler injected itself into a political/economic environment not always favorable to the American company's self-interest. The French government at first welcomed foreign investment, but by the early 1960s, with a resurgence of nationalism under Charles de Gaulle, the government became suspicious of foreign control. Chrysler gained its majority interest in Simca by buying stock outside of France and out of reach of French exchange controls, which outraged the French government. At the time, the minister of finance stated, "it is not desirable that important sectors of the Common Market's economy be controlled by outside decisions." Following Chrysler's takeover of Simca, the French government discouraged further investment.[30]

Chrysler bought an interest in Simca to establish a position in the European market and to gain a supply of small cars to sell in the United States. Chrysler dealers in the United States sold only 7,280 Simcas in 1958, but an impressive 55,256 units the following year. This proved to be the peak for sales, which fell to 36,310 in 1960 and then to only 11,395 in 1962. Despite the disappointing sales record, Townsend remained optimistic that U.S. sales of Simca cars would improve.[31]

In 1958, Chrysler founded Chrysler International, S.A., a wholly owned subsidiary based in Geneva, Switzerland, to develop and coordinate Chrysler's overseas operations. By 1963, the division operated manufacturing or assembly plants in 11 countries—France, England, South Africa, Australia, Holland, Turkey, Greece, the Philippines, Mexico, Venezuela, and Argentina. Chrysler International's sales rose from 45,985 units in 1959 to 73,249 units in 1962, still not an enormous number. More important, Chrysler's share of American-built cars sold outside of North America jumped from 16.2 percent in 1958 to 22.3 percent in 1962. Its greatest sales successes were in the United Kingdom and its former colonies.[32]

Townsend's efforts to acquire European automobile companies extended beyond the borders of France. During the first half of 1962, the American company had tried without success to buy a substantial interest in the Leyland Group (Leyland Motors and Standard Triumph), which accounted for 43.5 percent of British automobile production at the time. Chrysler proposed an exchange of stock, leaving each company with 22.5 percent of the stock of the other company. Donald Stokes, the chairman of the Leyland board, expressed concerns about Chrysler's lack of market penetration in the United States and vetoed the deal.[33]

In June 1964, Chrysler bought a minority interest in Rootes Motors, the fourth largest British automaker—but a distant fourth, with only 12.6 percent of the market. Rootes had a history extending back to the end of the First World War, when brothers William Edward (1894–1964) and Reginald Claude (1896–1977) Rootes began as automobile distributers. In 1928, they bought a controlling interest in the Humber Company, maker of the Humber car. Over the years, they bought several established automobile companies, including Hillman, Sunbeam, and Singer. Rootes earned only small profits from 1956 onward and lost money in 1957, 1962, and 1963. It needed additional capital to survive when Chrysler appeared on the scene, an ideal suitor looking for a business marriage.[34]

Chrysler paid $35 million for 30 percent of the voting shares of Rootes stock and 50 percent of the nonvoting shares. Commentators on both sides of the Atlantic, *Business Week* and the *Observer,* thought this was a perfect marriage. With the approval of the Labour government, Chrysler purchased another 15 percent of the voting shares in Rootes in May 1965 for $33 million, raising its stake to 45 percent. Chrysler bought another 22.3 percent in January 1967 for

$23 million, giving it a majority interest. The British government tried to block the purchase by inviting British Leyland and British Motor Company to rescue the near bankrupt Rootes, but both refused, leaving the way clear for Chrysler.[35]

Chrysler's infusion of new capital into Rootes gave the company a temporary boost but did not solve the problems faced by the British manufacturer. Unpopular products reduced its share of the U.K. market from 12.6 percent in 1964 to a mere 6.6 percent in 1975, while nearly constant labor unrest cut production and reduced efficiency. During the years 1960 through 1967, Rootes earned substantial profits only in 1960, 1961, and 1964.[36]

Chrysler bought a 40 percent interest in the Spanish truck manufacturer Barreiros Diesel S.A. in 1963 for $19.8 million and spent an additional $36.7 million on Barreiros shares in 1967, giving it 77.1 percent of the equity in the firm. Chrysler invested $20 million in the company in 1967 and made a commitment to invest another $35 million, but Barreiros consistently lost money. Chrysler increased its share of the stock to 86 percent in 1969, and in 1970 renamed the firm Chrysler España S.A.[37]

In addition to the major investments in Simca, Rootes, and Barreiros Diesel, Chrysler created foreign-based subsidiaries that built more than a half-dozen assembly plants outside of Europe, including facilities in Venezuela (1959), South Africa (1959), Turkey (1962), the Philippines (1963), Peru (1964), Columbia (1965), and Brazil (1966). For the most part, Chrysler owned 100 percent of the stock in these subsidiaries. Exceptions included Chrysler Sanayi, A.S., which operated a truck plant in Istanbul, Turkey (60 percent ownership), the Columbian subsidiary (76 percent), and Chrysler's Brazilian operation (92 percent).[38]

Much of Chrysler's growth in the 1960s and early 1970s came from its overseas operations. The 1963 spike in sales of vehicles manufactured outside of North America reflects the inclusion of Simca's output for the first time, after Chrysler gained control of the French company (see table 12.2).

Chrysler's two large European operations dominated the scene. In 1967, for example, vehicle production from Simca (256,331 units) and Rootes (215,963) combined accounted for 80 percent of production outside of North America. This was still the case in 1970, but the two became less important in the years that followed as production from Rootes fell off sharply.[39]

North American Investment, Defense, and Space

Chrysler's core automotive business remained in North America, where it made substantial investments in the 1960s and early 1970s. Construction began in the early 1960s on an enormous stamping plant in Sterling Heights, Michigan, and an assembly plant in Belvidere, Illinois, with a capacity of 200,000 vehicles per

TABLE 12.2 Chrysler Global Sales, 1960–69

	Unit Sales	Unit Sales of Vehicles Manufactured Outside North America	Share of Total (%)
1960	1,183,311	46,348	3.9
1961	802,003	29,381	3.7
1962	892,299	18,811	2.1
1963	1,518,586	263,898	17.4
1964	1,807,258	326,211	18.1
1965	2,076,523	313,221	15.1
1966	2,134,024	406,978	19.1
1967	2,245,583	522,472	23.3
1968	2,610,016	637,145	24.4
1969	2,431,551	660,071	27.1

Sources: Chrysler Corporation annual reports, 1960–69, box "Annual Reports 1925–69," DCHC.

year. These both came on line in 1965, along with a new aluminum casting plant in Kokomo, Indiana. To further increase capacity, in 1968 the company began building an assembly plant in New Stanton, Pennsylvania (near Pittsburgh), with a capacity of 200,000 units a year. New Stanton was to cost $100 million and was to be completed by fall 1970.[40]

Under Townsend's leadership, Chrysler continued to work in the fields of defense and space, but government contracts became less important over time. The large contracts of 1952–58, which accounted for as much as 20 percent of Chrysler's revenues, largely disappeared. Between 1960 and 1963, defense and space work accounted for 7–10 percent of Chrysler's overall sales, stood at 5 percent in 1964–65, and then fell to only 2 percent in 1970. In January 1977, Chrysler's Defense Group employed only 4,275 at a time when the company's North American employment was more than 130,000.[41]

Chrysler continued to produce tanks, trucks, and other special-purpose vehicles. The company manufactured 6,292 M-48 tanks at Newark, Delaware, from 1952 to 1959 and then worked with the army to develop the replacement medium tank, the M-60. Design work began in 1958 and the first tank rolled off the assembly line at the Lenape Ordnance Depot in Newark, Delaware, in October 1959. The new model, powered by a V-12 air-cooled diesel engine, came equipped with a 105 mm main gun. Chrysler assembled the first 360 M-60 medium tanks at the Newark, Delaware, plant, but ended production there in October 1960. Work shifted to the Detroit tank arsenal in Warren, with the M-60A1 replacing the M-60 in spring of 1962. Chrysler's production of the M-60 series extended from 1959 through 1979, with a total output of 12,166 tanks.[42]

On the heels of its successful work on the Redstone missile booster, Chrysler took on the job of designing, building, and testing the first stage booster for the Saturn space vehicle. The National Aeronautics and Space Administration (NASA) selected Chrysler as the prime contractor for this 80-foot rocket in November 1961 and awarded a contract in August 1962 for the production and testing of 21 Saturn S-1 booster rockets. A modified contract had Chrysler complete 8 S-1 boosters and 12 copies of the more powerful S-1B booster. Design and production took place at the NASA Michaud plant, where Chrysler had made engines for the M-48 tank in the early 1950s. Chrysler delivered the first S-1 booster in December 1963, right on schedule.[43]

The first Chrysler-built S-1 booster helped launch a scientific satellite on 25 May 1965. Three successful Saturn-1B booster launches followed in February-August 1966. Chrysler-built boosters lifted the first two Apollo spacecraft into earth orbits, with an unmanned flight in January 1968 and the first manned flight on 11 October 1968. Additional boosters were later used in NASA's Skylab program in 1973, to transport Skylab crews up to the orbiting space station. Chrysler's involvement in the Saturn program served NASA well and brought the automaker a degree of prestige, but had little long-term impact on its core vehicle business. The same can be said for Chrysler's intriguing and expensive flirtation with a turbine-powered car.[44]

The Turbine Car

One potentially significant automotive engineering breakthrough that came to full fruition under Townsend—the turbine engine automobile—brought Chrysler a good deal of positive publicity but few concrete benefits. The company seemed on the verge of a competitive breakthrough when it unveiled the Chrysler Turbine Car in May 1963.

The *Saturday Evening Post* predicted that Chrysler would produce gas turbine vehicles in volume in 1966 or 1967. In a *Ward's Quarterly* interview in 1965, Lynn Townsend said of the gas turbine engine, "It stands the greatest chance of becoming a new engine concept of anything being worked on in the industry today. I have high hopes. I think it's terrific." *Ward's* optimistically predicted that Chrysler would offer a limited-production turbine car to the general public by the 1967 model year.[45] Chrysler's rivals, however, were highly skeptical about the likelihood of a production turbine car. General Motors' chairman, Frederic G. Donner, dismissed turbine engines as impractical, while Ford's president, Arjay Miller, believed that their use would be limited to trucks.

The use of turbine technology was well established in other applications. Hydraulic turbines (turbines that harnessed the power of falling water) had been used in France and the United States since the 1820s and 1830s. Engineers and millwrights had designed machines with fanlike curved blades that formed a wheel and efficiently transferred the force of water to a drive shaft. In the 1880s, inventors Charles Parsons (Great Britain) and Carl De Laval (Sweden) developed practical steam turbines. The gas turbine, by contrast, uses the explosive power of expanding gas released from burning a mixture of fuel and compressed air in a combustion chamber. The escaping gas hits the blades of the turbine wheel, producing rotary power that is transmitted to the car's wheels.[46]

Chrysler's engineers were well aware of the potential advantages of the gas turbine engine over the conventional internal combustion engine. With 80 percent fewer parts, the gas turbine engine would need less maintenance and have a longer life expectancy. It would face no problems in starting in cold weather, require no warm-up, and use no antifreeze because it is air-cooled. It would operate free of vibration and noise. Theoretically, the turbine engine would be more economical to operate over the long run. It would weigh 300 pounds less than conventional engines and could burn gasoline, diesel fuel, or kerosene.[47]

Chrysler was not the first American automobile company to try gas turbine engines. One unsubstantiated story had Henry Ford experimenting in the 1920s with a gas turbine engine that blew up. One of Chrysler's engineers, George Huebner Jr., began designing an automotive gas turbine engine as early as 1939. General Motors produced the turbine-powered Firebird I show car in 1954, and Ford installed Boeing gas turbines in a Thunderbird and a full-size Ford the same year. In 1955, Ford showcased the Model 701 (Ford Mystere) turbine car.[48]

Chrysler nevertheless led the way in gas turbine research starting in the mid-1950s. The company announced on 25 March 1954 that it had successfully road tested a gas turbine engine of its own design in a 1954 production model Plymouth, an industry first. The company displayed this car at the Waldorf-Astoria in New York on 7–11 April and then demonstrated the car at the Chelsea Proving Grounds on 16 June 1954. The 100 hp engine was equipped with a heat exchanger, or regenerator, that reused hot exhausts and resulted in fuel economy comparable to that of piston engines. A year later, Chrysler engineers installed the same engine in a 1955 Plymouth Belvedere four-door sedan, which Chrysler's drivers tested on Detroit streets.[49]

Chrysler's turbine engineers completed a historic cross-country endurance test in March 1956 using a standard production model 1956 Plymouth four-door sedan equipped with essentially the same engine used earlier. The endurance test began on 26 March at the Chrysler Building in New York and ended at the Los Angeles City Hall on 30 March. Two engineering research teams of four men each shared the driving duties and kept records of the car's fuel usage and performance. They completed the trip of 3,020 miles with only two minor repairs needed along the way. The car generally cruised at 40–45 mph and averaged 13 mpg using standard gasoline and diesel fuel.

The first gas turbine cars had essentially the same engine, still an experimental prototype in most respects. Chrysler's engineers labeled it the "first generation engine"; seven additional engine generations followed, the last of these designed and tested in 1977–81. The 50-car test program of 1963–66 used the fourth generation engine. The engineers struggled for more than a quarter-century to improve the engine's fuel mileage, performance, and reliability, but the gas turbine engine never went into service in a standard line of production cars at Chrysler.

After the 1956 cross-country endurance test, Chrysler's engineers designed the second generation engine, featuring an improved compressor, with efficiency increased from 70 percent to 80 percent; a modified regenerator or heat exchanger, which reclaimed 90 percent of the heat from the exhaust gas; and an improved burner. This new engine was installed in a 1959 Plymouth four-door hardtop, which in December 1958 made an economy test run of 576 miles from Toledo to Woodbridge, New Jersey, via the Ohio, Pennsylvania, and New Jersey turnpikes. The car averaged 19.39 miles per gallon of diesel fuel on the trip east, but only 17.17 miles per gallon on the return trip from New Jersey to Highland Park. Still, this was an noticeable improvement over the 13–14 mpg of the 1956 cross-country run.[50]

Chrysler equipped a 1962 Dodge Dart with a third generation turbine engine and sent it on a coast-to-coast test run of 3,100 miles from New York to Los Angeles 17–31 December 1961. The acceleration lag from idle to full-rated output was only two seconds, down from seven seconds on the first generation engine. A 1962 Plymouth Fury equipped with this engine, along with the Turbo Dart, began extensive "consumer reaction tours" of dealerships at ninety American cities starting in January 1962. Public response to these turbine cars was so positive that Chrysler announced on 14 February 1962 that it would build 50–75 turbine-equipped cars and offer them to select users for testing.[51]

The turbine engine that would power the cars used in this national test program was the fourth generation engine, an improved version of the previous model. It featured a centrally located burner and two regenerators instead of one. The engine was more compact than the one it replaced and weighed 410 pounds compared to the third generation's 450. Chrysler claimed it was more lively and quieter. Most of the major size and performance specifications were largely unchanged.[52]

Chrysler began its limited production turbine car program on 14–15 May 1963 in New York City with unveilings at the Essex House and the Waldorf-Astoria Hotel and a ride-drive program for the press at Roosevelt Raceway on Long Island. These all-new two-door hardtops had a body designed by Elwood Engel at Chrysler, but had been built by Ghia of Italy. The resemblance to Engels's 1961 Ford Thunderbird design is striking. The turbine cars were to be

Stylist Elwood Engel with a 1963 Chrysler Turbine Car. Courtesy of DCHC.

assembled at a rate of one a week at the engineering facilities in Highland Park, where Chrysler also built and tested the engines, until all 50 were finished by October 1964. Starting on 29 October 1963, these cars would be given to motorists to drive for a three-month period, at no charge. The driver would pay for fuel, but Chrysler would insure the vehicles and perform all maintenance free of charge. Over a two-year period, a total of 203 motorists drove the turbine cars, with the last handing her vehicle back to Chrysler on 28 January 1966. The first motorist to participate in the program was Richard E. Vlaha and the last was Patricia Anderson, both from the Chicago area.[53]

Chrysler carefully monitored the performance of the forty-six turbine cars actually put into the hands of the motoring public and compiled detailed records of every aspect of the program. The company's marketing and consumer research department conducted in-depth interviews with the turbine car users within two weeks after the motorist was finished with the car. The majority of users cited three major advantages of the turbine car over conventional vehicles—the smooth, vibrationless operation, reduced maintenance requirements, and ease of starting in all conditions. However, many from the test group complained about slow acceleration from a standing start, poor fuel economy, and noise levels produced by the engine.[54]

Roger Huntington, an engineer writing about Chrysler's turbine engine in *Ward's Quarterly* in winter 1965, believed that Chrysler's engineers had overcome all of the basic problems inherent in turbine cars with their fourth generation engine. The use of improved regenerators resulted in fuel economy comparable to that of piston engines, varying the pitch of the turbine wheel guide vanes improved acceleration, and new alloys greatly reduced the cost of the turbine wheels and other components.[55]

To address the complaints about the fuel economy and performance of the turbine test cars, Chrysler's engineers developed a fifth generation engine, with larger regenerators and higher cycle temperatures than the previous engines. The company planned a limited production run of 500 turbine-equipped 1967 Dodge Charger coupes, but plans had to be scrapped because the engine failed to meet government-mandated emissions standards. A sixth generation engine followed, but work on the project was greatly curtailed in 1969, when Chrysler assigned more of its engineers to work on improving vehicle emissions to comply with the federal Clean Air Act of 1967. The sixth generation engine was field-tested in a single 1966 Dodge Coronet from 1966 until early 1973, but this car was not displayed for public viewing.[56]

Turbine car development and the efforts to expand into overseas markets never produced the long-term benefits Townsend had hoped for. In many respects, these efforts to expand and diversify became distractions, spreading Chrysler's already-thin executive talent pool even thinner. Townsend's impressive successes in the early 1960s faded, and in the later years of his administration, especially in 1969–75, the missteps became more frequent—and Chrysler suffered accordingly.

Chapter 13

THE LYNN TOWNSEND ERA

THE LEAN YEARS, 1969–79

The lack of profits [at Chrysler Corporation] has created a liquidity problem. That means that the already-debt-laden company will have to scramble for several hundred million dollars in outside financing in the coming months to pay for an ambitious capital spending program dictated both by Chrysler's internal five-year plan to overhaul its product line and by government orders to improve the fuel efficiency and safety features of its vehicles. The latest squeeze at Chrysler had caused some renewed handwringing by outsiders about the corporation's long-term ability to survive.

—Washington Post

In sharp contrast to his early tenure at Chrysler, Lynn Townsend's later years saw little success and much disappointment in the company's performance. His management systems and his management style corrected many fundamental weaknesses the company faced in 1961 when he assumed the presidency. In many respects, his first seven years were easy ones because he could quickly fix glaring problems such as badly styled cars, overstaffing, and a poor corporate image. Chrysler expanded under Townsend into areas the company's management was ill suited to operate. The diversion of resources into international automotive ventures and into domestic real estate was both a drain on capital and a distraction from the core North American car and truck business. Chrysler lacked an adequate pool of managers to efficiently operate the many new ventures that Townsend began during his early years.

From 1969 on, Chrysler failed to produce enough high-quality, stylish, and appropriately sized cars and trucks to appeal to the North American market. At a time when Volkswagen and the Japanese automakers were selling cars practically free of defects and both Ford and General Motors were improving the quality of their vehicles, Chrysler's products were often shoddy. The strategies and policies of Lynn Townsend and his management team of John J. Riccardo and Eugene A. Cafiero were the source of Chrysler's weak products. Townsend retired in 1975, but decisions made under his watch led directly to the sales and financial crisis of 1975–78 and Chrysler's near bankruptcy.

THE ANATOMY OF DECLINE

The downturn of Chrysler's fortunes, as chronicled by national business magazines, was remarkably rapid. Fast on the heels of an optimistic November 1968 *Fortune* article, "Chrysler's Well-Ordered Comeback," in July 1969, *Business Week* ran "What's Wrong at Chrysler," criticizing the company's failure to produce small cars. Suddenly, none of the industry observers saw much hope for the number three automaker. *Fortune* ran a lengthy analysis in April 1970: "Chrysler's Private Hard Times." *Business Week* followed with "Chrysler Tries without a Mini" in September 1970 and "How Chrysler Fights a Skid" the following April. The stream of gloomy commentaries continued, with a December 1973 *Forbes* article, "What's Wrong at Chrysler?" attacking the company's failure to develop small cars.[1]

Were these negative perceptions and even more negative forecasts about Chrysler's future justified? Overall performance, as seen in table 13.1, was mediocre at best after 1968.

Except for 1972 and 1973, these were not good years for Chrysler. High sales volumes simply did not translate into earnings, and huge losses in 1974 and 1975 did not bode well for the future.

Chrysler's troubles were the result of a combination of influences, many of these beyond the automaker's control. The energy crisis of 1973–75 was perhaps the most important factor. Deteriorating labor relations with the UAW and with the company's younger workers was another. Increased federal government regulation was the most troublesome issue.

On the heels of his initial successes as Chrysler's president, Lynn Townsend replaced George Love as chairman of the board on 1 January 1967 and named Virgil E. Boyd to the presidency. Boyd, also originally trained as an accountant, had served as vice president of automotive sales at American Motors Corporation before coming to Chrysler in February 1962. The managerial restructuring of January 1967 had included the promotion of John J. Riccardo to Boyd's former position as group vice president–U.S. and Canadian Automotive.

Townsend's choice raised many eyebrows because Riccardo was another accountant and Townsend's protégé. More important, Townsend had passed over Robert Anderson, who had worked for Chrysler since 1946 and had shown his ability to manage engineering, product planning, and manufacturing. Seeing quite clearly that he had no future at Chrysler, Anderson left early in 1968 to become executive vice president at North American Rockwell Corporation, later president and chairman.[2]

At Townsend's request, Boyd took an early (and unwanted) retirement on 8 January 1970, serving as a scapegoat for the company's poor performance in 1969–70. As part of the managerial realignment of January 1970, Riccardo

TABLE 13.1 Chrysler Corporation Performance, North American Market, 1968–79

| | Unit Production | Market Share* (%) | Net Earnings† | | |
			Total ($)	On Sales (%)	On Capital Invested‡ (%)
1968	1,972,871	16.3	290,728,807	3.9	14.1
1969	1,771,480	5.1	88,771,222	1.2	4.2
1970	1,713,672	16.1	(7,603,020)	(0.2)	(0.4)
1971	1,778,311	14.3	83,659,587	1.1	3.8
1972	2,013,470	4.3	220,455,261	2.3	8.9
1973	2,230,014	13.0	165,500,000	2.8	9.7
1974	1,782,285	13.4	(41,400,000)	(0.6)	(1.6)
1975	1,585,950	12.2	(259,500,000)	(3.0)	(8.6)
1976	2,076,649	13.6	422,600,000	3.5	11.7
1977	2,011,646	12.2	163,200,000	1.2	5.6
1978	1,878,411	11.3	(204,600,000)	(1.6)	(31.6)
1979	1,414,066	10.1	(1,097,300,000)	(9.6)	(169.9)

Sources: Chrysler Corporation annual reports, 1968–79, box "Annual Reports 1968–98," DCHC; and "Financial and General Fact Book," February 1986, DCHC.
Note: Losses are indicated in parentheses.

*As measured by new car and truck registrations.
°After taxes.
‡Defined as stockholders' equity and surpluses.

named his own replacement as group vice president–U.S. and Canadian Automotive: Eugene Cafiero, a low-ranking vice president in charge of Latin American operations. Riccardo, who served as Chrysler's president until 1 October 1975, in effect named the unknown Cafiero as his eventual successor.[3]

John J. Riccardo (2 July 1924–) had grown up in Little Falls, New York, the son of an Italian immigrant who worked as a laborer. After the Second World War, he enrolled at the University of Michigan, where he earned a master's degree in economics. In 1950, he took a job with the accounting firm of Touche, Ross, where he first became Lynn Townsend's protégé. Townsend left Touche, Ross for Chrysler in 1957; Riccardo followed two years later. With the older man's patronage, Riccardo received promotions at Chrysler almost every year until he reached the post of group vice president–U.S. and Canadian Automotive on 20 April 1967, in charge of all of North American automobile production and sales. His rapid rise in the company hierarchy earned him the nickname "the Rocket." In many respects, Riccardo was simply a younger Townsend—a very bright, brusque, hard-nosed, demanding manager.[4]

When difficult times came, Townsend ordered draconian—and short-sighted—cutbacks. When Chrysler faced sales slumps and losses in 1969–71 and 1974–75, Townsend ordered sharp reductions in spending on new plants and delays in new product development. The result was the postponing of the new products the company needed to regain its lost sales. Chrysler's capital expenditures of $647 million in 1969 fell to only $250 million in 1971. After allowing capital expenditures to recover to $629 million for 1973, Townsend slashed spending to $384 million for 1975. In contrast, General Motors and Ford routinely kept capital spending stable during downturns in sales.[5]

Townsend's management strategy included the belief that anyone could do any job, regardless of expertise or experience. In discussing his choices of vice presidents, Townsend told a *Fortune* writer, "You'll see engineers selling, book-keepers in other jobs, and a lawyer as v.p. of finance." When he appointed John J. Riccardo group vice president–U.S. and Canadian Automotive in April 1967, Riccardo had been at Chrysler only 8 years; managers at General Motors would normally need close to 30 years to reach that position. When Lee Iacocca came to Chrysler, he was shocked to see so many vice presidents in jobs they knew nothing about: "I have never seen anything like it. The vice-presidents were all square pegs in round holes. Townsend and his people had taken guys who had performed well enough in one area and had moved them around at will. Their attitude was that a guy with talent could climb any mountain. After a few years of being shuffled around, everybody at Chrysler was doing something he wasn't trained for. And believe me, it showed."[6] Townsend saw his own success at president and chairman of Chrysler, despite his background in accounting, as evidence that specialists were not needed. The performance of his handpicked executives suggests otherwise.

BIG CARS, SMALL CARS, MUSCLE CARS (AND A CARTOON BIRD)

Chrysler's product line consisted mainly of stodgy, conservative, middle-of-the-road cars. They reflected the preferences of Elwood P. Engel, the vice president for styling from November 1961 through 1972. He officially retired in 1973, but stayed on as a consultant until July 1974. In evaluating Engel's career, Lamm and Holls noted, "Elwood Engel did not leave a vast array of memorable designs at Chrysler. He's remembered as the man who removed the tailfins from Chrysler products, although they were nearly all gone by the time he arrived." Reflecting Townsend's desire to end the styling excesses of the 1950s, Engel became the "anti-Exner" stylist as much as anything else. The 1964 models were the last to offer pushbutton controls for the automatic transmission, a Forward Look trademark. The company explained that eliminating this feature would make owners of other brands feel more comfortable when they test-drove a Chrysler product. Engel's designs seemed to closely imitate the simple, austere look of his successful 1961 Ford Thunderbird.[7]

At the same time, Chrysler Corporation made a substantial commitment to improve styling by building a state-of-the-art styling and design center at the Highland Park headquarters. Designed by the architect Minoru Yamasaki, the complex was a set of interconnected buildings that housed the offices of product planning, advanced engineering, and styling, but also included two body studios and a domed showroom for viewing clay models of proposed car designs under ideal lighting conditions. When Lynn Townsend officially dedicated the facility on 2 August 1972 as the Walter P. Chrysler Building, he also renamed the General Office Building the K. T. Keller Building.[8]

Chrysler's sales fell off in the late 1960s, beginning most noticeably with the 1969 models. The market was gradually moving toward smaller cars by the late 1960s and did so sharply in 1973–75. Chrysler, however, did not produce a true subcompact car until its Dodge Omni/Plymouth Horizon "twins" first appeared in the 1978 model year. The decision to delay making a subcompact would not have caused so much damage to the company if it had sold enough of the more profitable full-sized models—but it didn't.

The all-new 1969 full-sized Chrysler products did poorly because of poor quality. A rushed and rocky launch of the new models resulted in dozens of design defects that went unnoticed until they reached the customer. The cars were badly assembled, often with the wrong parts. To make matters worse, Chrysler's new computerized ordering system failed. Cars went to the wrong destinations with the wrong options installed. At one point, 200 Chrysler New Yorkers, luxury behemoths weighing more than two tons, left the factory with standard transmissions and with no air conditioning, power steering, or power brakes.[9]

Quality problems were serious enough that Riccardo established an office of consumer affairs in mid-February 1971, with vice president Byron J. Nichols in charge. Customers could pass on their complaints about Chrysler products to Nichols, but only after all other attempts to get relief had failed. These efforts seemed like a "smoke and mirrors" strategy to deal with serious problems. Chrysler had quietly dropped its 5-year/50,000-mile warranty on the drive train for the 1971 models, reverting to the previous 12-month/12,000-mile coverage. Buyers of new Chrysler vehicles lost the extended warranty and got Byron Nichols instead.[10]

Business commentators constantly harped on Chrysler's lack of small cars or plans to build small cars. In 1969, Chrysler had no competitive response to the newest small cars from its competitors, the Ford Maverick and the American Motors Javelin. Planning for the Ford Pinto, Chevrolet Vega, and AMC Gremlin were well under way by mid-1969, and all three were in the showrooms by fall 1970. Townsend remained skeptical of the wisdom of building a subcompact.[11]

Even by the end of 1973, Chrysler had not yet committed to build a subcompact. Lynn Townsend told *Forbes,* "The subcompacts are just too small. The American people won't climb into them. They have to give up too much in creature comfort. I think even a compact's a little small. I would think that probably the most popular car size you'll see 15 years from now will be like our intermediates today."[12] Instead, Chrysler introduced all-new full-sized 1974 models, the first complete redesign since the 1969 model year.

In the fall of 1973, following the Yom Kippur War, the Organization of Oil Exporting Countries (OPEC) imposed an oil embargo on Israel's supporters, including the United States. Gasoline shortages and a tripling of prices in the United States in 1974 dried up demand for large cars. As a result of these drastic shifts in the car market in 1974 and 1975, Chrysler's sales plummeted and its financial losses skyrocketed.

The company did not concentrate exclusively on full-sized cars. Starting with the introduction of the 1960 Valiant and the 1961 Dodge Lancer, rebadged in 1963 as the Dodge Dart, Chrysler had success with its compact-sized cars in the 1960s. As was the case with all of the Big Three's compacts, Chrysler's offerings suffered in comparison with foreign cars in size, weight, and fuel economy. Between 1960 and 1975, the Valiant grew by 16 inches and gained 500 pounds.[13]

Chrysler nevertheless did well in the compact car market from 1961 to 1975. Sales of the compact Valiant and Lancer/Dart accounted for roughly one quarter of all domestic sales of compact cars from 1961 to 1965, approximately 16 percent 1966–69, and peaked at 41 percent in 1974. Profit margins on compacts, however, were much smaller than from full-sized cars, and Chrysler's profit margins on all of its products were much lower than those of its competitors. For 1973, for example, Chrysler earned net profits of only 3 percent of sales, while Ford earned 5 percent and General Motors 7 percent.[14]

Chrysler also enjoyed considerable—but short-lived—success with niche cars, especially sporty cars and "muscle cars," but these were not products that appealed to the broad auto-buying public. The company introduced the 1964 Plymouth (Valiant) Barracuda as a mid-1964 model to compete with the Corvair Monza and the Ford Mustang, easily the most successful of the early "pony" cars. By 1967, Chrysler also had to compete with the Mercury Cougar, Pontiac Firebird, and Chevrolet Camaro, among others.[15]

Product planners at Chrysler recognized that the automobile market was changing significantly in the early 1960s. In discussing the origins of Barracuda, product planner H. E. Weiss noted that by 1960, the car market had shifted because of the appearance of the first wave of the "postwar baby boomers," which quickly became a surge of young people reaching driving age. Increased affluence among middle-class families meant that the one-car family would become the exception. By late 1962, Ford had decided to build the Mustang to capture this youth market and Chrysler moved ahead to build the Barracuda.

The first Barracuda was in essence a Valiant with new upper body sheet metal with "fastback" styling. Barracuda used the Valiant platform because it had shown excellent handling and was the right size. Chrysler management approved the Barracuda program for introduction as a 1965 model, but when Ford accelerated its Mustang program to achieve a mid-1964 model introduction, Chrysler followed suit. One result was that the first Barracudas used the 1964 Valiant instrument cluster.[16]

Introduced at the New York Auto Show in April 1964, Barracuda sold 23,443 copies in its brief initial model year and a more impressive 64,596 of the 1965 models, but only 38,029 in 1966. The Barracuda was never a real competitor for Mustang. Combined sales for Barracuda during its first two and one-half model years stood at 126,068 units, versus 1,167,019 for Mustang. Although Mustang offered a fastback version starting in 1965, the overwhelming majority of Mustangs were "notchbacks" and convertibles. Chrysler discontinued Barracuda in April 1974 with sales in its final year of 11,734 units versus sales of 459,000 Valiants (including 277,000 Valiant Dusters).[17]

A Dodge fastback named Charger appeared in showrooms on 1 January 1966, but sold only 53,000 units during its first two years in production. Sales in 1968 (96,000) and 1969 (90,000) were more impressive. Popularity of the Charger peaked in 1973, with sales of 119,318 units. Charger was easily Chrysler's most popular muscle car. A 1969 Charger, the "General Lee," was a star on the hit TV program, "The Dukes of Hazzard," which ran between January 1979 and August 1985. Charger lasted until 1978, but by then, a smaller engine had turned its muscle to flab.[18]

Automobile writer Brock Yates suggested to Robert Anderson, Chrysler/Plymouth Division general manager, that Plymouth needed to drop a powerful engine into a stripped-down no-frills body to appeal to the youth market. Anderson gave the task to Jack Smith, Plymouth's product planning manager, who decided to put two high-performance packages into a Belvedere body—a standard 383-cid V-8 engine and an optional Hemi engine. Gordon Cherry, one of Smith's staff members, often watched Saturday morning cartoons with his kids and one of their favorites (and his) was Warner Brothers' *Road Runner*. This uncatchable bird, the state bird of New Mexico, accelerated quickly, could stop on a dime, went "beep beep," and always eluded Wile E. Coyote.[19]

1964 Plymouth Barracuda, Chrysler's first muscle car. Courtesy of DCHC.

Jack Smith registered the Road Runner name with the Motor Vehicle Manufacturers Association (MMVA) and then opened talks with Warner Brothers over the rights to use the cartoon character. Warner Brothers could not protect the Road Runner name because it was a real bird, but it did own the cartoon character. Chrysler agreed to pay Warner Brothers $30,000 a year for the rights to use the Road Runner images for the first two years and $20,000 a year thereafter.[20]

Before Road Runner appeared, adorned with cartoon logos in the exterior trim, Jack Smith had to overcome the strong objections of Richard Macadam, the head of Plymouth styling, to putting a cartoon figure on one of his cars. The dealer or the customer installed the first Road Runner logos. In the 1969 models, permanent colorful cartoons appeared all over the car. They even put a Wile E. Coyote decal on the air cleaner. The product planners sent out demonstration tapes of the famous bird's "beep beep" sound in an effort to develop a horn that would duplicate it. Spartan, a firm from Flora, Illinois, received the horn contract.[21]

The car was a phenomenal sales success for a specialized niche vehicle. The product planners would have been pleased with sales of 15,000 units for the 1968 model year, the first. Instead, customers bought 44,599 Road Runners. Sales received another boost when the editors of *Motor Trend* named Road Runner its 1969 Car of the Year. Sales peaked with the 1969 model (84,420) and then fell off the next year to only 43,404 copies.[22]

Plymouth Road Runner's cartoon logo decal. Courtesy of DCHC.

Another marketing success in the early 1970s was the Duster, a barebones two-door coupe that qualified as a muscle car because of the available engines. Besides the standard in-line Six, customers could choose a 318-cid V-8 or a 340–cid V-8 with a four-barrel carburetor. Either V-8 engine made Duster a fast car. Introduced as the Valiant Duster in the 1970 model year, the car appealed to young buyers. The base model had a factory price of only $2,162 versus $2,896 for the base Road Runner and $4,216 for a well-equipped Plymouth Fury Grand Coupe. Chrysler even developed its own logo peculiar to Duster, a cartoon character resembling a tornado churning up dust, with only two eyes visible.[23]

By any measure, Duster was a great sales success. The Plymouth Division produced 268,000 Valiants in the 1970 model year and 217,192 of these were Dusters, including 24,817 Duster 340s. Duster sales dropped slightly in the 1971 model year, recovered in 1972, and then climbed to an all-time peak of 281,378 units for 1974, when combined Valiant sales stood at 459,083 units. Duster sales for 1975, the last year Plymouth produced this car, fell off to only 120,000 copies. Duster's replacement for 1976 was the ill-fated Plymouth Volare.[24]

The appeal to youth had several dimensions. In analyzing the design of the 1970 models, Elwood Engel pointed out the importance of "fun" names like Road Runner and Duster, along with the use of bright, wild colors in appealing to youth. Available colors on the 1970 models included Tor-Red and Go-Mango

Red, Lemon Twist and Banana Yellow, Vitamin C and Hemi Orange, Sublime and Lime-lite Green, and In-Violet and Plum Crazy Purple. The high-performance engines that provided the muscle for muscle cars was, of course, the other essential ingredient.[25]

Chrysler did well in selling sporty and muscle cars, at least for a while. The share of those niche cars in Chrysler's overall sales jumped from only 3.6 percent in 1965 to a peak of 13.7 percent in 1970. Gasoline shortages, increased federal rules regarding emissions and safety, and skyrocketing automobile insurance rates on muscle cars starting in the early 1970s hurt sales. From 1973 to 1975, combined sales of these specialty cars fell from 174,127 units (7.9 percent of the total) to 30,812 units, only 2 percent of total sales. This was another case where Chrysler focused on a dying market segment.[26]

Styling became less important after 1968 because Chrysler's chronic financial problems produced severe cuts in styling staffs and because downsizing the company's offerings became the overriding priority in the 1970s. Because of changed circumstances and personalities, Chrysler's stylists lost much of their influence and independence. Both Virgil Exner in the 1950s and Elwood Engel in the 1960s enjoyed considerable power, but this was not the case for Richard G. Macadam, who served as Chrysler's director of design from 1972 to 1974 and as vice president for design from 1974 to 1979.

Macadam had studied mechanical engineering at the University of Delaware, but then moved into the fine arts, attending the Pennsylvania Academy of Fine Arts and the School of Art in Philadelphia. He took a job working with Richard Teague at Packard's styling department in 1954, moved with Teague to Chrysler in 1957, but then worked at General Motors' styling operation under Bill Mitchell. He returned to Chrysler in 1961, moving quickly up the corporate ladder. Engel put Macadam in charge of all the Chrysler/Plymouth studios in 1968 and named him director of design in 1972.

There is no distinctive car styling "statement" associated with Macadam. His early work at Chrysler included the 1967 Barracuda and the 1968 Plymouth Road Runner. Designer John E. Herlitz completed work on the 1970 Barracuda under Macadam's general supervision. In his later years as vice president, Macadam managed the styling for the K-cars and the first minivans, hardly notable designs in terms of appearance. In November 1979, Lee Iacocca hired Don DeLaRossa, formerly at Ford, as a design consultant and named him vice president of product design in February 1980. Macadam left Chrysler shortly thereafter to work for National Cash Register Corporation.[27]

When demand for Chrysler's big cars and muscle cars virtually disappeared in 1974 and 1975, the company's sales plummeted. The future looked particularly grim because the company did not have the resources to develop the new products needed for survival, particularly subcompact cars. As the smallest of the Big Three carmakers, Chrysler found the changed business environment of the 1960s and 1970s particularly burdensome. The corporation's greatest challenge was complying with new federal regulations on automobile emissions and safety without enduring prohibitively high costs.

THE CHANGING BUSINESS ENVIRONMENT

The most threatening change in the business climate for all American automakers, but especially for Chrysler, was the imposition of federal standards for automobile emissions. California led the nation in mandating reductions in tailpipe emissions, primarily hydrocarbons, carbon monoxide, and nitrogen oxides. The California legislature enacted regulations in 1959 reducing hydrocarbon emissions on cars sold in California starting with the 1963 model year. All tailpipe emissions were to be reduced by the 1966 model year. The U.S. Congress followed California's lead. The Motor Vehicle Air Pollution and Control Act of 1965 imposed California's standards nationally for the 1968 model year, with additional reductions of emissions by 1970. Two major pollutants, hydrocarbons and carbon monoxide, would be reduced by 30 percent from "normal" levels prior to regulation.[28]

The regulatory earthquake that shook the auto industry was the passage of Senator Edmund Muskie's Clean Air Act in December 1970 mandating a 90 percent reduction in emissions of hydrocarbons and carbon monoxide from the 1970 standards by 1975 and a similar decline for oxides of nitrogen by 1976. Muskie and his "experts" naively believed that these reductions could be easily achieved. After intense lobbying, in 1973 the Environmental Protection Agency (EPA) granted the automakers a two-year extension to meet the 1975–76 standards, recognizing that the original schedule was unreasonable.[29]

Starting in the early 1960s, Chrysler's engineers successfully modified engine performance to sharply reduce emissions, but in the end their efforts were wasted. Charles Heinen and his engineering staff at Chrysler first developed engine modifications they dubbed the "Chrysler Clean Air Package," introduced on a few models in 1966 and on all 1968 Chrysler cars. The "package" included a positive crankcase ventilation (PCV) system, which Chrysler had pioneered; a "lean carburetor"; a modified distributor; and improved vacuum controls. The company later introduced a vapor saver system on all of its 1971 models and an improved electronic ignition system (phased in starting in 1971), which further reduced pollution by eliminating misfiring.[30]

Unfortunately for Chrysler, the 1970 Clean Air Act specified that control devices to reduce emissions had to work perfectly for 5 years or 50,000 miles, which in effect mandated catalytic converters and ruled out Chrysler's approach.

As a result, the company had to use catalytic converters to meet the 1977 model year standards. The converters came from General Motors, which had invested heavily in their development. For General Motors, with its large number of vehicles, using an add-on device such as a catalytic converter was the most economical way to reduce emissions. The giant automaker had its own parts manufacturing operations and would be the largest buyer of these devices. James Flink estimated that the 1977 model year emissions system cost GM only $200 per car, but twice that figure for Chrysler.[31]

Automobile safety was the second area in which government regulation affected Chrysler and the other producers. Federally mandated safety standards grew out of hearings held by the U.S. Senate in 1965 following the publication of Ralph Nader's book, *Unsafe at Any Speed,* an attack on the auto industry's safety record. Nader singled out the Chevrolet Corvair for attention, but broadly attacked the entire industry for its indifference to safety issues.

The National Traffic and Motor Vehicle Safety Act of 1966 established an agency, the National Highway Traffic Safety Administration (NHTSA), charged with setting safety standards for new cars starting with the 1968 model year. NHTSA adopted 17 standards for the 1968 models and 28 for 1969. The car companies, including Chrysler, complained about the cost of these features, but they did not resist the regulations. For the most part, the new safety features involved reasonably straightforward engineering solutions.[32]

Chrysler's leaders consistently argued that these regulations were more costly to Chrysler because of its relatively small size. When Lee Iacocca approached Congress in 1979 for a bailout of Chrysler, he claimed that government regulation was a major cause of the company's demise. His financial staff estimated that complying with emissions and safety standards for cars, emission standards for its plants, and federal Occupational Safety and Health Administration (OSHA) rules cost Chrysler at least $700 million from 1974 to 1979. With Chrysler losing money in 1973–75 and laying off thousands, the only engineers it could afford to employ were those working on emissions research. This affected the company's ability to bring new products to market in the late 1970s and accelerated its slide toward bankruptcy.[33]

The (Mis)Managers: Townsend's Legacy and Successors

Under Lynn Townsend's leadership, Chrysler had enjoyed a robust recovery in the early 1960s, reasonably solid success through 1968, and then endured mostly a downward ride on the roller coaster from 1969 to 1975. Under his successors, the downturn continued through the near bankruptcy of 1980. The problems that surfaced after 1969 were largely the result of unpopular automotive prod-ucts—large cars when customers wanted smaller cars, muscle and other niche cars that quickly lost their appeal, stylistically unappealing vehicles, and prod-ucts that suffered from shoddy engineering and even worse assembly. To be sure, the changed regulatory environment after 1965 cost Chrysler dearly and probably affected its profits more than was the case for General Motors or Ford.

Beyond policy decisions Townsend made during his first seven or eight years as president of Chrysler, his choices of the executives who would succeed him largely determined the company's direction in the 1970s. John J. Riccardo, who ran North American automotive operations (1967–70), served as president (1970–75), and finally became chairman (1975–79), was Townsend's protégé. Between coming to Chrysler in 1959 and April 1967, he held nine positions, some for as little as two months. In the process, he ended up supervising men he had previously reported to. John Riccardo became president of Chrysler a little more than 10 years after joining the company. Like Townsend, he was an accountant with little real understanding of the automobile industry.[34]

A feature story in the *Detroit Free Press* in August 1971 described Riccardo's daily "management by the numbers" routine as the head of Chrysler. The article could have appeared 10 years earlier with Townsend's name inserted in place of Riccardo's. He would spend the first hours of his day looking at more than a dozen daily reports on production, sales, cash flow, and so on, comparing these with the target numbers. Riccardo noted, "ultimately, it is all reduced to num-bers. The basic measurement very simply is profits. Under our system that is the determination of the success of a business enterprise, and profits are numbers."[35]

After Chrysler lost money in the last quarter of 1969, Townsend ordered massive cost-cutting to reduce Chrysler's break- even point. Riccardo was the point man, laying off 12,000 North American employees in early 1970. His critics believed him to be a ruthless, cold-hearted moneyman. He and Townsend were both accused of being nothing more than "bean counters" with no real understanding of cars or passion for them.[36] Looking at the careers and decisions of both men, there is a good deal of truth to those observations.

For the first half of the 1970s, the Chrysler management team consisted of Townsend (chairman), Riccardo (president), and Eugene A. Cafiero, who held the third most important position, group vice president of U.S. and Canadian automotive operations. With Townsend's retirement as chairman on 30 Septem-ber 1975, Riccardo succeeded him and Cafiero became president, a position he held until Lee Iacocca replaced him on 2 November 1978. Cafiero was born on 13 June 1926 in Brooklyn, the son of a truck driver. He graduated from Dart-mouth College in 1946 with a degree in psychology. He worked briefly as a steel salesman for the David Smith Steel Company before coming to Ford Motor Company in 1949 as a management trainee. Cafiero went to work for the Briggs

Manufacturing Company in 1952 and then joined Chrysler the following year when the company bought Briggs. His first job for Chrysler was coordinator of forward planning in the automotive body division.

Unlike Townsend and Riccardo, Cafiero had extensive experience in manufacturing and product development. He was part of a team that brought Chrysler's new Twinsburg, Ohio, stamping plant into production in 1958–59. Cafiero served as manager of the New Castle, Indiana, forge and foundry in 1961–63 and was general plants manager of Chrysler's Power Train Group in 1965–67. His quick rise to the number three spot in Chrysler's hierarchy reflected his reputation as a cold, hard-nosed manager who solved problems.[37]

It is nearly impossible to assess Cafiero's effectiveness in improving Chrysler's manufacturing quality because he was operating under very difficult circumstances from 1970 to 1975. Both the automotive press and general business publications applauded his efforts, but could not point to any notable accomplishment. The cutbacks in capital investment and product planning in 1970 and 1971, followed by similar cuts in 1974–75, did not give Cafiero many resources to work with. It is ironic that after the two accountants, Townsend and Riccardo, mismanaged Chrysler to the brink of disaster, they brought in a manufacturing expert to bail out the corporation. There was little Cafiero could accomplish before 1975, when he became president.[38]

Any long-range assessment of Lynn Townsend's tenure at the Chrysler helm must include all of his major decisions. The failed effort to make Chrysler a multinational producer was one of Townsend's strategic blunders, perhaps the most important. The final fate of the overseas investments was a fire sale in 1978 to Peugeot. Another important mistake was the decision to diversify into real estate, which diverted resources away from Chrysler's core business. Finally, Townsend's rigid commitment to "production for the sales bank" created serious problems for the company after 1965.

One of Townsend's ventures outside of the automobile business was Chrysler Realty Corporation, established as a subsidiary in 1967 to manage Chrysler's 250 company-owned dealerships. Within a year, however, Chrysler Realty began expanding into a variety of land-development projects. One of the new ventures was a new "model" city to be built on a 1,700-acre parcel in suburban Troy, Michigan. Other projects included townhouses in Ann Arbor, Michigan; luxury housing in Bloomfield, Michigan; and the Big Sky Resort in Montana.[39] Most of these developments produced only modest profits, and the Big Sky project in Montana proved disastrous. At best, Chrysler Realty was another distraction from the company's core business.

Lynn Townsend's decision to manufacture cars for a "sales bank" rather than in response to dealer and customer orders was the most wrong-headed decision of his tenure at Chrysler. All of the car companies faced unpredictable fluctuations in demand for their products because of seasonal variations in demand and changes in the business cycle. General Motors and Ford produced some cars "for inventory," but the vast majority were based on firm orders from customers or dealers. They adjusted to changes in demand by shutting down their factories or by running them overtime. Townsend, however, set factory production schedules with the goal of "rationalizing" inventories of parts and components and smoothing the flow of funds internally. It led to enormous "sales bank" inventories in years of falling demand. In mid-February 1969, for example, during one downturn, Chrysler held an inventory of 408,302 cars, a 102-day supply at the then-current selling rate.[40]

The sales bank damaged Chrysler in a variety of ways and greatly demoralized the production staff, the sales force, and the dealers. This system tied up hundreds of millions of dollars of working capital in unsold cars. Townsend's focus on meeting quarterly production targets meant that the factories shipped too many hastily assembled cars. A quality control man at Dodge Main said, "We shipped cars at the end of a quarter we never should have. In the last hour of overtime work on an end-of-the-quarter shift, we'd ship out hundreds of dogs." Dealers would order the fewest cars possible, knowing that Chrysler would eventually offer hefty discounts to reduce its inventory. Customers would wait until the end of the model year to enjoy fire-sale prices. Above all else, the sales bank system isolated and insulated Chrysler from its customers.[41]

Lynn Townsend's final two years as chairman were not happy ones. After achieving a record North American production (until 1994) of 2.2 million vehicles in 1973, the company suffered a 30 percent decline in sales by 1975. Market share fell to about 12 percent, the lowest it had been since 1962. More important, an operating loss of $41.4 million in 1974 ballooned into a loss of $259.5 million in 1975. Auto industry observers and financial analysis began to question Chrysler's long-term viability for the first time in two decades.[42]

In a desperate effort to boost sales and reduce its whopping inventory, Chrysler offered customers rebates. Announced in Superbowl advertising in January 1975 by sports announcer and Chrysler spokesperson Joe Garagiola, the rebates broke new ground. In the past, Chrysler would extend "factory incentives" (discounts) to the dealers, who might or might not pass those discounts on to the customer. Under this new program, dubbed the Car Clearance Carnival, Chrysler would send a $200 rebate check to anyone who bought or leased a 1975 Plymouth Duster or Dodge Dart Swinger. The pitch was, "buy a car, get a check."

The program worked, reducing the inventory by 50,000 vehicles. Chrysler reinstated rebates for the month of May and again for July through November in an effort to boost sales.[43] Rebates, however, can be a double-edged sword;

they help sell cars, but once customers become accustomed to rebates or expect them, they will not buy a car without one.

Lynn Townsend met with the press in July to announced his retirement, effective 1 October 1975. John Riccardo would succeed him as chairman and Eugene Cafiero would become president. He gave a lengthy interview to the *Detroit Free Press* in mid-August 1975, in which he reflected on his years at Chrysler. When reminded about the criticism that he was a finance man, not an auto man, Townsend replied, "You don't have to have an engineering degree to be successful in this industry." When asked about his greatest accomplishments at Chrysler, Townsend focused on three—the internationalization of the company, the corporate identity program, and Chrysler Realty Corporation. While we can certainly question the long-term viability of Chrysler's international operations and Chrysler Realty, Townsend's corporate identity program was a great success and was imitated by the other auto companies.[44]

THE SLIDE TO BANKRUPTCY: PRODUCTS, 1975–79

Lynn Townsend left his successors John Riccardo and Eugene Cafiero a badly weakened Chrysler Corporation destined to struggle in the short run. The company needed to bring new, attractive products to market to reverse its declining sales and shrinking market share. Townsend's cost-cutting efforts of late 1974 and 1975 resulted in layoffs of so many designers and engineers that every new product introduced was delayed. In the fall of 1977, for example, Chrysler had no new products to sell. In June 1978, Chairman John Riccardo announced the company's plans to invest $7.5 billion in the next five years to remake its entire line of cars and to modernize most of its plants. The *Fortune* analyst who wrote of these plans suggested that Riccardo had no choice but to "bet the company," but questioned if Chrysler had the financial wherewithal to complete the plan.[45]

Sales rebounded in 1976–77 from the recession levels of 1974–75, and the company enjoyed modest earnings. Sales, however, fell 7 percent in 1978, and the company suffered losses of nearly $205 million. The performance that year was especially ominous because the industry as a whole enjoyed its best year ever, with sales of 12.9 million vehicles. The crisis of 1978 became a near fatal disaster in 1979, in part because of another Middle East oil crisis in the spring and a national economic recession. When Chrysler's sales in 1979 fell 30 percent below the 1977 level and captured only 10 percent of the market, the company lost nearly $1.1 billion. All the car companies lost money in 1979, but Chrysler suffered more than the others.

The company did not go down without a struggle during these years and

Eugene Cafiero (*left*) and John Riccardo (*right*) with a 1975 Dodge Charger SE Coupe. Courtesy of DCHC.

introduced several new models, not all of them successful. The Chrysler Cordoba appeared in fall 1974 as a 1975 model. The new offering, a "personal luxury coupe," was smaller than the standard-sized Chrysler, with a wheelbase of 115 inches versus 124 inches. Cordoba had a smaller engine than Newports and New Yorkers (318 cid versus 400 cid) and less weight, so it delivered better fuel economy. The sales results were impressive: 150,000 units of the 1975 models, 120,000 in 1976, a peak of 183,000 in 1977, and a still-robust 125,000 for 1978. For 1975–77, Cordoba accounted for more than half of the Chrysler nameplate sales and single-handedly revived the division.[46]

One of the new models that defined the Chrysler Corporation in the 1970s were the 1976 model Dodge Aspen/Plymouth Volare twins, introduced in fall 1975. Chrysler appeared to have made a very successful sales coup with these upscale luxury compacts. Combined sales for the 1976 Aspen/Volare were

1978 Dodge Aspen used by the Phoenix police force. Courtesy of DCHC.

511,068 units and an impressive 695,064 for the 1977 models. The frosting on the cake came in February 1976, when *Motor Trend Magazine* gave the Aspen/Volare line its Car of the Year Award. Naturally, Chrysler immediately used the award in the advertising for the line.[47]

The Aspen/Volare line, which began on such a positive note, soon became victim to design defects that had come from the premature, hasty launch of the new line in fall of 1975. As a result of the severe cutbacks in engineering staff in 1974 and 1975, many components of the new car line were not adequately tested. By mid-1977, customers' complaints about defects became a flood: brakes failed, hoods would suddenly pop open while the car was moving, the car would stall when the driver stepped on the gas pedal. By fall of 1977, Chrysler recalled more than 3.5 million Aspens and Volares and spent more than $200 million fixing them.

The Center for Auto Safety, a consumer advocate organization established by Ralph Nader in 1970, gave the car line its Lemon of the Year Award for 1977. The problems with defects continued. In May 1978, Chrysler recalled 1.2 million Aspens and Volares to repair the suspension system, the fourth recall in six months. The impact in the marketplace was disastrous, with sales of 695,064 for the 1977 models falling to 454,485 in 1978, a boom year for the rest of the U.S. auto industry. Sales then slipped another 100,000 units for 1979.

One early problem, premature rust-through on front fenders, was not subject to a safety recall and remained a lingering complaint and the subject of litigation. Chrysler finally signed a consent agreement with the Federal Trade Commission in April 1980 to replace rusted front fenders on the 1976 and 1977 models or reimburse customers who had already done so. The cost to Chrysler was $45 million. The ill-fated line ended with the 1980 models, replaced by Chrysler's K-cars.[48]

Before Omni/Horizon finally arrived in early 1978, Chrysler provided its dealers with a limited number of subcompact cars through a patchwork of "captive imports." The 1970s patchwork included Mitsubishi-made Dodge Colts and Plymouth Arrows and the Plymouth Cricket made by Rootes in 1971. The Dodge Colt and the Plymouth Arrow enjoyed some success, with sales of 78,972 units in 1976, 118,475 in 1977, and 101,336 for the 1978 model year. Chrysler's sales of captive imports peaked in 1979, with combined sales of 165,084 cars from five models—the Dodge Colt and Challenger and the Plymouth Arrow, Champ, and Sapporo.[49] This arrangement gave Chrysler's dealers small, fuel-efficient cars to sell.

Chrysler's European (Simca) connections finally led to the Omni/Horizon. Its designers began work in 1974 on a replacement for the Simca 1100, using the same wheelbase (99.2 inches) and dubbed the "C2." In spring 1975, when Chrysler faced a serious sales slump, very little demand for its larger cars, and approaching federal fuel economy standards, the company's top executives decided to move ahead with a front-drive subcompact for the American market. The C2 in France and the U.S. version, the "L-Car," would be developed as a joint program.

The American subcompact, which became Omni/Horizon, received formal approval in July 1975. These all-new cars were to appear as 1978 models, which meant that development had to be compressed into about 30 months instead of the normal 48 months for new models. Buying engines from Volkswagen instead of designing a new engine from scratch saved Chrysler at least a year. Chrysler's engineers did, however, design an automatic transmission for the Omni/Horizon. American consumers demanded automatic transmissions, even on a subcompact model. Although the Chrysler and Simca engineers worked closely together and helped each other in designing their respective cars, Omni/Horizon shared little with the European version in terms of mechanical components or sheet metal.[50]

The Omni/Horizon was the first American-made front-drive subcompact car and featured a transverse-mounted 1.7-liter four-cylinder overhead-cam engine made by Volkswagen. These boxy hatchbacks closely resembled the popular Volkswagen Rabbit. Front-wheel drive made for greater interior room and better handling than the competitive rear-drive subcompacts such as the Ford Pinto

1978 Dodge Omni subcompact car. Courtesy of DCHC.

or Chevrolet Chevette. Chrysler had reasserted its engineering leadership, this time with a subcompact car.

The arrival of Omni/Horizon in December 1977, long after the other 1978 models had debuted, guaranteed extensive coverage in the automotive and general press. The fact that this was the first domestic front-drive subcompact helped as well. The reviews came fast and furious early in 1978 and offered mainly high praise for the new car lines. In January 1978, reviews appeared in *Auto Reports, Car and Driver, Mechanix Illustrated, Popular Mechanics, Road and Track,* and *Ward's Auto World.* Additional reviews followed in February in *Road Test, Motor News,* and *Motor Trend.* More detailed reports appeared in *Car and Driver* in March, *Popular Mechanics* in April, and in *Consumers Research* in May.[51]

Reinforcing and confirming the praise heaped on Omni/Horizon by various automotive magazines, *Motor Trend* gave the car line its 1978 Car of the Year Award in February 1978. Besides recognizing the cars as the first domestic front-drive subcompacts, this enthusiasts' magazine praised the handling characteristics of Omni/Horizon and the interior roominess, especially headroom and legroom for rear seat passengers. Even the dash layout received special praise because instruments were laid out logically and easy to read. Exterior styling had "a distinctive flair that sets it apart from similar smaller front-drives."[52]

Then came the bombshell. Consumers Union (CU), a well-respected independent product testing institution, held simultaneous press conferences on 14

June 1978 in Washington, D.C., and New York City in which they previewed and explained their upcoming evaluation of Omni/Horizon in the July 1978 issue of *Consumer Reports.* In that evaluation, they branded Omni/Horizon as "unacceptable" based on two road tests in which the cars exhibited "unpredictable and dangerous handling during some abrupt maneuvers."[53]

The CU condemnation did little damage to Omni/Horizon's reputation or sales over the long run. Chrysler Public Relations had sufficient time to blunt the potentially devastating effects on Omni/Horizon's reputation. The company immediately issued a press release condemning the first CU test as having "no relationship to highway driving." They duplicated the second CU test at the Chelsea Proving Grounds, and the cars maneuvered around the cones flawlessly. In a bold move, Chrysler also petitioned the NHTSA and its Canadian equivalent, Transport Canada, to conduct independent tests of Omni/Horizon's handling.[54]

Virtually all the newspapers that carried the CU story also carried Chrysler's rebuttal evidence, including its tests at Chelsea. The car magazines that had tested Omni/Horizon handling with good results, including *Car and Driver,* attacked both the methods and the motives of Consumers Union regarding Omni/Horizon. In fast order, Transport Canada and NHTSA exonerated Omni/Horizon.[55]

The Consumers Union episode caused only minor damage; the new models were an enormous success for Chrysler. Sales for the (shortened) 1978 model year totaled more than 188,000 units, reached 304,000 units for 1979, and climbed to nearly 310,000 for the 1980 model year, making the line one of Chrysler's few sales successes of this period. The addition of sporty two-door hatchback coupe versions, the Omni 024 and the Horizon TC3, for the 1979 model year further boosted sales. The company could have sold more, but was limited by its contract with Volkswagen, which provided for only 300,000 engines a year. Chrysler did not have its own four-cylinder engines (2.2 liter) for Omni/Horizon until the 1981 model year.[56]

The last new model launch, that of the full-sized 1979 model Chrysler New Yorker, Chrysler Newport, and Dodge St. Regis, was yet another example of poor management. These totally redesigned luxury cars, with improved fuel efficiency, were aimed at the resurgent market for large cars. Early planning, which began in 1975, was delayed because of staff cuts and Cafiero's indecision about design details. By September 1977, the program was eight months behind schedule. At the time of new model introductions in fall of 1978, advertising and promotions for the new car lines went forward as if production were on schedule, but dealers had no cars to sell. The company repeated the Airflow disaster of 1934, with Eugene Cafiero clearly responsible for the fiasco. Dealers finally received the new models in quantity in January, but Chrysler had lost another opportunity.[57]

Chrysler also remained in the tank business into the early 1980s. Production of the M-60 continued at the Warren, Michigan, tank plant through 1982. More important, the U.S. Army awarded the company a contract in November 1976 to develop the new XM1 (M1) Abrams main battle tank. The contract brought Chrysler sales of about $4 billion over the length of the M1 program. This 60–ton tank, powered by a 1,500 hp Chrysler-designed turbine engine, was initially produced at the army's Lima, Ohio, tank plant. Production began there in May 1979, with the first two tanks delivered to the army on 28 February 1980. The initial plans called for the production of 7,058 XM1 tanks in the 1980s. But Chrysler's defense operations, mainly its tank contracts, also fell victim to the financial crisis of 1979 and beyond. The automaker sold Chrysler Defense, its subsidiary, to General Dynamics in March 1982 for $239 million, yielding (net of taxes) $172 million for Chrysler's coffers.[58]

In a critical article written a decade after the initial XM1 contract award, Richard Mendel argued that this contract was really the first government bailout for Chrysler. The army had asked Chrysler and General Motors to develop competing designs for the new tank and the General Motors entry was clearly superior. In addition, GM's tank used a proven diesel engine and was less costly than Chrysler's design, with its unproven turbine engine. Over strong army objections, Secretary of Defense Donald Rumsfeld gave the contract to Chrysler in November 1976.[59] The army ended up getting a tank with serious design flaws that took years to correct. However, over time the XM1 and later versions of this tank showed their mettle. This was the main battle tank that won the stunning victory in Operation Desert Storm in February 1991.

THE SLIDE TO BANKRUPTCY: FINANCIAL CRISIS, GOVERNMENT REGULATION, AND NEW MANAGEMENT, 1975–79

The fundamental crisis that Chrysler faced in 1979 that led to the U.S. government loan guarantees was financial. Chrysler faced mounting operating losses, had exhausted its financial reserves, had large long-term debts, and found most financial institutions increasingly unwilling to loan it funds either long- or short-term. As the year went forward, Chrysler found it increasingly hard to pay its bills and began to face the prospect of not meeting its payroll as well. The automaker had to finance its losses while simultaneously trying to implement the first part of the $7.5 billion of investments in new products and plants Riccardo had announced in June 1978.

Bankers were understandably nervous about Chrysler's situation. Its long-term debt had jumped from $250 million in 1960 (14 percent of shareholders' equity) to $791 million in 1970 (37 percent of equity). By 1970, Chrysler had more long-term debt than General Motors. Chrysler's long-term obligations jumped again to nearly $956 million in 1973 and to $1.24 billion (42 percent of equity) in 1977. Long-term debt was slightly under $1 billion at the end of 1979, nearly double shareholders' equity in the company.

Chrysler also needed to assure itself adequate working capital to continue operations. Its lead banker, Manufacturers Hanover Trust Company of New York, sometimes referred to as "Manny Hanny," got Chrysler through many of its short-term crises. Manny Hanny orchestrated a new revolving credit arrangement in April 1977, whereby Chrysler received $560 million in bank credit from 95 domestic banks. The company also reached an agreement with international banks in 1977 to provide it with an additional $263.5 million in revolving Eurodollar credits, and a new stock issue in 1978 raised another $200 million. Despite these long-term loans and provisions for short-term credits, Chrysler nevertheless had to sell off many of its assets starting in 1976 just to remain solvent.[60]

The process began in 1976 and accelerated in 1978 and 1979 in the face of growing losses and mounting debts. In 1976, Chrysler sold the unfinished New Stanton, Pennsylvania, factory to Volkswagen of America. More important was the sale of the Airtemp Division, which had lost money for years, to Fedders Corporation in February 1976. Fedders bought the nonautomotive air-conditioning assets for $18 million in cash, $10.5 million in notes, and $30 million in Fedders preferred stock, for a total sale price of $58.5 million.[61]

The company's involvement in real estate ventures through Chrysler Realty was scaled back after 1975 and in September 1979, the parent company sold its real estate operation to ABKO Realty. The new owners agreed to maintain the 750 dealerships Chrysler Realty owned. In January 1980, Chrysler sold its Marine Division as well, except for the marine engine operations.[62]

Chrysler also had to sell all of its international operations outside of North America. The company's international operations were never well integrated or well managed and were for the most part only marginally profitable. Chrysler sold a bewildering mixture of vehicles worldwide. In 1974, the company operated 35 manufacturing and assembly plants in 11 countries outside of North America. After the company bought a 15 percent equity interest in Mitsubishi Motors Corporation in 1971, Chrysler sold Mitsubishi models all over the world, along with scores of cars carrying the names of Humber, Hillman, Sunbeam, and Simca.[63]

The foreign operations were losing money by the early 1970s and contributing to the automaker's growing financial troubles in North America. The investments in Europe in particular never generated the profits Townsend had expected. For 1970, Chrysler's European operations had combined sales of $1.2 billion, but lost $36 million.[64] Chrysler's late entry into Europe meant that it could acquire only marginal companies. Only Simca made profits on a consistent basis.

The Rootes operation in Britain was a constant drain on Chrysler. Over the years 1966–76, Chrysler's U.K. operations made combined profits of only $27 million in four years, but cumulative losses of $188 million over the rest. After losing $35 million in 1974 and $71 million in 1975, Riccardo took drastic action. In early November 1975, he presented the British government with an ultimatum—Chrysler would liquidate its British holdings by the end of the year and throw roughly 55,000 people out of work unless the government nationalized Chrysler UK or provided massive financial aid to keep it afloat. The Labour government, acting under duress, agreed to a bailout package. The government would provide Chrysler UK with $325 million to cover losses and loan guarantees in 1976–79 and Chrysler would invest an additional $126 million.[65]

In August 1978, Chrysler Corporation announced that it had sold its entire European automobile operations, Chrysler France (Simca); Chrysler UK (Rootes), and Chrysler España (Barrieros S.A.) to Peugeot-Citroen for $230 million in cash and 15 percent of Peugeot's stock, estimated to be worth $200 million. Peugeot became the largest automobile manufacturer in Europe, with annual sales of 2.2 million units. Peugeot loaned Chrysler $100 million in January 1980, with Chrysler's Peugeot stock serving as collateral. In a single deal, John Riccardo sold off one-quarter of his company's car-building capacity worldwide and effectively ended Lynn Townsend's vision of Chrysler as a major player in the global auto industry.[66] The long-term impact on Chrysler's sales "mix" can be seen from table 13.2.

While Chrysler's international presence certainly shrank noticeably in 1978, it did not disappear, mainly because of its ongoing relationship with Mitsubishi Motors and continuing operations in Mexico. In 1979, Chrysler's sales of 270,405 Mitsubishi vehicles worldwide (165,000 in North America), combined with 91,785 vehicles assembled in Mexico, accounted for nearly all of its international business. The alliance with Mitsubishi Motors, which began when Chrysler acquired a 15 percent stock interest in 1971, became even stronger in the 1970s and 1980s and continues to this day. The two automakers reached an agreement on 31 January 1978 whereby Mitsubishi would supply Chrysler with 1,250,000 engines for the K-body car for the 1981 through 1985 model years.[67]

Despite raising more than $600 million in cash by liquidating various pieces of its operations from 1976 to 1979, increasing its long-term debt, and extending its short-term lines of credit, Chrysler was headed toward bankruptcy by the spring of 1979. Losses of over $1 billion in 1979 pushed the company to the

TABLE 13.2 Chrysler Global Sales, 1970–79

	Unit Sales	Unit Sales of Vehicles Manufactured Outside North America	Share of Total (%)
1970	2,434,398	720,726	29.6
1971	2,662,517	884,206	33.2
1972	3,028,212	1,014,742	33.5
1973	3,402,413	1,172,399	34.5
1974	2,762,842	980,557	35.5
1975	2,475,597	889,647	35.9
1976	3,130,307	985,267	31.5
1977	3,068,692	961,215	31.3
1978	2,211,535	354,462*	16.0
1979	1,796,465	382,399	21.3

Sources: Chrysler Corporation annual reports, 1970–79, box "Annual Reports 1968–98," DCHC.

*Reflects the sale of overseas operations.

brink. The company's leaders, John Riccardo and Lee Iacocca, warned the Carter administration of this eventuality and began asking for federal help. They argued that Chrysler needed temporary financial assistance from Washington because federal regulations had caused Chrysler's problems.

The severe gasoline shortages that came out of the 1973–74 OPEC oil embargo against the United States and other countries brought on the last onerous federal regulation of the automobile in this period. Congress passed the 1975 Energy Policy and Conservation Act, which mandated corporate average fuel efficiency (CAFE) standards for the industry. Average gas mileage for each company's fleet of new cars would rise sharply to 27.5 mpg for the 1985 model year. Combined CAFE for the American car companies was a dismal 13 mpg in 1973. The fuel economy standards proved to be more costly to the U.S. auto industry than the emissions standards because improved CAFE had to be achieved within the framework of the EPA's standards for tailpipe emissions.[68]

Riccardo predicted that the CAFE standards would affect Chrysler more than Ford or General Motors and would damage competition. Independent analysts agreed. In November 1978, the U.S. Department of Transportation's own think tank, the Transportation Systems Center, issued a report, *The Effects of Federal Regulation on the Financial Structure and Performance of the Domestic Motor Vehicle Manufacturers.* The report argued that Chrysler would be forced to take on enormous new debt to achieve the CAFE mandates, possibly threatening the company's survival.[69]

Early in 1979, Harbridge House, a Cambridge, Massachusetts, think tank, published a study, *Corporate Strategies of the Automotive Manufacturers,* that it had completed for NHTSA. Its report concluded that even a minor recession over the next eight years would likely destroy the ability of either American Motors or Chrysler to make the investments needed to fulfill the CAFE standards. Two minor recessions or a severe economic downturn would make compliance impossible.[70] This study, commissioned by the regulators, confirmed what John Riccardo had been saying all along—that federal regulations discriminated against smaller car companies like Chrysler and threatened their very existence.

Federal regulations, however, were not the only reason Chrysler faced a sales and financial crisis starting in the late 1970s. The company had long suffered with an extremely weak management team, a legacy of Lynn Townsend's years in power. For all of his faults, John Riccardo recognized that Chrysler's survival depended on bringing in stronger leaders than the ones in place in 1978. He and Eugene Cafiero had been a managerial odd couple to say the least. The two men, who had had fundamental disagreements about policy right from the beginning, began feuding openly in meetings and by 1977 were no longer on speaking terms.

In July 1977, Cafiero announced that he was quitting Chrysler to accept a chief executive's position at another major (unnamed) company, but instead of welcoming an end to what had become a destructive relationship, Riccardo convinced Cafiero to stay. Riccardo may have feared that Cafiero's departure would mean his own demise as well. An uneasy truce remained in place for more than a year, but Chrysler's deteriorating position by fall 1978, combined with the availability of Lee Iacocca, brought Cafiero's demotion. On 31 October, Riccardo informed him that he was no longer president and offered him the largely ceremonial job of vice chairman of the board.

John Riccardo's decision to bring Lee Iacocca to Chrysler was perhaps his only stroke of genius during his tenure as chairman. Riccardo and the Chrysler board introduced Lee Iacocca as the company's new president and chief operating officer on 2 November 1978. Cafiero remained as vice chairman of the board until 1 March 1979, when he left the company to become president and CEO of the ill-fated DeLorean Motor Corporation. Riccardo was to serve as chairman for only one more year, but his health problems and Chrysler's deteriorating condition speeded up the timetable. Riccardo announced his resignation as chairman on 18 September 1979, and Iacocca succeeded him two days later. The Lynn Townsend era had finally come to a close.[71]

Chapter 14

LEE TO THE RESCUE, 1978–83

Lee is a *reconteaur [sic]* extraordinary, and not only can he quip with the best, but he can pun with the worst. If knowledge really is power, he is omnipotent. This, together with the ability he has developed in managing and directing school affairs, will prove a great asset in his career in engineering.

—*Comus,* Allentown High School's yearbook

Between the appointment of Lee Iacocca as its president on 2 November 1978 and the end of 1983, the Chrysler Corporation went through a traumatic and turbulent reversal in its fortunes. In five years, the nearly dead automaker revived and was well on the road to a healthy future life. Day-to-day accounts of those times can be found in several excellent books and will not be repeated here.[1]

In many important ways, this monumental recovery was the work of one remarkable man—Lido (Lee) Anthony Iacocca. Iacocca emerged from the Chrysler rescue as the most easily recognized and admired corporate executive in the United States, a mythological figure in many respects. The Chrysler Corporation, now part of DaimlerChrysler, still bears the imprint of those difficult years and of Iacocca's work.

Chrysler's struggle to survive began a year before the start of a deep national economic recession from 1979 to 1982 that included soaring energy prices and gasoline shortages, double-digit inflation, and automobile loans at 20 percent and higher. This was the longest, deepest downturn in auto sales since the Great Depression. Combined sales of cars and trucks in the United States for all companies, domestic and foreign, fell from 15.4 million units in 1978 to 10.5 million in 1982. The Big Three and American Motors suffered even greater declines because foreign automakers increased their share of the American market during these years, from 15.2 percent in 1978 to 25.0 percent in 1982.

Table 14.1 shows the immensity of Chrysler's sales and financial crisis of

1978–82 and its remarkable recovery in 1983–84. Contrasting years in which the production volumes were similar, for example, 1980 with 1982, reveals the stunning turnaround in performance in this brief period. By its own calculations, the company reduced its break-even sales volume from 2.4 million units in 1979 to 1 million by 1982. By the early 1980s, Chrysler was much smaller, leaner, and more efficient than just a few years earlier. The company employed an average of 142,239 workers in its North American operations in 1978, but in 1983 had only half that number (70,409).[2] Chrysler's remarkable turnaround is impossible to imagine without the dynamic team of managers that began running Chrysler under the overall direction of Lee Iacocca.

TABLE 14.1 Chrysler Corporation Performance, North American Market, 1977–84

			Net Earnings†		
	Unit Production	Market Share* (%)	Total ($)	On Sales (%)	On Capital Invested‡ (%)
1977	2,011,646	12.2	163,200,000	1.2	5.6
1978	1,878,411	11.3	(204,600,000)	(1.6)	(31.6)
1979	1,414,066	10.1	(1,097,300,000)	(9.6)	(169.9)
1980	910,352	9.1	(1,709,700,000)	(19.9)	(256.0)
1981	1,011,864	9.5	(475,600,000)	(4.8)	(73.4)
1982	967,682	9.9	170,100,000	1.7	257.3
1983	1,301,348	9.9	700,900,000	5.3	99.9
1984	1,824,428	11.1	2,380,000,000	12.2	72.0

Sources: Chrysler Corporation, *Nineteen Eighty-Four Report to Shareholders,* box "Annual Reports 1968–98," DCHC; and "Financial and General Fact Book," February 1986, DCHC.
Note: Losses are indicated in parentheses.

*As measured by new car and truck registrations.
† After taxes.
‡ Defined as stockholders' equity and surpluses.

Lee Iacocca and the New Management Team

Chrysler Corporation named Lee Iacocca president and chief operating officer on 2 November 1978 and less than a year later named him chairman of the board and chief executive officer. Chrysler was able to hire Iacocca, a proven automotive executive, because he was without a job after Henry Ford II fired him as president of Ford Motor Company on 13 July 1978. Two weeks after Iacocca's firing, a reporter asked Riccardo if Chrysler had contacted Iacocca about him joining the company in an executive capacity. Riccardo gingerly dodged the question: "Mr. Iacocca is a very fine, outstanding automobile man. I think he's one of the best businessmen around. But this is a different organization. This isn't Ford, this is Chrysler. We have our team in place."[3]

Three and one-half months later, John Riccardo introduced Lee Iacocca as Chrysler's new president. Iacocca quipped, "Johnny called me and said, very simply, how about coming and giving me a hand? I said, 'OK' and here I am." Iacocca was upbeat and optimistic, while admitting he did not know much about Chrysler's situation. Still, he thought that "with a little good planning and a little bit of luck and with a little Divine guidance," Chrysler would soon earn profits again.[4]

The life of Lido Anthony Iacocca (1924–) is an American success story. Born in Allentown, Pennsylvania, he was the son of Italian immigrants Nicola and Antoinette Iacocca. Lee's drive, ambition, and lack of patience mirrored his father's qualities. His father operated a pair of successful hot dog restaurants in Allentown in the early 1920s, opened a car rental agency, invested successfully in real estate, and operated two movie theaters. Contracting rheumatic fever in the tenth grade, Lee Iacocca had to give up sports—he turned to reading instead. He excelled in high school, graduating twelfth in a class of over 900.[5]

Iacocca wanted to enlist in the armed forces after high school, but was declared unfit because of his history of rheumatic fever. He studied engineering at Lehigh University in Bethlehem, Pennsylvania, after he failed to win a scholarship to Purdue, his first choice. Iacocca completed Lehigh's program in mechanical engineering, took economics and business courses in his senior year, and graduated in 1945 with high honors. By attending eight straight semesters, with no summer vacation, he finished in three years. He went on to earn a master's degree at Princeton University in engineering. Ford Motor Company hired him into its engineering training program, and Iacocca began working at the River Rouge complex in Dearborn in August 1946. He remained with Ford for 32 years.[6]

Iacocca endured Ford's tough "Rouge Loop Course," in which engineering trainees spent nine months at the Rouge learning all the basic manufacturing operations involved in making cars. Disenchanted, he left engineering and went over to Ford's sales operation, selling trucks in Chester, Pennsylvania. Selling was Lee Iacocca's calling. Iacocca became a Ford zone manager in Wilkes-Barre in 1949.

The engineer-turned-salesman came to the attention of Ford headquarters through his imaginative "$56 a month for a '56 Ford" campaign, which boosted sales in Pennsylvania. Ford brought Iacocca to Dearborn in December 1956 to manage Ford Division's national truck marketing program. A year later, Iacocca took over car marketing and by 1960 was doing both jobs. In December 1960, Henry Ford II named him general manager of the Ford Division. At age 36, Iacocca was directing the production and sales of 80 percent of Ford Motor Company vehicles.[7]

His most famous achievement at Ford was the development of the Mustang, which Iacocca directed in conjunction with product planners Don Frey and Harold Sperlich. Introduced in April 1964, Mustang enjoyed record sales of nearly 419,000 units in its first 12 months and earned Ford profits of $1.1 billion (in 1964 dollars) in its first two years alone. In a remarkable public relations coup, the Mustang and Iacocca were the cover stories of both *Time* and *Newsweek* in the same week in April 1964. Iacocca credited the news coverage for the sale of 100,000 additional Mustangs that year.[8]

Iacocca did not lose his magic touch in developing successful new products following Mustang. He revitalized the languishing Lincoln-Mercury Division with the brand-new Mercury Couger and Mercury Marquis for 1967, followed by the Lincoln Mark III, which debuted in April 1968. Henry Ford II promoted Iacocca to the position of executive vice president–North American Automotive Operations in October 1967 and in December 1970 named him president of the Ford Motor Company—the position from which he fired him some seven and a half years later.[9]

The precise reasons behind Henry Ford's decision to fire Iacocca in July 1978 will never be known with any confidence. In April 1977, Henry Ford II created a three-member office of the chief executive, with Ford as chairman and CEO, but with Philip Caldwell serving as vice chairman and CEO in Ford's absence. Iacocca remained president, but was in effect demoted to the number three position of power. In June 1978, Henry Ford II added his younger brother, William Clay Ford, to the office of the chief executive, demoting Iacocca to the number four spot. A little more than a month later, Henry Ford II summarily fired Lee Iacocca, offering no explanation for the decision.[10]

Iacocca had dozens of job offers from major American corporations. John Riccardo and Chrysler director J. Richardson Dilworth first talked with Iacocca in early August about coming over to Chrysler as its president. The Chrysler Board of Directors officially hired him as president on 2 November. Riccardo agreed to serve as chairman and CEO until 1 January 1980 at the latest. Iacocca would earn $360,000 a year at Chrysler, the same as his Ford salary, and Chrysler would make up the $1.5 million of his Ford severance package he would forfeit by working for a competitor.[11]

Iacocca's arrival at Chrysler was not viewed by everyone as an automatic quick fix to the company's deep-seated problems. Iacocca had to address three major weaknesses at Chrysler—an extremely weak management team, an unappealing lineup of cars and trucks, and production costs much higher than at

Lee Iacocca taking the helm at Chrysler, November 1978. Courtesy of NAHC.

Ford or General Motors. Analysts Ronald Glanz and Donald DeScenza believed that Iacocca's greatest challenge would be to attract the capital needed to up-grade Chrysler's products and plants.[12]

Iacocca was shocked to discover just how dysfunctional Chrysler's manage-ment system was. Ironically for a company that had long been led by accoun-tants, there was no effective system of financial analysis in place. Townsend's accounting system generated daily figures for production and sales but none of the information needed for long-range cost analysis and planning. Most of the top executives were simply not very competent. Iacocca's observations about the existing managers were accurate, if brutal: "The place [Chrysler Corporation] had become known as a last resort: if someone couldn't hack it elsewhere, he could always go to Chrysler. Chrysler executives had a better reputation for their golfing abilities than for any expertise with cars."[13]

Within a few weeks of coming in as Chrysler president, Iacocca began a massive overhaul of the company's top executive ranks. Within a year, he had replaced virtually all of the vice presidents he had inherited. Most of the new executives came from outside of Chrysler, mainly from Ford. As president of Ford, Iacocca had initiated a system for reviewing the performance of about 100 top managers each quarter. He kept the results in a set of black notebooks, so this became known as the "black book" review system. When he left Ford in 1979, Iacocca asked William Clay Ford for permission to take his black notebooks with him and Ford agreed. The new Chrysler president could consult this detailed record of the top Ford executives. In recruiting many of Ford's brightest young talents, he gained sweet revenge for his firing by Ford.[14]

The worst of the problems Iacocca faced were unattractive, inappropriate products, an out-of-control purchasing system, lack of financial controls, a faltering marketing and sales system, and high-cost, poor-quality manufacturing.

Upgrading product planning was a fairly simple task. An old friend of Iacocca's, Harold (Hal) Sperlich, had been in charge of product planning at Ford until Henry Ford II fired him in December 1976. Sperlich had come to Chrysler in March 1977 as an executive assistant to the vice president for engineering. In late November 1978, Iacocca named him group vice president in charge of all product planning and engineering. Iacocca also brought in retired Ford styling director Don R. DeLaRossa as a design consultant in November 1979 and named him vice president for product design three months later.[15]

To straighten out Chrysler's chaotic purchasing system, Iacocca convinced J. Paul Bergmoser, who had been vice president for purchasing at Ford, to come out of retirement. Bergmoser was a tough negotiator and a disciplinarian who had reduced Ford's procurement costs while maintaining quality. He came to Chrysler as a consultant in January 1979 and Iacocca named him executive vice president for procurement and supply in June 1979. Bergmoser became president of Chrysler Corporation in September 1979 when Iacocca became chairman and served in that post until May 1981. He remained heavily involved in procurement.[16]

Iacocca brought in financial experts from Ford as the solution to the lack of financial controls at Chrysler. The most important was Gerald Greenwald, 44, who resigned his job as head of Ford Venezuela to become Chrysler's controller in April 1979. Greenwald agreed to take the position on a temporary basis only, because he wanted to remain in operations. Robert S. (Steve) Miller Jr., 38, and

Frederick W. Zuckerman, 45, both Ford finance men, came over at the same time. In September 1979, Greenwald became executive vice president for finance and was perhaps the second most important executive after Iacocca in orchestrating Chrysler's financial rescue.[17]

Iacocca also wanted to strengthen the areas of marketing, sales, and dealer relations. He convinced marketing genius E. F.(Gar) Laux, who had retired from Ford in June 1969, to join him at Chrysler in March 1979. Laux took the post of vice president for marketing and three months later became executive vice president for sales and marketing. Iacocca also recruited other young executives from Ford—Jerry H. Pyle, 42; John K. Givens, 39; and Joseph A. Campana, 42. Iacocca's ability to convince these rising stars to leave Ford and bet their futures on Chrysler is a testament to his powers of persuasion.[18]

Finally, a major area of major concern was Chrysler's rightly deserved reputation for poor manufacturing quality, which hurt sales and produced high warranty costs. Iacocca named Richard A. Vining executive vice president for manufacturing in November 1978. A graduate of the Chrysler Institute of Engineering, Vining had worked for Chrysler since 1948 in a variety of manufacturing management positions. Iacocca later promoted Stephan Sharf, who had served as vice president of the engine and casting division, to the post of executive vice president for manufacturing in January 1981.

Iacocca hired Richard E. Dauch, a manufacturing executive at General Motors and at Volkswagen of America, to improve the quality of Chrysler's factory production. He joined Chrysler in April 1980 as executive vice president of diversified operations. Dauch became executive vice president for manufacturing at Chrysler in 1985 and remained with the company until he retired in 1991. The drive to improve quality also involved Bergmoser, who reinstituted tight quality control standards for parts and components supplied from the outside. The primary objective was to assure that the new front-wheel drive K-cars, introduced for the 1981 model year, would be of better quality than previous Chrysler products.[19]

In addition to the revamping of the executive corps, Iacocca made two major changes in Chrysler's operations in the first six months he was on board. On 1 March 1979, he announced that the company had replaced its two advertising agencies, Young & Rubicam, which handled the Chrysler/Plymouth account, and Batten Barton Durstine & Osborne (BBDO), which had the Dodge account, with a single agency, New York–based Kenyon & Eckhardt (K & E). The new ad agency received a five-year contract worth $120 million a year, an unprecedented agreement in the automobile industry.[20]

Iacocca knew and respected the top K & E executives from his Ford days, when the agency had done an outstanding job of promoting the Ford Mustang and Lincoln/Mercury products. K & E had created the slogan "Ford Has a

Better Idea" and the highly successful use of the cougar for the Mercury Cougar cars and then for the entire Mercury line, through the "Sign of the Cat" promotion. The agency understood the emotional significance of cars and trucks to their owners and the importance of symbols in selling them. Right after coming to Chrysler, they reintroduced the symbol of the ram and the slogan, "Ram-Tough" for Dodge trucks.[21]

Kenyon & Eckhardt changed the focus of Chrysler's advertising and got the public's attention. They made Lee Iacocca the company's pitchman and the embodiment of Chrysler's comeback. When Iacocca first came to Chrysler, the Young & Rubicam ad agency asked him to appear on television ads, but he refused, confining himself to signing a series of print advertisements in August and September 1979 that explained Chrysler's troubles and the need for government aid. At the urging of the K & E executives, he did a series of television ads in late 1979 promoting Chrysler products. With some coaching, he became an effective pitchman, with classic tag lines, including "if you can find a better car—buy it." Kenyon & Eckhardt's research found that the public considered Iacocca sincere and credible. He frequently appeared in Chrysler print and television ads from 1980 to 1983, and *Advertising Age* named him Adman of the Year for 1983 in recognition of his impact.[22]

The second major reform was the elimination of the sales bank. By spring 1979, Iacocca understood how the sales bank worked and what a cancer it was on Chrysler's health. He and Gar Laux announced the cancellation of the traditional discounts and rebates used to clear unsold cars from the sales bank. Iacocca needed the rest of the 1979 model year to eliminate the sales bank. He pledged that, starting with the 1980 models, production would be geared to firm orders from customers or from dealers.

With Iacocca revamping the company's management and its internal operations in 1979, Chairman Riccardo continued to direct the company's external relations with its bankers, the federal regulators, and with Congress. He tried to convince Congress that federal emissions, safety, and fuel efficiency regulations had created Chrysler's financial problems and therefore it should provide relief. He remained optimistic that Congress and the Carter administration would help Chrysler.[23] His strategy to rescue the ailing company was simple, consistent, but ultimately counterproductive.

Riccardo spent the spring and summer of 1979 lobbying Congress and the Carter administration for assistance. He wanted a two-year delay in the imposition of stricter emissions standards. In July and August, Riccardo aggressively pushed for an immediate cash advance of $1 billion against future tax credits, but to no avail. Critics in Congress blamed incompetent management, especially Riccardo's, for Chrysler's condition and would not consider any type of aid as long as Riccardo remained at the helm.[24]

Chrysler's problems, real and perceived, seemed only to get worse as the summer waned. An article in the *Wall Street Journal* in early August pointed out that Chrysler might soon be in technical default of its 1977 loan agreement, when it received $500 million in credits from its banks but agreed to maintain working capital of at least $600 million. Its working capital had already slipped below $800 million and was moving even lower. Loans from General Motors Acceptance Corporation (GMAC) of $230 million and a $500 million loan from Household Finance Corporation in mid-August were stopgap measures.[25]

In mid-September 1979, Treasury Secretary G. William Miller turned down Chrysler's request for an aid package that included federal guarantees for $1.2 billion in loans. The next day, in a surprise announcement, John Riccardo resigned as Chrysler's chairman. He cited his deteriorating health as one reason for the move. Heart problems had surfaced in May, when he was briefly hospitalized for what his doctors described as "cardiac insufficiency." Riccardo stepped down mainly because he recognized that his continued high-profile presence was hurting Chrysler's chances for survival. In his statement to the press, he conceded: "In the minds of many, I am closely associated with the present management of a troubled company. It would be most unfair to the new management and to the employees of Chrysler if my continued presence as chairman should in any way hinder the final passage of our request for federal loan guarantees." Two days later, the Chrysler board of directors named Iacocca chairman and J. Paul Bergmoser president, ending the Townsend-Riccardo administration, which had spanned some 18 years.[26]

To the Edge of the Abyss: The Loan Guarantees

By summer 1979, Chrysler's future had become the subject of speculation in the automotive press. Possible mergers with other automobile companies came up frequently. The 25 June 1979 issue of *Automotive News* announced the imminent purchase of Chrysler by Volkswagen A.G. The German company would buy Chrysler's stock for $15 a share, although it recently traded at a mere $8. Volkswagen officials and Iacocca vehemently denied the story. To be sure, Iacocca had talked with the head of Volkswagen, Toni Schmuecker, about the advantages of producing identical cars on both sides of the Atlantic. Iacocca raised the prospect of a global merger, which he dubbed "the Grand Design," and which would include a Japanese automaker as well. As Chrysler's situation further deteriorated, Volkswagen quickly lost interest.[27]

In the end Chrysler found little help from foreign car companies. Instead, it turned to its employees, suppliers, banks, and to Congress for a helping hand. The United Automobile Workers, led by President Douglas Fraser, became more actively involved in Chrysler's fate by the middle of 1979. In late July, Fraser announced that Chrysler would not be the UAW's strike target for bargaining for a new contract in the fall. Blaming federal emissions and safety regulations for Chrysler's problems, Fraser called on the federal government to invest in the company by taking $1 billion in Chrysler stock, roughly one-third of the total. Direct assistance from the union was another matter. The UAW flatly rejected Chrysler's call for a two-year freeze on wages and benefits.[28]

Throughout much of 1979, many of Chrysler's bankers, congressional conservatives, publications such as the *Wall Street Journal,* and business groups suggested that bankruptcy and reorganization under Chapter 11 of the Bankruptcy Reform Act of 1978 was a better alternative than a public bailout of Chrysler. Those suggesting this strategy believed Chrysler should turn itself into a small car specialist, akin to American Motors. This notion, however, was fatally flawed. Once it had declared Chapter 11 bankruptcy, Chrysler would no longer have been able to sell its products for lack of consumer confidence and it would have had to liquidate its assets. Besides, a small company making only small cars would suffer both from the lack of economies of scale and from small profit margins.[29]

By early August 1979, Riccardo concluded that a federal government rescue package was Chrysler's only hope for survival. Operating losses continued to mount and the company was running out of cash. In March 1979, Manufacturers Hanover Bank had assembled a syndicate of more than 100 banks to extend Chrysler a $560 million line of credit. By July, the company had already used $408 million of the total. Riccardo formally requested federal assistance through regulatory relief and $1 billion in tax credits in early August, sending shock waves through the banking and financial communities. In mid-August 1979, Secretary of the Treasury G. William Miller announced the Carter administration's rejection of Riccardo's tax credit scheme. Instead, Miller proposed a loan guarantee package for Chrysler of up to $750 million.[30]

Many in Congress argued that federal loan guarantees for Chrysler would set a dangerous precedent, but such a precedent, dangerous or not, had already been set. In recent years the federal government had guaranteed bank loans for the Penn Central Railroad (1970), Lockheed Corporation (1971), and New York City (1978), among others. In his November 1979 testimony before the U.S. Senate Banking Committee, Lee Iacocca reminded Senator William Proxmire (R-Wisconsin) that the federal government had granted Wisconsin-based American Motors substantial tax credits, waivers, and special treatment on five occasions since 1967.[31]

The loan guarantee story was a two-act play. In the first act, the Treasury Department, Congress, and President Jimmy Carter agreed to legislation whereby the federal government would guarantee $1.5 billion in loans to Chrysler, on the condition that the automaker raise an additional $2 billion through concessions, economies, and loans. The House of Representatives and the Senate passed slightly different Chrysler loan bills on 18 and 19 December 1979 respectively, and a conference committee hammered out a compromise bill that both houses approved on 21 December. President Carter signed the Chrysler Loan Guarantee Act on 6 January 1980, concluding the first act of the drama.

In many respects, getting the loan guarantee legislation passed was the easy part. Political maneuvering, lobbying, and public relations campaigns brought the first act to a close. However, the second act of the drama—putting the required aid package together to qualify for the loan guarantee—did not end until 24 June 1980. Only then did the Chrysler Corporation, in the death throes of bankruptcy, satisfy the requirements of the legislation and receive its first transfusion ($500 million) of badly needed financial plasma.

Chrysler initially presented a rescue plan to the U.S. Treasury in mid-September calling for loan guarantees of $1.2 billion. The company projected that it would fall $2.1 billion short of the resources it needed to pay for new product development in 1980–82, but could raise $900 million in additional capital without federal aid. The difference, $1.2 billion in financing, would have to be guaranteed by the government. Treasury Secretary G. William Miller quickly rejected the scheme, in part because the plan included no specifics about the source of the $900 million Chrysler claimed it could raise on its own. His strongest complaint, however, was the lack of any firm concessions from the UAW, state governments, suppliers, or banks.[32]

With Iacocca leading the charge, Chrysler launched an effective, nonstop public relations campaign for federal government assistance starting in September 1979, followed by lobbying and political arm-twisting that lasted until the passage of the loan guarantee legislation. The company enlisted its 19,000 suppliers and 4,700 dealers in the campaign to change public opinion and to influence members of Congress. In announcing salary cuts of up to 10 percent for Chrysler's 1,700 top managers, Iacocca and Riccardo agreed to cut their own salaries to $1 a year until the company became profitable.[33]

To counter negative perception about the company, Kenyon & Eckhardt launched a campaign to shift public opinion in favor of the loan guarantees. The advertising campaign was aimed at convincing the car-buying public that Chrysler was only asking for a helping hand, not a handout, and that the company was reforming itself and developing new, fuel-efficient vehicles to guarantee its long-term future. One of the first ads, which appeared in the *Wall Street Journal* in mid-September under Iacocca's signature, featured the headline, "Chrysler's Problems Ultimately Won't Be Solved in Congress, the Treasury or the Banks. But in the Marketplace."[34]

Lee Iacocca's opening testimony on 18 October 1979 before the House Banking Committee, which was considering a loan guarantee bill, laid out Chrysler's basic argument for passage. Given some breathing room, Chrysler would introduce fuel-efficient cars and return to profitability. Bankruptcy was not an option, nor was a merger with another car company. A Chrysler bankruptcy would result in the loss of more than 500,000 jobs nationally and directly affect over 2 million people. In the first year alone, bankruptcy would cost federal, state, and local governments $10 billion in welfare and unemployment payments, lost taxes, pension liabilities, and other costs. Iacocca made essentially the same argument before the U.S. Senate a month later.[35]

The Chrysler chairman greatly exaggerated the likely permanent job losses from a bankruptcy, based on the most pessimistic view of the general health of the automobile industry. A Department of Transportation study completed in early September estimated that bankruptcy would produce direct job losses at Chrysler of 100,000, plus additional unemployment of 140,000–200,000 at Chrysler's suppliers and dealers, yielding a maximum loss of 300,000 jobs. Iacocca based his estimates on a study completed by Data Resources in August 1979 for the Congressional Budget Office, which estimated short-term unemployment at 500,000. Chrysler's own estimate of jobs saved through 1981 as a result of its survival (330,000) are more in line with the Department of Transportation estimate given above.

On 2 November 1979, the Carter administration announced its support for Chrysler aid. The federal government would guarantee $1.5 billion in loans provided Chrysler generate about $2 billion from economies and financial assistance from other sources. Chrysler would have to develop a detailed survival plan covering the period through the end of 1983 and would need government approval for major investment and product decisions. The administration agreed to a higher figure for the loan guarantees than the company's request for $1.2 billion based on a reassessment of the automaker's situation. Chrysler had just announced losses of $461 million for the third quarter.[36]

Political maneuvering, lobbying, and compromises finally led to the passage of the Chrysler Loan Guarantee Act of 1979 on 21 December 1979. Passage came in part because of systematic and unrelenting lobbying by Chrysler's dealers and suppliers, the UAW, and the bankers. Douglas Fraser, the president of the UAW, was skilled and tireless in lobbying for passage. The Speaker of the House, Thomas (Tip) O'Neill, gave an impassioned speech on behalf of the bill from the floor of the House.[37]

Chrysler needed nearly six months to assemble all the concessions from its constituents to satisfy the requirements of the Chrysler Loan Guarantee Act. The company was finally able to draw down the first $500 million in guaranteed loans on 24 June 1980 and used another $300 million on 31 July. The company

Chrysler Loan Guarantee Act signing, 7 January 1980. *Seated,* Lee Iacocca; *immediately behind, right to left,* Douglas Fraser, President Jimmy Carter, Michigan senator Don Riegle, and Michigan congressman Jim Blanchard. Courtesy of DCHC.

resorted to draconian cutbacks, strong-arm tactics with suppliers, and other "quick fixes" to weather 1979 and the first half of 1980. Layoffs of thousands of white-collar workers at a time became the order of the day. Between 17 December 1978 and 7 September 1980, a 21-month period, Chrysler laid off 10,000 white-collar workers, including managers, some 32 percent of the its white-collar labor force.[38]

The Loan Guarantee Act required a package of about $2 billion in concessions or aid for Chrysler from sources outside of the federal government. The major elements were wage concessions from the UAW ($462.5 million) and from salaried workers ($125 million); new loans or lower interest payments from both U.S. and foreign banks ($650 million); tax abatements, loans, or grants from state and local governments ($250 million) and concessions from suppliers and dealers ($180 million). Chrysler was to raise $50 million through a new stock issue and sell off $300 million in assets.[39]

The UAW led the concessions parade even before there was loan guarantee legislation in place. The union reopened its contract with Chrysler in October 1979 and agreed to wage concessions amounting to $203 million over three years. The workers would receive the same pay raises as their fellow workers at Ford or GM, but the "kick-in" dates would be delayed for several months. The contract also allowed Chrysler to defer $200 million in pension contributions until later.

The agreement set another important precedent as well— Iacocca nominated UAW president Douglas Fraser for a seat on the company board of directors. At the annual shareholders' meeting in May 1980, Fraser was elected to the Chrysler board by an overwhelming majority vote. (Although Iacocca denied that he had nominated Fraser as part of the concessions deal, Fraser claims this was the case.) Fraser accepted the board seat, but did not participate in board discussions of bargaining strategies vis-à-vis the UAW. He would, however, discuss and vote on all other matters relating to corporate policies and planning, including plant closures, new technology, and hiring practices.[40]

Douglas Fraser's election to the Chrysler Board of Directors was controversial. The *New York Times* ran a long feature article on the controversy on the eve of Fraser's election. Most corporate and labor leaders interviewed recognized Chrysler's unique circumstances. Thomas A. Murphy, the chairman of General Motors, was the most critical: "Directors, in my judgement, should not be elected because they represent some particular constituency. That is the wrong way to go." While Iacocca carefully avoided any reference to Fraser's union position in announcing the nomination, Fraser made it clear that he saw himself as a representative of the workers' interests. One of his priorities was to convince Chrysler management to develop a more humane way of handling plant closings.[41]

The Loan Guarantee Act called for UAW concessions of $462.5 million, but the $203 million already granted in October would count against the total. In five days in early January, Fraser and his negotiators reached a new agreement with Chrysler that achieved the additional savings ($259.5 million) Chrysler needed. UAW members received an employee stock ownership plan (ESOP) from Chrysler, as required in the loan guarantee legislation. Chrysler put $162.5 million in stock into a fund, a share of which workers could claim based on their length of service, but only when they quit or retired.[42]

During the early months of 1980, Chrysler stayed afloat simply by not paying its bills and convincing its creditors to accept delayed payments. In mid-January, $100 million due to suppliers went unpaid; at the end of the month, Chrysler stopped paying Japanese banks for the Mitsubishi cars they had financed; and in mid-February, suppliers agreed to wait until mid-April for $150 million owed them.[43]

The burden of lining up the package of concessions fell on Gerald Greenwald and Steve Miller. They slowly assembled the pieces, including pay concessions from nonunion workers; aid from Indiana ($39 million), Delaware ($5 million), and Michigan ($150 million loan); and $200 million in loan guarantees from the Canadian government. When aid was available in the form of cash, the company used it to pay outstanding bills. On 25 April 1980, Chrysler laid off another 6,900 salaried staff, for a projected savings of $200 million a year.[44]

The banks remained the final, frustrating stumbling block to completing the aid package. The loan guarantee legislation mandated that the banks, both domestic and foreign, provide Chrysler with $650 million in aid, primarily in the form of new loans. Gerald Greenwald and Steve Miller originally hoped to have all the banks signed on by early April. The most difficult lenders to persuade were the foreign banks and the smallest of the American banks. A handful of banks could have derailed the entire loan guarantee train. In June, Chrysler simply stopped paying its suppliers, who could have pushed the company over the edge by insisting on payment or by refusing to ship supplies or parts. They did neither. Finally, on 19 June, Steve Miller convinced the last holdout, the North Little Rock, Arkansas, Twin City Bank, which had loaned Chrysler $78,000, to come on board.[45]

After frantic work by armies of lawyers to assemble all the paperwork and a fire in the Westvaco Building on Park Avenue in Manhattan that threatened the documents, Chrysler and the Loan Guarantee Board officially announced their agreement on the loan guarantees shortly after noon on 24 June 1980. The underwriting syndicate headed by Salomon Brothers had already sold the offering of $500 million in government-guaranteed notes in one day. Later that afternoon, Steve Miller deposited a check for $486,750,000 into Chrysler's account at Manufacturers Hanover Bank and the company could start paying its bills again.[46]

The first guaranteed loan was only the beginning of a relationship between Chrysler and the Loan Guarantee Board that lasted for more than three years. The company quickly drew down another $300 million in loan guarantees on 31 July 1980. Chrysler had to submit operating and financial plans on a regular basis to the board for its approval as long as any loans were outstanding. Board authorization was required for all contracts larger than $10 million and for the sale of any asset worth more than $5 million. At least once a month for more than three years, Iacocca reported to the Loan Guarantee Board in Washington on Chrysler's plans and progress. He had to explain and justify all of Chrysler's major decisions. The Loan Guarantee Board was not like the pliant boards of directors that Iacocca customarily dealt with.[47]

On the eve of the first loan drawdown and its attendant negative publicity, Chrysler's showroom traffic and sales suffered. Leo-Arthur Kelmenson, the CEO of Kenyon & Eckhardt, suggested to Iacocca an aggressive advertising campaign to counteract the bad publicity associated with the loan guarantee. He also wanted the car-buying public to view Chrysler more favorably *before* the launch of the K-cars in late summer. He urged Iacocca to do a 30–second television spot with Frank Sinatra. The ad, which emphasized that Chrysler had the financing in place to stay in business and the kind of cars that the American public wanted, aired in late July.[48]

THE K-CAR AND THE CONTINUING STRUGGLE

Conventional wisdom holds that Chrysler's new front-wheel drive compact car introduced in fall 1980, the so-called K-car (Dodge Aries and Plymouth Reliant), quickly and single-handedly brought the company back to health. Nothing could be further from the truth. The new models had a rocky initial launch and had modest sales for most of the time they were in production. Chrysler frequently offered rebates to sell the K-cars.

The company suffered enormous losses for 1980 and 1981, and even the modest profits earned for 1982 reflected the sale of Chrysler's defense operations and not operating profits from motor vehicle production. Chrysler extracted additional concessions from its stakeholders in early 1981 and engaged in severe belt-tightening in both 1981 and 1982 to remain afloat. Without the K-car, the company certainly would not have survived, but this car line did not single-handedly turn the company around. It was more significant because it served as the platform for virtually all of Chrysler's new products from 1981 to 1985 and beyond.

The "K-body" was the code name for the replacement model for the ill-fated Dodge Aspen/Plymouth Volare. Chrysler used the "K-car" moniker so successfully in its advertising that the actual model names, Dodge Aries and Plymouth Reliant, were not widely recognized. This was the car Hal Sperlich and Iacocca unsuccessfully urged Henry Ford II to consider in the mid-1970s— a six-passenger, front-wheel drive vehicle with excellent fuel economy. This was a more risky and expensive new model for Chrysler than a conventional rear-wheel drive design because virtually all of the major components were brand new. According to Sperlich, using a front-wheel drive design added about $300 million to engineering and tooling costs.[49]

Iacocca announced preliminary plans for the K-cars in June 1979, including the decision to produce the models at the Jefferson Avenue plant in Detroit and at the Newark, Delaware, assembly plant. Chrysler spent $50 million at Newark and $100 million revamping the aged Jefferson Avenue plant, which would be equipped with 90 welding robots (Unimates), an automated framing system (Robogate), and a variety of computer-controlled quality control systems. Other major investments in plant and equipment included $120 million at the Kokomo, Indiana, transmission plant to make transaxles for the K-car and $150 million at the Trenton, Michigan, engine plant for the 2.2-liter four-cylinder engine that would be standard equipment on the new models.[50]

The company also implemented improved methods for "debugging" the new models before they reached customers. Service engineers assisted with the launch at both Jefferson Avenue and Newark for a period of four to twelve weeks. The first 100 K-cars to come off the assembly line were taken to the Chelsea Proving Grounds for 5,000 miles of testing for quality and durability. K-cars were not delivered to dealers until the engineers at Chelsea signed off. Another set of cars was shipped to 22 select dealerships for intensive quality checks.[51]

K-car production was distinct from that of earlier Chrysler products in that the company and the union established a cooperative joint program to improve quality, formally called the Product Quality Improvement (PQI) Program. It involved joint union-management meetings to discuss quality issues and the establishment of a quality committee at each plant. The key was worker input into changing production practices to improve quality. Richard Vining, Chrysler's vice president for manufacturing, and those who succeeded him supported the program, as did Douglas Fraser and Marc Stepp, the head of the UAW's Chrysler Department. Stepp's standard line to workers was, "no quality, no sales . . . no sales, no jobs." This was indeed a New Chrysler Corporation.[52]

The launch of the K-cars was a time of heady optimism. The company predicted sales of about 500,000–600,000 units in the first model year. The first K-cars came off the line at Jefferson Avenue on 6 August and from the Newark factory on 3 September. In Detroit, Iacocca simply gushed: "This is K-day for Chrysler, it's D-day for Detroit, and it's a new day for America." The optimism seemed well founded. Iacocca revealed that fleet buyers liked the cars so much that Chrysler had to cut off its advance orders at 45,000 units.[53]

Early sales of the K-cars were far below the numbers Iacocca had predicted. First of all, the factories had production glitches with the new robotic welding machines and other new technologies. The company wanted 35,000 cars in dealers' showrooms on Introduction Day (3 October), but instead had only 10,000. Iacocca blamed Richard Vining for these problems and forced his "early retirement" in January 1981. Stephan Sharf, a Chrysler insider who successfully managed the development and production of the new four-cylinder 2.2-liter engine at the Trenton, Michigan, engine plant, became executive vice president for manufacturing.[54]

But the production glitches proved to be a minor problem for the K-cars. Iacocca, Gerald Greenwald, and Gar Laux committed a fundamental marketing mistake in introducing the K-car. After pricing the base models of Aries and Reliant ($5,880) well below GM's base X-car, the Chevrolet Citation Hatchback ($6,270), they shipped a large share of the units loaded with options. What had been advertised as an economy car simply wasn't. Customers walked into dealerships to find K-cars priced from $9,000 to over $10,000, including destination charges and taxes. Reeling from the sticker shock of a five-figure price

1981 Plymouth Reliant, the first K-car. Courtesy of DCHC.

tag, made worse by high interest rates on car loans, they walked out of the showrooms and looked elsewhere.[55]

By mid-November, Iacocca realized the seriousness of the marketing blunder and began to take corrective action. First, Chrysler increased the production of the base model coupe ($5,880) and introduced a base model four-door sedan at $5,980. More important, the company created a reasonably well-equipped, moderately priced K-car with vinyl bench seats and the five most popular options—automatic transmission, power steering, wheel covers, AM radio, and white sidewall tires. The result was a coupe priced at a more reasonable $6,595 and a four-door sedan at $6,695. Sales eventually revived, but amounted to only 307,000 units for the 1981 model year, only half of the volume predicted.[56]

High interest rates and a continuing national economic recession also hurt sales. In July 1980, at the time of the K-car launch, the prime interest rate was 11 percent, the lowest it had been in 18 months. By early October, it had climbed to 13.5 percent, and it reached 21 percent by the end of the year. To counteract this development and to jump-start K-car sales, Iacocca introduced a unique incentive system for new car buyers. Chrysler offered a cash rebate based on the difference between the cost of a car loan at 13 percent and the total payments the buyer would have to pay on the loan at the going interest rate.[57]

The K-cars received *Motor Trend*'s 1981 Car of the Year Award in February 1981. The editors explained, "In this part of the new decade, Passenger Comfort, Ride & Drive, Styling & Design and, most important, Dollar Value are more relevant than all-out performance. In these classes, the K-car simply outscored its competition." *Motor Trend* tested seven cars for the competition. Plymouth Reliant-K finished first and Dodge Aries-K second in the overall rankings, so the magazine awarded them the honor jointly. The editors ended the test report with the observation: "Chrysler has used the K-car catch term at every opportunity, including its national advertising. In an American sort of way, the K-car has become a pop symbol of hard work, truth and the idea that Yankee ingenuity is still around." *Popular Science*'s automotive editor, Jim Dunne, said of the K-cars: "If Chrysler could have designed a car that was right for today's market just three weeks ago instead of three and a half years ago, they still would have designed this car."[58]

K-car sales for the 1982 through 1985 model years averaged only about 260,000 units and never topped the annual sales records of the Aspen/Volare twins in 1976–79. However, the real significance of the K-cars for Chrysler went beyond the sales, revenues, and profits generated. The K-car platform, including the drive train and other components, served as the basis for most new Chrysler products introduced in 1982 and the years that followed.

Chrysler reintroduced the Imperial nameplate in the 1981 model year after dropping it after the 1975 model year. The plan was to sell 25,000 Imperials annually and to earn a profit of $5,000 per car, yielding earnings of $125 million a year on an investment of only $75 million. The new model was a mid-sized, two-door, "personal luxury car," which came in only one body style with only one available option, a powered "moon roof," and a sticker price of about $18,000. The car carried a special 24-month/30,000-mile warranty that covered everything except tires and included free service and maintenance.[59]

The new Imperial had a glitzy launch on 11 August 1980 at the Windsor, Ontario, assembly plant. Lee Iacocca drove the first Imperial off the line and then presented it to singer Frank Sinatra, the "Chairman of the Board" who had appeared in Chrysler ads and had accepted only $1 for his services. Imperial sales, however, were disappointing for the three years the model survived—7,225 units (1981), 2,329 units (1982), and 1,427 units (1983), for a grand total of only 10,981 units.[60]

The production and marketing glitches that accompanied the launch of the K-car and the disappointing sales of the new Imperial, combined with continued high interest rates and the national economic recession, ruled out any substantial recovery for Chrysler in 1980. The company lost $1.71 billion for the year, but was not alone in its suffering. Ford had losses of $1.5 billion for 1980 and General Motors finished the year $763 million in the red.

Chrysler experienced a second major cash crisis in November and December 1980, after barely surviving the first half of the year. The struggling company entered the fall selling season with 100,000 leftover 1980 models in stock. With interest rates climbing to 20 percent at the end the year and growing economic uncertainty, dealers cut back on their orders and fleet buyers hedged on taking deliveries of their previous orders. With sales plummeting, Chrysler shut down the Belvidere Omni/Horizon plant for all of the December and both K-car plants for most of the month. At year's end, the automaker was operating only two of its five assembly plants, hardly a picture of a company on the rebound.[61]

With Chrysler's cash flow crisis continuing, Iacocca and Greenwald met with the Loan Guarantee Board in early December 1980 and requested a quick draw-down of the remaining $700 million in unused guaranteed loans. They wanted to get the loans before the new Republican administration of Ronald Reagan took office in January 1981. Treasury Secretary Miller agreed to consider additional loan guarantees in the amount of $400 million only, preferring to hold the last $300 million in reserve to help attract a potential merger partner for Chrysler. As a requirement for additional loan guarantees, the company would need to get another set of contributions from labor, suppliers, and the banks.[62]

From December 1980 through February 1981, Lee Iacocca, Gerry Greenwald, and Steve Miller assembled a new package of concessions amounting to more than $1 billion. The key UAW concession was a 21-month wage freeze plus the end of COLAs through the end of the agreement in September 1982. This amounted to wage concessions of $622 million. In December 1980, Iacocca gave the union an ultimatum that has become a Detroit legend: "It's freeze time, boys. I've got plenty of jobs at seventeen dollars an hour; I don't have any at twenty. Do you want 'em?" The UAW Chrysler workers approved the concessions on 30 January 1981 by a three to two margin.[63]

The other "partners" in Chrysler's future also granted further concessions in time for the company to receive $400 million in guaranteed loans on 27 February 1981. Salaried workers gave up another $161 million through September 1982. Suppliers agreed to an across-the-board retroactive price cut of 5 percent for the first quarter of 1981 and a price freeze for the rest of the year, estimated to cost them about $72 million. The Canadian government guaranteed an additional $200 million in loans to Chrysler. The bankers nearly killed the agreement by refusing to grant additional concessions, but finally agreed to restructure Chrysler's long-term debts. They converted $560 million of debt into Chrysler preferred stock. The remaining debt, some $740 million, could be paid off by Chrysler at 30¢ on $1.[64]

Even with the last round of concessions and $400 million in guaranteed loans cobbled together in February 1981, Chrysler's long-term viability remained uncertain. In March, Iacocca explored a possible merger of Chrysler and Ford Motor Company, but Ford's chairman, Phillip Caldwell, dismissed the idea and did not even allow his own board time to study the proposal in detail. On 11 April, he publicly announced Ford's rejection of the merger proposal.[65]

Chrysler faced another crisis in November 1981, when its cash balance stood at only $1 million, mere pocket change for a firm spending $50 million a day. It operated the rest of the year with a cash balance of under $10 million, but kept its cash flow problems secret. Iacocca decided against returning to the Loan Guarantee Board for the remaining $300 million in loans, in part because this would trigger another sales crisis. He concluded that Chrysler needed to sell off one more major asset to boost its cash reserves. He decided to sell Chrysler Defense, which was mainly the tank operation, and asked Lehman Brothers to find a buyer. Although the division was earning profits of $60 million a year, it was peripheral to Chrysler's core business. In February 1982 General Dynamics Corporation bought Chrysler's defense operations for $340 million.[66]

Chrysler continued to suffer through recession conditions in 1982, when it sold only 968,000 vehicles. The company offered factory rebates in March in an effort to jump-start sales. These ranged from $300 on many of the imports and smaller cars to $2,000 on Imperial and Dodge Ramcharger trucks. Rebates of $600–750 on different versions of the Plymouth Reliant K and Dodge Aries K must have been particularly painful. The advertisements began with the challenge, "If You Can Find a Better Rebate, Take It. If You Can Find a Better Car, Buy It."[67]

The company's financial recovery began in 1982, when it earned a modest profit, but really had to wait until the national economy enjoyed a healthy recovery in 1983. Chrysler's production in 1982 (967,682 units) was down 4 percent from 1981, but was 6 percent above the disastrous performance of 1980. Robust sales of 1.3 million vehicles in 1983, combined with the company's lean cost structure, brought large profits ($701 million) despite the payback of $1.2 billion in guaranteed loans that year. The dramatic turnaround in Chrysler's fortunes vindicated Iacocca and the federal loan guarantee program, while creating a new set of problems for Chrysler.

THE RETURN TO PROFITS

At first glance, the company seemed to return to profitability in 1982, when it posted earnings of $170 million for the year. The results for the entire year were nothing to crow about—operating losses of $69 million became a net profit of $170.1 million for the year only because of the sale of Chrysler Defense. This was nevertheless an impressive result in a seriously depressed economy where U.S. automakers sold only 5.8 million vehicles, the lowest sales in 21 years, and Chrysler made fewer than 1 million of the total.[68]

The company's apparent recovery brought increased restlessness and resentment among unionized workers over their continuing sacrifices. By summer of 1982, when the UAW prepared for negotiations for the contract due to expire in September, Douglas Fraser made it clear that the union wanted to close at least part of the $3-an-hour wage gap between Chrysler workers and those at Ford and General Motors. In September, the company and the union reached a tentative agreement that provided no pay increases other than cost-of-living allowances. Fraser and the other UAW leaders worried about the reactions of the membership to this contract—and for good reason.

The UAW Chrysler Council narrowly recommended approval, but the rank and file rejected the agreement in early October by a two to one margin. Fraser presented the workers with a referendum in which they could vote to continue negotiations or strike. The American UAW members chose the former, but the Canadian workers went on strike. At the end of December 1982, Chrysler and the UAW agreed to a new one-year contract that gave American workers an immediate pay raise of 75¢ an hour, with Canadian workers getting an increase of $1.15 an hour. In return, the UAW gave up the profit-sharing plan that was supposed to run for another year.[69]

Chrysler become profitable again in 1983 in part because the company continued to cut its overhead costs and its break-even point. With continuing wage and other concessions in place, its operating costs remained low. Once the K-car production and pricing glitches were corrected, the new models started making money for the corporation. More important was the introduction of successful new vehicles, all based on the K-car platform and therefore done "on the cheap," in both the 1982 and 1983 model years.

Chrysler had adopted an innovative front-wheel drive design for its 1978 Omni/Horizon line of subcompacts, but this was a single one-time experiment. With the K-cars, the New Chrysler Corporation committed itself to becoming a front-wheel drive car company. Using front-wheel drive design was the fastest and most cost-effective way to meet federal gas mileage standards. Front-wheel drive let the designer eliminate the drive shaft and the center hump on the floor and make the car "bigger on the inside and smaller on the outside." Downsizing and eliminating the drive shaft also brought weight savings. Lower weights and more efficient drive trains meant in turn that smaller engines could power the vehicle.[70]

A direct comparison of the 1981 Dodge Aries K (four-door sedan with the base engine and manual transmission) with the 1976 Dodge Aspen, its predecessor, illustrates the impact of front-wheel drive. The Aries K was 13 inches shorter

(99.6 versus 112.5 inches) and nearly 900 pounds lighter (2,300 versus 3,190 pounds). The K-car was adequately powered by a four-cylinder 135 cid engine that developed 84 brake hp, while the Aspen came equipped with a six-cylinder in-line engine with 225 cid and 100 brake hp. The EPA mileage ratings were 26 mpg city/41 mpg highway for the Aries K versus 20 city/27 highway for the Dodge Aspen.[71]

Iacocca, Sperlich and company took the K-car platform, particularly the drive train, and used it as the basis for a series of new cars introduced in the 1982 model year and beyond. The K-car begat the all-new Chrysler LeBaron and Dodge 400 series for the 1982 model year, well-disguised upscale cars that sold well in their first year—more than 90,000 LeBarons and 31,449 Dodge 400s. Iacocca also reintroduced the convertible, which no American company had made since 1976. Acting on a whim, he decided to produce a convertible version of the new LeBaron. Chrysler's marketing researchers projected sales of 3,000 convertibles in the first model year, but the company sold 24,000.

Chrysler used the same design formula again in the 1983 model year, with the introduction of the Chrysler E Class, Dodge 600, and the Chrysler New Yorker, all using front-wheel drive. The three new models for 1983 generated additional sales of just under 100,000 units combined. The Chrysler LeBaron Town & Country convertible, with simulated wood panels on its body sides, followed in January 1983. In the fall of 1983, the company introduced the Dodge Daytona/Chrysler Laser sports cars, also based on K-car mechanical components. By the 1983 model year, all but three Chrysler models were front-wheel drive.[72]

Chrysler's remarkable recovery was evident when it repaid all of the federally guaranteed loans in the spring and summer of 1983, some seven years ahead of schedule. In June 1983, Chrysler paid back the $400 million loan it had made in February 1981. This loan carried a whopping interest rate of 14.9 percent versus the comparatively cheap rates of 10.35 percent and 11.4 percent on the first two loans of $500 million and $300 million.[73]

Iacocca then decided to repay all of the remaining loans in the summer of 1983. He announced the payback at the National Press Club in Washington, D.C., on 13 July 1983. Ironically, this was the five-year anniversary of Iacocca's firing by Henry Ford II. A month later, on 15 August, he presented a check for $813,487,500 to Chrysler's bankers, repaying the loans in full.

However, one sticky issue remained. As part of the original loan guarantee program, Chrysler granted the federal government warrants (options) to buy 14.4 million shares of Chrysler stock at $13 a share, at a time when Chrysler common stock sold for less than $10 a share. Three years later, when its shares sold for about $30, the company would have to issue another 14.4 million shares of stock.

In May 1983, Chrysler asked the Treasury Department to return the warrants

The "Gang of Ford" and friends at the Washington, D.C. National Press Club, 13 July 1983, announcing the repayment of the guaranteed loans. *Left to right,* Gerald Greenwald, Douglas Fraser, Lee Iacocca, Senator Don Riegle, Hal Sperlich, and Michigan governor Jim Blanchard. Courtesy of WRL.

at no cost, since it had repaid the loans early. When the government offered the warrants on the open market, Salomon Brothers, acting on behalf of Chrysler, bought the warrants for more than $21 a share. For Chrysler, the loan guarantee program was hardly a "bailout." The monetary cost of borrowing $1.2 billion was staggering—$404 million in interest payments to the lenders, $33 million in fees to the government, $67 million in other legal and banking fees, and $311 million to buy back the stock warrants—for a grand total of $815 million.[74]

The return to prosperity brought a worsening in relations with the UAW. In June 1983, the UAW insisted that the existing contract be reopened before it expired in January 1984. Negotiations began in July, with the company offering a one-year contract with an increase of $1.42 an hour and the union demanding $2.42 over two years and parity with workers at Ford and GM by the end of the contract. New UAW president Owen Bieber announced in August that the union would strike Chrysler if there was no new contract in place. Not wanting to disrupt the launch of the company's new minivans in January 1984, Iacocca pushed hard for an agreement, which came in early September 1983. The company granted its workers their pay demands and restored the "annual improvement" pay raise of 3 percent as well.[75]

After the death of Iacocca's wife, Mary, in mid-May 1983 from complications resulting from diabetes, speculation began that Iacocca would leave Chrysler once he had repaid the guaranteed loans. The Chrysler Board of Directors, well aware of Iacocca's value to the company, worried that another corporation would lure him away. At the end of 1983, they offered him a lucrative three-year contract, which he accepted.[76]

The board increased his base salary, approximately $365,000 per year for 1981 and 1982, to $475,308 (1983), $569,838 (1984), and $667,455 (1985). Under the terms of his contract, Iacocca also earned incentive pay of $625,000 for 1983 and $950,000 for 1984. As a result, his final salary for 1983, slightly more than $1.1 million, was more than double his 1982 pay. When the profits from exercising his stock options ($4.3 million) are taken into account, his total compensation for 1983 was roughly $5.4 million. For 1984, Iacocca earned $1,519,838 from his base salary and incentive pay combined, but the value of stock options he exercised in 1984 is not known. The Chrysler board also gave him 150,000 shares of Chrysler common stock on 2 November 1986 and another 50,000 shares on 8 December 1987. In addition, he had an option to buy another 300,000 shares in 1986 and 100,000 in 1987, all at the price of $28 per share.[77]

Douglas Fraser was the lone Chrysler director to vote against Iacocca's new contract, characterizing the compensation as scandalous and insensitive to the Chrysler workers who had sacrificed so much since 1978. In typical Doug Fraser style, he asked, "how much pasta can the man eat, anyway?"[78] Because of this generous pay package, and for other reasons as well, Lee Iacocca remained as Chrysler's CEO through the rest of the 1980s. Perhaps this monetary compensation was an appropriate reward for his work in reviving the corporation.

CHRYSLER'S REVIVAL IN PERSPECTIVE

The number three American automaker survived the crisis of 1978–83 and went on to earn healthy profits for most of the rest of the 1980s. The federal loan guarantee program worked, Chrysler avoided bankruptcy, and thousands of workers, including those employed by suppliers, kept their jobs. In time, the banks and other lenders recovered most of the value of their loans, and stockholders enjoyed dividends and rising share prices as well. The New Chrysler Corporation survived because it transformed itself into a smaller, leaner, and much more efficient operation than before. Survival involved traumatic adjustments, including the permanent layoff of more than a third of the company's workers and the closing of dozens of plants. One key to Chrysler's recovery was a dramatic improvement in the quality of the vehicles it manufactured. Another was the reform and modernization of the company's entire management structure.

A primary result of Chrysler's survival was the preservation of jobs, but lost jobs were also the principal cost of the company's new lease on life. Average North American employment, which stood at 142,239 in 1978, fell to a low of 66,412 for 1982, a decline of 53 percent. The following year, the company increased employment slightly to 70,409, but produced nearly 334,000 more vehicles than in 1982. To be sure, Chrysler employment then jumped to 84,973 in 1984, an increase of 21 percent, but production increased some 40 percent.[79]

The layoffs hit blue-collar workers harder than white-collar workers and employees in the greater Detroit area harder than elsewhere. Average employment of hourly workers fell from 105,469 in 1978 to 44,114 in 1982, a decline of 58 percent. In contrast, the number of salaried employees fell from 36,770 to 21,298 over the same period, a significant retrenchment of 42 percent, but much less than that experienced by the factory workers. The Detroit area was especially hard hit by layoffs, simply because most of Chrysler's plants were there. In early 1978, Chrysler employed 81,700 in greater Detroit, some 57 percent of its North American payroll. By June 1980, the numbers had already fallen to 47,200 and would fall even further over the next two years.[80]

The precise number of plants permanently closed or sold is not easy to determine, in part because of inconsistencies in the counts found in different sources. A summary of facilities compiled in August 1979 indicated a total of 50 plants in the United States and Canada. In a September 1980 report submitted to the Loan Guarantee Board, Chrysler claimed to have already closed 9 plants of a total of 53, but intended to shut down another 23 of the 44 remaining facilities.[81]

The number of plants that Chrysler disposed of by closure or sale by the end of 1983 was not the 32 predicted in September 1980, but more like 21. The long-term advantages of the plant closings for Chrysler were enormous. The company saved money by increased outsourcing. Harold Sperlich explained Chrysler's cost advantages in a September 1983 interview. Chrysler made only 30 percent of its parts in-house, versus 55 percent for Ford and 70 percent for General Motors, and most of Chrysler's parts came from nonunion low-wage plants. Lee Iacocca made similar observations in remarks he made to security analysts in December 1983.[82]

A crude indicator of productivity at Chrysler is the number of vehicles produced per worker over the course of the company's crisis and recovery, shown in table 14.2.

Part of the remarkable jump in the average number of vehicles per worker

TABLE 14.2 Chrysler Corporation Vehicle Production and Employee Costs, 1977–84

	North American Unit Production	Average Number of Employees	Units Produced per Employee	Average Hourly Costs per Employee* ($)
1977	2,011,646	143,411	13.95	12.50
1978	1,878,411	142,239	13.20	14.11
1979	1,414,066	121,806	11.61	16.49
1980	910,352	90,195	10.09	19.14
1981	1,011,864	76,522	13.22	19.52
1982	967,682	66,412	14.57	20.18
1983	1,301,348	70,804	18.48	20.60
1984	1,824,428	84,973	21.47	21.67

Sources: Chrysler Corporation, "Financial and General Fact Book," February 1986, DCHC.

*Includes fringe benefits.

between 1980 and 1984 reflects the fact that much of the workforce in 1980 worked only part-time, while 1984 employees were typically working overtime hours. The improvement between 1977, the last "normal" year of production, and 1984 is perhaps a better indicator or the difference between the "old" and the "new" Chrysler Corporation. The figures also illustrate the modest pay raises Chrysler gave its employees in a period of double-digit inflation, due entirely to the various wage concessions extracted from union workers.

Iacocca and his manufacturing staff had to improve the quality of the company's vehicles if there was any hope of improving sales. Chrysler measured the quality of its vehicles by counting "conditions per hundred" (C/100), which is simply a count of the number of defects or problems reported by customers. This is at best an imprecise measure of quality because the "conditions" may range from a serious defect, such as the failure of engine mounts, to a minor paint defect. Furthermore, it is probably an understatement of quality problems because all customers might not report all defects, particularly if they were numerous.

A case in point was the record of the "R-body" cars, the Dodge St. Regis/ Chrysler Newport/Chrysler New Yorker, all-new cars introduced as 1979 models and delivered to showrooms months late because of a botched launch. For the first full year of R-body production, Chrysler's quality engineering staff predicted 1,077 conditions per hundred, which meant that each car had, on average, nearly 11 defects. For every car that had only 4 or 5 defects, there was another that might have 15. The manufacturing division was committed to reducing the rate to 740 C/100 for the 1980 models and to 590 C/100 the following year. In contrast, the Japanese auto companies consistently delivered vehicles with fewer than 200 conditions per hundred.[83]

Improvements in the real and perceived quality of Chrysler products came as a result of the commitment by Iacocca and his executives to change. The internal discussions regarding quality goals for the two new 1981 model introductions—the Chrysler Imperial (Y-body) and the K-cars—show the changed attitudes of the new managers. In October 1979, some 10 months before the launch of the Imperial, E. W. Gaynor of the corporate sales staff noticed that the company's quality targets for the new Imperial were 630 C/100 for the 1981 model year and 500 C/100 for the 1982 models. Gaynor complained to his bosses in sales that these defect targets were unacceptably high, especially for a luxury car. Once Chrysler president Paul Bergmoser got wind of these "targets," he notified George Butts, the vice president in charge of quality, that these were simply unacceptable quality goals for the new Imperial.[84]

The detailed monitoring of quality issues by Chrysler's highest officials was a clear sign that improved quality was a top priority. In November 1980, Bergmoser complained to Butts about his failure to improve the K-car's quality record: "I do not believe that we can continue building 'K' cars for the next three years at levels of 400–450 defects per hundred." In mid-February 1981, Stephan Sharf sent Sperlich a detailed explanation of how they were fixing K-car power brake problems, including the specific dates when changes would be implemented at the assembly plant. At the end of the month, Sharf sent Bergmoser a four-page memo outlining the ongoing quality improvements being made to the K-car. In addition to changes in the power brakes, Sharf identified 13 defects already fixed or in the process of correction.[85]

Chrysler's remarkable recovery in 1980–83 would not have happened without federal government assistance. The loan guarantee program alone represented a significant change in federal government policy toward Chrysler. In the final two years of the Carter administration and the first year of the Reagan administration, Chrysler received significant regulatory relief and preferential treatment from Washington. First, in June 1979, the Department of Transportation lowered the fuel economy standard for pickup trucks and vans by eight-tenths of a mile per gallon. In August 1979, the EPA exempted half of the company's 1981 production from the new standard of 3.4 grams of CO emissions allowed per mile traveled and instead allowed 7 grams, the previous standard. In March 1980, the EPA announced that the same exemption would apply to the four-cylinder engines that would power the K-cars.[86]

Although the Reagan administration strongly opposed the loan guarantee program, it nevertheless aided Chrysler and the auto industry in other ways.

Because of U.S. government pressure, the Japanese Ministry of International Trade and Industry (MITI) announced "voluntary" export limits. For the year starting 1 April 1981, Japan would limit its car exports to the United States to 1.68 million units and would limit any growth in the following year to 16.5 percent of the growth in the American market. The previous year, the Japanese had exported more than 2 million cars to the United States and had taken more than 25 percent of the market. The voluntary export restraints remained in effect until 1994, but had less significance over time as the Japanese car companies began to assemble their products in the United States.[87]

Chrysler's revival in 1980–83 was a monumental struggle that succeeded only because of the willingness of all of the members of the Chrysler "family" to make painful sacrifices—including organized labor represented by the UAW; salaried workers; Chrysler's venders; the company's dealers, many of which did not survive the crisis; the stockholders, who saw their dividends disappear while the value of their stock plummeted; Chrysler's lenders, primarily its banks; and the many provincial, state, and local governments who granted loans or forgave taxes. The revival also depended on the extraordinary talents and hard work of Chrysler's executives and especially of Lee Iacocca. He revived the company, recast it, and went on to run it for another decade.

Chapter 15

LEE'S COMPANY, 1984–92

The T115, to be known as the Dodge Caravan and Plymouth Voyager, is no woozy frolic in the outlands of automotive design. Rather, it is a sparkling example of the kind of thinking that will power Detroit out of its rut and may very well serve to accelerate Chrysler's drive back to the big time. As a box on wheels, the T-115 is that good.

—Car and Driver

The Chrysler Corporation enjoyed mixed success during Lee Iacocca's final nine years as chairman. The company earned more than $1 billion each year for the half-decade of 1984 to 1988. From the peak earnings of $2.38 billion in 1984, however, profits fell every year through 1991, when the automaker suffered losses of $795 million, the first time it had finished in the red since 1981. After making a profit of $723 million in 1992, Chrysler then suffered extraordinary losses of $2.55 billion for 1993. To be sure, this was not the same poorly managed, inefficient company that nearly went bankrupt in the early 1980s, but Iacocca and his management team nevertheless made some costly errors that brought the company into another serious financial crisis. Chrysler's overall performance is summarized in table 15.1.

Some of Chrysler's problems resulted from ill-advised and costly efforts to diversify and to establish new partnerships. This is not to suggest that the company spent all its funds on new acquisitions. It launched meaningful efforts to cut costs and improve quality. Plant modernization continued apace, and Chrysler opened a new design center, Chrysler Pacifica, in California in 1983 and a second proving ground in Arizona in 1984. Another major commitment to the core automobile business was the building of a new engineering and design facility, the Chrysler Technology Center, in Auburn Hills, Michigan, completed in 1991. Chrysler's purchase of American Motors Corporation (AMC) in 1987 was motivated in large part by the desire to add the Jeep brand to the Chrysler lineup. AMC became an important component of Chrysler's efforts to speed new product development.

TABLE 15.1 Chrysler Corporation Performance, North American Market, 1984–1993

	Unit Production	Market Share* (%)	Net Earnings†		
			Total ($)	On Sales (%)	On Capital Invested‡ (%)
1984	1,824,428	11.1	2,380,000,000	12.2	72.0
1985	1,869,060	11.8	1,610,000,000	7.7	38.6
1986	1,856,404	11.7	1,389,000,000	6.3	26.3
1987	1,917,132	12.3	1,290,000,000	5.1	19.8
1988	2,219,615	14.3	1,050,000,000	3.4	13.8
1989	2,108,322	13.8	359,000,000	1.2	5.0
1990	1,734,162	12.3	68,000,000	0.3	0.1
1991	1,572,882	12.4	(795,000,000)	(3.0)	(13.0)
1992	1,839,528	13.1	723,000,000	2.2	9.6
1993	2,124,069	14.4	(2,551,000,000)	(6.2)	(37.4)

Source: Chrysler Corporation, *Report to Shareholders, 1985–1993,* box "Annual Reports 1968–98," DCHC.
Note: Losses are indicated in parentheses.

*As measured by new car and truck registrations.
†After taxes.
‡Defined as stockholders' equity and surpluses.

Chrysler's fundamental failing during these years was its weak line of cars and trucks. Often, the company had little to offer in new products and when it did, the models frequently met a lukewarm reception from the public. With the company using its resources for diversification, there was little available for product development. The failure to develop new lines of popular vehicles in large measure rests with Lee Iacocca. He remained committed to making cosmetic (and cheap) remakes of the K-car platform of 1980, a strategy that proved unworkable in the late 1980s. Iacocca also remained rigidly committed to the boxy, chrome-laden style of the K-car and its spinoffs.

Just as Lee Iacocca and his handpicked management team should be credited with the nearly miraculous revival of Chrysler in 1978–83, so were they responsible for the mistakes and missteps of these later years. Virtually all of the top executives who were in place in 1983 remained for most of the decade. But by the time Iacocca and his board of directors came to choose his successor in mid-March 1991, they went outside the corporation and picked Robert J. Eaton from General Motors, in part because almost all of Iacocca's lieutenants had left Chrysler.

Hal Sperlich walked away in January 1988 after unsuccessfully opposing Chrysler's purchase of American Motors Corporation, and Gerald Greenwald resigned in May 1990 to become CEO of United Airlines. Bennett Bidwell, who had come to Chrysler in June 1983, began working as a part-time consultant to Chrysler in spring 1990 and retired early in 1991. Iacocca fired Richard Dauch, his manufacturing guru, in April 1991 and then forced Steve Miller, the financial whiz, to "retire" in March 1992. In choosing Eaton as Chrysler's new CEO, Iacocca deliberately passed over Robert A. Lutz, who had come to Chrysler from Ford in 1986.

AUTOMOTIVE PRODUCTS: THE INNOVATIVE MINIVAN AND THE K-CAR CLONES

Except for the rear-wheel drive Chrysler Fifth Avenue, Dodge Diplomat, and Plymouth Gran Fury, which survived through the 1989 model year, Chrysler shifted over to front-wheel drive vehicles exclusively in the 1980s. One of the new products, the minivan (Dodge Caravan and Plymouth Voyager), introduced in January 1984, was a breakthrough vehicle that redefined the automotive market. Minivans became Chrysler's most important single product after 1984, bringing consistent sales and profits. The company would not have prospered without them. They marked the beginning of a shift toward a new and profitable product mix at Chrysler that featured minivans, light trucks, and sport utility vehicles. This allowed Chrysler to prosper during a time when it was not offering a full line of competitive cars.

With the exception of the minivan, Chrysler developed no notable new products until the introduction of the Jeep Grand Cherokee and the LH series of sedans in the 1993 model year. The offerings were K-car clones or spinoffs, with wheelbases extended or shortened from the original dimensions, but with the same mechanical components. This product strategy, perfected by Iacocca and Sperlich at Ford, saved product development costs, but after a decade of reskinning, Chrysler's cars looked old and outdated.

Chrysler Corporation struggled just to name the new product, reflecting the innovative character of these vehicles. The report to shareholders for 1982 called them "T-Wagons" (Tech Wagons), and the next two annual reports labeled them "mini-wagons." During their early life, they also carried the badges T-van, midi-van, and garageable van, in part because they defied the usual categories. From 1985 onward, Chrysler consistently called them "minivans," shorthand for "miniaturized vans."[1]

What set the new Chrysler minivan apart were its dimensions. The minivan had more interior space than standard station wagons, permitting seven-passenger seating. The passenger compartment was 48 inches in height and 60 inches wide, but with 48 inches between the wheel wells in the rear, providing room for a standard 4-by-8-foot sheet of plywood. A key design requirement was that the vehicle be "garageable," small enough to fit into a standard garage. At just over 64 inches tall, the minivan was 15 inches lower than the next-smallest van on the market (the Dodge Ram Wagon). As *Car and Driver* put it, a bit indelicately, using front-wheel drive allowed the designers to lower the floor "to a point where even Shelley Winters could hop aboard without splitting her capri pants." Front-wheel drive also permitted excellent fuel economy, with top EPA ratings of 24 mpg city and 38 mpg highway.[2]

The minivan went through a gestation period of more than a decade before its birth at Chrysler in January 1984. At Ford, Iacocca had discovered during the Arab oil crisis of 1973 that Hal Sperlich was developing a remarkable new vehicle: a small front-wheel drive van they dubbed the "Mini/max," for minimum (exterior) size, maximum (interior) space. Using an engine and transmission from Honda, Sperlich built a prototype, which he hid from Henry Ford II. Iacocca commissioned market research to assess its viability in the market. The research noted three minimum requirements for the Mini/max to be successful—the floor would have to be low enough for women to want to drive it, the vehicle would have to fit in a standard garage, and it would need to have its engine mounted well ahead of the driver, to provide crush space in an accident.

Iacocca and Sperlich tried in vain to sell the concept to Henry Ford II. The market researchers suggested sales of 800,000 of these minivans a year by the late 1970s. Henry Ford II, however, was unwilling to risk the large investment that would be required to bring such a radically new vehicle into production. The Mustang, which borrowed heavily from the Ford Falcon, cost only $75 million, but the Mini/max would carry a price tag of at least $600 million.[3]

The minivan that emerged in January 1984 also had roots within Chrysler before Sperlich joined the company, in the 1977 plans for a "Supervan," code-named "S-Van," intended to be a rear-wheel drive passenger van. Chrysler's corporate decision of February 1980 to become a front-wheel drive company ended further debate over drive trains. The vehicle would seat seven passengers, fit into a standard garage, and have the feel of a car rather than a truck. The engine would be placed in front in a short, stubby nose that enabled drivers, including women, to see the front of the hood. Adding a Pentastar hood ornament eliminated any confusion. The designers gave the new vehicle a rear lift gate, rather than split rear doors, and an easy-opening sliding passenger-side door.[4]

The minivan required an investment of nearly $700 million, including the $400 million Chrysler spent to modernize and automate the Windsor assembly

1984 Dodge Caravan. Courtesy of DCHC.

plant that built it. Most of the investment in Windsor was tied up in 125 robots and a $110 million paint shop. The minivan was not a K-car clone, although it used key common components. The two product lines shared the base four-cylinder 2.2-liter Chrysler engine, with a Mitsubishi-made 2.6-liter four available as an option with the automatic transaxle. Chrysler lacked the funds to develop a more powerful six-cylinder engine for the minivan, so the designers limited its wheelbase to 112 inches and overall length to 176 inches, the size of a compact car. Although management approved the minivan project in early 1980, the lack of funds during that time delayed the planned fall 1982 introduction for 15 months. On 2 November 1983, the first T-Wagons, as they were still called, rolled off the Windsor assembly line.[5]

Enthusiasts' magazines gave the minivan favorable reviews. *Car and Driver* (May 1983) pulled no punches, calling it "a sparkling example of the kind of thinking that will power Detroit out of its rut and may very well serve to accelerate Chrysler's drive back to the big time." *Road and Track* (September 1983) offered similar comments: "The T-wagon is a success because it is a straightforward, honest vehicle. Honest in the sense that it is designed to be utilitarian. Yet, it is clean and pleasant to look at. It doesn't pretend to be what it's not."[6] By the time of the official "roll-off" of the first minivans from the Windsor assembly plant, sales momentum was already building. Chrysler struggled over the next three years to satisfy the demand for these innovative vehicles.

Production for calendar year 1984 amounted to 190,516 units, then increased to 220,046 in 1985 and to 226,047 in 1986. Chrysler finally increased production in 1987 by opening a second plant to produce a longer wheelbase minivan (119 inches versus 112 inches) for the 1988 model year, dubbed the Dodge Grand Caravan, Plymouth Grand Voyager, and Dodge Mini Ram Van. The extended versions had to await the availability of a more powerful engine, a 3.0-liter V-6 manufactured by Mitsubishi.

The company spent $381 million to convert the St. Louis assembly plant 2 to produce the extended minivans. Production of the large rear-wheel drive cars moved from St. Louis to the American Motors Corporation plant in Kenosha, Wisconsin. The first extended minivans came off the line at the St. Louis plant on 24 March 1987. Chrysler's total minivan production then increased to nearly 294,000 units in calendar year 1987, jumped to 393,000 in 1988, and to 468,000 units for 1989. The extended versions have accounted for half of the total numbers sold since 1988. The addition of the luxurious Chrysler Town & Country version for the 1990 model year further boosted the appeal of this vehicle. In 1992, Chrysler's minivan sales amounted to 565,000 units and accounted for 27 percent of the company's total sales volume.[7]

Chrysler's position in the automotive market deteriorated in the 1970s and 1980s in several fundamental ways. A series of national surveys conducted by Toledo's Rogers National Research measured the corporate loyalty of new car buyers—that is, their willingness to buy a new car from the same corporation as their previous new car. The study made early in the 1979 model year showed General Motors enjoying the greatest loyalty (84.6 percent), followed by Ford (59.5 percent), with Chrysler a distant third (36.3 percent). Only American Motors (26.5 percent) fared worse. By 1989, Chrysler's loyalty rate had improved slightly to 38 percent, Ford's fell to 54 percent, and General Motors' fell off sharply to 59 percent.[8]

Rogers National Research also tracked the age of new car buyers, and their studies did not bode well for Chrysler. The median age of buyers of new Chrysler cars climbed from 42 years in 1979 to 47 years in 1989. Over the same period, the same figures for Ford increased from 39 years to 45 years, while the median age of buyers of new General Motors vehicles leaped from 41 to 49 years. In contrast, buyers of new Hondas were consistently 10 years younger than buyers of Chrysler products.

These numbers, however, hide a significant gain made by Chrysler starting in 1984, mainly because they do not include minivans. Buyers of Chrysler minivans in early 1984 had a median age of only 39. The growing appeal of Chrysler products to younger buyers is even more clearly evident in 1989. The median age of minivan buyers had crept up to 40, but the demographics from the growing light truck and sport utility vehicle side were even more encouraging.

The median age of buyers of Dodge Dakota pickup trucks was 38 years, while buyers of all Jeep products had a median age of only 37 years.[9]

Chrysler dominated the market for minivans from 1984 into the late 1990s, capturing half the total sales. It did so by constantly improving the product and by paying attention to customers' needs. Besides offering an extended version of the base model for the 1988 model year, Chrysler reskinned and revamped its minivans for 1991. The new versions featured restyled interiors, freshened exteriors, improved steering systems and front suspensions, driver's-side air bags and two additional options—antilock brakes and all-wheel drive. After conducting consumer research in December 1988 about the desirability of integrated child safety seats and the types consumers preferred, Chrysler introduced the child safety seat as an option on its 1992 minivans and more than 100,000 minivan customers ordered them.[10]

Chrysler kept a large share of the minivan market because the competition proved remarkably inept in producing attractive alternatives. Competitors turned over the design job to their truck engineers, who predictably developed rear-wheel drive trucklike vehicles. Ford introduced the Aerostar, based on the Ranger pickup truck, as a 1986 model and it sold poorly. Ford's first front-wheel drive minivan, the 1992 Mercury Villager, did better. In 1984, General Motors introduced rear-wheel drive minivans, the Chevy Astro and the GMC Safari, but these never caught on. GM followed in 1989 with a front-drive, plastic-bodied minivan, the APV, in Chevrolet, Pontiac, and Oldsmobile versions. With their wedge-shaped noses and huge windshields, the APVs were styling disasters, derisively called "Dustbusters." In 1993, GM sold a total of 81,628 copies of their plastic minivans, in contrast to Chrysler's sales of 565,000 units.

The Japanese also failed to cut into Chrysler's dominant position in minivans until the late 1990s. The Toyota Previa, Nissan Access, Mazda MPV, and Mitsubishi Van were either too small, too slow, or too expensive to draw many customers. Honda did not offer a competitive vehicle until the end of the 1990s.

Chrysler's product line in the mid-1980s, outside of minivans, consisted of a series of "new" models based on the K-car platform, but with varying sheet metal. The company introduced the 1984 Chrysler Laser/Dodge Daytona twins in the fall of 1983. These were front-wheel drive sport coupes with optional turbocharged engines. Production for the 1984 model year was a solid 112,984 units, fell to 98,385 in 1985, and further to 81,000 in 1986. Chrysler discontinued the Laser version after 1986 and redesigned the Daytona, which became a specialty performance car.[11]

Chrysler's new 1985 H-cars, the Chrysler LeBaron GTS (Grand Touring Sedan) and Dodge Lancer, were five-door hatchback sedans. These twins used a stretched version of the K-car platform, with the wheelbase extended from 99.6 inches to 103.1 inches, and a new body. Model year 1985 production of

1987 Dodge Dakota, official truck of the Indianapolis 500. Courtesy of DCHC.

106,636 units increased in 1986 to 125,454 copies, but then fell off sharply to 65,669 in 1987 and to only 23,554 units in 1988. The last H-body cars—the Dodge Lancer and the Chrysler LeBaron GTS, continued through 1989, the last year of production.[12]

Chrysler continued the same general product strategy for the rest of the 1980s. After introducing nothing new for the 1986 model year, in 1987 the company brought out the compact Dodge Shadow/Plymouth Sundance twins, based on a downsized K-car chassis. Shadow/Sundance easily had the longest successful run of any of the K-car spinoffs of the 1980s. Production for the 1987 model year of 151,735 units climbed to a peak of 203,893 units in 1989, fell to just under 148,000 in 1991, but then rebounded to 188,791 units in 1993. In their last model year of 1994, the Shadow/Sundance twins sold a respectable 145,438 units.[13]

Continuing its moves into new market segments, Chrysler also introduced the Dodge Dakota mid-sized pickup truck in 1987. It was designed to appeal to customers who wanted a truck smaller than conventional pickups but larger than the compact trucks. Produced at the "Dodge City" truck assembly complex in Warren, Michigan, the Dakota offered as an option a brand-new 3.9-liter V-6. The Dakota, combined with the popular minivans, was another successful move into the light truck market.[14]

For 1988, Chrysler introduced the full-sized, front-wheel drive Chrysler New Yorker and Dodge Dynasty, designated as "C-body" cars. A new Mitsubishi 3.0-liter V-6 (136 hp) was standard on the New Yorker and an option for the

Dynasty. These were popular cars at first, with Chrysler producing 126,518 units in the initial year and over 238,000 in 1989 model year. The New Yorker lasted only three years, the victim of high oil prices and the brand-new Chrysler Imperial and New Yorker Fifth Avenue models introduced in 1990. The Dodge Dynasty version hung on through the 1993 model year, when Chrysler made only 65,805 of them.[15]

The 1989 model year saw the last introduction of popular new vehicles by Chrysler until the 1993 model year. The Dodge Spirit/Plymouth Acclaim (A-bodies) were to be the corporation's new family sedans for the 1990s. These were also front-wheel drive cars based on the K-car platform and replaced Dodge Aries/Plymouth Reliant. Production of Spirit/Acclaim amounted to 145,933 units for the 1989 model year and then climbed to about 210,000 units for both in 1990 and 1991. Production (and sales) then dropped every year until 1995, when Chrysler assembled only 55,342 copies.[16]

The new front-drive Chrysler Imperial and Chrysler New Yorker Fifth Avenue debuted in 1990, along with the Chrysler Town & Country minivan. This was also the last year of Dodge Omni/Plymouth Horizon production, the end of a remarkable 13-year run. The Imperial and Fifth Avenue, dubbed Y-bodies, lasted only four years and never sold 60,000 units combined in any year. Chrysler introduced no new domestically produced models for the 1991 model year and only the Dodge Stealth high-performance sports car for 1992. This was a three-year drought with no significant new model introductions, which severely damaged Chrysler's sales, revenues, and profits.

The cars introduced in 1989 and 1990, the Spirit/Acclaim and the Imperial/New Yorker Fifth Avenue, were stylistic and mechanical throwbacks to the 1981 K-cars. The Spirit/Acclaim twins, with their boxy shape, seemed particularly dull and ugly when compared to the Japanese competition. Automotive writers such as David E. Davis of *Automobile* bashed Chrysler for continuing to design cars "with smoke and mirrors" from K-car parts.[17]

Luckily, Chrysler's vehicle lineup did not come exclusively from North American sources. Besides supplying Chrysler with million of engines in the 1980s and 1990s, the Mitsubishi Motors Corporation also provided millions of cars and light trucks, which Chrysler sold as captive imports. The Mitsubishi vehicles gave Dodge and Plymouth dealers additional economical cars to sell. Chrysler's sales of imports averaged about 100,000 units per calendar year from 1983 to 1985, increased to about 120,000 per year 1986 to 1989, and then declined to roughly 65,000 annually 1990 to 1992. Over the entire decade of 1983–92, about 80 percent of all the sales came from the Mitsubishi-made Dodge/Plymouth Colt and Dodge/Plymouth Colt Vista, subcompact coupes and station wagons respectively. Starting in 1991, Mitsubishi also made the Dodge Stealth.[18]

Lee Iacocca and Alejandro de Tomaso, the head of Maserati, formed an alliance in 1984 to jointly produce a car that combined Chrysler mechanical components with a Maserati body. After many delays, the "Chrysler TC (Turbo Convertible or Touring Convertible) by Maserati" debuted as a 1989 model. Assembled in Italy, this convertible two-seater sold for $30,000 at about 300 carefully selected Chrysler dealers. Iacocca had hoped to sell between 5,000 and 10,000 per year, but over the three-year run from 1989 through 1991, customers bought a total of only 7,299 units. He squandered $500 million on a vehicle that was supposed to create a new image for Chrysler, but utterly failed to do so.[19]

The automotive press was merciless in its criticisms of the Chrysler TC. Lindsay Brooke's review in *Automotive Industries* (April 1988) criticized the model for poor design and poor quality. The June issue of *Motor Trend* made a frequently repeated observation—the Maserati TC looked remarkably like the Chrysler LeBaron GTS convertible. Since the two cars were mechanically alike, why pay $30,000 for the Italian import? A *Detroit News* review in April 1989 pointed out that the sumptuous leather interior appointments were interrupted by the K-car's cheap plastic parts. Only *Road and Track* gave the TC grudging approval.[20]

Chrysler's weak offerings, especially in model years 1989–92, were the result of too-long reliance on a product formula that had worked in the early 1980s. Over time, potential customers recognized reskinned K-cars for what they were. The "look" of Chrysler's cars reflected Iacocca's styling preferences and prejudices—and these were increasingly out of touch with the tastes of the car-buying public. The lack of all-new products also reflected the lack of resources available for such expensive investments. Funds were not available in part because the nonautomotive diversification that Iacocca promoted starting in 1985 drained away resources.

New Directions and Automotive Alliances

Chrysler's moves to diversify were not unique in the auto industry. With memories of the devastating automotive recession of 1979–82 still fresh, all of the auto companies began to diversify in the mid-1980s once they had surpluses to spend. They reasoned that diversifying their businesses would boost the prices of their traditionally undervalued stock. General Motors bought Electronic Data Systems (EDS) Corporation in 1984 for $2.5 billion and the following year acquired Hughes Aircraft for $5.2 billion. Ford acted similarly, buying the rental car company Hertz ($1.3 billion), First Nationwide, a chain of savings and loans ($493 million), and the Associates, a consumer finance company ($3.4 billion).[21]

Chrysler had teamed with Allied-Signal to bid $3 billion for Hughes Aircraft, but lost out to General Motors. In mid-June 1985, Chrysler announced its purchase of Gulfstream Aerospace, the leading producer of corporate jets (Iacocca's favorites) in the United States, for $637 million. Chrysler's *1986 Report to Shareholders* boasted that the airplane company already had 100 orders in hand for its newest business jet, the Gulfstream IV.[22]

Chrysler also expanded its involvement in financial services in a major way in 1985. Chrysler Financial Corporation (CFC) formed a joint venture with General Electric Credit Corporation and bought E. F. Hutton Credit Corporation in July for $125 million, renaming the operation Chrysler Capital Corporation. Late the same year, on 22 November, CFC acquired FinanceAmerica Corporation and BA Financial Services Corporation, merging them to form Chrysler First. Chrysler Capital Corporation was engaged in financing capital equipment, while Chrysler First was involved in wholesale and retail financing and consumer lending. As a result of these acquisitions, CFC became the fourth largest nonbank financial company in the United States, with $16 billion in assets.[23]

Chrysler's second major high-tech acquisition came in August 1987, when it bought Electrospace Systems for $367 million. This electronics contractor, based in Richardson, Texas, specialized in supplying communications and electronic command and control systems to military and civilian customers. In October 1987, Chrysler created a new subsidiary, Chrysler Technologies Corporation, consisting of Gulfstream Aerospace and Electrospace Systems.[24]

Many of Chrysler's new ventures were more directly related to its core vehicle business. In 1983, the company opened its Pacifica Advanced Product Design Center in Carlsbad, California. The Japanese auto companies, starting with Toyota in 1973, had established design operations on the West Coast, and Chrysler was the first of the American companies to do the same. The designers at Chrysler Pacifica worked mainly on concept cars and sports cars, including the Plymouth Prowler.[25]

In April 1984, Chrysler began building a new proving grounds in Wittmann, Arizona, some 32 miles northwest of Phoenix. Completed in October 1985 at a cost of $12 million and dedicated in January 1986, the Arizona Proving Grounds enabled Chrysler to test vehicles under high-temperature, high-altitude, and dry desert conditions, particularly important for cooling and air-conditioning systems. The company used the grand opening of the Arizona Proving Grounds for the national press preview of the 1987 Dodge Shadow and Plymouth Sundance.[26]

Iacocca revealed an initiative known as the Liberty Project in March 1985. This was Chrysler's response to General Motors' Saturn Project, announced early in 1983. In 1985, GM chairman Roger Smith established the Saturn Corporation, an entirely independent division within General Motors. Saturn was to design and build an all-new small car using cutting-edge technology and innovative work arrangements to compete against the Japanese. Saturn was a household name by 1985 and brought the parent company lots of positive publicity.[27]

In announcing the Liberty Project to a group of security analysts in Detroit, Iacocca was clearly trying to blunt GM's publicity "bounce" from Saturn. Liberty's goals were twofold—to improve the quality of Chrysler's vehicles and to reduce their cost by roughly one-third. Statements by Chrysler officials, including Iacocca, concerning the Liberty Project were contradictory throughout 1985 and 1986. They flip-flopped on the issue of making a new line of Liberty cars and where Chrysler would build them. Chrysler's 1985 annual report explained that the Liberty Project had three goals—to produce a small, efficient car for the 1990s, to reduce the cost of building cars by at least $2,500, and to keep Chrysler on "the leading edge" of new technologies.[28]

Because the Liberty Project was a top-secret research project from the beginning (and still is to this day), its accomplishments are not easy to determine. Liberty contributed to the design of the Diamond-Star Motors Eagle Summit and Plymouth Colt Vista cars. Many of the components for the LH family sedans, including the transmissions, were the outgrowth of Liberty research.[29]

Chrysler also entered into a joint venture with Mitsubishi Motors Corporation to manufacture small cars in a new plant near Bloomington, Illinois. After the Reagan administration announced in early 1985 the expiration of the Voluntary Restraint Agreement on automobile exports from Japan, Chrysler strengthened its alliance with Mitsubishi. On 7 October 1985, the two companies announced the formation of a joint venture, Diamond-Star Motors Corporation, to produce up to 180,000 small cars per year in the United States. The name was a combination of the Mitsubishi Motors symbol (Three Diamonds) and the Chrysler Pentastar. They considered sites in five Midwestern states, but opted for Normal, Illinois, because that state's incentive package was the best.[30]

Under the joint venture, each partner would invest equally to build and equip the plant and to launch the new vehicles. They would split the production on a 50–50 basis. At the groundbreaking for the new factory on 18 April 1986, Diamond-Star Motors (DSM) announced that production would be 240,000 cars annually from a workforce of 2,900. The 2-million-square-foot plant was finished in January 1988, with production starting later that year. The first cars assembled there were two-door specialty sports cars—the Plymouth Laser/Eagle Talon/Mitsubishi Eclipse, introduced in January 1989 as 1990 models. Production in 1991 included the Eagle Summit, previously imported from Japan.[31]

When Chrysler's sales and profits fell sharply in 1989 and 1990, the company sold off some of its assets to raise cash and to concentrate on its core business.

Iacocca announced in early December 1989 that Chrysler would sell Gulfstream Aerospace, Electrospace Systems, and Airborne Systems. On 13 February 1990, Chrysler announced the sale of Gulfstream for $825 million. The company was not, however, able to find a buyer for Electrospace Systems or Airborne Systems.[32]

Chrysler also began pulling back from its relationship with Mitsubishi almost as soon as it had committed itself to Diamond-Star Motors. The Detroit company sold 45 percent of its 24 percent equity stake in Mitsubishi in 1989, reducing its equity share to 13 percent. Chrysler gained $503 million ($309 million after taxes) from the transaction. In late October 1991, Chrysler sold its 50 percent interest in Diamond-Star Motors to Mitsubishi, realizing a $205 million profit, plus its original investment of $100 million, for a cash infusion of $305 million. Chrysler, however, continued to buy half of the production of Diamond-Star.[33]

These acquisitions are not the entire list of Chrysler's ventures into new ventures. The company also bought the Italian automaker Lamborghini in 1987 and various financial services companies in the late 1980s and early 1990s. Chrysler acquired Thrifty Rent-a-Car Systems in June 1989 and by the end of 1990, had combined Thrifty with other recent acquisitions, Snappy Car Rental, and Dollar Rent a Car Systems, into a new subsidiary, Pentastar Transportation Group. However, the most important acquisition came in March 1987, when Chrysler announced its purchase of a controlling interest in the American Motors Corporation (AMC) from the French automaker Renault.[34]

THE PURCHASE OF AMERICAN MOTORS CORPORATION

In buying American Motors Corporation in 1987, the Chrysler Corporation was, in a curious way, drawing together many of the tangled tendrils of Walter P. Chrysler's complicated automotive past. The major reason Chrysler wanted AMC was its Jeep Division, which American Motors had acquired from Kaiser Jeep Corporation in 1970. Kaiser Jeep in turn had emerged from Kaiser-Willys (1953–63), which had evolved from Willys-Overland (1908–53), the company Walter P. Chrysler helped revive in 1920. The American Motors Corporation was the result of the merger in 1954 of the Hudson Motor Car Company (1909–54) and Nash-Kelvinator Corporation (1937–54). Earlier, the Chalmers Motor Company begat Hudson and, along with Maxwell Motor Corporation, the Chrysler Corporation in 1925.

Nash-Kelvinator Corporation was the product of a merger between Kelvinator, a Detroit appliance manufacturer, and Nash Motor Company (1916–37), established in Wisconsin by Charles W. Nash, who originally hired Walter

Chrysler to work at Buick in 1912. George Mason was another string in these tangled tendrils. After working for Walter P. Chrysler at Maxwell and at Chrysler Corporation from 1921 to 1926, Mason served as the president of Kelvinator (1928–36), then as president of Nash-Kelvinator (1936–54) and chairman (1948–54). The purchase of American Motors in 1987 involved Walter P. Chrysler's company buying up the remains of the automobile enterprises of Charles W. Nash, John North Willys, the founders of Hudson, and George Mason.[35]

There is not sufficient space to give the histories of the Nash, Hudson, or Kelvinator companies adequate treatment here, but a brief history of American Motors Corporation is needed to place the 1987 buyout in context. George Mason died five months after the formation of AMC and George W. Romney, who had worked at Nash since 1948, became president, general manager, and chairman of American Motors. Romney closed the Hudson factory in Detroit and moved all production to the Nash plants in Kenosha and Milwaukee, Wisconsin. The Hudson and Nash nameplates disappeared in 1958, replaced by Rambler.

At the urging of George Romney, who once labeled the gas-guzzling full-sized cars of the Big Three "dinosaurs of the driveway," American Motors became a small-car specialist. Overall sales, 114,087 units in 1957, nearly doubled in 1958 to 217,332, making AMC the only auto company to increase sales in 1958. American Motors sold 401,446 cars in 1959 and nearly 486,000 in 1960, its all-time peak sales year. Rambler American registrations increased from 42,196 units in 1958 to 120,603 in 1960, when the compact car accounted for one-quarter of AMC's sales. George Romney left the company in 1962 to successfully run for governor of Michigan.

Roy Abernathy replaced Romney as chairman from 1962 to 1966 and the company went into relative decline, with sales of only 250,000 cars in the late 1960s. Roy D. Chapin Jr., the son of one of the founders of the Hudson Motor Car Company, served as chairman of the board and CEO of American Motors 1967–78. AMC introduced the compact 1970 Hornet and the subcompact Gremlin in April 1970, but they were only marginally successful. Under Chapin's leadership, AMC sold off its Kelvinator operations in 1968 and acquired Kaiser Jeep Corporation in 1970. The company struggled to survive in the 1970s and 1980s. American Motors introduced the subcompact Pacer as a 1975 model and the Eagle in 1981, but these products did not stem the flow of red ink. AMC sold its military truck division, AM General, in 1983 to raise cash to continue operating.

The French automaker Renault spent $500 million in 1979 and 1980 to gain a controlling interest of 46.1 percent of American Motors stock. In time, Renault invested a total of $785 million in AMC, with few tangible results. AMC produced American versions of two Renault models, the Alliance and the Encore, starting in 1982, but these did not sell particularly well. The later Medallion and Premier fared no better. Since 1979, AMC earned modest profits ($15.5 million) in only one year (1984), then lost $125 million in 1985 and $111 million in the first nine months of 1986. Renault also had large losses in its European operations by the mid-1980s ($1.6 billion in 1985 alone), so it was eager to sell American Motors.[36]

Before Chrysler bought American Motors, it had already established a working relationship with the company. American Motors had used Chrysler's three-speed Torqueflite automatic transmissions for many years. Chrysler and AMC reached an agreement in June 1986 whereby AMC would assemble the full-sized rear-wheel drive M-body cars—the Chrysler Fifth Avenue, Dodge Diplomat, and Plymouth Gran Fury—at its Kenosha, Wisconsin, assembly plant starting in February 1987. As part of the agreement, the State of Wisconsin provided more than $3 million to assist Chrysler in training the 2,700 workers who assembled the new product.[37]

Beginning in the fall of 1986, Chrysler also talked with AMC about assembling its L-body cars (Dodge Omni/Plymouth Horizon) at AMC's idle Kenosha Lake Front plant starting in November 1987. Chrysler planned to convert the Belvidere, Illinois, plant to produce its new full-sized, front-wheel drive C-body cars, the Chrysler New Yorker and the Dodge Dynasty. Chrysler wanted to make the L-body cars at Kenosha from 1987 through 1992. These talks dragged on because AMC was at the same time asking for concessions from the UAW and aid from Wisconsin to bring a new Jeep model to Kenosha.[38]

Before the negotiations about L-body production at Kenosha began, Chrysler held secret discussions with Renault about acquiring part or all of AMC. Iacocca met with Renault chairman Georges Besse in June 1986 to discuss cooperative ventures. Chrysler initially expressed an interest in buying only the Jeep part of AMC's business, but Besse would only discuss selling American Motors as a whole. Iacocca and Besse's successor, Raymond Levy, resumed their talks in New York on 5 February, and the two companies reached an agreement on 9 March in Paris after three days of around-the-clock marathon negotiations. Bennett Bidwell, Chrysler's vice chairman, informed AMC's Joseph Cappy of the merger agreement with Renault in a letter, providing him with a copy of the letter of intent of 9 March 1987 signed by Chrysler and Renault.[39]

The agreement, which was subject to Chrysler completing a thorough examination of AMC's books, products, and facilities, might have been derailed by several nettlesome problems. AMC's "baggage" included aging facilities at Kenosha and Toledo, Ohio, militant and uncooperative UAW locals at both plants, an unfunded pension liability of more than $600 million and, most important, $1.9 billion in lawsuits resulting from rollovers of the Jeep CJ model. Chrysler took on the pension liabilities, and Renault and Chrysler agreed to share equally the costs of the rollover lawsuits.[40]

The merger proposal was simple. Chrysler would buy the Renault stock by issuing $200 million in 10-year bonds paying 8 percent interest. Owners of AMC's remaining common and convertible preferred shares would receive Chrysler common stock worth $522 million. In the letter of 9 March, the two parties clearly stated that the deal was contingent on two other developments—Chrysler acquiring substantially all of the remaining AMC stock and Renault receiving a "fairness opinion" from a reputable investment banking firm. Once these conditions were met, Renault would vote all of its shares for the merger. Chrysler would assume $767 million in AMC long-term debt and pay Renault an additional $35 million for AMC's finance subsidiary. This came to a total purchase price of $1.5 billion, but did not include the unfunded pension liability of more than $600 million.[41]

In late March, AMC officials informed the New York Stock Exchange that, in light of the Chrysler merger proposal, they would postpone the annual stockholders' meeting scheduled for 29 April and would delay issuing the annual report for 1986. The AMC stockholders' meeting did not take place until 5 August. The AMC board could not act until it received a report from the investment firm of Shearson Lehman Brothers on 19 May 1978 that Chrysler's merger proposal was fair to the AMC stockholders. The AMC board of directors' proxy statement regarding the merger, dated 2 July 1987, unanimously recommended that the stockholders approve the merger. At the special stockholders' meeting held on 5 August 1987, the stockholders concurred, making the merger official.[42]

Once the Chrysler takeover was settled, AMC executives and white-collar workers were rightly concerned about their future job prospects. Within months of the AMC purchase, with sales of its own vehicles doing poorly, Chrysler began laying off salaried workers. Iacocca announced in late October that he planned to reduce the combined salaried workforce of 38,000 by at least 9 percent (3,500 workers) before the end of the year and then by 3 percent per year after that. Most of the layoffs came from the AMC salaried force of 5,700. Employees at AMC's technical center in Detroit, including engineers and technicians, took the brunt of the first wave of layoffs.[43]

At the end of October 1987, Chrysler laid off one shift at the Kenosha plant making the rear-wheel drive vehicles, with the loss of 1,400 jobs, but 1,000 of these workers would be rehired within a month to staff a second shift producing the Omni/Horizon twins. In late January 1988, Chrysler announced it would close the Kenosha assembly plant, permanently idling 5,500 workers. This facility had assembled automobiles since 1902, when Thomas B. Jeffery built his first car, the Rambler, at that location. Production of the Omni/Horizon would also be shifted to Detroit. State and local officials in Wisconsin, along with Governor

Tommy Thompson, accused Chrysler of breaking its word to keep the plant open for five years.[44]

After four months of bitter negotiations, the UAW won its Kenosha workers an acceptable compensation package from Chrysler in early May 1988. In essence, Chrysler agreed to repay the workers most of the $60 million in concessions that they had granted American Motors. Workers would get a lump sum ranging between $5,000 and $10,000. They would also receive 24 weeks of supplemental unemployment benefits (SUB). Because the American Motors SUB fund was bankrupt, they would not have received any benefits without this settlement. Both the local and national UAW leadership accepted this package as the best possible agreement, given all the circumstances.[45]

The purchase of AMC impacted Chrysler in several fundamental ways. One immediate effect was an increase in long-term debt by $1 billion to $3.3 billion at the end of 1987. On the bright side, adding Jeep vehicles to the product line helped convert Chrysler in the 1980s from a generic manufacturer of cars and some trucks to a specialist in minivans and light-duty trucks. Trucks and vans accounted for about 20 percent of Chrysler's total production in 1981–83, with the share jumping to 28.8 percent in 1984 after the introduction of the minivan. The non-automobile portion of Chrysler's sales leaped dramatically to 50.3 percent in 1987 with the addition of the extended minivans, the Dakota pickup, and Jeep. In roughly five years, the Chrysler Corporation had drastically altered its product mix and therefore its customer base. More important, it had specialized in market segments where the Japanese had minimal presence.[46]

Over the long run, however, the engineering and product-planning people who moved over to Chrysler from AMC had the greatest impact. The key person was Francois J. Castaing, one of only a handful of Renault executives who stayed with Chrysler after the buyout. He was an engineer who had run Renault's Formula One racing team at one time and had the post of group vice president for product and quality at AMC. He came over to Chrysler as vice president of Jeep and truck engineering, but then served as vice president of vehicle engineering from 1988 through 1997. Castaing and Robert Lutz became friends and allies, contributing to the departure of Hal Sperlich and his supporter Jack Withrow, Chrysler's chief engineer.

Castaing brought with him several talented AMC engineers, including John Nemeth, who was AMC's product development chief, and Chris Theodore, who was in charge of engine engineering at AMC. Both played vital roles in the development of Chrysler's all-new minivan that debuted in 1996. More important, Castaing came to Chrysler with the preliminary plans for a new Jeep Grand Cherokee, code-named the ZJ. Chrysler's product planners wanted to develop a new sports utility vehicle based on the Dakota pickup platform, but the superior AMC design won out. This showed that the tiny AMC engineering group, working as a "platform group," could produce an outstanding vehicle.[47]

RETHINKING THE VEHICLE DESIGN PROCESS: PLATFORM TEAMS, THE LH, AND THE CHRYSLER TECHNOLOGY CENTER

Chrysler, much like the other American automobile companies, typically needed 60 months from the initial concept approval to bring an all-new vehicle to market. The major functional divisions that were ultimately involved in the development process—styling, engineering, finance, manufacturing, and marketing—worked independently and sequentially, each beginning its work only after another division had finished. Manufacturing, for example, had little input into the design and engineering process, but simply had to build the product it was given. Each of these "chimneys" became a self-perpetuating empire. Conflicts were "resolved" based on which side had the most political clout. Problems with new models often did not come to the surface until late in the design process, resulting in costly redesign work.

One of the features of American Motors that appealed to Lee Iacocca was its ability to do "lean engineering" in new vehicle development. Its engineering staff, fewer than 700 in total, developed more generalized knowledge and relied on extensive teamwork. At the time of the buyout of American Motors, Chrysler had a staff of 6,000 engineers.[48]

Chris Theodore noted the differences in how the two firms developed new vehicles: "Because of our size at AMC we had to operate with tiny groups, which were forced to make major decisions. The design guys, the manufacturing and financial guys—everybody—had to work together. There was no other way. . . . It was only natural that Francois [Castaing] would try to implement the smaller, more flexible units that had worked for him."[49]

The team approach to product development had support within Chrysler as well. In the 1980s, the company established the Youth Advisory Committee, consisting of its own young white-collar employees, to advise the top executives on how to capture the youth market. Many younger executives within Chrysler viewed the Honda Motor Company as a model company in terms of its operations and its products. In late 1987, Chrysler named 14 of these advisors to a Honda Study Team, charged to recommend to top management Honda practices that Chrysler should copy.[50]

The Honda team spent five months examining "the Honda way" with great care, making several trips to the Honda offices in Marysville, Ohio. Their report of February 1988 included a scathing attack on Chrysler's entire management culture. The team strongly urged a move toward genuine teamwork in all areas of corporate operations. More specifically, the Honda team strongly urged the implementation of multidisciplinary teams to develop new products.[51]

Francois Castaing, Robert Lutz, and Tom Gale, Chrysler's vice president for product design, favored the platform team approach for new vehicle development, in the belief that better products would result. Iacocca agreed to experiment with the platform team concept only because he desperately wanted to speed up the introduction of Chrysler's new mid-sized family sedans, the LH models, while reducing the development costs. Chrysler needed to develop simultaneously the LH cars, the Jeep Grand Cherokee, and a new Dodge Ram pickup, but lacked the staff to do so. The K-car required a team of 2,000 to bring it to market in 1981. In contrast, the platform group for the LH began with 850 members, but soon shrank to 744. Platform teams for later products typically had fewer than 800 members.[52]

Iacocca knew that the LH platform was vital to Chrysler's survival in the 1990s. Insiders nervously joked that "LH" really stood for "Last Hope" for Chrysler. Incorporating the innovative "cab-forward design" developed by Tom Gale, these mid-sized models were Chrysler's competitive answer to the Ford Taurus/Mercury Sable. By extending the vehicle cabin forward, the designers created an enormous passenger compartment compared to the overall vehicle silhouette. The base of the windshield was located directly above the front wheels.

The first conceptual version of the LH, attributed to Hal Sperlich and Jack Withrow, had the V-6 engine mounted crosswise in the engine compartment. Castaing wanted the engine mounted in the more conventional longitudinal position, claiming this would reduce noise and vibration. Mounting the engine in a transverse position also ruled out future use of the platform for rear-wheel drive versions of the LH. Castaing assembled a group of engineers called the "Iron Eagle" team, which took a prototype Eagle Premier and within a month mounted the V-6 engine in the longitudinal configuration. He showed this version to the top management and at a meeting of the corporate product planning committee in January 1989, Iacocca approved Castaing's design. Chrysler's challenge was to produce the new vehicle by June 1992, in only 42 months instead of the usual 60. This could be achieved only through the use of platform teams. On 5 February 1989, Chrysler officially announced the reorganization of its engineering design operations by platform group. Within the month, Lutz and Castaing held two huge meetings with the entire engineering staff of 6,000 to explain the new scheme.[53]

Castaing appointed Glenn Gardner to head the LH platform team. Gardner, who was managing the Diamond-Star Motors plant at the time, had also directed the design of the first minivans and the Dodge Dakota pickup. Gardner's LH team did not work at Chrysler's engineering center in Highland Park, but instead moved into a building in a dreary industrial park on Featherstone Road in Auburn Hills, Michigan, in the shadows of the planned Chrysler Technology Center. Part of the platform team concept included seeking input from the

manufacturing side, not just from plant engineers but from foremen and line
workers as well. This required a different approach from manufacturing, which
under Richard Dauch had remained staunchly traditional. Lutz convinced Iacocca to replace Dauch, who abruptly quit in April 1991. Iacocca named Dennis
Pawley, who had successfully managed the Mazda assembly plant in Flat Rock,
Michigan, in the mid-1980s, as Dauch's replacement.[54]

Castaing and Lutz initially created three platform groups—the large car LH
group under Gardner; a small-car group headed by Bob Mercel, which in time
produced the Neon; and a minivan group led by John Nemeth, another AMC
veteran. A fourth platform group responsible for truck and Jeeps emerged a bit
later. The top executives decided that the platform teams were too important to
be left in the control of the engineers. In mid-January 1991, Chrysler named
four of its top managers as supervisors of the platform groups—Castaing ran
the Jeep/truck group; Tom Gale oversaw the minivan group; Tom Stallkamp,
Chrysler's purchasing chief, managed the LH team; and Ronald Boltz, vice
president for product strategy, was in charge of the small-car platform group.[55]

The platform team system was not universally welcomed by the engineering
staff. There was widespread skepticism that the new system would work. Some
saw the restructuring move as nothing more than an effort by Lutz and Castaing
to consolidate their power within Chrysler. There was resentment against the
AMC newcomers imposing their ideas on the veteran Chrysler engineers. Many
of the senior engineers believed (rightly) that they would lose power and perks
under the platform system. Sensing resistance, Castaing and Lutz asked senior
managers to submit names of potential team members, but promised that no
one would be forced to join. They then went ahead and reassigned Chrysler's
6,000 engineers to platform groups.

Some engineers quit, convinced that Chrysler would not survive the engineering "reforms." The more vocal opponents were moved to backwater jobs or
forced into retirement. Some of the malcontents wrote anonymous letters to
Iacocca warning him that the platform teams were not working and that none
of the desperately needed new products—the LH sedans, the new Jeep Grand
Cherokee, and the Dodge Ram pickup—would be ready on time. Late in 1990,
Iacocca demanded that Lutz fire Castaing and hire a new vice president of
engineering. Lutz explained that the complaints reflected the loss of power that
managers faced under the new system. Platforms groups were teams, not hierar-
chies. The corporation was reinventing the way it developed new vehicles and
some people would be hurt by the changes. Lutz reassured Iacocca that all the
products were on time and on budget. Castaing and the platform team system
remained in place.[56]

Strictly speaking, the first new Chrysler vehicle produced under the platform
group system was the 1993 Jeep Grand Cherokee, introduced in April 1992. This

1993 Jeep Grand Cherokee. Courtesy of DCHC.

was the model already under development at Jeep when Chrysler bought AMC in 1987. For Grand Cherokee, Chrysler built the state-of-the-art Jefferson North plant in Detroit. Chrysler insisted that the UAW agree to a so-called modern operating agreement (MOA) as a condition for its investment of $1 billion. The MOA provided for fewer union stewards, a reduction of job classifications from 98 to 10, and the organization of workers into teams. By any measure, the Grand Cherokee was an enormous success for Chrysler. Production of 214,406 units for the 1993 model year climbed steadily to a peak of 310,507 for the 1996 models.[57]

The LH models appeared in June 1992, some 42 months after approval, as Iacocca demanded. The required investment fell from the original projection of $2.5 billion to $1.5 billion—still a hefty commitment. Production of the LH models (Chrysler Concorde, Dodge Intrepid, and Eagle Vision) started off at a healthy 168,130 units for the 1993 model year and then jumped to roughly 270,000 units for both the 1994 and 1995 model years.[58]

The all-new Dodge Ram pickup truck, introduced at the 1993 Detroit Auto Show as a 1994 model, was the third major platform team success. Chrysler had not completely redesigned the Dodge full-sized pickup since 1972 and company engineers nicknamed it Festus, after an aged TV cowboy. In the early 1980s, a new pickup was sacrificed so the company could develop the minivan. Tom Gale's design staff produced a striking, aggressive-looking pickup with a front end that resembled big-rig trucks. In customer surveys, potential buyers either

1993 Chrysler Concorde, one of the cab-forward LH models. Courtesy of DCHC.

loved the look or hated it. There was no middle ground. Lutz, Gale, and the platform team went ahead and the new truck was a hit. In its first year, Dodge Ram's share of the full-sized truck market jumped from 7 percent to 15 percent. The success of the Jeep Grand Cherokee, the LH, and the Dodge Ram pickup speaks volumes to the effectiveness of this team approach. Platform teams brought out these nicely styled, well-engineered products on time and within budget.[59]

The platform groups also brought important unintended changes to Chrysler's product development process. Although senior executives periodically reviewed the progress of the LH models, Lutz, Castaing, and Gardner kept them at arm's length from the team members. For the most part, Gardner politely ignored their suggestions. Even when Gale, Lutz, and Iacocca agreed that some change was needed, they could no longer order changes by virtue of their position—they had to convince the team members. Within the platform teams, the various parts of the corporation had to share power. Engineering, a dominant force within Chrysler from the Zeder-Skelton-Breer days, was simply one among equals, while product planning lost much of its power with the departure of Sperlich. The stylists gained considerable power and prestige, particularly because their work was seen as Chrysler's salvation.[60]

Part of the fundamental changes brought to Chrysler's engineering operations during Iacocca's final years with the company was the construction of the Chrysler Technology Center (CTC) in Auburn Hills, Michigan, some 20 miles north of the Highland Park headquarters. In October 1986, Iacocca first announced the construction of the technology center and the transfer of 5,000 employees from Highland Park by 1990. The company softened the blow to Highland Park by moving about 1,000 of its employees located elsewhere into the empty Highland Park offices, a process referred to as "backfilling." Chrysler asked Highland Park to approve the move, so that the company could receive $84 million in tax incentives from Auburn Hills. Highland Park reluctantly agreed, and Chrysler in turn gave the city an aid package of $14 million spread over eight years.[61]

The CTC was Iacocca's brainchild. He believed that the company needed a state-of-the-art facility where designers and engineers could work together in an attractive and safe environment. Iacocca simply wanted to bring together engineering and design staffs that were located in dozens of buildings scattered all over metropolitan Detroit. He argued that the outdated facilities at Highland Park, combined with their location in a grim, crime-infested inner-city area, hampered the corporation in recruiting the best young engineers, especially women. The company scaled back the original plans to spend $1.5 billion on the CTC to $1 billion, but Iacocca nevertheless pushed the project forward.[62]

Chrysler Corporation's 1988 annual report described the CTC as a 3.2-million-square-foot complex with an adjacent 47-acre industrial park where suppliers could locate research facilities. Construction began in 1989 and the financing for the complex was arranged in May 1990, when Chrysler completed a $1.1 billion sales and leaseback arrangement with Manufacturers Hanover Bank. Officially dedicated on 15 October 1991, the CTC was 90 percent occupied by the end of 1992, with 6,200 employees located there. By then, a pilot plant was in operation at the CTC, along with the evaluation road (test track). Although the master plans for the complex included a large suppliers' park at the southern edge of the property, Chrysler's suppliers never moved there.[63]

Many both within and outside the corporation viewed the CTC as a pyramid, a monument to Chrysler's pharaoh, Iacocca the Magnificent. The company's public relations staff, especially Michael Morrison, Iacocca's speechwriter, tried to minimize negative perceptions of the CTC. In January 1989 and again in January 1991, Morrison argued against naming the CTC, presumably after Iacocca, until Chrysler's financial condition improved.[64] The Chrysler board had not named the CTC after Iacocca by the end of 1992, while he was still chairman, and the rapid deterioration in Iacocca's relationship with the Chrysler board after his departure then ruled out the possibility.

Lee Iacocca enjoyed much success during his first six or seven years at Chrysler—the rescue of the company from bankruptcy and its return to profits; the K-car and its many clones; and the minivans, to name the major achievements. The new products introduced during his final days at Chrysler—the Jeep Grand Cherokee, the LH sedans, and the Dodge Ram pickup—were enormously successful as well. One can argue that the purchase of American Motors and the building of the CTC were brilliant long-range moves. Iacocca, however, also made serious mistakes during the middle period of his tenure, including most of the acquisitions he championed for the sake of diversification. His most glaring failure in his final years was his unwillingness to retire and to provide for an orderly managerial succession.

THE MANAGEMENT TEAM AND THE SUCCESSION STRUGGLE

Chrysler's chairman faced several public relations problems or crises in the last part of his tenure and did not always handle them skillfully. The closing of the Kenosha, Wisconsin, factory was one such misstep. The other major examples were his continuing attacks on the Japanese auto industry, an odometer-tampering case that developed in 1987, and the defective Ultradrive transaxles introduced by Chrysler in 1989. Iacocca also presided over an unstable and badly divided top management team during the last four or five years of his tenure as chairman. Much of this chaos was of his own creation and it clouded the succession to his position.

From 1983 until his retirement in 1992, Lee Iacocca engaged in a strident campaign against what he labeled the "unfair" trade practices of the Japanese automakers and the Japanese government. He called for strong unilateral actions against Japan by Congress and the president, including increased tariffs on Japanese imports and strict import quotas. Observers in the United States and Japan saw Iacocca as the leading American "Japan basher" of the 1980s.

Iacocca's most famous attack came after he and the CEOs of Ford and General Motors, along with the UAW's Owen Bieber, accompanied President George Bush on a trade mission to Japan in early January 1992. Right after his return to Detroit, on the eve of the North American Automobile Show, Iacocca delivered a speech, "Trade with Japan and U.S. Economic Policy," to more than 3,000 at an Economic Club of Detroit luncheon on 10 January 1992. He explained how the Japanese could actually lose money on their cars exported to the U.S. market:

> You see, they operate from a *sanctuary*. They have almost no competition at home and they won't allow any foreign competitor to be a factor in their market. In total, all foreign auto makers from all over the world have only three percent of the Japanese market. In Europe, foreign companies have 15 percent, and in the United States they have a whopping 35 percent of our car and truck market.
>
> Japan should immediately drop its trade barriers and open its market to foreign goods and stop dumping their vehicles on the American market at artificially low prices.[65]

The national news media reported his comments and roundly criticized them. A *New York Times* editorial called Iacocca the "Excuse Maker" and dismissed his attacks as unfair Japan bashing. The *Wall Street Journal* suggested that his explanation of minuscule Jeep sales in Japan was deliberately misleading. Toyoo Tate, Mitsubishi's chairman, found Iacocca's attacks offensive and hypocritical. After all, by increasing its purchases of engines and cars from Mitsubishi, Chrysler Corporation was adding to the trade deficit.[66]

The most embarrassing problem that Chrysler faced in the late 1980s was an odometer fraud scandal that first broke on 24 June 1987. The U.S. Attorney for the Eastern District of Missouri announced that a federal grand jury had indicted Chrysler and two of its high-level officials for odometer fraud. The two Chrysler employees, Allen F. Scudder and Frank J. O'Reilly, had managed all of Chrysler's assembly plants in the 1980s. The indictment charged Chrysler and the two executives with disconnecting odometer cables on more than 60,000 new vehicles over a period of 18 months ending 31 December 1986. These cars were allegedly driven up to 400 miles before the factory reconnected the odometers. The indictment also alleged that Chrysler had repaired many of these cars after they were involved in accidents and sold them as new. The two men faced jail terms of up to a year, plus fines, while the indictment sought $120 million in fines against Chrysler.[67]

Since 1949, Chrysler had allowed the executives at its assembly plants to drive brand-new cars home and elsewhere with the odometers disconnected. The company claimed that this practice was an important part of its quality assurance system to test cars for defects. After Congress passed legislation (the Motor Vehicle Information and Cost Savings Act) in 1973 prohibiting odometer tampering, Ford and General Motors stopped disconnecting odometers, but Chrysler did not.[68]

The first official Chrysler response was a press release issued 24 June 1987 denying that the company or its employees had done anything illegal or improper in disconnecting odometers. A week later, Iacocca held a press conference in Highland Park to engage in damage control. He again denied that Chrysler had done anything illegal. Still, Chrysler would take corrective actions. For cars that had their odometers disconnected, the company would extend the existing warranty from five years/50,000 miles to seven years/70,000 miles. Chrysler sent out letters announcing the program to owners of cars known to have had the odometer disconnected.[69]

Despite Iacocca's efforts, the case did not go away. In mid-December 1987, Chrysler offered to pay at least $500 to each of the owners of about 32,000 vehicles that were driven with disconnected odometers. The U.S. District Court in St. Louis took more than a year to agree to this settlement, which ended a class-action lawsuit against Chrysler. The company mailed $500 checks to the

27,000 customers they were able to locate in February 1990, for a total of $13.8 million. In August 1990, a U.S. Federal District Court judge in St. Louis found Chrysler guilty of fifteen counts of mail fraud in this case and fined the company $7.6 million. The charges stemmed from Chrysler's use of the U.S. mail to deliver fraudulent vehicle titles to customers. The fines and other payments came to a total of $21.4 million, and the company estimated it spent another $30 million on the extended warranties it offered.[70]

Chrysler had another potential disaster on its hands as a result of design defects in its innovative electronically controlled four-speed transaxle introduced on many of its 1989 models. Iacocca pushed the transmission into production against the advice of his engineers, who wanted more time to refine the design. The Ultradrive Transaxle often left the driver in second gear, which company engineers called the "limp mode." *Consumer Reports,* never a friend of Chrysler, claimed that 20 percent of Chrysler's 1989 minivans and 10 percent of the 1990 models equipped with the Ultradrive experienced major transmission problems. The transaxle suffered from a variety of design defects, including seals that leaked. On Iacocca's orders, Lutz gave the assignment of fixing the transaxle to Chris Theodore, one of the AMC engineers. He and a small team of engineers took care of the problems, but in the meantime, Chrysler paid out hundreds of millions of dollars to placate angry customers.[71]

Chrysler also suffered from instability in the top management ranks during Iacocca's last five years at the helm. A *Wall Street Journal* article of late November 1989 that examined Chrysler's problems, including the lack of new products, pointed out the "managerial musical chairs" of the previous two years as a major source of weakness. The (involuntary) departure of chief product planner Harold Sperlich, chief engineer Jack Withrow, and longtime marketing chief Joseph Campana were major losses. A July 1990 *Fortune* article noted that the seven top executives at Chrysler were all renegades of one sort or another. All of them saw themselves as the future CEO, but none of them were particularly good managers.[72]

Lee Iacocca must shoulder the blame for most of Chrysler's managerial chaos and confusion during his last years as chairman. He hired Robert Lutz from Ford in 1986 largely to weaken Hal Sperlich. He deliberately created rivalries between Bidwell, Sperlich, Greenwald, Miller, and Lutz. His managerial style came to mirror the methods of Henry Ford II, which Iacocca had hated so much during his days at Ford.[73]

The management crisis at Chrysler began with the hiring of Robert A. Lutz as executive vice president of Chrysler Motors in 1986. Lutz had had a distinguished career in the auto industry before coming to Chrysler. He first worked for General Motors and ran its European sales operations. Lutz left GM in 1972 to go to BMW as sales director and then joined Ford Motor Company in 1974.

After serving as chairman of Ford of Europe, Lutz became Ford's executive vice president for international operations and a director of the company in 1982. After clashing with Harold A.(Red) Poling, Ford's president, Lutz resigned from Ford on 3 June 1986, and Iacocca announced his appointment as Chrysler's executive vice president the next day. Iacocca hired Lutz primarily to drive Harold Sperlich out the door.[74]

Once on board, Lutz and Francois Castaing allied themselves against Sperlich, with Iacocca's blessing. Sperlich, who by his own admission was acerbic, clashed openly with Iacocca over the AMC purchase. In early January 1988, Iacocca took away Sperlich's control of product planning and on 21 January, Sperlich announced his "retirement" at age 58. In an interview with *Ward's Auto World* more than eighteen months later, Sperlich admitted that he quit because he was unhappy with the direction in which Chrysler was moving.[75]

Gerald Greenwald, who joined Iacocca at Chrysler in 1979, left Chrysler at the end of May 1990. Greenwald was almost exclusively a financial expert and a general businessman, with no particular knowledge of cars. Industry analysts assumed that he would be the next chairman. Iacocca said as much to Greenwald, who expected Iacocca to retire in late 1989 at the customary age of 65. When this did not happen and Iacocca announced that he would serve at least until the end of 1991, Greenwald concluded that Iacocca would never step aside so he could become chairman.[76]

In January 1990, the unions representing pilots, mechanics, and other workers at United Airlines, who planned to take over United through an employee stock ownership plan (ESOP), offered Greenwald a job. To hire him to arrange the takeover, they offered Greenwald a $5 million "signing bonus," a $1.1 million annual salary, a bonus payment of $1.2 million if the plan succeeded, plus the permanent job of CEO. Even if the financial plan failed, Greenwald would receive an additional payment of $4 million. Greenwald, who was earning $1 million a year at Chrysler, took the United job at the end of May 1990. The United Airlines deal fell apart by fall 1990 and Greenwald, with his $9 million cash in hand, joined the investment banking firm of Dillon, Read as a managing director.[77]

Iacocca denied any responsibility for Greenwald's sudden departure and used it to his own personal advantage. With no obvious successor waiting in the wings, in mid-July 1990 Iacocca extracted a supplemental pay package from his board of directors. He would receive an additional 62,500 shares of stock for every quarter he remained as chairman beyond December 1991. Depending on the value of the stock, this deal could bring him another $25–40 million a year.[78]

Bennett Bidwell, who joined Iacocca at Chrysler in June 1983, began a reduced work schedule in spring 1990. In serving as chairman of Chrysler Motors in 1988 and 1989, Bidwell held the number three position within Chrysler, after

Iacocca and Greenwald. However, in the spring of 1990, his doctor ordered him
to slow down and Iacocca agreed that Bidwell, 63, could reduce his work load.
He retired in the spring of 1991, but stayed on as a consultant. Unlike the other
members of the "Gang of Ford," Bidwell was not fired, in part because he was
never a threat to succeed Iacocca and he remained staunchly loyal to him.[79]

After Greenwald left Chrysler in May 1990, Steve Miller and Robert Lutz
became the leading candidates to replace Iacocca as chairman and CEO. Miller
and Lutz, who did not particularly like each other, declared a truce, each stating
publically that he would gladly serve under the other man. The Chrysler board
rejected Miller as the future CEO, but felt that he and Lutz might make an
effective team. Miller, however, made a fatal mistake. He met with the outside
directors on 30 September 1991 to discuss the succession possibilities at Chrysler.
He put into writing, in what became known as "the black letter," his assessment. Miller strongly criticized Iacocca's recent decisions and urged the board
to force him out as soon as possible. Incensed by Miller's statements, Iacocca
forced him to "retire" in March 1992. Of the "Gang of Ford," only Lutz survived, and Iacocca made certain that Lutz would not succeed him.[80]

Within two years after Bob Lutz arrived at Chrysler in June 1986, he became
the object of Iacocca's paranoia. The chairman became suspicious of the powerful alliance of Lutz and Castaing, which had restructured Chrysler's engineering
operations into platform teams. He was offended by Lutz's all-too-public criticisms of the K-car clones. Iacocca attacked Castaing and Lutz by delaying their
pet project, the Viper high-performance sports car, until May 1990. Iacocca
demanded that Lutz fire Castaing, but to his credit, Lutz refused. Ironically, in
his final years at Chrysler, Iacocca became just like Henry Ford II. He feared
that if Lutz ever became his successor, he would destroy his reputation as Chrysler's savior. As the other contenders for Iacocca's job left Chrysler, the aging
chairman became adamant that the board of directors choose "anybody but
Lutz" to replace him.[81]

The question of management succession at Chrysler was more complex than
necessary because Iacocca wanted to control the process and because he was
reluctant to leave. After Greenwald left Chrysler, only Lutz and Miller were
viable inside candidates to replace Iacocca. In mid-December 1990, Chrysler
announced that a reclusive California investor named Kirk Kerkorian had
bought nearly 10 percent of the company's shares. Fearing a hostile takeover
attempt, the Chrysler board pushed Iacocca to announce his retirement and to
name a successor.

In spring of 1991, Iacocca and Bidwell courted Roger Penske, who had successfully run a racing team, a string of car dealerships, and a diesel engine manufacturing company. In early June, after he discovered that Iacocca planned to
stay on as chairman through 1993, Penske rejected the overture. The Chrysler

board grew impatient with Iacocca after his public statement in late August that Chrysler would not even start to look for a successor until late 1992. Following its regular meeting on 5 September 1991, the Chrysler Board of Directors announced that Iacocca would retire at the end of 1992 and that the board would soon pick his successor.[82]

By late fall of 1991, Iacocca was promoting Gerald Greenwald as his replacement, but the board suspected that Greenwald would simply serve as Iacocca's puppet. After Lutz threatened to quit if Greenwald got the job and Miller threatened to quit if Lutz left, the board rejected Greenwald. Within Chrysler, opposition to Lutz was by no means limited to Lee Iacocca. Other executives and board members thought that Lutz put his own ambition and ego above the long-term best interests of the company. The solution to this dilemma for the Chrysler board and for Iacocca was to go outside of the company for its new leader.[83]

Their choice was Robert J. Eaton, who had served as president of General Motors Europe since June 1988. Eaton had worked for GM since 1963 and had held a variety of positions reflecting his training as a mechanical engineer. Iacocca interviewed him in Detroit in late December 1991, as did several Chrysler directors in January 1992. Following another interview in February 1992, the Chrysler board named Eaton vice chairman and chief operating officer on 16 March 1992. Although clearly disappointed that he was not chosen, Robert Lutz promised to stay at Chrysler and to support Eaton.[84]

After retiring as CEO, Iacocca would remain on as a board member and as chairman of Chrysler's executive committee for two years. Eaton's contract clearly defined the limits of Iacocca's power after he retired. The *Wall Street Journal* recognized that Eaton was a compromise choice of a board that would have faced serious internal dissension had it selected either Lutz or Greenwald.[85]

Several business publications openly questioned how well Eaton would fare with both Iacocca and Lutz still on board at Chrysler. As a *Fortune* article noted: "The odds on Eaton's survival may be no better than Chrysler's as an independent automaker. Iacocca treats heirs apparent the way Henry VIII treated his wives. Says one well-placed former Chrysler executive: 'The longer Lee lives with this guy, the longer he has to find fault with him.'" *Business Week* interviewed several former Chrysler officials, who all predicted that Eaton and Lutz would both fight to maintain power and that Iacocca would use this as an excuse to ask the board for a postponement of his retirement. No such struggle ensued. Lutz and Eaton worked cooperatively and Iacocca retired as scheduled. After retiring, Iacocca fought with the Chrysler board over details of his compensation package and continued his efforts to undermine Lutz. Finally, in September 1993, Iacocca resigned his director's position, thus cutting his ties with Chrysler and ending an era.[86]

IACOCCA IN PERSPECTIVE

Assessing Lee Iacocca's time at Chrysler is difficult at best. There are at least three Iacoccas—the "savior" who led Chrysler in 1978–83 through its government-guaranteed loans and near bankruptcy to a return to profits; the leader who made several unwise and costly acquisitions while strangling new product development in 1984–88; and the "Imperial Iacocca" of 1988–92, unwilling to groom a successor or gracefully give up power.

First of all, Lee Iacocca deserves credit for the survival of the Chrysler Corporation in 1978–83. He helped with the passage of the Loan Guarantee Act, though he did not orchestrate it—Michigan's senators and congressmen and Douglas Fraser did most of the work. However, once the legislation passed, Iacocca deserves credit for assembling the concessions packages that allowed Chrysler to get the guaranteed loans. He single-handedly rebuilt public confidence in Chrysler's vehicles. Iacocca did much to bring the K-cars to market and to develop the minivans, which proved to be Chrysler's salvation from 1984 on. He attracted an able corps of executives, mostly from Ford, to rebuild and strengthen all of the major aspects of Chrysler's business—product planning, manufacturing, marketing, sales, and finance. His managerial skills and charisma combined to save Chrysler and return it to profitability. No other automotive leader could have done this.

Lee Iacocca became an American folk hero and business icon, a symbol of the American "can-do" spirit in the 1980s. He came to represent and personify the Chrysler Corporation, a feisty underdog that ultimately fought its way back from the edge of defeat to become a winner, against all odds. He was antiestablishment and honest, sometimes brutally honest. Iacocca's fame was greatly enhanced with the publication of *Iacocca: An Autobiography* (1984), which sold 2.6 million hardcover copies in four years. He received invitations for more than 3,000 speaking engagements in 1984 alone. Publications such as the *Saturday Evening Post* (October 1984) and *Time* (1 April 1985) recognized him as an American folk hero. His supporters and admirers promoted him in 1984 and 1988 as a potential presidential candidate.[87]

Iacocca's belief that Chrysler faced unfair treatment was often justified. His attacks on unreasonable government regulation and unfair competition from the Japanese often fell on receptive ears. He was incensed when NHTSA proposed easing the corporate average fuel efficiency standard for 1986 from 27.5 to 26 mpg, mainly because Ford and General Motors were unable to meet the standard and would face substantial fines. Iacocca argued that while Chrysler invested billions to successfully meet the standard, Ford and GM consciously decided to sell higher-profit, gas-guzzling cars instead. Changing the standard was unfair to Chrysler and unfair to America.[88]

Iacocca was seen by the general public as a generous and public-spirited man. He donated all of his book earnings from *Iacocca* ($3 on each copy sold) to the Lee Iacocca Foundation, which supported research on diabetes, a factor in his wife's death in 1983. He helped raise $40 million for the Iacocca Institute (Lehigh University), a research center that addressed issues of America's international competitiveness. His most famous work came as the chair of the Statue of Liberty–Ellis Island Centennial Commission in 1982–86. He helped raise $305 million to restore the Statue of Liberty and buildings on Ellis Island, only to be fired unceremoniously by telegram in February 1986 by Secretary of the Interior Donald Hodel, on orders from President Reagan's chief of staff Donald Regan. According to Iacocca, Regan had strongly disliked him when Regan chaired the Chrysler Loan Guarantee Board, so the firing was purely personal.[89]

During the middle years of his tenure as Chrysler's CEO, from 1984 to 1988, Iacocca made a series of wrong-headed decisions that cost the company dearly. He diverted much of the profits from the K-cars, minivans, and other products into the purchase of non-automotive businesses like Gulfstream Aerospace, Electrospace Systems, and firms offering a variety of financial services. These purchases drained resources away from the development of new products, which Iacocca discouraged in the first place. He instead preferred that Chrysler simply produce additional clones of the K-car platform, saving money but resulting in outmoded, unattractive offerings. Iacocca's mishandling of the odometer tampering crisis also damaged Chrysler's reputation. The one exception was his decision to buy American Motors, against the advice of his lieutenants.

It is unfortunate that the mistakes Iacocca made during his last few years in power, his increasingly imperial and imperious management style, his unlimited ego, his rigid thinking about automotive design, and his inability to give up power gracefully detract from his overall contributions to the Chrysler Corporation.

Throughout his years at Chrysler, Iacocca was always interested in earning money, retaining power, and protecting his legacy. Many viewed his salary and benefits while CEO at Chrysler as obscene. He earned more than $14.5 million in salary, bonuses, and stock options in 1992, his last year at the helm. That was the third-largest payout in U.S. automotive history. The first- and second-largest payouts were also Iacocca's—$20.6 million in 1986 and $17.9 million in 1987. His reluctance to give up power caused chaos in Chrysler's management and damaged the company he headed. Even as he prepared for retirement, Iacocca's desperate efforts to preserve his legacy caused him to foster dissension in the corporation.[90]

For all of his faults, which became more apparent and more damaging in his last years at the head of Chrysler, Iacocca was nevertheless one of the most dynamic of the company's leaders and one of the most successful. In many respects, he was the CEO who most resembled Walter P. Chrysler. Iacocca had a broad understanding of automotive engineering, styling, marketing, and sales. He compensated for his areas of weakness, mainly in manufacturing and in finance, by hiring some of the best specialists in those areas and depending on their judgment. Iacocca introduced platform teams and successfully revamped the product lineup to help generate enormous profits in the 1990s. Much like Walter P. Chrysler, he was a natural-born, charismatic leader. Although the two men lived in very different eras and faced very different problems and challenges, they were both visionaries and risk-takers with the ability to imagine bright futures and the tenacity and talent to get there.

Chapter 16

CHRYSLER INTO DAIMLERCHRYSLER, 1993–2000

November 17, 1998 saw the birth of DaimlerChrysler—a child with extraordinary genes and extraordinary potential. It has been said that there are only two things we can give our children: one is roots, the other is wings. DaimlerChrysler has roots that are the envy of our industry. Our people are giving it wings.

—*DaimlerChrysler: Merger of Growth* (annual report)

Robert Eaton succeeded Lee Iacocca as chairman of the Chrysler Corporation on 1 January 1993 and was at the helm for the next six years. During his tenure, Chrysler introduced a steady stream of extremely popular and profitable products ranging from the high-powered Viper sports car to the subcompact Neon. The dynamic, innovative, forward-looking management team assembled earlier by Iacocca—including Robert Lutz, Francois Castaing, Thomas Gale, and others—remained firmly in control of the automaker's key operations. Sales hovered around 2.5 million vehicles and Chrysler captured roughly 15 percent of the North American market. Net earnings after taxes never fell below $2 billion a year from 1994 through 1997. Under Eaton, Chrysler was enjoying the exhilarating "upside" of its usual roller-coaster ride.

This is not to suggest that Chrysler was Camelot. There were internal disagreements over policy decisions and ongoing friction and clashes between some top executives. This is a normal circumstance in an industry ruled by men with enormous egos. One fly appeared in the Chrysler ointment in the person of investment tycoon/stockholder Kirk Kerkorian who, along with his ally Lee Iacocca, launched a crude and unsuccessful bid to take over the company in April 1995. Once Eaton and his board had rebuffed this effort, Chrysler Corporation seemed headed for continued successes.

Chrysler and the venerable German automaker Daimler-Benz A.G. made a surprising joint announcement in London on 7 May 1998—the two companies would merge, thus creating a giant automobile company operating on a global stage. The controlling boards of both companies approved the merger on 18

September 1998 and on 17 November 1998, shares of the new corporation, DaimlerChrysler A.G., began trading on stock exchanges worldwide. Chrysler Corporation no longer existed as an independent business entity. The decision by Chrysler's Bob Eaton to begin merger discussions with Daimler-Benz and then to consummate the marriage surprised Chrysler insiders and automobile industry observers alike.

PRODUCTS, PERFORMANCE, AND PROSPECTS

Chrysler produced an impressive stream of successful new products in the 1990s: the 1993 Jeep Grand Cherokee, introduced in April 1992; the 1993 LH models (Chrysler Concorde, Dodge Intrepid, and Eagle Vision) in June 1992; the 1994 Chrysler New Yorker and Chrysler LHS models; the 1994 Dodge Ram truck, which first appeared at the Detroit Auto Show in January 1993; the 1995 compact Plymouth and Dodge Neon, introduced in January 1994; the 1995 model Chrysler Cirrus and Dodge Stratus; all-new 1996 model minivans, introduced at the January 1995 Detroit Auto Show; the all-new 1997 Jeep Wrangler, available in early 1996; the 1997 Plymouth Breeze, which appeared in showrooms in January 1996; an all-new 1997 model Dodge Dakota pickup truck; the 1998 Dodge Durango, a mid-sized sports utility vehicle; the all-new 1998 Chrysler Concorde and Dodge Intrepid; the all-new 1999 model Jeep Grand Cherokee, introduced in spring 1998; and, finally, the Chrysler 300-M and the reworked Chrysler LHS, both 1999 models introduced in 1998. Two specialty cars also deserve mention—the Dodge Viper (1992) and the Plymouth Prowler (1997)—because they brought Chrysler Corporation positive notoriety among automobile enthusiasts.

All these vehicles were products of Chrysler's platform teams. Most incorporated at least one major design or styling innovation. The designers applied the "cab-forward design" principle, first used in the 1993 LH family sedans, to the longer 1994 Chrysler New Yorker and LHS models, the 1995 Chrysler Cirrus and Dodge Stratus, the compact Neon (1995 model), and the 1997 Plymouth Breeze. At the end of the decade, the second generation of Jeep Grand Cherokee, Dodge Dakota pickup truck, and LH family sedans made their appearance, along with the Dodge Durango sport utility vehicle.

Two lines of high-volume vehicles were vital to Chrysler's success—the compact Dodge/Plymouth Neon, introduced as a 1995 model, and the all-new minivans that debuted as 1996 models. Chrysler designed a new compact car to replace the dull Dodge Shadow/Plymouth Sundance models introduced in the 1987 model year so that the company could maintain an acceptable corporate average fuel efficiency (CAFE) rating for its full line. This was a tough challenge, given the Japanese advantage in high-quality small car designs and the small profit margins inherent in small cars.

Bob Lutz tapped veteran engineer Bob Marcell to head a small platform team to begin work on a design. In a meeting of Chrysler's top executives, including Iacocca, on 31 July 1990, Marcell offered an emotional appeal for approval of the project. He cited the example of his hometown of Iron River, Michigan, devastated by its inability to compete in the global iron ore industry. The U.S. auto industry and Chrysler in particular should not simply concede the small car market to the Japanese, but should apply its genius to recapturing that segment. The appeal impressed Iacocca, and in April 1991 he gave his final approval for a new small car.[1]

Bob Marcell's team displayed a cab-forward, bug-eyed compact idea car called the Neon at the Detroit Auto Show in January 1991. The model had the code designation PL because the goal was to combine the interior space of Chrysler's P cars—the Dodge Shadow and Plymouth Sundance—with the low cost of the earlier L subcompact cars—the Dodge Omni and Plymouth Horizon. Marcell could assemble his team from scratch, but faced severe cost restrictions. The new cars were to sell from between $9,000 and $13,000, with most at the lower end of that range. The corporation gave him only $1.3 billion for the development and initial production of Neon. In contrast, General Motors spent $4.5 billion, including the cost of an entirely new factory, to bring out its Saturn line.[2]

The Neon platform team used several unconventional methods to reduce costs. They would produce the car in the existing plant at Belvidere, Illinois, and would use as much existing machinery as possible. The Dodge and Plymouth versions would be identical, saving the company millions. To save shipping costs, Marcell built a small stamping plant next to the assembly plant. By reducing the number of dies required to produce the stampings for Neon compared to Shadow/Sundance from 597 to 370, Marcell saved $42 million. The team reduced the numbers and variety of screws, bolts, and other fasteners from 530 to 358, simplifying assembly. More important, the Neon had steering/suspension systems, engines, and manual transmissions superior to those in the Shadow/Sundance. In most respects, it was a worthy competitor for the Japanese compacts.[3]

One Neon design decision nicely illustrated how Chrysler's corporate culture had changed under the influence of the platform teams. Chrysler's top executives made a traditional "walk-around" look at Neon prototypes in the company's styling dome in the spring of 1992. Iacocca, Lutz, Gale, and the others liked what they saw, with one exception. The Neon team had replaced the large oval buglike headlights of the Neon idea car with narrow rectangular lights. Iacocca thought the new model's face had lost its charm, its "cute" appearance.

1991 Dodge Neon concept car. Courtesy of NAHC.

Lutz and Gale agreed with Iacocca, but Marcell and his team members were incensed that the bosses would undermine a key underlying principle of platform teams—that the higher-ups would trust a team's judgment and not interfere. Marcell also argued that the change in the headlights would cost an additional $20 million and might delay the model's introduction.

Five years earlier, Iacocca would have ordered the changes, whatever the cost, and the designers would have followed orders. This time, he broke with past habits and said nothing more. Instead, Gale and Lutz tried to convince Marcell to listen to the arguments for the round headlights and to reconsider the design, but Gale promised Marcell that he would live with the team's final decision. The Neon platform team still opposed the change, but found that the cost of redesign would be only $7 million and that using round headlights would save a like amount because they were cheaper to make. In time, Marcell changed his mind and the top management got its way through persuasion, not intimidation. Gale, Lutz, and even Iacocca recognized that their commitment to the platform team system would lose credibility if they meddled in team decisions.[4]

Chrysler officially introduced the Neon to the press on 5 September 1993, and the first copies rolled off the assembly line in Belvidere on 10 November 1993. Neon debuted in January 1994 as a 1995 model, with a base price less than $9,000. It varied only slightly in dimensions and styling from the 1991 idea car.

Iacocca's instincts about the headlights were right. Both the press and the buying public fell in love with the cute Neon face. *Automobile Magazine* named the Dodge/Plymouth Neon its 1994 Automobile of the Year. Calendar year production in 1994 was 136,529 units, but then jumped to 327,225 units in 1995. Neon production in 1996 slipped slightly to 278,429 units and to 247,046 units for 1997, impressive numbers in a market segment Chrysler had nearly abandoned. In contrast, production of the Dodge Shadow/Plymouth Sundance twins had peaked at 203,891 units in the 1989 model year and then fell to 145,438 units for the 1994 model year, their last.[5]

Chrysler reworked the minivan in the mid-1990s to keep its dominant position in that market segment. The company's production of 485,522 minivans in calendar year 1990 and 480,598 units in 1991 accounted for half the industry total. Chrysler remained the dominant minivan manufacturer in part because the other automakers continued to blunder in their efforts to produce a competitive product. Ford, General Motors, and the Japanese took misstep after misstep, producing rear-wheel drive trucklike vans that customers did not buy.

Chrysler updated the T-115 with totally reskinned 1991 models of the Plymouth Voyager and Dodge Caravan, code-named "AS." Sales of the AS suffered for a short time because of its problem-plagued electronic four-speed Ultradrive transaxle. A team of engineers led by Chris Theodore quickly fixed the Ultradrive problems and sales recovered nicely. Combined calendar year production of Chrysler's minivans rose steadily from 480,598 units in 1991 to 615,754 in 1994. The company's share of the combined minivan market slipped to 43 percent by late 1994, causing temporary distress within Chrysler. An all-new 1996 model minivan, code-named "NS" and scheduled for a full introduction in March 1995, was designed to allow Chrysler to retain its dominant position in this increasingly competitive market segment.[6]

Initial planning for the NS got under way in early 1990, with a small platform team of 20 headed by John Nemeth, former product development chief at American Motors. The team's broad goal was to develop a vehicle that would give Chrysler global minivan dominance into the twenty-first century. They struggled with the dual goals of keeping the basic size characteristics of the previous models while improving on interior space, gas mileage, driver/passenger visibility, and safety. The number, location, and type of doors were critical design issues for the team. Product quality, especially the "fit and finish" of the body, would be a major concern throughout the development process. The team estimated that they would need $2.25 billion to design the NS and bring it into production. They also projected that it would remain in production until 2006, but with periodic cosmetic changes.[7]

The NS platform team debated door configuration options for well over a year. Chrysler conducted market research in the fall of 1991 on this question, asking 300 current owners of Chrysler minivans for their views. They conducted the research in Chicago and in San Mateo, California. Asked about their willingness to pay an additional $300 for a driver's-side rear door, 85 percent answered positively, and two-thirds of the participants preferred a sliding door. The platform team decided to offer a sliding driver's-side door as an option. Once Chrysler introduced the NS models, 90 percent of the customers ordered the extra door and Chrysler decided to produce four-door models exclusively, offering the three-door version on a special-order basis only. The new Ford Windstar minivans, otherwise very competitive with Chrysler's minivans, did not initially offer a fourth door, briefly giving Chrysler a tremendous marketing advantage.[8]

In spring 1991, John Nemeth retired from Chrysler and Chris Theodore replaced him as the minivan team leader. Tom Gale became the project "godfather," exercising overall supervision from a distance. The planning and development process was a long one, even with the platform team—"theme approval" in April 1991, followed by "concept approval" on 23 September 1991, and "program approval" in May 1992. By the latter date, the financial experts had set the first official budget (subject to later changes) at $2.1 billion. The team proudly showed its first NS prototype to Eaton, Lutz, Gale, and the rest of the top management on 24 November 1992. The schedule for bringing the new minivan to market was firmly set by then. "Job one" would come off the assembly line in January 1995 and the official "rollout" would begin in March 1995, when dealers would have at least 13,000 of the new minivans on their lots.[9]

The investment Chrysler made in the NS models was greater than originally estimated, in part because the company enlarged its production goals. A decision to increase combined production at the two North American plants (Windsor and St. Louis) from 560,000 to 670,000 units per year added $300 million to the budget, while $200 million more was added for a European version. Adding in the advertising costs for the NS minivans drove the project budget to $2.8 billion, easily the greatest investment Chrysler had ever made in any product.[10]

The minivan team faced serious last-minute glitches, including a problem with body panels not fitting properly. Chrysler's dealers faced a shortage of the new models in March through June of 1995, traditionally their best-selling period. Largely because of the production glitches, calender year production in 1995 was only 452,619 units, down 26 percent from the previous year. Sales in 1995 were split nearly evenly between the older AS models (214,257 units) and the NS versions (249,310 vehicles). Production of 741,751 minivans in North America in 1996, an astonishing 29 percent of all Chrysler-made vehicles, proved the popularity of the NS and the value of the investment.[11]

Two of Chrysler's new cars of the 1990s, the Dodge Viper and the Plymouth Prowler, reflected the company's willingness to try radical, risky designs, although in limited-production, expensive models. Both appeared initially as automobile show "concept cars," with little apparent likelihood that they would ever become production vehicles. Viper and Prowler brought Chrysler Corporation much publicity and prestige while generating a good deal of showroom traffic. They reaffirmed the company's styling vigor and audacity. These were captivating vehicles that car enthusiasts appreciated, proof that "car guys" who took risks ran Chrysler. We cannot measure their contribution to Chrysler's image, but most observers agreed that it was substantial.

Bob Lutz loved overpowered, extremely fast sports cars like the Shelby Cobra of the 1960s. The Dodge Viper was the result of his notion that Chrysler should marry its planned V-10 engine for the future Dodge Ram pickup with a two-seat sports car body to produce a concept car to display at the auto shows. Tom Gale and Francois Castaing supported Lutz in his quest for a performance sports car. They named it the Dodge Viper and unveiled the car at the Detroit Auto Show of January 1989. Public reaction was enthusiastic and overwhelming. Hundreds of letters poured into Chrysler, many containing unsolicited deposits on a car that was yet to be considered for production.[12]

Early in 1989, Lutz and Castaing assembled a team of 80 volunteers to work on Viper, the first real platform team of the new era. They collaborated in a large room appropriately called "the snake pit," and quickly devised a plastic-bodied "super car" powered by an aluminum V-10 engine (488 cid), with a six-speed transmission. Lutz had to convince Iacocca to spent $80 million to produce a few sports cars that would sell for upwards of $50,000 each.[13]

The Viper project was briefly a pawn in the increasing struggle between Iacocca and Lutz. Iacocca delayed approval of Viper until May 1990, perhaps because he was afraid it would succeed, in sharp contrast to his Maserati fiasco. The Viper team had the first hand-assembled cars ready for sale in late 1992. Although Viper had a list price of $60,000, the factory could not begin to supply the demand for the car. The Viper GTS coupe joined the original roadster in 1996, with equal success. Production in 1992 was a mere 162 units, but jumped to 1,046 in 1993 and peaked at 3,083 for 1994. Viper production for 1995–97 averaged about 1,700 units. More important, Viper brought prestige and increased showroom traffic to Dodge. It epitomized Bob Lutz's love of cars.[14]

The retro-styled Plymouth Prowler, a tribute to the street hot rods of the 1950s, had less broad impact than Viper, but also illustrated the company's willingness to be stylistically daring. Chrysler introduced the low-slung purple Prowler at the 1996 Detroit Auto Show, with Eaton and Lutz appearing with the car as the Blues Brothers. This innovative aluminum-body car had a list price of only $39,000 and was almost impossible to get.[15]

The steady stream of popular, hot-selling products that began pouring from Chrysler in the early 1990s quickly improved the company's overall financial health, as table 16.1 illustrates. The combined profits of more than $12 billion for 1994–97 for a small company like Chrysler were impressive results by auto industry standards.

TABLE 16.1

Chrysler Corporation Performance, North American Market, 1991–97

	Unit Production	Market Share* (%)	Net Earnings†		
			Total ($)	On Sales (%)	On Capital Invested‡ (%)
1991	1,572,882	12.4	(795,000,000)	(3.0)	(13.0)
1992	1,839,528	13.1	723,000,000	2.2	9.6
1993	2,124,069	14.4	(2,551,000,000)	(6.2)	(37.4)
1994	2,448,518	14.3	3,713,000,000	7.5	34.7
1995	2,399,752	14.3	2,025,000,000	4.1	18.5
1996	2,516,354	15.9	3,525,000,000	6.1	30.5
1997	2,451,000	14.9	2,805,000,000	4.9	24.7

Source: Chrysler Corporation, *Report to Shareholders, 1991–1997,* box "Annual Reports 1968–98," DCHC.
Note: Losses are indicated in parentheses.

*As measured by new car and truck registrations.
† After taxes.
‡ Defined as stockholders' equity and surpluses.

In March 1998, the Chrysler Corporation announced an agreement to merge with the venerable German automaker Daimler-Benz, creating Daimler-Chrysler, but with Chrysler clearly the junior partner in the new corporation. Chairman Robert Eaton spearheaded the merger and received very strong support from his directors. Given Chrysler's spectacular performance in the 1990s, the merger seemed inexplicable to industry insiders and outsiders alike. Eaton, however, looked over the horizon and saw dark clouds, largely invisible to others. He foresaw Chrysler's management "dream team" breaking up and other threats to Chrysler's prospects for future success in an increasingly competitive global auto industry.

ROBERT EATON, THE "DREAM TEAM," AND THE MANAGERIAL RECORD

Assessing Robert Eaton's term as Chrysler's CEO is fraught with difficulties. He was quiet, shy, reserved, and definitely low key, a manager more than a leader,

Robert J. Eaton at a luncheon in Detroit, 21 February 1994. Courtesy of DCHC.

the polar opposite of Lee Iacocca or Robert Lutz. Observers often described him as a loner, with few confidants within Chrysler. He became the CEO of a company that he knew nothing about and spent the first year at Chrysler learning about Chrysler. Eaton did not rely on browbeating and intimidating his executives as had Iacocca. He did not shoot from the hip, but instead came to decisions through exhaustive study of the issues.[16]

To the surprise of most industry insiders, Eaton and Lutz not only did not feud, they worked together reasonably well. Lutz could have been an immediate threat to Eaton, who did not bring a single loyalist with him when he came over from General Motors. Lutz clearly was disappointed to be passed over in favor of Eaton, but did not need to be convinced to stay on. He really had no other options if he wanted to keep the power and salary he enjoyed as the number two in command at Chrysler. "The two Bobs," as they were called, stayed out of each other's way and avoided conflicts. Eaton let Lutz run product development, engineering, and manufacturing, the heart of Chrysler, and publically acknowledged Lutz's role in developing the company's spectacular product line.[17]

Bob Eaton reassigned some of his top executives during his early years as CEO, but the key members of the dream team he inherited from Iacocca—Bob Lutz, Francois Castaing (engineering), Tom Gale (styling), and Dennis Pawley (manufacturing)—remained in place. Eaton never got close to any of these men and increasingly clashed with them. Instead, he groomed and empowered two mid-level managers—Jim Holden and Thomas Stallkamp.

In 1994, Eaton put Holden, who had spent his entire career at Chrysler in sales, in charge of Chrysler's product quality, a chronic weakness at the number three automaker. In August 1995, he asked Holden to study a possible merger with Daimler-Benz. Eaton also developed a good working relationship with Thomas Stallkamp, who had served as vice president for procurement and supply since 1990. Eaton orchestrated Stallkamp's appointment as Chrysler's president and chief operating officer in December 1997. In part, Stallkamp got the job by default. Dennis Pawley had withdrawn from consideration, while Castaing's feuding with both Eaton and Lutz eliminated him as a candidate. Neither Eaton nor Lutz thought that Tom Gale would be an effective president. He was a brilliant designer, but was not aggressive enough to wield authority.[18]

Bob Eaton wanted Chrysler to expand its international presence through increased sales efforts and joint ventures with European or Asian automakers. He put Tom Gale in charge of expanding international sales in 1993 and Gale held that job, while still managing product design at Chrysler, through 1996. In 1992–95, the company's international revenues had quadrupled to $3.6 billion annually, but still accounted for only 7 percent of Chrysler's sales. In 1996, Francois Castaing took charge of international operations and Gale returned exclusively to design work. By then, Gale and Castaing's close working relationship and alliance had turned into a bitter rivalry.[19]

Starting in 1997, the Chrysler dream team began to unravel. Bob Lutz would reach Chrysler's mandatory retirement age of 65 in February 1997, but Eaton wanted him to remain on board to maintain a degree of stability in the top management ranks. The Chrysler board waived the rules and allowed Lutz to remain as vice chairman to manage product development. He was no longer president and had little direct control over operations. Dennis Pawley merely wanted to be left alone to run the factories and began planning for retirement. Castaing had grown tired of being characterized as an engineering expert with no other interests, so he agreed to take over international operations from Tom Gale. Castaing increasingly feuded with Eaton, Gale, and Lutz and resigned in December 1997, when Eaton chose Stallkamp as Chrysler's new president.[20]

Chrysler completed its move out of Highland Park when it opened its new world headquarters in suburban Auburn Hills in 1996. The opening of the Chrysler Technology Center (CTC) in mid-October 1991 had marked the first phase of this historic move. Less than a year later, on 9 September 1992, Lee Iacocca announced the construction of a new corporate headquarters next to the CTC. Lutz explained that the growing reliance on platform teams made the 25-mile trip between Highland Park and Auburn Hills increasingly costly and disruptive. The move transferred 4,500 employees to the new facilities. The City of Highland Park accepted a $90-million economic aid package from Chrysler to help mitigate the impact of the move. The package included $30 million in tax payments and economic development funds and a commitment to spend $60 million to clear and clean up the vacant property before giving it to Highland Park.[21]

The platform team system brought Chrysler greater agility in vehicle design and savings in time and money. A new computer-aided design/computer-aided manufacturing (CAD/CAM) system eased the products design/introduction process. Chrysler adopted a single unified computer program known as CATIA—computer-aided three-dimensional interactive application—developed by Dassault Systems, a division of the French aircraft manufacturer Avions Marcel Dassault. Honda and Toyota had used the system starting in the early 1980s and Castaing had employed it in some limited applications at American Motors. Nevertheless, it had not spread very widely because it required its users to be skilled in mathematics and because it was mainframe-based.

IBM and Dassault Systems united in the late 1980s to make CATIA more user-friendly and to move it to individual PCs. By 1993, Chrysler had installed 2,500 CATIA work stations for its engineers and designers and helped its suppliers to install a similar number. CATIA enabled fully integrated "virtual" design and testing of parts and components and the dies and machinery needed to build them. Chrysler used CATIA in a limited way starting in 1991 in the design of the NS minivans and found that it brought enormous time savings throughout the design process. The company's 1996 annual report claimed that the 1998 Chrysler Concorde/Dodge Intrepid were the first vehicles entirely developed with CATIA. The elapsed time between the initial concept approval and the actual product launch fell from 38 months for the 1993 Concorde/Intrepid/Vision to only 24 months for the 1998 Dodge Durango.[22]

Two significant developments severely tested Bob Eaton's leadership—a crisis involving alleged safety defects in minivan rear liftgate latches, which first surfaced in November 1994, and the Kirk Kerkorian/Lee Iacocca effort to complete a leveraged buyout of Chrysler Corporation, launched in April 1995. The National Highway Traffic Safety Administration (NHTSA) shocked Chrysler by announcing in November 1994 that the agency was investigating reports of failures of rear liftgate latches on Chrysler's T-115 and AS minivans in certain crash situations. NHTSA had received reports of fifty-one crashes in which latches failed, resulting in the ejection of seventy-four passengers and the deaths of twenty-five.

NHTSA threatened to force a recall of more than 4 million minivans for a retrofit of a stronger latch. Chrysler was legally within its rights in designing the rear liftgate latch to resist less pressure (750 pounds) than the 2,500 pounds mandated by NHTSA for passenger doors; there were in fact no federal standards for the rear liftgate. The outstanding safety record of Chrysler's minivans did not matter, nor did the fact that all of the fatalities involved unbelted passengers. The revelation that Chrysler could have strengthened the latch on the AS models with a minuscule investment of only $125,000, but chose to avoid the added expense, put the company in an indefensible position.

On 27 March 1995, Chrysler announced an agreement with NHTSA to offer owners of the 1984–89 T-155 models and the 1990–95 AS models a stronger latch, all at no charge to the customer. The average cost (parts and labor) of a replacement latch was about $30 and the program would have been costly had it involved all 4 million minivans. Fortunately for Chrysler, some of its minivans were no longer in use and most owners did not seem concerned about latch safety. The company estimated that only 200,000 customers would take advantage of the offer. NHTSA, however, insisted that Chrysler replace at least 60 percent of the latches, roughly 2.5 million, or face the threat of a mandatory recall. The company finally agreed to spend $14 million on consumer awareness programs in 1996 if it did not reach that goal. Still, Chrysler extricated itself from this problem at minimal cost.[23]

Right on the heels of the announcement of the minivan latch settlement, a more serious threat came to Bob Eaton—a proposed leveraged buyout of Chrysler, which billionaire financial mogul Kirk Kerkorian announced on 12 April 1995. His Las Vegas–based Tracinda Corporation offered to buy the entire 90 percent of Chrysler's stock that he did not already own for $55 a share, a 40 percent premium over the trading price of $39. The proposed $22.8 billion deal would be the second largest involving an American corporation. Lee Iacocca was one of Kerkorian's fellow investors and an ally in this effort. The attempted buyout surprised Bob Eaton and the Chrysler directors, who viewed it from the outset as a hostile action.[24]

Kerkorian was a 77-year-old financier who owned the MGM Grand, a gambling conglomerate, and had amassed a personal fortune of several billion though risky corporate acquisitions. At various times, he had owned Trans International Airlines and Western Airlines; Hollywood movie studios, including Metro-Goldwyn-Mayer, Columbia Pictures, and United Artists; and the MGM Grand and Flamingo hotels in Las Vegas. He loved to gamble.[25]

Kerkorian believed that Chrysler's stock price and the dividends on that stock were artificially low, given the company's profits. He began buying Chrysler stock in earnest in 1990, paying only about $10 a share, and quickly acquired 9.8 percent of the common stock. Kerkorian first met Iacocca in the chairman's New York office in December 1990. The two men gradually became friends and then business allies. Iacocca brought to the partnership with Kerkorian his Chrysler shares, worth about $50 million, but more important, his alleged prestige and stature with shareholders. Kerkorian, who knew nothing about the automobile business, believed that Iacocca's visible presence in the partnership would make a friendly takeover possible. Kerkorian was mistaken. Iacocca's return to the top at Chrysler would have set off a stampede of top executives for other jobs and an investor panic.[26]

Kerkorian believed that Chrysler share prices were artificially low because the dividends were too low, given the automaker's profits and cash surplus. In November 1994, when Chrysler shares were selling in the mid-$40s, the company had salted away $4.2 billion cash to weather the inevitable next downtown in sales. Kerkorian demanded an increase in the dividend from the current level of 25¢ per quarter and a two-for-one stock split. Eaton countered by announcing an increase in the quarterly dividend to 40¢ cents a share and a $1 billion stock buyback program. These moves were only the opening skirmishes in what four months later would become a full-fledged battle.[27]

Kerkorian's belief that he could effect a friendly takeover was mistaken. More important, Kerkorian's associates at Tracinda had not lined up the financing for the deal. Kerkorian planned to finance part of the takeover by draining Chrysler's cash surplus. To announce the deal without having investors committed to finance it was a monumental blunder.[28]

In the weeks following the Kerkorian announcement, Chrysler counterattacked, threatening never to conduct business again with any bank or brokerage house that cooperated with Kerkorian. The strategy worked. Kerkorian was unable to get a single investment bank to come on board. Ironically, he approached the German automaker Daimler-Benz to enlist its aid in his efforts, but the new Daimler CEO, Jürgen Schrempp, flatly rejected the idea. On 31 May 1995, Tracinda Corporation announced that Kerkorian had withdrawn his $55-a-share offer to buy Chrysler. Phase one of the Kerkorian struggles had ended.[29]

Kerkorian, however, did not give up the struggle. By late August 1995, he bought additional Chrysler shares and owned 14.1 percent of the stock. On Labor Day, he announced that Jerry York, former chief financial officer at Chrysler in the 1980s, would become vice chairman of Tracinda. Kerkorian dropped another bombshell on 25 October 1995 when he demanded that York be given a seat on the Chrysler board and that Tracinda have a say in naming two additional directors. Following long negotiations, the two sides reached an agreement on 7 February 1996.

One of Kerkorian's executives, James Aljian, would get a board seat instead of Jerry York. Kerkorian agreed to a five-year stand-down, during which he would buy no more Chrysler stock and would refrain from any negative remarks about Chrysler Corporation. The company agreed to pay Iacocca half the value of his remaining stock options, or $21 million. Kerkorian would sever all ties with Iacocca, who also had to agree to a five-year gag order on public statements about Chrysler. Iacocca complained that he really deserved a payout of $53 million, so Kerkorian paid him the difference of $32 million out of his own pocket to shut him up and to complete the deal.[30] Sadly, this was Lee Iacocca's final dealing with the company he had directed for fourteen years.

One unexpected result of the Kerkorian takeover was a series of high-level secret talks between Chrysler and the German automaker Mercedes-Benz. Two days after the Kerkorian announcement of 12 April 1995, Helmut Werner, the CEO of Mercedes-Benz and an old friend of Bob Eaton, suggested that the companies could work together. Top officials from Chrysler (Eaton, Lutz, Tom Denomme, and Gary Valade) and from Mercedes-Benz (Werner, Dieter Zetsche, and Jürgen Hubbert) met secretly in New York City on 17 April. Werner was not thinking about a merger of the two companies, but instead proposed several joint ventures in the emerging economies of Asia and Latin America.

The talks continued until 9 October 1995, when Eaton and Werner met with Jürgen Schrempp, the new chairman of Daimler-Benz, in Stuttgart, Germany. Daimler-Benz was the holding company that controlled the automobile operation, Mercedes-Benz, and additional businesses producing heavy trucks, railroad equipment, and aircraft. Schrempp attacked the plans developed by Werner and Eaton as ill conceived. Schrempp killed any plans for a joint venture and sent Eaton back to the United States. But nonetheless, this initial high-level contact between the two automakers had laid the foundation for serious merger talks two years later.[31]

CHRYSLER INTO DAIMLERCHRYSLER

On 7 May 1998, Daimler-Benz A.G. and the Chrysler Corporation announced the merger of the two firms, forming DaimlerChrysler A.G., the fifth largest automaker in the world. Bill Vlasic and Bradley A. Stertz chronicle the negotiations that led to the merger and the consummation of this union in great detail in their book *Taken for a Ride: How Daimler-Benz Drove Off with Chrysler*. There is no need to repeat that twisting, complicated story here, except in a summary fashion.

Following the collapse of talks between Chrysler and Daimler-Benz in November 1995 about joint ventures, neither company discussed partnerships with other auto companies for two years. Although both corporations enjoyed robust sales and profits in 1996 and 1997, Bob Eaton and Jürgen Schrempp had independently concluded by June 1997 that their respective companies needed to merge with another automobile company. Eaton was concerned about Chrysler's ability to survive as an independent firm in an increasingly global market against much larger competitors, especially General Motors, Ford, and Toyota. Schrempp wanted Daimler-Benz to double its revenues over the next decade, but knew that it could not accomplish that goal if it remained a producer of luxury cars only. Each did extensive research suggesting that the other company would be an ideal merger partner.[32]

Schrempp, in Detroit for the Detroit Auto Show, breached the possibility to Eaton in January 1998. At that point, Schrempp was also considering Ford as a partner; he met with Alex Trotman, Ford's chairman. The Ford family quickly vetoed this plan. Chrysler and Daimler-Benz began serious merger talks on 12 February 1998 in Geneva, and these negotiations continued at various venues, most notably New York City, London, and Stuttgart. The Chrysler board, which had been kept informed of the talks, formally agreed to the merger idea, at least in principle, on 7 April. Schrempp presented the merger deal to the Daimler management board, which endorsed it on 3 May 1998. The Chrysler board did the same two days later, after a last-minute disagreement over the name of the combined corporation, a dispute that threatened to kill the deal. Schrempp wanted Daimler-Benz-Chrysler and Eaton preferred Chrysler-Daimler-Benz: they compromised on DaimlerChrysler. Bob Eaton and Jürgen Schrempp announced the merger in London on 7 May 1998 at 7:00 A.M.[33]

Chrysler held its last annual shareholders' meeting on 22 May 1998 in Englewood, Colorado. It lasted only an hour and a half and the main business was a tribute to Lutz, who was retiring in July. Both Chrysler and Daimler-Benz held special shareholders' meetings on 18 September 1998 to ratify the merger, with 98 percent of Chrysler's shareholders and 99 percent of Daimler's approving. One notable fly appeared in the merger ointment before the merger was fully consummated. The executive committee of the Standard and Poor's Corporation announced on 1 October that DaimlerChrysler would not be included in the S & P 500 stock index because the firm was not incorporated in the United States. This meant that the managers of American mutual funds tied to the S & P index would be forced to sell their shares in DaimlerChrysler. This was not a good omen for future share values.[34]

The Chrysler board of directors met for the last time on 5 November in New York City. Chrysler stock traded on the New York Stock Exchange for the last time on 12 November 1998; after the close of trading, the Chrysler Corporation no longer existed as a corporate entity. The following Tuesday, 17 November, Eaton and Schrempp bought the first shares of DaimlerChrysler stock at the opening of trading on the New York Stock Exchange. The marriage was fully consummated, at least in a narrow legal sense.

Even a cursory look at the details shows that this "merger of equals" was in fact a takeover. At the onset, the former Daimler stockholders owned 57 percent of the shares in the new company. More important, the new entity was a German corporation and a majority of its management board came from the Daimler-Benz side.[35] A judicious assessment of the long-term results of the merger is impossible until more time has passed, but the merged company's early years have witnessed disappointing financial results, sudden and disturbing changes in the top management of the Chrysler operations, and much public controversy.

DAIMLERCHRYSLER'S STRUGGLES

Noting the two year anniversary of the formation of DaimlerChrysler A.G., on 26 November 2000 the *New York Times* ran a long analysis of the automaker's situation entitled, "This 1998 Model is Looking More Like a Lemon." The Chrysler Group, a division of DaimlerChrysler, had losses in the third quarter 2000 of $512 million, with no prospect of a quick turnaround. This was Chrysler's first quarterly loss in nine years. DaimlerChrysler shares, which had peaked at $108 in January 1999, had fallen to $40 in late November 2000. Jürgen Schrempp, DaimlerChrysler's chairman, had just fired James Holden, the American president of the Chrysler Group. Holden's replacement, veteran Daimler-Benz executive Dieter Zetsche, fired several of the remaining top American Chrysler officials right after taking control. The "dream merger" of two years earlier had become a nightmare.[36]

What had happened in only two short years? On the surface, the Chrysler Group appeared to perform well in 1998 and 1999 before the sharp reversal of fortune in 2000. Combined vehicle sales in North America increased strongly in 1998 to 2.81 million units (versus 2.45 million in 1997) and then grew slightly to 2.95 million units in 1999. Profits for the Chrysler Group remained healthy at roughly $5 billion a year in 1998 and 1999. Then the (former) Chrysler Corporation suffered operating losses of $1.75 billion in 2000, followed by losses of $3.96 billion in the following year.[37]

The *New York Times* and other observers of the Chrysler Group's troubles have focused on the rapid departure of the 1990s "dream team" from Chrysler right before the merger and shortly thereafter. The loss of a dozen key executives, who either took early retirement in their late fifties or were forced out by Jürgen Schrempp, changed the working dynamics of the American management team. Many of them left Chrysler because they found the new management structure and culture dominated by the Germans unacceptable. The merger brought severe disruptions in the way that Chrysler had operated, with few discernable benefits. Still, the more serious wounds Chrysler endured after the merger were self-inflicted. The American executives leading the Chrysler Group in 1999 and 2000 made a series of purchasing, design, and marketing blunders which damaged Chrysler's sales and profits.[38]

The loss of Chrysler's independent status and the overbearing, domineering management style of Jürgen Schrempp and the Daimler-Benz executives accelerated whatever "natural" exodus of American managers might have otherwise occurred. Despite the public statements that the merger of Chrysler and Daimler-Benz was a "merger of equals," it was not. The management board that emerged after the retirement of Dennis Pawley in December 1998 had seven Americans and ten Germans. More important, Schrempp was aggressive and assertive when disagreements occurred and Bob Eaton was passive, almost withdrawn much of the time. The Germans, especially Schrempp, were authoritarian in their demeanor and did not tolerate criticisms from the American executives, who soon understood that they were junior partners at best.[39]

The departure of Steve Harris, Chrysler vice president for public relations, was typical of the pattern that developed. Harris had come to Chrysler from American Motors in 1987 with the Chrysler buyout of AMC and became vice president in 1998 before the merger. He had worked in automotive public relations for thirty-one years and was widely respected by journalists covering the industry. With the creation of DaimlerChrysler, his German counterpart, Christoph Walther, became his boss with control over all corporate communications. Harris bristled at the way public relations was handled under Walther. Press releases were written in German, then translated into English and went out in the morning in Germany, usually around 2 A.M. in the United States. Harris announced his resignation on 3 February 1999 to become vice president of global communications at General Motors.[40]

The exodus of top management which began before the merger of Daimler and Chrysler became a stampede after the merger was completed. Francois Castaing had retired at age 52 in December 1997 and Bob Lutz followed in July 1998. Chris Theodore, senior vice president for platform engineering, resigned in March 1999 to take a position at Ford Motor Company and Chrysler's senior vice president for international manufacturing, Shamel Rushwin, joined Theodore in defecting to Ford. The first earth-shaking departure came when Eaton fired Chrysler president Thomas Stallkamp in September 1999 and replaced him with James Holden. Stallkamp had served as president since January 1998 and had coordinated Chrysler's efforts to integrate with Daimler-Benz following the merger. He had become increasingly critical of the new DaimlerChrysler management board and of the behavior of the Germans, particularly their lavish spending habits. Eaton, with Schrempp's support, fired Stallkamp to eliminate the criticism and to clear the way for Holden to move up the management ladder. Eaton may have wanted to do this before his own retirement early in 2000. Stallkamp was permitted to stay on until the end of 1999 as vice chairman of DaimlerChrysler, a largely ceremonial post.[41]

Bob Eaton's announcement of his retirement as co-chairman of Daimler-Chrysler on 26 January 2000 was another turning point in the evolution of the

merged company. At the time of the merger, Eaton had announced his inten-
tion to retire after three years, but stayed for only fifteen months after the
merger was consummated.

The departure of Chrysler executives was accelerated by the brutal candor of
Jürgen Schrempp in discussing the "merger of equals" in an interview with the
Financial Times on 30 October 2000. Schrempp revealed his real intentions in
merging the two companies: "We had to go a round-about way, but it had to
be done for psychological reasons. If I had gone and said Chrysler would be a
division (of DaimlerChrysler), everyone on their side would have said, 'There is
no way we can do a deal.' But it's precisely what I wanted to do."[42]

With the Chrysler Group suffering losses in the third quarter of 2000, Schrempp summarily fired James Holden as Chrysler's president on 15 November
2000, replacing him with Dieter Zetsche, long-time Daimler executive and
Schrempp loyalist. Theodore Cunningham, vice president for sales and marketing, was fired along with Holden. Within three months, most of the remaining
executives from the old Chrysler Corporation were gone. Thomas Gale and
John Herlitz, twin gurus of styling and design, retired in December 2000 and
Arthur Liebler, senior vice president for global marketing, resigned the following
February.[43]

On the heels of Schrempp's statement and the firing of Holden, stockholder
Kirk Kerkorian filed a lawsuit against DaimlerChrysler AG in late November
2000 seeking $9 billion in damages and a reversal of the merger of 1998. He
claimed that Schrempp fraudulently induced him and other Chrysler shareholders to agree to a merger instead of an acquisition, which would have brought
them more compensation than they received from the "merger." The other
owners of Chrysler Corporation shares followed suit the next day, asking for $8
billion in damages.[44]

The bad news for the Chrysler Group did not end with the arrival of Dieter
Zetsche as the new president. On 30 January 2001, Zetsche announced plans to
eliminate 26,000 Chrysler jobs or 20 percent of its workforce within three years,
the permanent closure of six plants, and a 15 percent reduction in production
capacity. This stiff medicine was needed to reverse the disastrous results of 2000.
The American Chrysler leaders, especially James Holden, had made a series of
miscalculations and mistakes that put Chrysler in jeopardy. Their production
plans and sales forecasts were based on the unrealistic assumption that the company would gain market share at a time when the other automakers were introducing attractive minivans and SUVs, Chrysler's two most important lines.
Instead, Chrysler's North American market share fell from 16.7 percent in 1999
to 15.7 percent a year later.

Holden and his lieutenants made two serious marketing blunders. They failed
to anticipate the enormous demand the popular PT Cruiser would generate,

resulting in severe shortages. The most costly blunder, however, was the handling of the introduction of the all-new 2001 model minivans. Worried that they might be caught with few minivans to sell, as happened in 1995, they built far too many of the 2000 models in the first eight months of the year. With an excess of perhaps 200,000 units of the old models, Chrysler had to offer customers rebates of $3,000 to clear the old minivans from the inventory before the 2001 models appeared. Customers took advantage of the bargains but as a result, demand for the new and more expensive 2001 minivans was well below projections. Chrysler was forced to offer rebates of $4,000 on the new models as well. The net result was the loss of most of the profits on this key product, operating losses for the Chrysler Group in the third quarter of 2000, and the management purge that followed.[45]

Of course, one can speculate about how the Chrysler Corporation might have performed had it remained an independent entity in 1998 and beyond. Blaming Chrysler's recent troubles on the merger and the actions of the Daimler-Benz leaders is simplistic and unfair. In many respects the downturn of 2000 and 2001 is merely a return to the downward phase of the roller- coaster ride that Chrysler has experienced since the 1950s. Perhaps the old management team of Lutz, Castaing, Gale, Pawley, and others might have avoided the errors made by James Holden and his management team. Still, the key mistakes of 1999 and 2000 were made by Chrysler's American executives already in place or in the wings when the merger took place. Under Dieter Zetsche, the Chrysler Group has already turned the corner, earning a small profit of $111 million in the first quarter of 2002, with projections of respectable profits for the entire year.[46]

CHRYSLER CORPORATION: A RETROSPECTIVE

Chrysler's history consists of four distinct segments. The first included the early success and rapid growth of the company between 1925 and 1935 under the visionary leadership of Walter P. Chrysler. The second, extending from 1935 through 1950, was a period when the company struggled and barely maintained its position as the number two producer. The third period, from 1950 to 1978, was largely a time of crisis and decline. The fourth, from Iacocca's arrival in 1978 to 1998, saw the company recover and prosper by remaking itself into a manufacturer of front-wheel drive cars, minivans, sport utility vehicles, and trucks.

In its first decade, the Chrysler Corporation was innovative. It took risks, and taking those risks paid off in rapid growth. Introducing any new line of cars in 1924 was risky business, but Walter Chrysler's introduction of the expensive but lightweight Chrysler Six, sold by the Maxwell Motor Corporation, challenged existing marketing principles. The Chrysler Six was packed with new features, offered speed and excellent handling, and was stylish to boot. Walter Chrysler's business decisions of 1928—the purchase of Dodge and the introduction of the Plymouth and DeSoto lines—were risky and, taken together, unprecedented. Even in the midst of the Depression, Chrysler continued to lead the industry in automotive engineering. The "Floating Power" Plymouth and especially the unsuccessful Airflow cars showed Walter Chrysler's iconoclasm and ingenuity.

The Chrysler Corporation maintained its position as the number two automaker under the stewardship of K. T. Keller (1935–50), but made no significant advances. The second half of the 1930s brought struggles with organized labor, a severe recession in 1938, a damaging strike in 1939, and the beginnings of the conversion to war work. Chrysler's very successful war production effort included manufacturing innovations and showcased Keller's great skill as a production man. Chrysler struggled to reconvert to civilian work in the immediate postwar years, but lost its competitive edge in the market of newly designed automobiles starting in 1948. Chrysler's cars remained static, reflecting Keller's preference for tall boxy designs until the 1954 model year. The disastrous strike of 1950, largely the result of Keller's rigid conservatism, foretold the permanent loss of the number two position in the American automobile industry starting in 1953.

The third period in Chrysler's history, and the longest, was the roller-coaster ride extending from 1950 to 1978. Chrysler's relatively small size meant that it could shift policies, programs, and products more quickly than its larger competitors. Chrysler developed a more nimble management than General Motors or Ford largely out of necessity. It had more innovative, risk-taking, swashbuckling leaders than its competitors, but their mistakes and miscalculations produced more frequent crises—the company faced a serious financial crisis at least every ten years from 1950 through 1978. During the period, Chrysler was easily the smallest and least profitable of the Big Three automakers, with the smallest cash reserves and the smallest margin for errors.

Over the lengthy stretch between K. T. Keller's retirement in 1950 and Lee Iacocca's arrival as a "white knight" in 1978, the company suffered from weak management at the top. None of the men who served in the interim—Colbert, Townsend, or Riccardo—shared Walter Chrysler's breadth of knowledge or his vision. Colbert was a brilliant but erratic salesman, while Townsend and Riccardo were accountants—"bean counters," in auto industry parlance.

Chrysler's leaders have managed the company's core automotive business poorly since the Second World War. Financial crises typically resulted in severe cuts to the engineering and design staffs, damaging new product development. The tendency to rush new models to market before they were ready proved disastrous. From the 1957 model line to the Dodge Aspen/Plymouth Volare, Chrysler suffered in the marketplace from self-inflicted wounds. Lynn Townsend's expensive overseas acquisitions drained resources away from the core vehicle business. In the late 1970s, Chrysler sold these assets at fire-sale prices to raise cash to avoid bankruptcy.

With Iacocca's arrival in 1978, Chrysler reinvented itself in several ways. Iacocca purged the top managers and installed bright, brash iconoclasts in their place. The company jettisoned its outmoded factories and modernized the rest. Cost accounting and other basic business practices were updated. Chrysler revolutionized the way in which it designed new products through the platform teams. Finally, Chrysler abruptly changed the products it made. The company recognized and exploited the emerging niche markets for minivans, sport utility vehicles, and light-duty trucks before the other American automakers. Chrysler's competitors began to challenge its dominance of these niche markets in the mid-1990s, and perhaps the company would not have survived in the global marketplace long after 2000 on its own.

Despite or perhaps because of its size disadvantage, Chrysler kept its position as one of the industry's leading engineering innovators long after the departure of the engineering trio of Zeder, Skelton, and Breer. The company can boast of a long list of automotive firsts since 1950, including the hemispherical combustion chamber V-8 engine (1951), alternating current generator (1960), gas turbine automobile (1963), electronic spark advance control (1976), and electronically

controlled automatic transaxle (1989). Chrysler has introduced a remarkable collection of innovative vehicles since 1950, including the 1955–57 Forward Look
models, the muscle cars of the 1960s and early 1970s, the 1978 model front-
wheel drive Dodge Omni/Plymouth Horizon, the 1981 model front-wheel drive
Dodge Aries/Plymouth Reliant, the revolutionary 1984 model minivans, the
1993 Jeep Grand Cherokee, and the "cab forward" automobiles of the 1990s.

NOTES

Chapter 1

1. Walter P. Chrysler and Boyden Sparkes, *Life of an American Workman* (New York: Dodd, Meade, 1950), 99–109. Chrysler's autobiography was originally published in serial form in the *Saturday Evening Post* between 19 June and 14 August 1937. Unfortunately, none of the dozens of illustrations were reproduced in the book version. Until recently, this was virtually the only source of information on the first 35 years of Walter Chrysler's life, and most of it is based on his recollections when he was in his early 60s. Interviews he gave the press starting in the late 1920s recall the same basic facts of his early life. Vincent Curcio's *Chrysler: The Life and Times of an Automotive Genius* (New York: Oxford University Press, 2000) is an exhaustive biography that adds much detail to Chrysler's autobiography, but does not contradict it in any substantial way. I have relied almost exclusively on *Life of an American Workman* in recounting Chrysler's career before he began working in the automobile industry in 1912. He probably embellished certain incidents of his childhood or youth, but the first two-thirds of his autobiography is quite detailed and refreshingly honest about his youthful weaknesses and indiscretions. However, I view his accounts of key incidents during his automotive career with much more skepticism and have found his version of his accomplishments untrustworthy and incomplete. For example, he makes no reference to the Airflow (perhaps deeming it best forgotten) in his autobiography.
2. Chrysler and Sparkes, *Life of an American Workman,* 24–26, 30–32.
3. Ibid., 37–39, 43.
4. Ibid., 45–47, 60–61.
5. Ibid., 41, 111.
6. Ibid., 71.
7. Ibid., 95 for both quotations.

8. Ibid., 73–76.

9. Ibid., 51–53, 57–76, passim, 83–93.

10. Ibid., 95–99.

11. Ibid., 111.

12. Ibid., 113–15.

13. Ibid., 117–23.

14. Ibid., 123–27.

15. Ibid., 132–33. Quotation from p. 133.

16. Ibid., 134–36; O. D. Foster, "'Watch the Terminals; Not the Way Stations'—Chrysler," *Forbes*, 1 February 1925, 541, 554; and Terry B. Dunham and Lawrence R. Gustin, *The Buick: A Complete History*, 4th ed. (Kutztown, Pa.: Kutztown Publishing, 1992), 416.

17. Chrysler and Sparkes, *Life of an American Workman*, 139–40.

18. Ibid., 141–43. The text of Storrow's letter to Chrysler dated 27 July 1916 is reproduced in Henry Greenleaf Pearson, *Son of New England: James Jackson Storrow, 1864–1926* (Boston: Todd, 1932), 143.

19. "Walter P. Chrysler, The Man Who Worked His Way to the Presidency of the Buick Motor Co.," *Timken Magazine*, February 1917, 617. Durant's recollections of convincing Chrysler to stay at GM can be found in "Memorandum, the Chrysler Incident" and "The Chrysler Story," both in folder D74–2.1A, William C. Durant Papers, SA/KU. For Chrysler's account, see Chrysler and Sparkes, *Life of an American Workman*, 143–45. Lawrence R. Gustin, *Billy Durant: Creator of General Motors* (Grand Rapids, Mich.: Eerdmans, 1972), 181–83, repeated Durant's version, while Bernard W. Weisberger, *The Dream Maker: William C. Durant, Founder of General Motors* (Boston: Little, Brown, 1979), 200–201, reiterated Chrysler's account.

20. Chrysler and Sparkes, *Life of an American Workman*, 145.

21. Ibid., 146–48.

22. Ibid., 153–56.

23. Dunham and Gustin, *The Buick*, 107–9.

24. Ibid., 111–12; and *Report of General Motors Corporation for the Fiscal Year Ended December 31, 1918*, 3, vertical files, General Motors Company, NAHC.

25. Alfred P. Sloan Jr., *My Years with General Motors*, ed. John McDonald and Catherine Stevens (Garden City, N.Y.: Doubleday, 1964), 116–48.

26. Arthur Pound, *The Turning Wheel: The Story of General Motors through Twenty-Five Years, 1908–1933* (Garden City, N.Y.: Doubleday, 1934), 89, 179, 203; Alice Lethbridge, *Halfway to Yesterday* (Flint, Mich.: Genessee County Historical and Museum Society, 1974), 114–15; Ronald Edsforth, *Class Conflict and Cultural Consensus: The Making of a Mass Consumer Society in Flint, Michigan* (New Brunswick, N.J.: Rutgers University Press, 1987), 75; and Janet L. Kreger, Nomination of the Civic Park Historic Residential District to the National Register of Historic Places, 1 November 1978, continuation sheets 13–14, found in the files of the Michigan Historical Center, Lansing, Michigan.

27. Chrysler and Sparkes, *Life of an American Workman*, 157–63; Gustin, *Billy Durant*, 201; and Weisberger, *The Dream Maker*, 253–54.

28. Chrysler and Sparkes, *Life of an American Workman*, 161–63; and Sloan, *My Years with General Motors*, 50, 317.

29. Walter P. Chrysler to John J. Carton, 28 October 1919, folder 14, box 15, John J. Carton Papers, BHL; Walter P. Chrysler to Charles F. Kettering, 28 October 1919 and Kettering

to Chrysler, 3 November 1919, "W. P. Chrysler, 1919," folder 87–11.17–66, Charles F. Kettering Papers, SA/KU.

30. Chrysler and Sparkes, *Life of an American Workman,* 163–65; and "Willys Seeks to Lead Field: Walter P. Chrysler Joins Motor Interests with Plans for Big Production," *Detroit Free Press,* 6 January 1920, 1.

31. "An Appreciation Tendered to Mr. Walter P. Chrysler by the Membership of the Kiwanis Club, the Rotary Club, the Exchange Club of Flint, Michigan at a Dinner January 22, 1920 at Flint Country Club, Flint, Michigan" and "Songs, Appreciation of Walter P. Chrysler," folder 77–7.4–1.15.1, Charles Stewart Mott Papers, SA/KU.

32. "Walter P. Chrysler, Former Manager of the Buick Motor Co.: An Appreciation by the Rev. J. Bradford Pengelly, Rector of St. Paul's Episcopal Church," *Flint Weekly Review,* [?] January 1920, folder 77–7.4–1.15–1, Charles Stewart Mott Papers, SA/KU. Half of the newspaper's masthead is missing and a search of a half-dozen archives in Flint and throughout Michigan failed to turn up copies of this weekly newspaper before 1933.

33. "Re Chrysler," folder D74–2.1A, William C. Durant Papers, SA/KU.

34. William C. Durant, "My Autobiography," folder D74–2.1A and letter, S. E. Miller to W. C. Durant, 8 January 1940, folder D74–2.1C, William C. Durant Papers, SA/KU. The others named on the dedication page were Arthur G. Bishop, R. Samuel McLaughlin, DeWitt Page, S. Sidney Stewart Jr., and Nathan Hofheimer. Durant identified Hofheimer as the person "who came to my assistance at the time of my real need and to whom I am at this time greatly indebted."

35. Chrysler and Sparkes, *Life of an American Workman,* 165 and Curcio, *Chrysler,* 307–8.

CHAPTER 2

1. The most useful general histories of the American automobile industry during the formative years of 1900 to 1925 include George S. May, *A Most Unique Machine: The Michigan Origins of the American Automobile Industry* (Grand Rapids, Mich.: Eerdmans, 1975); James J. Flink, *America Adopts the Automobile, 1895–1910* (Cambridge, Mass.: MIT Press, 1970); Edward D. Kennedy, *The Automobile Industry: The Coming of Age of Capitalism's Favorite Child* (New York: Reynal & Hitchcock, 1941); John B. Rae, *American Automobile Manufacturers: The First Forty Years* (Philadelphia: Chilton, 1959); and Donald Finlay Davis, *Conspicuous Production: Automobiles and Elites in Detroit, 1899–1933* (Philadelphia: Temple University Press, 1988).

2. Thomas E. Bonsall, *More Than They Promised: The Studebaker Story* (Stanford: Stanford University Press, 2000), 122–23.

3. Chrysler and Sparkes, *Life of an American Workman,* 170–71; Carl Breer, *The Birth of Chrysler Corporation and Its Engineering Legacy,* ed. Anthony J. Yanik (Warrendale, Pa.: Society of Automotive Engineers, 1995), 65; and Carl Breer, "The Three Engineers: Zeder-Skelton-Breer," 138, DCHC.

4. Breer, *Birth of Chrysler Corporation,* 65–70; and Owen R. Skelton reminiscence, "Origins of Chrysler Corporation and the First Chrysler Car," 1–2, DCHC. The undated Skelton reminiscence covers the years 1920–23 only.

5. "Plan to Market Chrysler Six," *Automobile Topics,* 21 August 1920, 23; and "Chrysler's Name Is Given to New Plant," *Automobile Topics,* 30 October 1920, 1275. The photograph

is reproduced in Breer, *Birth of Chrysler Corporation,* 72, and the engineering drawings are in the DCHC.

6. Chrysler and Sparkes, *Life of an American Workman,* 179–80. This enormous plant, with one building enclosing 2.1 million square feet, and the intended arrangement of the production processes are described in detail in Paul L. Battey, "Designing a Modern Automobile Plant," *Iron Age* 9 March 1922, 652–56 and 16 March 1922, 713–16.

7. *Automobile Manufacturer,* March 1922, 31. Breer, *Birth of Chrysler Corporation,* 75, identifies Rayal Hodgkins from the Cleveland Tractor Company as Zeder-Skelton-Breer's contact, but says that the new venture would produce the "Zeder" car; folder "Zeder," box "Logos," DCHC; and James M. Laux, "Rollin H. White," in *Encyclopedia of American Business History and Biography: The Automobile Industry, 1896–1920,* ed. George S. May (New York: Facts on File, 1990), 448–49.

8. Eugene W. Lewis, *Motor Memories: A Saga of Whirling Gears* (Detroit: Alved Publishers, 1947), 70, 129–31; Davis, *Conspicuous Production,* 88–89; and E. R. Thomas-Detroit Company, articles of association, 2 May 1906, in minutes of meetings of the board of directors, DCHC.

9. E. R. Thomas-Detroit Company, minutes of meetings of the board of directors, meetings of 8 July 1907, 15 November 1907, 3 December 1907, and 30 July 1908; minutes of stockholders' meetings, meeting of 15 June 1908; and Chalmers-Detroit Motor Company, minutes of stockholders' meetings, meetings of 29 July 1909 and 26 January 1910, DCHC.

10. Lewis, *Motor Memories,* 70–71; and "Chalmers Celebrates Anniversary of His Coming to Detroit," *Detroit News,* 16 November 1915, 2.

11. Memoranda, Hugh Chalmers to C. A. Pfeffer, 31 July 1916; Chalmers to Paul Smith, 3 July 1916; Chalmers to C. A. Pfeffer, 11 September 1916; Chalmers to Woodruff, 6 November 1916; Chalmers to Woodruff, 25 November 1916; and Chalmers to Mr. Morse, 19 January 1917, DCHC.

12. Chalmers Motor Company and Maxwell Motor Company, Indenture of Lease, September 1, 1917, DCHC; "Chalmers Owners to Vote on Lease," *Automobile Topics,* 1 September 1917, 375–76; "Chalmers Lease Is Taken By Maxwell: Unique Arrangement Ratified by Both Parties and Management Passes—Walter E. Flanders Now Heads Joint Enterprise," *Automobile Topics,* 15 September 1917, 609; Davis, *Conspicuous Production,* 89–90; and Rae, *American Automobile Manufacturers,* 114–15.

13. May, *A Most Unique Machine,* 298–300; Rae, *American Automobile Manufacturers,* 52–54; and "History of Chrysler Corporation in New Castle," New Castle, Indiana plant files, DCHC.

14. The best summary of the United States Motor combination is Anthony J. Yanik, "U.S. Motor: Ben Briscoe's Shattered Dream," *Automobile Quarterly,* 36 (February 1997): 52–69.

15. Davis, *Conspicuous Production,* 153–54; and Walter E. Flanders, "Why We Chose the Name Maxwell," *Automobile,* 20 March 1913, 90–91. More on the life of Walter Flanders can be found in Anthony J. Yanik, *The E-M-F Company: The Story of Automotive Pioneers Barney Everitt, William Metzger, and Walter Flanders* (Warrendale, Pa.: Society of Automotive Engineers, 2001).

16. Kennedy, *The Automobile Industry,* 129; Nick Baldwin, *World Guide to Automobile Manufacturers,* (New York: Facts on File, 1987) 317; Rae, *American Automobile Manufacturers,* 143–44; "Chrysler," *Fortune,* August 1935, 31; Davis, *Conspicuous Production,* p. 154; and J. C. Holmes, "History of the Maxwell Organization," *Maxwell-Chalmers Circle,* May

1923, 2. The profit figures are drawn from the Maxwell Motor Company annual reports and consolidated general balance sheets, 31 July 1915–31 July 1919, DCHC.

17. "Chrysler Takes Helm at Maxwell, Will Direct Affairs under New Manager," *Motor World,* 18 August 1920, 35, 42; Rae, *American Automobile Manufacturers,* 143–44; Davis, *Conspicuous Production,* 154–55; Chrysler and Sparkes, *Life of an American Workman,* 177; B. C. Forbes, "Chrysler Tells How He Did It," *Forbes,* 1 January 1929, 30; "Chrysler," *Fortune,* 33; and the Budget Office of the Highland Park Manufacturing Division, Chrysler Corporation, "A History of Events Leading Up to the Formation of the Chrysler Corporation," 4 September 1952, 15, DCHC.

18. Maxwell Motor Company, and Chalmers Motor Corporation, "Plan and Agreement of Readjustment, August 30, 1919," box "Chalmers/Maxwell 1," DCHC. Signatories representing the Maxwell Motor Company stockholders were Harry Bronner, James C. Brady, John R. Morron, and Elton Parks. The representatives of the Chalmers Motor Corporation stockholders were Jules S. Bache, Hugh Chalmers, and J. Horace Harding.

19. Richard M. Langworth and Jan P. Norbye, *The Complete History of Chrysler Corporation, 1924–1985* (New York: Beekman House, 1985), 14, 17; Baldwin, *World Guide to Automobile Manufacturers,* 317; Maxwell Motor Corporation minutes, vol. 2, directors' meetings of 27 April 1922 and 21 December 1922; Maxwell Motor Corporation and Chalmers Motor Corporation, consolidated balance sheets, years ended 31 December 1921, 31 December 1922, and 31 December 1923; and Chalmers confidential bulletin no. 1, signed by Joseph Fields, director of sales, 14 December 1922, DCHC.

20. Langworth and Norbye, *The Complete History of Chrysler,* 16–17; Kennedy, *The Automobile Industry,* 135; 1922 advertisement, "The Good Maxwell," in the "1922 Maxwell" folder in the Maxwell records, DCHC; and Tad Burness, *Cars of the Early Twenties* (New York: Galahad, 1968), 171.

21. Breer, *Birth of Chrysler Corporation,* 70–73; Beverly Rae Kimes, "John North Willys: His Magnetism, His Millions, His Motor Cars," *Automobile Quarterly* 17 (third quarter 1972): 314; and Skelton, "Origins of the Chrysler Corporation and the First Chrysler Car," 3–4.

22. "Chrysler," *Fortune,* 112; Skelton, "Origins of the Chrysler Corporation," 5; and "Chrysler Series (B), December 20, 1922," folder 13, Walter Miller Papers, DCHC.

23. B. E. Hutchinson journal entry, 30 March 1923, Chrysler folder, box 29, B. E. Hutchinson Papers, HIA.

24. "Agreement, Maxwell Motor Corporation and Walter P. Chrysler, June 1, 1923," in Maxwell Motor Corporation minutes, vol. 3, DCHC; Maxwell Motor Corporation and Subsidiaries, consolidated balance sheet, 31 December 1923 and 31 December 1924; and *Motor Age,* 3 January 1925, 52.

25. Skelton, "Origins of the Chrysler Corporation," 6; and Breer, *Birth of Chrysler Corporation,* 77–79.

26. Donald C. Critchlow, *Studebaker, The Life and Death of an American Corporation* (Bloomington: Indiana University Press, 1966), 89; Bonsall, *More Than They Promised,* 122; Chrysler and Sparkes, *Life of an American Workman,* 182; Rae, *American Automobile Manufacturers,* 145; Lewis, *Motor Memories,* 72–73; and Allen B. ("Tobe") Couture's untitled reminiscences, 11–13, DCHC. The Couture typescript, some 14 pages long, dates from around May 1975. The originality and authenticity of this reminiscence is open to question. Nearly half (pages 5–8, 10, and 13) is taken verbatim from Skelton's reminiscence, or both come from a third source. The remainder, however, consists of detailed descriptions

of test-drives Couture made with various Willys and Chrysler prototypes. None of these descriptions appear elsewhere. The Zeder quote is from Norman Beasley and George W. Stark, *Made in Detroit* (New York: Putnam, 1957), 300.

CHAPTER 3

1. *Saturday Evening Post,* 8 December 1923, 75; 15 December 1923, 67; 22 December 1923, 67; and 29 December 1923, 65–66.
2. Gregg D. Merksamer, *A History of the New York International Auto Show* (Atlanta, Ga.: Lionheart Books, 2000), 64–66; Clyde Jennings, "The Premier of Motor Car Shows Will Open 1924 Season in New York Saturday," *Motor Age,* 3 January 1924, 10–13; and "Wave of Buyers Floods Armory; Prospect Lists Swell as Attendance Grows; Better Values Bring Stimulus to Trade," *Automobile Topics,* 12 January 1924, 954–60, 967, 1002.
3. Chrysler and Sparkes, *Life of an American Workman,* 182–84.
4. *The Tenth Annual Directory, New York Automobile Show, January 5 to January 12, 1924, Armory* (Detroit: Detroit Free Press, 1924), 7–8, 39; "New York National Automobile Show on Single Vast Floor an Unrivaled Panorama of Superbly Beautiful Cars," *Motor Vehicle Monthly,* February 1924, 56; "Much of Mechanical Interest in New York Show," *Motor Age,* 10 January 1924, 16; Maxwell-Chrysler-Chalmers confidential bulletin no. 25, 26 December 1923, DCHC; and *New York Times,* 6 January 1924, 16.
5. Maxwell Motor Corporation minutes, vol. 3, meeting of the subcommittee of the board of directors, 28 January 1924; and Maxwell Motor Corporation and Subsidiaries, consolidated balance sheet, 31 December 1923.
6. Skelton, "Origins of the Chrysler Corporation," 6.
7. Chrysler and Sparkes, *Life of an American Workman,* 185–88.
8. Kennedy, *The Automobile Industry,* 162–63: Langworth and Norbye, *The Complete History of Chrysler,* 28–29; "Chrysler Six Appears with Seven Bearing Crankshaft," *Automotive Industries,* 27 December 1923, 1290–92; "Chrysler Puts out a Six in Own Name: Brand New Product Offered Those Who Want a Better Car—Is Remarkable Performer, Highly Developed," *Automobile Topics,* 29 December 1923, 639–43, 650; and see also "Chrysler Six Built for Performance and Economy," *Automobile Trade Journal,* 1 December 1923, 68–70; and H. A. Tarantous, "The Chrysler, a Remarkable Six," *Motor,* February 1924, 44–45, 74, 76.
9. "Chrysler," *Fortune,* 33–34, 112.
10. James Dalton, "New York Show Is Greatest Ever! Its Success Assured," *Automotive Industries,* 10 January 1924, 58; P. M. Heldt, "Four-Wheel Brakes Are Most Striking Mechanical Feature of Show," *Automotive Industries,* 10 January 1924, 64–65; and "Wave of Buyers Floods Armory," 967.
11. "Orders for Lockheed Brakes for Test," 10 December 1923; "License Agreements Signed and to Be Signed," 15 August 1923–23 March 1924; licensing agreement between the Hydraulic Brake Company and the Paige-Detroit Motor Car Company, not dated; Chalmers confidential bulletin no. 8, 17 October 1923; "Four Wheel Brakes Offered on Chalmers Cars: Lockheed Hydraulic System Adopted for Current Models—Installed at Extra Price of $75," *Automobile Topics,* 3 November 1923, 1159–60; and "Chalmers Adopts Lockheed Four Wheel Hydraulic Brakes," *Automobile Trade Journal,* 1 December 1923, 55.

12. Breer, *Birth of Chrysler Corporation*, 79–84.

13. "Power without Precedent in the New Chrysler Six," *Saturday Evening Post*, 2 February 1924, 55; "Only Bodies by Fisher Conform to Chrysler Standards," *Saturday Evening Post*, 8 November 1924, 63; and Maxwell-Chrysler confidential bulletin no. 94, 23 October 1924, DCHC.

14. Breer, *Birth of Chrysler Corporation*, 85. The winged radiator cap first appeared in the Maxwell-Chrysler confidential bulletin no. 80, 27 August 1924, DCHC.

15. Pamphlet "Chrysler Six Sets New Mt. Wilson Record," in "1924 Chrysler Literature," DCHC.

16. Maxwell-Chrysler confidential bulletin no. 111, 5 February 1925, DCHC.

17. Albert R. Bochroch, *Americans at LeMans: An Illustrated History of the 24 Hour Race from 1923 to 1975, with Emphasis on American Drivers and Cars* (Tucson, Ariz.: Aztex Corporation, 1976), 23, 26–27; David Hodges, *The LeMans 24–Hour Race* (London: Temple Press Books, 1963), 9, 18, 21, 27; and Roger Lebric, *Les 24 heures du Mans: Histoire d'une grande bataille pacifique et sportive* (Paris: Automobile-Club de L'Ouest–LeMans, 1949), 115, 124. A more specialized book is Ray Jones and Martin Swig, *Chrysler in Competition: European Road Racing 1925 to 1931* (San Francisco: Automobilia, 1997).

18. George S. May, ed., *Encyclopedia of American Business History and Biography: The Automobile Industry, 1920–1980* (New York: Bruccoli Clark Layman, 1989), 316–17; and *Maxwell-Chalmers Circle*, November 1922, 1.

19. For Taylorism, see Daniel Nelson, *Frederick W. Taylor and the Rise of Scientific Management* (Madison: University of Wisconsin Press, 1980). The best discussion of Taylorism in federal arsenals is Hugh G. J. Aitken, *Scientific Management in Action: Taylorism at Watertown Arsenal, 1908–1915* (Cambridge: Harvard University Press, 1960).

20. David A. Hounshell and John Kenly Smith Jr., *Science and Corporate Strategy: Du Pont R & D, 1902–1980* (New York: Cambridge University Press, 1988), 141–43.

21. Memoranda, William Robert Wilson to G. W. Mason, works manager, 6 September 1922; G. L. Paullis to George W. Mason, 2 July 1923; George Mason to Messrs. Morgana, Downey, Koerner, Clark, R. K. Mitchell, O'Brien, Taylor, and Paullis, 1 August 1924; and G. H. Fennell, plant engineering, to G. L. Paullis, paint department, Highland Park plant, 23 January 1926; and G. L. Paullis to G. W. Mason, 1 December 1923, folder "Duco High Bake Enamel Paint," box "Duco Paint," DCHC.

22. George W. Mason Collection, Heritage Presentation File, DCHC.

23. Langworth and Norbye, *The Complete History of Chrysler*, 29; and Breer, *Birth of Chrysler Corporation*, 93–94.

24. Nicholas Kelley, oral reminiscences, interview by Wendell Link, 20 February 1953, leaves 243–44, Columbia University Oral History Collection; Maxwell Motor Corporation, plan and agreement, 15 April 1925; Maxwell Motor Corporation minutes, vol. 5, special meeting of the board of directors, 16 April 1925; annual meeting of the stockholders, 21 April 1925; and general meeting of the stockholders, 24 June 1925, DCHC; Langworth and Norbye, *The Complete History of Chrysler*, 30; Thomas S. LaMarre, "From Model B to Big Three: Chrysler's Amazing Ascent," *Automobile Quarterly* 32 (April 1994): 22; and Chrysler Corporation, News Relations Office, "Presidents of the Chrysler Corporation," October 1972. The Maxwell Motor Corporation consolidated balance sheet, dated 31 December 1924 and included in the plan of April 1925, suggests the relatively weak financial position of the company. In contrast with total liabilities of $65,442,814, including capital stock liabilities of $57,678,871, the firm's tangible assets, including real estate and cash, came to only

$40,442,814. Maxwell's assets included $25 million in "Goodwill," more than one-third of the firm's total assets.

25. "Founders of Chrysler Corporation," Chrysler Corporation general history files, DCHC.

26. "Chrysler Corp. Buys American Motor Body," *Automobile Topics,* 5 September 1925, 301.

27. Michael Lamm and Dave Holls, *A Century of Automotive Style: 100 Years of American Car Design* (Stockton, Ca.: Lamm-Morada, 1996), 28, 44, 152–54.

28. Construction details are taken from Charles K. Hyde, historical report on the Chrysler Jefferson Avenue plant submitted to the Historic American Engineering Record, National Park Service (HAER no. MI-24-A), March 1993 and historical report on the Chrysler Center (Chrysler Highland Park plant) submitted to the Historic American Engineering Record, National Park Service (HAER no. MI-142 and MI-142-A through MI-142-J), May 1997. Information on the transfer of production from Highland Park to Jefferson Avenue is from "Highlights of Chrysler Accomplishments for 1928," *Chrysler Motoring,* January 1929, 10–11.

29. Building construction dates are taken from Charles K. Hyde, historical report on the Chrysler Center (Highland Park) submitted to the Historic American Engineering Record, National Park Service (HAER no. MI-142, MI-142-B, C, D, E, and F), May 1997. For the Chrysler Engineering Building, see "Chrysler Adds a New Building: $1,000,000 Structure Will Be Used to House Engineering Staff and Equipment," *Detroit News,* 1 July 1928, section 10, p. 1; and E. Y. Watson, "New Chrysler Building Open: Many Auto Magnates among Thousands Who Inspect $1,000,000 Plant," *Detroit News,* 3 July 1928, 5.

30. Chrysler Corporation, *Six Years' Progress of Chrysler Motors* (Detroit: Chrysler Corporation, 1929), 3 (found in the Chrysler Corporation vertical files, NAHC, and in the DCHC); and Cullen Thomas, "Chrysler: The Early Years," *Automobile Quarterly* 6 (summer 1967): 100.

31. Langworth and Norbye, *The Complete History of Chrysler,* 34.

32. Sales brochures, Chrysler Four (1925) and Chrysler 58 (1926); Chrysler confidential bulletin no. 164, December 1925, DCHC.

33. Thomas, "Chrysler: The Early Years," 100; "The New Chrysler Imperial," *Automobile Topics,* January 1926, 878–79; "Chrysler Produces a Car of Speed and Power," *Automobile Topics,* 2 January 1926, 712–15, 726–27, 732; "Chrysler Demonstration a Thriller: Speed, Short Stops and Curves on High Keep Observer 'Interested'—Riding Qualities Superb," *Automobile Topics,* 2 January 1926, 715, 725; and "Car Displays Show Improved Bodies and Engines," *Automobile Topics,* 16 January 1926, 994.

34. "Wide Open—But for Only 400 Miles: Bulletins on the Full Distance," *Motor Age,* 3 June 1926, 17; and *Another Chrysler Achievement* (Detroit: Chrysler Sales Corporation, 1928).

35. Leslie S. Gillette, "Chrysler Introduces the Model '50,'" *Automotive Industries,* 19 August 1926, 284; and "Chrysler to Offer New Light Model," *Automobile Topics,* 7 August 1926, 1213.

36. Hodges, *The LeMans 24–Hour Race,* 18; Bockroch, *Americans at LeMans,* 26–27; and Thomas, "Chrysler: The Early Years," 98.

37. "Serves the Entire Market," *Automobile Topics,* 6 February 1926, 1308; "Chrysler Dealers Sell 18 Million Dollars' Worth of Chrysler '60' in First Sixty Days," *Automobile Topics,* 17 July 1926, 906; "The New Chrysler '50' Opens the Entire Motor Car Market to Chrysler

Dealers," *Automobile Trade Journal,* 1 September 1926, 48–49; "Announcing the New Finer Chrysler '70,' Further Widening the Gap between Chrysler and All Other Motor Car Franchises," *Motor World Wholesale,* 14 October 1926, inside front cover; "Announcing the Illustrious New Chrysler 72: A Personal Message to Every Motor Car Dealer from Walter P. Chrysler," *Automobile Topics,* 20 August 1927, 166–67; "How Was Business Last Season, Mr. Motor Car Dealer?" *Automobile Trade Journal,* 1 August 1927, 51; "One Contract—Four Great Lines: A Type and Price for Every Prospect," *Automobile Topics,* 17 September 1927, 544–45; and "You Need These Advantages Which Only Chrysler Can Give," *Automobile Trade Journal,* 1 April 1928, 56–57.

38. Chrysler confidential bulletin no. 300, 10 May 1927; and "Chrysler Adding Marine Engines to His Output," *Detroit News,* May 1927, section 10, p. 1.

CHAPTER 4

1. John C. Gourlie, "Dodge-Chrysler Merger Unites Two Great Properties," *Automotive Industries,* 9 June 1928, 863.
2. C. T. Schaefer, "What's in a Name?" *Motor Life,* October 1926, 35, 47.
3. Clarence M. Burton, *The City of Detroit, Michigan, 1701–1922* (Chicago: S.J. Clarke, 1922), 3:250 and 4:308, 311. The Dodge brothers applied for a patent (in both their names) for a "Bicycle-Bearing," on 20 July 1895, and the U.S. Patent Office issued the patent (serial no. 567,851) on 15 September 1896.
4. "Dodge Bros.' New Establishment: One of the Most Complete Machine Shops in Michigan—Everything New and Up to Date. Builders of Specialized Machinery and High Speed Pleasure Yachts," *Detroit Free Press,* 1 September 1901, section 2, p. 6; May, *A Most Unique Machine,* 119; "Dodge Brothers as Quality Producers of Cars," *Automobile Topics,* 13 June 1914, 379; and George S. May, *R. E. Olds: Auto Industry Pioneer* (Grand Rapids, Mich.: Eerdmans, 1977), 157–59.
5. Allan Nevins and Frank Ernest Hill, *Ford: The Times, the Man, the Company* (New York: Charles Scribner's Sons, 1954), 237–40, 251, 272; Jean Maddern Pitrone and Joan Potter-Elwart, *The Dodges: The Auto Family Fortune and Misfortune* (South Bend, Ind.: Icarus Press, 1981), 17–19; and Caroline Latham and David Agresta, *Dodge Dynasty: The Car and the Family That Rocked Detroit* (New York: Harcourt, Brace, and Jovanovich, 1989), 51–54.
6. Grant Hildebrand, *Designing for Industry: The Architecture of Albert Kahn* (Cambridge, Mass.: MIT Press, 1974) barely mentions the Dodge factory. The archives of Albert Kahn Associates include the original drawings for the major buildings. For a detailed history of Dodge Main, see Charles K. Hyde, "'Dodge Main' and the Detroit Automobile Industry, 1910–1980," *Detroit in Perspective: A Journal of Regional History* 6 (spring 1982): 1–21.
7. Burton, *The City of Detroit,* 1:582; "The Tremendous Plant Created by the Dodge Brothers," *Michigan Manufacturer and Financial Record,* 8 August 1914, 1, 5–7; and "Wonderful Plant of the Dodge Brothers in Detroit," *Michigan Manufacturer and Financial Record,* 26 April 1914, 1.
8. Letter, James Couzens to the Dodge brothers, 21 April 1906, box 1, Dodge brothers correspondence, accession 893, HFMGV; and Latham and Agresta, *Dodge Dynasty,* 65–66.
9. "Agreement between the Ford Motor Company and the Dodge Brothers, July 1913," folder 7, box 1, "Agreements and Notes," accession 95, HFMGV.

10. "Dodges Will Manufacture Cars," *Motor World*, 23 May 1912, 28; and "Dodges to Manufacture a Six: Car to Appear Soon, Despite Rumors of Its Abandonment—Relations with Ford Company Remain Unchanged," *Motor World*, 22 August 1912, 5.

11. B. C. Forbes and O. D. Foster, *Automotive Giants of America: Men Who Are Making Our Motor Industry* (New York: B.C. Forbes, 1926), 121–30; and Sinclair Powell, *The Franklin Automobile Company* (Warrentown, Pa.: Society of Automotive Engineers, 1999), 54–55, 116.

12. Allan Nevins and Frank Ernest Hill, *Ford: Expansion and Challenge, 1915–1933* (New York: Charles Scribner's Sons, 1957), 88–90, 103–4, 110; and David L. Lewis, *The Public Image of Henry Ford: An American Folk Hero and His Company* (Detroit: Wayne State University Press, 1976), 99–102.

13. David Smith, "How John and Horace Made Good: The Untold Story of the Dodge Boys," *Detroit Free Press,* 17 April 1966, 13; Pitrone and Elwart, *The Dodges,* 63.

14. "The Tremendous Plant Created by the Dodge Brothers," 5; Niran Bates Pope, *Dodge Brothers Works* (Detroit: Dodge Brothers, 1919), 18; Thomas J. Holleman and James P. Gallagher, *Smith, Hinchman & Grylls: 125 Years of Architecture and Engineering, 1858–1978* (Detroit: Wayne State University Press, 1978), 75, 84, 94; *National Cyclopedia of American Biography* (New York: James T. White, 1926), 19:267; and H. Cole Estep, "How Dodge Brothers Plant Was Reorganized," *Iron Trade Review,* 6 May 1915, 913–16. For a comprehensive history of the Dodge plant in Hamtramck, see Hyde, "'Dodge Main' and the Detroit Automobile Industry," 1–21.

15. Pope, *Dodge Brothers Works,* 5; "Dodge Brothers Reveal the Car They Will Make," *Automobile Topics,* 7 November 1914, 905.

16. "The Tremendous Plant Created by the Dodge Brothers," 1.

17. Pitrone and Elwart, *The Dodges,* 65.

18. "Dodge Bros. Car Makes Its Debut: Official Announcement and Presentation to Public Is Made Today. New Machine Launched on Market at Big Plant with Luncheon as Feature," *Detroit News,* 14 November 1914, 1, 20.

19. "Dodge Bros. Out with All Year Car: Is First Winter Model Company Has Built," *Detroit News,* 17 September 1915, 20; Dodge Brothers winter car brochures for 1916, 1917, and 1918 models; and Dodge sales brochure, 1924 models, DCHC. The special tops were made by the Rex Manufacturing Company of Connersville, Indiana.

20. Lamm and Holls, *A Century of Automotive Style,* 31–34.

21. Gilbert F. Richards, *Budd on the Move* (New York: Newcomen Society in North America, 1975), 7–10; and Stan Grayson, "The All-Steel World of Edward Budd," *Automobile Quarterly* 16 (fourth quarter 1978): 354–57.

22. Thomas A. McPherson, *The Dodge Story* (Osceola, Wis.: Motorbooks International, 1992), 7–23; Don Bunn, *Dodge Trucks* (Osceola, Wis.: Motorbooks International, 1996), 11–15; and "Dodge Bros. Offer Commercial Model: Design Based on Passenger Car Chassis, but Several Parts Are Strengthened and Tires Are Bigger—Many Delivered to Government," *Automobile Topics,* 24 November 1917, 249.

23. A. H. E. Beckett, "'Charge of the Light Brigade,' Motorized Motor Cars Turn Tide for Pershing's Men in Chihuahua Skirmish," *Motor Age,* 1 June 1916, 21; and Robert L. Rosekrans, "Bandits, Bullets, Battles—Dependability Is Born amid Violence as 'Old Betsy' Chugs on Stage," *Dodge News,* January 1964, 4–5.

24. Pitrone and Elwart, *The Dodges,* 77–80; Burton, *The City of Detroit,* 4:311–12; "Dodges

Build Huge Plant: Work Under Way on Munitions Factory; Contract Reported for $20,000,000," *Detroit News,* 31 October 1917, 1; "Acres of Concrete Laid for Floor of Munitions Factory," *Detroit News,* 2 December 1917, real estate section, p. 2; and Holleman and Gallagher, *Smith, Hinchman & Grylls,* 94, 211. One of Horace Dodge's notebooks, entitled "Operations on 155 MM Howitzer Sleigh and 155 MM Rifle Cradle," lays out the 77 and 38 distinct consecutive operations, respectively, needed to produce these components. The notebook, dated 1918, is found in box "Dodge Brothers 4," DCHC. Pitrone and others, including this author, have erroneously credited the Dodge brothers with manufacturing the French 75 mm artillery piece, easily the most famous large gun of the First World War. All of the direct evidence from the Chrysler Historical Collections and elsewhere, including photographs and contracts, refer only to two 155 mm versions.

25. Lloyd E. Griscom, *The Automotive Pioneers: Industrious Adventurers* (Palmyra, N.J.: S.J. Publications, 1967), 95; Burton, *The City of Detroit,* 3:253; and *National Cyclopedia of American Biography,* 19:267.

26. Burton, *The City of Detroit,* 4:312.

27. Ford encouraged Horace Lucien Arnold and Fay Leone Faurote to publish *Ford Methods and the Ford Shops* (New York: Engineering Magazine, 1915), which praised the operations of the Ford Highland Park plant. The most thorough discussions of Ford's breakthroughs are Stephen Meyer III, *Labor Management and Social Control in the Ford Motor Company, 1908–1921* (Albany: State University of New York Press, 1981), 9–36; and David A. Hounshell, *From the American System to Mass Production, 1800–1932: The Development of Manufacturing Technology in the United States* (Baltimore: Johns Hopkins University Press, 1984), 217–61.

28. Quoted in "Dodge Brothers as Quality Producers of Cars," 383.

29. Arnold and Faurote, *Ford Methods and the Ford Shops,* 5, 77–83, 114; "How Dodge Brothers Plant Was Reorganized," 909–16, 946b; and Nevins and Hill, *Ford: The Times, the Man, the Company,* 644.

30. "Dodge Brothers as Quality Producers of Cars," 383.

31. Ibid.; and "The Tremendous Plant Created by the Dodge Brothers," 6. Because the Dodge Brothers production records have not survived, we cannot compare production line speeds or productivity at Dodge with that achieved at the Ford Motor Company.

32. Burton, *The City of Detroit* 3:254.

33. Pitrone and Elwart, *The Dodges,* 113.

34. *Detroit News,* 13 December 1920.

35. Letter, William G. Mather, president of the Cleveland-Cliffs Iron Company, to John F. Dodge, 23 December 1919, box 1, Dodge brothers correspondence, 1904–1920, accession 893, HFMGV; and Nevins and Hill, *Ford: Expansion and Challenge,* 208–10.

Chapter 5

1. Dodge Brothers, directors' minutes, special meeting of 29 January 1920; special meeting of 28 May 1920; and annual stockholders' meeting, 20 July 1920, box "Board Minutes," DCHC.

2. Dodge Brothers, directors' minutes, special meeting of the board of directors, 27 November 1920, box "Board Minutes," DCHC.

3. "Effort to Buy Dodge Plant Likely: New York Interests Long Have Sought It; Death of Both Brothers May Make Efforts Successful, Detroit Bankers Feel," *Automotive Industries,* 16 December 1920, 1237, 1239.

4. Dodge Brothers, directors' minutes, special meetings of 31 December 1921 and 15 March 1922, box "Board Minutes," DCHC; "People Given Parks by Dodge Brothers," *Automobile Topics,* 9 September 1922, 323.

5. Dodge Brothers, directors' minutes, special meeting of the board of directors, 15 August 1922, box "Board Minutes," DCHC; and McPherson, *The Dodge Story,* 34–35.

6. "Dodge Brothers Have All-Metal Business Coupe," *Motor World,* 7 June 1922, 33; "New Dodge Brothers All-Steel Coupe," *Motor Age,* 8 June 1922, 12; "Dodge Brothers out with Its New Coupe," *Automobile Topics,* 10 June 1922, 301; and "All-Steel Business Sedan Being Produced by Dodge," *Automotive Industries,* 14 September 1922, 539.

7. "Death Breaks Life-Long Triad of Triumphant Graham Brothers," *Automotive Industries,* 20 August 1932, 246; Rae, *American Automobile Manufacturers,* 163–64; Jeffrey L. Godshall, "The Graham Brothers and Their Car," *Automobile Quarterly* 13 (first quarter 1975): 80–82; and "Graham Brothers Company Minute Book," 15 January 1917–10 March 1919, box "Board Minutes," DCHC.

8. F. J. Haynes, "The Sound Progress of Dodge Brothers Business," speech delivered in August 1924, box "Dodge History 4," DCHC.

9. Dodge Brothers, directors' minutes, meetings of 26 August 1924, 16 December 1925, 14 April 1926, and 25 January 1928; Dodge Brothers, *Annual Report to the Stockholders for the Year Ended December 31, 1925,* 7; *Annual Report to the Stockholders for the Year Ended December 31, 1926,* 6; American Appraisal Company, "Grand Summary, Graham Brothers Properties," 31 December 1925; all found in banker's box "Dodge Brothers 2," DCHC; and "Dodge Brothers Big Program Is Launched, Buys Truck Unit as Graham Brothers Enter Management," *Automobile Topics,* 28 November 1925, 215.

10. Lawrence H. Seltzer, *A Financial History of the American Automobile Industry* (Boston: Houghton Mifflin, 1928), 12; *The American Car since 1775* (Kuntztown, Pa.: Automobile Quarterly, 1971), 140, 141.

11. Manufacturers' Appraisal Company, "Appraisal, Dodge Bros. Detroit, Mich., March 31, 1925," banker's box "Dodge Brothers 2," DCHC.

12. "Dillon Read Group Buys Dodge Motors for over $175,000,000 *[sic]*: Sale for All Cash, Biggest on Record, Ends a Keen Battle with General Motors," *New York Times,* 1 April 1925, 1, 2; Forbes and Foster, *Automotive Giants of America,* 131–33; Kennedy, *The Automobile Industry,* 170–72; Dodge Brothers, directors' minutes, stockholders' meeting, 7 April 1925; special meeting of the stockholders, 30 April 1925; and special meeting of the board of directors, 30 April 1925, banker's box "Dodge Brothers 2," DCHC.

13. William Z. Ripley, *Main Street and Wall Street* (Boston: Little, Brown, 1927), 86–87; and Kennedy, *The Automotive Industry,* 171. Ripley cites the Dillon, Read takeover of Dodge as an outrageous example of financiers removing control of corporations from the rightful owners, the stockholders. Apparently, this was a common technique in American business in the 1920s.

14. Dodge Brothers, *Annual Report to the Stockholders for the Year Ended December 31, 1926,* 3; directors' minutes, meetings of 14 April 1926 and 21 July 1926, box "Dodge Brothers 2," DCHC; and Powell, *The Franklin Automobile Company,* 247–48, 254, 263.

15. Hugh Allen, *The House of Goodyear: A Story of Rubber and of Modern Business* (Cleveland:

Corday & Gross, 1943), 49–51; and John C. Gourlie, "New President Discusses Future Policies of Dodge," *Automotive Industries,* 22 April 1926, 677–79.

16. Dodge Brothers, *Annual Report to the Stockholders for the Year Ended December 31, 1926,* 6; and McPherson, *The Dodge Story,* 48–52.

17. Dodge Brothers, *Annual Report to the Stockholders for the Year Ended December 31, 1927,* 6–7; "Dodge Brothers Now Has 5-Bearing Shaft," *Automotive Industries,* 23 September 1926, 512; and "New Dodge Brothers Engine," *Detroit News,* 1 May 1927, section 10, p. 1.

18. McPherson, *The Dodge Story,* 53–58.

19. "Financial Data concerning Automotive Manufacturers," *Automotive Industries,* 18 February 1928, 226; and John C. Gourlie, "Automotive Securities Gain 50% in Value in Year," *Automotive Industries,* 7 April 1928, 539–41.

20. L. L. Stevenson, "Orders Briefs in Dodge Deal: Supreme Justice Studies Injunction Plea in Fight to Stop Merger," *Detroit News,* 27 June 1928, 11.

21. "Operating Statement, Chrysler Corporation & Subsidiaries versus Willys-Overland & Subsidiaries, as of December 31st, 1927," statement dated 22 May 1928, box "Chrysler/ Dodge 1928," DCHC.

22. Dodge folders in box "Chrysler/Dodge, 1928," DCHC.

23. "Economic Advantage of the Plan," in box "Chrysler/Dodge, 1928," DCHC.

24. Forbes, "Chrysler Tells How He Did It," 30; Walter Boynton, "Chrysler-Dodge Combine Will Have 9,000 Dealers, Covering All the World," *Automotive Daily News,* 5 June 1928, 1–2; and Chrysler Corporation, *Six Years' Progress of Chrysler Motors,* 7. The last source gives an overall breakdown by location.

25. "The Big Three," *Automotive Daily News,* 4 June 1928, 4.

26. Chrysler and Sparkes, *Life of an American Workman,* 192–96; and Root, Clark, Buckner, Howland, & Ballantine, "The Clayton Act," 13 June 1928, in box "Chrysler/Dodge, 1928," DCHC.

27. Dodge Brothers, directors' minutes, meeting of 29 May 1928 and special meeting of 29 June 1928, box "Dodge Brothers 2," DCHC; Chrysler and Sparkes, *Life of an American Workman,* 192–96; George Hassett, "$450,000,000 Stock Involved in Merger: Consolidated Chrysler-Dodge Organization Will Be Third in Auto World, Trailing Only General Motors and Ford," *Detroit News,* 30 May 1928, 1–2; "Chrysler and Dodge Brothers Unite to Form Third Largest Producer," *Automotive Industries,* 2 June 1928, 853, 857; John C. Gourlie, "Chrysler-Dodge Merger Embraces 8000 Dealers," *Motor Age,* 7 June 1928, 32–33, 38; Gourlie, "Dodge-Chrysler Merger Unites Two Great Properties," 863–64; and Arthur M. Leinbach, "What the Chrysler-Dodge Merger Means to Security Holders: Terms of Consolidation Analyzed—Now Third Largest Automobile Manufacturer," *Magazine of Wall Street,* 16 June 1928, 304–5, 362–63. Dillon, Read's near failure to come up with 90 percent of all categories of stock is confirmed in Nicholas Kelley's oral reminiscences, interview of 20 February 1953, leaves 249–50.

28. "The Big Three," 4.

Chapter 6

1. "Dodge Senior Six Has New Body Lines, Increased Power," *Automotive Industries,* 8 September 1928, 331–33; and Walter P. Chrysler, "What Chrysler Engineers Have Found out about Dodge Brothers," *Literary Digest,* 13 October 1928, 71.

2. "Price Reduced on New Truck: Dodge Offers One-Ton Machine in Eight Styles for $745," *Detroit News,* 25 August 1929, section 6, p. 3; "Chrysler Pays Dodge Tribute: He Talks on Restoration of Prestige before Executives on First Anniversary," *Detroit News,* 15 September 1929, section 6, p. 5; Langworth and Norbye, *The Complete History of Chrysler,* 93; and "The Dodge Ram," folder "Dodge Ram," box "Emblems 3, Dodge," DCHC.

3. "Fargo Truck Production Figures," September 1928–November 1930, DCHC; "Fargo Introduces a New Line of Buses," *Automobile Topics,* 4 October 1930, 700–701, 706; "Col. A. C. Downey New President of Airtemp, Inc.," *Automobile Topics,* 28 June 1937, 330; and sales literature, Fargo Motor Company, NAHC.

4. "Pioneer Keller Talks on Cars and Fishing," *Detroit News,* 23 September 1958, 32.

5. Jeffrey L. Godshall, "DeSoto: Walter Chrysler's Stepchild," *Automobile Quarterly* 20 (first quarter 1982): 72–73; "DeSoto Six," *Automobile Topics,* 28 July 1928, 1065; and Chrysler Corporation, *Six Years' Progress of Chrysler Motors,* 7.

6. DeSoto advertisements, *Saturday Evening Post,* 21 July 1928, 41; *Automobile Topics,* 4 August 1928, 1156–57; and *Saturday Evening Post,* 4 August 1928, 60–61.

7. Godshall, "DeSoto: Walter Chrysler's Stepchild," 72–73; and "The New DeSoto Is Typical of Chrysler," *Automobile Topics,* 4 August 1928, 1122–25, 1134.

8. Beverly Rae Kimes, "Plymouth: Walter Chrysler's Trump Card," *Automobile Quarterly* 5 (summer 1966): 74, 80; Jeffrey I. Godshall, "Plymouth: The Years of Triumph," *Automobile Quarterly* 23 (second quarter 1985): 126; and advertisement, *Saturday Evening Post,* 7 July 1928, 103–4. All quotations are from the advertisement of 7 July 1928.

9. "Announcing the New Chrysler Plymouth," *Automobile Topics,* 7 July 1928, 717; identical advertisement, *Motor,* August 1928, 93; "Chrysler Plymouth: Share in the Tide of Plymouth Sales!" *Motor,* November 1928, 95; and "150 Dealers a Week Are Swinging to Plymouth," *Automobile Trade Journal,* July 1929, 210–11.

10. Kimes, "Plymouth: Walter Chrysler's Trump Card," 80.

11. "Highlights of Chrysler Accomplishments for 1928," *Chrysler Motoring,* January 1929, 10–11; and "Dodge Brothers, an Epic of Manufacturing," *Automobile Topics,* 30 December 1933, 429, 434.

12. Sloan, *My Years With General Motors,* 58–70, 149–56.

13. *Fourth Annual Report of Chrysler Corporation, Year Ended December 31, 1928.*

14. *Saturday Evening Post,* 13 April 1929, 52–53.

15. Chrysler Corporation, *Six Years' Progress of Chrysler Motors.*

16. "A Century of Progress in Ten Years," *Automobile Topics,* 30 December 1933, 410 and "Corporation's Products Handled by 6032 Foreign Dealers," *Automobile Topics,* 30 December 1933, 455.

17. Reginald M. Cleveland and S. T. Williamson, *The Road Is Yours: The Story of the Automobile and the Men behind It* (New York: Greystone Press, 1951), 252, 254, is the source of this tale, but suggests this happened in 1932 or 1933. They are mistaken, since Chrysler was recovering and actually growing in those years.

18. Langworth and Norbye, *The Complete History of Chrysler,* 45, 50; and *Saturday Evening Post,* 4 April 1931, 55.

19. *The Growth of Plymouth* (Plymouth Motor Corporation, 1934), 13; Gary Blonston, *Plymouth, Its First 40 Years* (Detroit: Chrysler-Plymouth Division, Chrysler Corporation, 1969), 21; and Kimes, "Plymouth: Walter Chrysler's Trump Card," 80.

20. Breer, *Birth of Chrysler Corporation,* 100–108; J. Russell Walsh, "'Floating Power' Free

Wheeling in 4–Cyl. Plymouth," *Automotive Daily News,* 3 July 1931, 1, 12; "Walter P. Chrysler Introduced Floating Power," *Automobile Topics,* 4 July 1931, 616–20; and E. Y. Watson, "'Floating Power' Short Circuits Car Vibration: Gives New Smoothness to 4–Cylinder Engine," *Detroit News,* 18 October 1931, section 1, p. 12. Breer's lengthy description at times confuses this breakthrough with the use of rubber engine mounts on the 1925 Chrysler models.

21. "Ford, Chevrolet, Plymouth," *Fortune,* October 1931, 86–87, 152.

22. Breer, *Birth of Chrysler Corporation,* 135–37; Blonston, *Plymouth, Its First 40 Years,* 22; and "Ford, Chevrolet, Plymouth," 86–87, 152.

23. "Chrysler Company Rehires 1,200 Men, "*Detroit News,* 17 July 1931, 32; E. Y. Watson, "Chrysler Operates at Capacity on New Plymouth Models: Assembly Lines Keep up 'Car-a-Minute' Volume," *Detroit News,* 26 July 1931, section 1, p. 10; "Chrysler Adds New Line, Uses 'Floating Power' Principle on All Its Cars," *Automotive Industries,* 9 January 1932, 58–59, 65; and "Citroën Signs with Chrysler: Makes Agreement for Use of 'Floating Power' Principle in French Cars," *Detroit News,* 10 April 1932, section 1, p. 10.

24. "Plymouth Breaks Cross-Country Record," *Automobile Topics,* 15 August 1931, 91; and Speed Record Certificates Issued by the Contest Board of the American Automobile Association, 13 February 1931, box "Racing-General," DCHC.

25. Langworth and Norbye, *The Complete History of Chrysler,* 60–61; and Godshall, "Plymouth: The Years of Triumph," 128.

26. Julian Lewis Watkins, *The 100 Greatest Advertisements, Who Wrote Them and What They Did* (New York: Moore Publishing, 1949), 108–11; and Roland Marchand, *Advertising the American Dream: Making Way for Modernity, 1920–1940* (Berkeley: University of California Press, 1985), 304, 307–8.

27. "Chrysler Bets on U.S. Future, Invests 9 Millions in New Plymouth as Evidence of Faith in Recovery," *Detroit News,* 3 November 1932, 1, 2; and "Chrysler Courageous," *Detroit News,* 5 November 1932, 6; "Chrysler 'Shoots the Works' in New Plymouth Plant," *Automotive Industries,* 4 February 1933, 138–42; Kennedy, *The Automobile Industry,* 258; and *The Growth of Plymouth,* 23.

28. Godshall, "Plymouth: The Years of Triumph," 130.

29. *The American Car since 1775,* 140–41.

30. Samuel C. Stearn, "The Financial History of the Chrysler Corporation," 22, typescript, box "Chrysler History 6," DCHC; "Chrysler Pay up 10 Per Cent," *Detroit News,* 22 July 1933, 1, 7; and "Trade Topics," *Detroit News,* 3 February 1934, 22.

31. "A Century of Progress in Ten Years: Celebrating the Tenth Anniversary of Chrysler Motors," *Automobile Topics,* 30 December 1933, 354–456.

Chapter 7

1. Breer, *Birth of Chrysler Corporation,* 143–44; and Howard S. Irwin, "The History of the Airflow Car," *Scientific American,* August 1977, 99.

2. Breer, *Birth of Chrysler Corporation,* 144–45; and "History of 'RD' Streamline Development," undated one-page summary found in folder "Miscellaneous Airflow," box "Airflow 4," DCHC. The photographic record of wind tunnel models is found in folder "Development of Airflow," box "Airflow 4," DCHC, and the summary of wind tunnel results are in "History of 'RD' Streamline Development."

3. George L. McCain, "How the Airflows Were Designed," *Automotive Industries*, 23 June 1934, 766–67, 769; Irwin, "The History of the Airflow Car," 101; Carl Breer, "The Automobile of Tomorrow," *Automobile Topics*, 30 December 1933, 389–90; Lamm and Holls, *A Century of Automotive Style*, 155; and Beverly Rae Kimes, "Chrysler from the Airflow," *Automobile Quarterly* 7 (fall 1968): 207–8.

4. Ross Roy, interview by Carole Royer, 10 December 1976, place not identified, side 2 of cassette tape in the DCHC.

5. Irwin, "The History of the Airflow Car," 101; Breer, "The Automobile of Tomorrow," 390; Lamm and Holls, *A Century of Automotive Style*, 155; and Breer, *Birth of Chrysler Corporation*, 149–50.

6. Bruce R. Thomas, "Trifon Special: Birth of a Classic," *Torque*, November 1965, 7–8. Fortunately, this car was saved from the scrap heap and is now owned by the Walter P. Chrysler Museum.

7. Handwritten notes, in pencil, undated, with no clear authorship, with a reference to an article published on 30 December 1933, found in box "Airflow 4," DCHC.

8. Breer, *Birth of Chrysler Corporation*, 151–55.

9. The medal is found in the DCHC.

10. William Jeanes, "1934 DeSoto Airflow: A Triumph That Failed—but Not for the Reason You Think It Did," *Car and Driver*, September 1985, 91; "Albanita!" *Special-Interest Autos*, February–March 1973, 51–54; *Ninth Annual Report of Chrysler Corporation, Year Ended December 31, 1933* (9 February 1934); and Breer, *Birth of Chrysler Corporation*, 159.

11. *Automobile Topics*, 16 December 1933, 268–69; 30 December 1933, 316–17; 6 January 1934, 490–91, 494–95; *American Automobile*, April 1934, 27; June 1934, 35; and *Fortune*, March 1934, 17; April 1934, 13; and June 1934, 39.

12. Chrysler Sales Corporation, confidential bulletin no. 909, 1 June 1934, DCHC.

13. Franklin B. Tucker, "The Airflow Story," *Antique Automobile*, November–December 1964, 53.

14. Breer, *Birth of Chrysler Corporation*, 157–62.

15. "Production Delays Are Likely to Hold January Output to 125,000 Units," *Iron Age*, 11 January 1934, 37–38; "Ford Increases Production as General Motors and Chrysler Are Delayed," *Iron Age*, 28 December 1933, 40; Joseph Geschelin, "Production of Airflow Bodies Demands Utmost of Welding Art," *Automotive Industries*, 11 August 1934, 166, 168; and Burnham Finney, "Chrysler Employs New Methods in Making Airflow Cars," *Iron Age*, 1 November 1934, 20.

16. Chrysler Sales Corporation, confidential bulletin no. 909; Sidney Fine, "The Tool and Die Makers Strike of 1933," *Michigan History*, September 1958, 297–323; Steve Babson, *Building the Union: Skilled Workers and Anglo-Gaelic Immigrants in the Rise of the UAW* (New Brunswick: Rutgers University Press, 1991), 163–67; "Production Delays Continue to Hold Back Automobile Industry," *Iron Age*, 21 December 1933, 35; and "Ford Increases Production as General Motors and Chrysler Are Delayed," 39.

17. Daily production report," summarized by month, December 1933 through December 1934, found in microfilm reel L-93, DCHC.

18. The ads in the *Saturday Evening Post* are "Three in a Row," 31 March 1934, 32–33; "Progress out of the *Common Sense* of the *Common People*," 28 April 1934, 38–39; "More Than a Million Car Owners 'Sat In,'" 12 May 1934, 40–41; "'When GM Does It You Know It's Going to Click,'" 26 May 1934, 40–41; and "Something Far Sounder Than 'Hunch,'" 9 June 1934, 34–35.

19. Michael Lamm, "Magnificent Turkey," *Special-Interest Autos,* April–May 1973, 56, quotes Fred Breer.

20. Lamm and Holls, *A Century of Automotive Style,* 155; Kimes, "Chrysler from the Airflow," 208; and *Safety with a Thrill,* Wilding Picture Productions, Detroit, directed by J. Cullen Landis, in the Chrysler Photographic Collection.

21. "Another Record for Chrysler Airflow," *Automobile Topics,* 1 September 1934, 180, 190; and "'Airflow' Time Trial Checked," *Detroit News,* 26 August 1934, section 4, p. 9.

22. Kimes, "Chrysler from the Airflow," 208; Irwin, "The History of the Airflow Car," 101; Godshall, "DeSoto: Walter Chrysler's Stepchild," 77; and Paul C. Wilson, *Chrome Dreams: Automobile Styling since 1893* (Radnor, Pa.: Chilton, 1976).

23. Lamm and Holls, *A Century of Automotive Style,* 54, 155–57; Irwin, "The History of the Airflow Car," 101–2; and Athel F. Denham, "Six Chassis Models in Chrysler 1935 Line," *Automotive Industries,* 29 December 1934, 802. Irwin illustrates the evolution of the Airflow grille from 1934 to 1937.

24. Tucker, "The Airflow Story," 52–53.

25. Lamm and Holls, *A Century of Automotive Style,* 54, 155.

26. "Chrysler," *Fortune,* 117, 122.

27. Dodge truck files, 1934–40, DCHC; and Bunn, *Dodge Trucks,* 74, 79, 84, 98.

28. Lamm and Holls, *A Century of Automotive Style,* 80, 157; Godshall, "DeSoto: Walter Chrysler's Stepchild," 78–79; Tucker, "The Airflow Story," 52; "Airstream Model Is Offered by DeSoto as Companion Line to the Airflow: Priced from $695 in Low Medium Field," *Automobile Topics,* 29 December 1934, 478–80; "Chrysler Refines Airflow Line, Adds Airstream Model Also," *Automobile Topics,* 29 December 1934, 484–88; Denham, "Six Chassis Models in Chrysler 1935 Line," 802–3, 806; Athel F. Denham, "Chrysler Airstream, New Airflow Running Mate," *Automobile Trade Journal,* January 1935, 36–38; Joseph Geschelin, "Advanced Styling Marks Chrysler 1936 Debut," *Automobile Trade Journal,* November 1936, 28–29; and "Four New Chryslers in 1936 Line," *Automobile Topics,* 28 October 1935, 571–73.

29. "Chrysler Makes Good," *Barron's,* 27 April 1936, 9; and "The Chrysler Bonanza," *Barron's,* 27 July 1936, 6.

30. A 1937 photograph of the Lynch Road plant final assembly lines claims that it "is the world's biggest assembly plant." See box "Lynch Road 1," DCHC.

31. "Chrysler: Engineering and Plymouth," *Fortune,* December 1940, 187.

32. "Rubber Mounting Used on Chrysler Marine Engine," *Automotive Industries,* 26 December 1931, 996.

33. *American Machinist,* Special Chrysler Issue, 20 May 1936, 487, 493, 497; Chrysler Corporation, quarterly financial statement, 30 June 1934, 2; Airtemp Division, Chrysler Corporation, press release, October 1965, box "Airtemp 1," DCHC.

34. *Tenth Annual Report of Chrysler Corporation, Year Ended December 31, 1934,* 3; "Chrysler Reveals Air Condition Plans: Plans Large Scale Production of Apparatus," *Detroit News,* 17 February 1935, section 4, p. 13; "Chrysler Takes over Airtemp as Subsidiary," *Detroit News,* 11 August 1935, section 4, p. 15; Stearn, "The Financial History of the Chrysler Corporation," 25, 29; and press release, Airtemp Division, Chrysler Corporation, October 1965, box "Airtemp 1," DCHC. Gail Cooper's recent book, *Air-conditioning America: Engineers and the Controlled Environment, 1900–1960* (Baltimore: Johns Hopkins University Press, 1998), makes no mention of Airtemp.

35. "Chrysler . . . means Number Three Corporation, Number Two Personality, and the first manufacturer in the automotive field to raise its rate of production above its figures for the great boom year of 1929." *Fortune,* August 1935, 37, 111; and "Of Arms and Automobiles," *Fortune,* December 1940, 60, 179–80.

36. John B. Rae, *The American Automobile: A Brief History* (Chicago: University of Chicago Press, 1965), 98.

37. Federal Trade Commission, *Report on Motor Vehicle Industry* (Washington, D.C.: United States Government Printing Office, 1939), 609–10.

38. *Detroit News,* 9 January 1938,section 1, p. 12; and Chrysler Corporation, directors' meeting of 12 April 1929, in looseleaf binders, "Chrysler Incentive Programs, 1929–1957," in box "Early Chrysler 1," DCHC.

39. "Of Arms and Automobiles," 179; and Chrysler Corporation, press release no. 34555, DCHC.

40. Richard P. Scharchburg, "Kaufman Thuma Keller," in May, *Encyclopedia of American Business History and Biography: The Automobile Industry, 1920–1980,* 235–41.

41. "Chrysler," *Fortune,* 111; and "Keller of Chrysler," *Time,* 16 October 1939, 88.

42. "B. E. Hutchinson Converted Intangibles into Real Assets," *Automobile Topics,* 30 December 1933, 416, 441; and biographical sketch, Hutchinson biographical file, DCHC.

43. "Chrysler," *Fortune,* 111; "Of Arms and Automobiles," 179.

44. "Analysis of Engineering Features—Comparison of Chrysler, General Motors and Ford Cars Showing First Model Year Used in Production," in file "Chrysler Firsts," box "Chrysler Early History 1," DCHC.

45. Breer, *Birth of Chrysler Corporation,* 91–133.

46. "Chrysler Adds a New Building," 1; and "A Century of Progress in Ten Years," *Automobile Topics,* 30 December 1933, 428–29.

47. "Fred M. Zeder's Genius behind Every Chrysler Motor Car," *Automobile Topics,* 30 December 1933, 415; Karla A. Rosenbusch, "One for All and All for One! Chrysler's Three Engineers," *Automobile Quarterly* 37 (March 1998): 72; and summary of the life of Zeder, typescript (five pages) in the Zeder file, box "ZSB," DCHC.

48. Rosenbusch, "One for All and All for One! Chrysler's Three Engineers," 72, 81.

49. Breer, *Birth of Chrysler Corporation* 1, 20–21; Rosenbusch, "One for All and All for One! Chrysler's Three Engineers," 73, 81; and Breer biographical file, box "ZSB," DCHC.

50. "Chrysler Adds a New Building," 1; Watson, "New Chrysler Building Open," 5; and booklet, "Published by the Chrysler Corporation in Commemoration of the Opening of the New Engineering Building, July 2nd, 1928," (Detroit: Chrysler Corporation, 1928), in box "Engineering 1," DCHC.

51. Construction details are taken from Hyde, report on the history and architecture of the Chrysler Highland Park plant. Chrysler Corporation, "New Worlds in Engineering" is found in box "Engineering 1," DCHC.

52. Breer, *Birth of Chrysler Corporation,* 137–38; "Chrysler Institutes a University of Experience," *Automobile Topics,* 30 December 1933, 388; and "The Story of the Chrysler Institute of Engineering," typescript (1954), box "Chrysler Institute 1," 10, DCHC.

53. "The Story of the Chrysler Institute of Engineering," 12–13, 17–20, 33–35; and Chrysler Institute yearbook, looseleaf notebook with photographs and biographical sketches of the first 24 students, box "Chrysler Institute 2," DCHC.

54. "The Story of the Chrysler Institute of Engineering," 29–31.

55. "The Story of the Chrysler Institute of Engineering," 37–38; "Chrysler Honored by Own Institute of Engineering," *Detroit News* 12 July 1933, 24; "49 At Institute Hear Chrysler: Social Aspects of Engineering Are Stressed at Graduation," *Detroit News,* 27 June 1934, 8. "Chrysler Institute March, Words by W. H. MacDuff, Music by Eduard Werner"; "Second Annual Commencement of the Chrysler Institute of Engineering, June 26, 1934"; and *The Exponent* (1938) (yearbook), all in box "Chrysler Institute 2," DCHC.

56. "First Woman Automotive Engineer to Retire after 42 Years with Chrysler," Chrysler Corporation, News Relations Office, press release no. 89 of 1979; Ronald L. Russell, "It All Started with Ginny . . . , First Woman Auto Engineer Retires," *Detroit News,* 3 April 1979, 3-C; "Female Auto Engineer Was a Pioneer" (obituary), *Detroit Free Press,* 22 November 1986, 8-D; *The Exponent* (1937) 26, 28; and *The Exponent* (1938), 20. The last two items are found in box "Chrysler Institute 2," DCHC. Her wartime work included teaching evening classes in mathematics, blueprint reading, and the use of precision instruments to new female employees. Her work as a teacher was featured in an article, "Wartime Teacher: Mary Sink Leads YWCA Course," *Chrysler War Work Magazine,* October 1942, 13.

57. "The Story of Chrysler Institute of Engineering," 21, 39–45.

CHAPTER 8

1. The best general history of labor in Detroit is Steve Babson et al., *Working Detroit: The Making of a Union Town* (Detroit: Wayne State University Press, 1986). For the emergence of the UAW in the 1930s, see Babson, *Building the Union.*

2. Chrysler Corporation, "The Men Who Make Chrysler Motors," booklet, 1930, library of the American Automobile Manufacturers Association, NAHC, 11–16.

3. Sidney Fine, *The Automobile under the Blue Eagle: Labor, Management, and the Automobile Manufacturing Code* (Ann Arbor: University of Michigan Press, 1963), 152–55; and Leo Huberman, *The Labor Spy Racket* (New York: Modern Age Books, 1937), 5, 12–13, 76–78, 165–69.

4. Daniel Nelson, "The Company Union Movement, 1900–1937: A Reexamination," *Business History Review* 56 (autumn 1982): 335–38; and Sanford M. Jacoby, *Employing Bureaucracy: Managers, Unions, and the Transformation of Work in American Industry, 1900–1945* (New York: Columbia University Press, 1985), 187–89, 221, 226–28.

5. "W. P. Chrysler Offers Employees Equal Voice with Management on Wages, Working Conditions" and "Employee Representation in the Plants of Chrysler Motors," October 1933, folder "Dodge Main Plant Works Council 1933–36," box 8, Zaremba Papers, Archives of Labor and Urban Affairs, WRL; and "Novel Union in Chrysler Plants," *Automobile Topics,* 14 October 1933, 408. Chrysler also announced the plan in its "Financial Statement of Chrysler Corporation, September 30, 1933," DCHC.

6. Fine, *The Automobile under the Blue Eagle,* 155–57. The operation of the elections was outlined in "Walter P. Chrysler Offers Employees Equal Voice with Management on Wages, Working Conditions."

7. Babson et al., *Working Detroit,* 66.

8. Steve Jefferys, *Management and Managed: Fifty Years of Crisis at Chrysler* (Cambridge: Cambridge University Press, 1986) 55–56; Fine, *The Automobile under the Blue Eagle,*

26–27; and "Chrysler," *Fortune,* 127. Jefferys claimed that the dingmen struck for two days in 1933, based on John Zaremba's memory and a printed call for support for the dingmen, erroneously dated "1933" in pencil, folder "Dodge Local 3, Miscellaneous," box 2, Ross Papers, WRL. The profit figures cited for Chrysler Corporation unambiguously tie the document to the strike of 30 April 1935.

9. Jefferys, *Management and Managed,* 20–21.

10. Ibid., 58–67, 71; Fine, *The Automobile under the Blue Eagle,* 337–41.

11. For an exhaustive analysis of the Flint sit-down strikes, see Sidney Fine, *Sit-Down: The General Motors Strike of 1936–1937* (Ann Arbor: University of Michigan Press, 1969).

12. Babson et al., *Working Detroit,* 86; "'Blacklist' Notations Sent to Washington: UAW Leaders Asserts that Information on Espionage Charged to Chrysler Corporation Was Withheld from Senators," *Detroit News,* 23 March 1937, 4; and Clarence McConnell, "Chrysler Files Fan a Dispute: Union Charges Bring 'Burglary' Retort," *Detroit Free Press,* 23 March 1937, 1, 3.

13. Clarence McConnell, "Doctor Called after 11–Hour Strike Parley," *Detroit Free Press,* 27 March 1937; "Major Events in Dispute with Chrysler," *Detroit Free Press,* 4 April 1937; "Pact Is Hailed as Master Plan to End Strikes," *Detroit Free Press,* 7 April 1937; "Text of Chrysler Agreement," *Detroit Free Press,* 15 April 1937; and Nicholas Kelley, oral reminiscences, interviews of 26 March 1953 and 30 March 1953, leaves 346–62.

14. "Union Agrees to Let Contract Go Unchanged: UAW Gives Up Fight for Wage Pledge; Locals to Vote," *Detroit Free Press,* 1 April 1939; "Telephone Conversation between K. T. Keller and John L. Lewis, Thursday, 3/31/38, 3:00 PM," folder 3, box 3, K. T. Keller Papers, NAHC. An accompanying note indicated that a "cylinder record" made the recording of the conversation. It is not clear that Lewis knew he was being recorded.

15. "Vote by Plants Listed," *Detroit Free Press,* 29 September 1939; Jefferys, *Management and Managed,* 244, n. 62; and Chrysler Corporation, *"Slowdown": A Documentary Record of the Strike in Chrysler Corporation Plants from Oct. 6 to Nov. 29, 1939* (Detroit: Chrysler Corporation, 1939), 6.

16. "Chrysler Corp. Gets Threat of General Strike," *Detroit Free Press,* 12 October 1939; "Chrysler Men Vote to Strike, Union Reports," *Detroit Free Press,* 16 October 1939; statement issued to the press by Herman L. Weckler, vice president in charge of operations of Chrysler Corporation, 8 October 1939; and an open letter "To the Distributors and Dealers of the Chrysler Corporation," from K. T. Keller, president, Chrysler Corporation, 12 October 1939, both reproduced in Chrysler Corporation, *"Slowdown": A Documentary Record,* 11–14, 16–21, 55–59; and Jefferys, *Management and Managed,* 83–84.

17. "Agreement Entered into on the 29th Day of November, 1939, between Chrysler Corporation and International Union, United Automobile Workers of America" (and nine local unions, listed separately), in Chrysler Corporation, *"Slowdown": A Documentary Record,* 203–11; and Stearn, "The Financial History of the Chrysler Corporation," 39, 42.

18. Lamm and Holls, *A Century of Automotive Style,* 54, 157–58; and Langworth and Norbye, *The Complete History of Chrysler,* 90–97.

19. Lamm and Holls, *A Century of Automotive Style,* 159–60; Langworth and Norbye, *The Complete History of Chrysler,* 98–103; and Chrysler Corporation, Engineering Division, "Chrysler Corporation Idea Cars and Parade Cars, 1940–1961," 1 November 1961, box "Idea Cars 2," 6–7, DCHC.

20. Langworth and Norbye, *The Complete History of Chrysler* 98–99; "Chrysler Is First American Car to Adopt the 'Fluid Drive,'" *Automotive Industries,* 24 December 1928, 319–20;

and "Chrysler's Fluid Drive Eliminates Shocks," *Automobile Topics,* 19 December 1938, 296.

21. Harold Katz, *The Decline of Competition in the Automobile Industry, 1920–1940* (New York: Arno Press, 1977), 345–47.

22. Erik Barnouw, *The Golden Web: A History of Broadcasting in the United States,* vol. 2, *1933 to 1953* (New York: Oxford University Press, 1968), 102; Sally B. Smith, *In All His Glory: The Life and Times of William S. Paley* (New York: Simon & Schuster, 1990), 92.

23. *Major Bowes Amateur Parade,* June 1937, in box "Chrysler History 2," DCHC; printed texts of Chrysler advertisements on the Major Bowes shows, 15 December 1938–27 November 1941, in box "Events, 1927/1940," DCHC; Chrysler Corporation print advertisements, 1936–42, DCHC; and "'Eulogy on the Late Walter P. Chrysler,' by Major Edward Bowes, Broadcast, August 22, 1940," in box "Walter P. Chrysler 2," DCHC.

24. "Mrs. Chrysler Critically Ill: Iron Lung Is Used after Hemorrhage Occurs," *Detroit News,* 8 August 1938, 1; "Mrs Chrysler Is Dead at 66: She Fails to Rally after Stroke," *Detroit News,* 9 August 1938, 1; "Della Forker Chrysler," *Detroit News,* 10 August 1938, 14; and Clifford Epstein, "Stroke Fatal to Chrysler on Long Island," *Detroit News,* 19 August 1940, 1, 9.

25. *Time,* 7 January 1929,, 37; Forbes, "Chrysler Tells How He Did It," 15–17, 30, 32.

26. Frazier Hunt, "The Man Who Bet on His Dreams," *Popular Mechanics,* August 1932, 194–98; letter from V. D. Anderson, circulation manager, addressed "Dear Friend," in box "Chrysler History (1924–1939)," DCHC.

27. "The Boy Mechanic," *Ben Webster's Page,* by Edward Alger, *Detroit News,* 22 April 1934, comic section; E. and I. Geller, "The Story of an Ambitious Man . . . Who Made Jobs for Thousands through Free Enterprise," *Detroit Free Press,* 23 January 1949, comic section.

28. Memorandum, Ray Ayer to Frank Wylie, manager of public relations–Dodge, 16 April 1964; Walter A. Chrysler Dies in East after Stroke," *Detroit Free Press,* 19 August 1940, 5; and Nicholas Kelley, oral reminiscences, leaves 354–55.

29. Nicholas Kelley, oral reminiscences, leaf 311.

30. Kennedy, *The Automobile Industry,* 312.

31. "High School Is Named for Walter P. Chrysler," *New Castle (Indiana) Courier-Times,* 4 February 1955; "$5,000,00 School Gets Amelia Earhart's Names," *Detroit News,* 9 February 1955, 11; Robert L. Wells, "Chrysler Kin, Officials Start Xway on E. Side," *Detroit News,* 30 January 1959, 3; and Lawrence Gareau, "Chrysler Freeway Link Opened amid Echoes of the Past," *Detroit News,* 27 June 1964, 3-A.

Chapter 9

1. Alan Clive, *State of War: Michigan in World War II* (Ann Arbor: University of Michigan Press, 1979), 18–24.

2. Nelson Lichtenstein, *Labor's War at Home: The CIO in World War II* (Cambridge: Cambridge University Press, 1982), 83–89.

3. Barton J. Bernstein, "The Automobile Industry and the Coming of the Second World War," *Southwestern Social Science Quarterly,* June 1966, 22–30; Gregory Hooks, *Forging the Military-Industrial Complex: World War II's Battle of the Potomac* (Urbana: University of Illinois Press, 1991), 103–4, 180.

4. Letter, Major R. Z. Crane to R. P. Fohey, secretary, Chrysler Corporation, 26 September 1939, Chrysler War Records, vol. 22, "General, 1938–1941," DCHC.

5. Chrysler War Records, vol. 22, "General, 1938–1941," 11 December 1939–26 September 1940.

6. Letter, K. T. Keller to Henry Morgenthau Jr., 23 May 1940 and miscellaneous communications, 27 February–7 March 1941, Chrysler War Records, vol. 22, "General, 1938–1941; and Clive, State of War, 19–20.

7. "How Chrysler Corporation Subcontracts More Than 50% of Its War Work," ca. 1944, Carl Breer reports, Chrysler War Records, vol. 22, "General, 1938–1941" and vol. 24, "General, 1943, 1944," 5 March 1943.

8. "Tank Plant Chronology"; folder "Chrysler at War," box "Defense 1"; and Chrysler War Records, vol. 22, "General, 1938–1941," entries dated 14 June 1941, DCHC.

9. "Americanizing the Deadly Bofors: Chrysler Reveals Dramatic Story of How It Became World's Largest Producer of Antiaircraft Gun," Automotive News, 7 February 1944, 24, 27; and "Chrysler-Made Guns Bag 32 Japanese Bombers," reported by the Incentive Division, U.S. Navy, Carl Breer reports, Chrysler War Records, vol. 22, "General, 1938–1941."

10. The Index of Information concerning War Work Performed by Chrysler Corporation 1939–1946 in the DCHC is 36 pages long and mostly single-spaced, with considerable duplication in listing war products.

11. Nevins and Hill, Ford: Expansion and Challenge, 238–47; and Pound, The Turning Wheel, 318–28.

12. "Super-Strong Helldiver Wing in Production at Chrysler," Automotive News, 20 March 1944, 15.

13. Wesley W. Stout, Mobilized (Detroit: Chrysler Corporation, 1949), 44, 57; and Wesley W. Stout, Bullets by the Billion (Detroit: Chrysler Corporation, 1946). The latter discusses in some detail the products and processes employed at the Evansville plant, especially the quick conversion from brass to steel cartridges (20–30).

14. Wesley W. Stout, A War Job "Thought Impossible" (Detroit: Chrysler Corporation, 1945), 19–31, 34.

15. Wesley W. Stout, The Great Detective (Detroit: Chrysler Corporation, 1946), 51–57.

16. Stout, Mobilized, 71–74; "New Marine Tractor Beats Tug and Cuts Costs," Detroit News, 25 July 1942, 4; "Now We Build 'Tugboats,'" Chrysler War Work Magazine, February 1943, 8–10; and "13 Ships a Day for Chrysler Corporation's 'Dry-Land' Shipyard," Chrysler War Work Magazine, March 1944, 12–13.

17. Stout, Mobilized, 74–90; "Chrysler Smoke Screen to Protect Our Invading Soldiers," Chrysler War Work Magazine, November 1943, 3–4; "Reflectors Made by Chrysler Cast Beam 20 Miles," Automotive News, 18 December 1944, 4; and "Twenty-Mile Tunnels through Darkness," Chrysler War Work Magazine, January 1945, 8–9.

18. Wesley W. Stout, Secret (Detroit: Chrysler Corporation, 1947), 51–59; and James Jones, "The Key to Chrysler's Return to Prosperity," Ward's Quarterly 1 (winter 1965): 58.

19. Chrysler War Records, vol. 23, "General, 1942," entry of 4 May 1942; Motor Cars to Munitions, special issue of American Machinist, 11 June 1942, 5–6; and "Chrysler Didn't Wait for New Machines; Revamped the Ones They Had," American Machinist, 11 June 1942, 549–61.

20. Chrysler War Records, vol. 24, "General, 1943, 1944," entry of 19 November 1943; and Gerald T. White, Billions for Defense: Government Financing by the Defense Plant Corporation During World War II (University: the University of Alabama Press, 1980), 49.

21. Statement of H. F. Diegal, Chrysler Corporation chief accountant, 17 October 1946, Chrysler War Records, vol. 25, "General, 1945, 1946"; vol. 48, "Tanks, 1945, 1946," entry for 18 June 1945; and entries of 7 September 1945 and 6 January 1946, Chrysler War Records, vol. 15, "Dodge-Chicago, 1945, 1946."

22. Automobile Manufacturers Association, *Freedom's Arsenal: The Story of the Automotive Council for War Production* (Detroit: Automobile Manufacturers Association, 1950), 193.

23. Wesley W. Stout, *"TANKS Are Mighty Fine Things"* (Detroit: Chrysler Corporation, 1946), 12–13, 16–18; "Tank Plant Chronology," in box "Defense 1"; report of R. P. Fohey, 15 August 1940; and miscellaneous materials from the files of E. J. Hunt and B. E. Hutchinson, Chrysler War Records, vol. 44, "Tanks, 1940, 1941."

24. Stout, *"TANKS,"* 20–21; reports of E. J. Hunt, 4 October and 18 October 1940, Chrysler War Records, vol. 44, "Tanks, 1940, 1941."

25. Memorandum from E. J. Hunt, 3 October 1941; and construction reports of H. S. Wells, 28 January 1941, 15 April 1941, Chrysler War Records, vol. 44, "Tanks, 1940, 1941."

26. Stout, *"TANKS,"* 23–26 and "Delivering No. 1 to the United States Army: Chrysler Corporation's First M3 Medium Tank, April 14, 1941," box "Defense 1," DCHC.

27. Reports of L. L. Colbert, 31 July and 8 August 1941; Stout, *"TANKS,"* 32–33; Chrysler War Records, vol. 44, "Tanks, 1940, 1941."

28. Note from Mr. Littel, Detroit Ordnance Department, 14 October 1941 and Chrysler Corporation letter, 17 November 1941, Chrysler War Records, vol. 44, "Tanks, 1940, 1941."

29. Supplements to tank contract W-ORD-416, 26 and 27 March 1942, Chrysler War Records, vol. 45, "Tanks, 1942" and "Shipments of War Products," Chrysler War Records, vol. 25, "General, 1945, 1946,"; and Stout, *"TANKS,"* 40–41.

30. Letter from L. A. Moehring, comptroller, 20 June 1944, Chrysler War Records, vol. 44, "Tanks, 1940, 1941"; entries of 17 October 1942 and 16 December 1942, vol. 45, "Tanks, 1942"; entry of 12 January 1943, vol. 46, "Tanks, 1943"; and Stout, *"TANKS,"* 34–36.

31. Chrysler Corporation public relations release, 24 April 1945, Chrysler War Records, vol. 25, "General, 1945, 1946"; "Roosevelt's Visit to Chrysler," *Detroit News,* 1 October 1942; "Presidential War Tour Makes History for Leak-Proof Security," *Detroit Free Press,* 2 October 1942; "Roosevelt Pays Tribute to the Genius of Chrysler," *Detroit Free Press,* 2 October 1942; and "President Saw Production Miracles in Detroit," *Detroit Times,* 2 October 1942.

32. Letter, L. A. Moehring, comptroller, to J. W. Lee II, public relations, 20 June 1944; Chrysler War Records, vol. 47, "Tanks, 1944"; end-of-the-year employment summaries, 31 December 1942, 31 December 1943, 31 December 1944, and 31 December 1945, found in the Chrysler War Records, vols. 23–25, "General, 1942–1945"; and Stout, *"TANKS,"* 62–63.

33. Summary dated 26 September 1946, Chrysler War Records, vol. 48, "Tanks, 1945, 1946"; Stout, *"TANKS,"* 49–50; and Automobile Manufacturers Association, *Freedom's Arsenal,* 199, 201.

34. Entries of 1 June, 1 July, 19 September, and 26 October 1945, Chrysler War Records, vol. 48, "Tanks, 1945, 1946."

35. Entries of 11 September 1941, 30 December 1941, and 2, 11, 13, 15 March 1942, Chrysler War Records, vol. 13, "Dodge-Chicago, 1941, 1942, 1943"; and Wesley W. Stout, *Great Engines and Great Planes* (Detroit: Chrysler Corporation, 1947), 18–19.

36. Entries of 27 February 1942, 18, 20, and 30 March 1942, 27 May 1942, and 2 July 1942,

Chrysler War Records, vol. 13, "Dodge-Chicago, 1941, 1942, 1943"; and "Dodge-Chicago Plant Division of Chrysler Corporation, for the Manufacture of Aircraft Engines," letter to the Chrysler stockholders, 14 December 1942, signed by K. T. Keller, Chrysler Corporation vertical files, NAHC.

37. Entries of 5 June 1942 and 19 August 1942, Chrysler War Records, vol. 13, "Dodge-Chicago, 1941, 1942, 1943"; Stout, *Great Engines and Great Planes,* 14–15; "The New Giant of Giants," *Chrysler War Work Magazine,* December 1942,: 8; and "New Plants of 1943: Dodge-Chicago Division of Chrysler Corporation," *Factory Management and Maintenance,* April 1944, B-73.

38. Entries of 4 March, 6 March, 17 March, 30 March 1942; and report of L. L. Colbert, 29 July 1942, Chrysler War Records, vol. 13, "Dodge-Chicago, 1941, 1942, 1943"; and Breer, *Birth of Chrysler Corporation,* 188–90.

39. Entries of 10 and 17 August 1942, 23 March 1943, 3 April 1943, and 4 September 1943, Chrysler War Records, vol. 13, "Dodge-Chicago, 1941, 1942, 1943"; and Stout, *Great Engines and Great Planes,* 16.

40. Entries of 15 October 1943 and 1 December 1943, Chrysler War Records, vol. 13, "Dodge-Chicago, 1941, 1942, 1943"; entries of 1 February 1944, 5 June 1944, 31 August 1944, and 6 October 1944, vol. 14, "Dodge-Chicago, 1944"; and "Shipments of War Products," vol. 25, "General, 1945, 1946."

41. Memorandum of R. H. Hetrick, general auditor, Dodge-Chicago plant, 1 August 1944, Chrysler War Records, vol. 14, "Dodge-Chicago, 1944."

42. Ibid.; and Stout, *Great Engines and Great Planes,* 22–23.

43. Entries of 15 August 1945, 6 September 1945, and 4 December 1945, Chrysler War Records, vol. 15, "Dodge-Chicago, 1945, 1946."

44. Entries of 7 September 1945 and 6 January 1946, Chrysler War Records, vol. 15, "Dodge-Chicago, 1945, 1946."

45. "The Story of Chrysler Institute of Engineering," 21, 39–45; "Wartime Teacher: Mary Sink," 13; and "Women Doing a Real Job in Engineering Laboratory," *Chrysler Tonic,* 2 February 1943, 1–6.

46. "More Than a Billion Bullets Already from Chrysler Corporation's Evansville Ordnance Plant," report to the stockholders, June 1943; Carl Breer reports, DCHC; K. T. Keller, "Since the Start of the War," *Chrysler War Work Magazine,* April 1945, 3–4; K. T. Keller. "Industrial Logistics," *Logistics,* July 1946, 5–9; and Chrysler War Records, vols. 23–25, "General, 1942–1946." The records include lists of peak employment by plant for 1942–45.

47. Clive, *State of War,* 60; Howell John Harris, *The Right to Manage: Industrial Relations Policies of American Business in the 1940s* (Madison: University of Wisconsin Press, 1982), 52; Jefferys, *Management and Managed,* 92; and Lichtenstein, *Labor's War at Home,* 98–102.

48. Jefferys, *Management and Managed,* 93–98; Lichtenstein, *Labor's War at Home,* 130–31; and "'Beyond the Facts and the Records' War Labor Board Panel Admittedly Ignores the Evidence and Rewards Union Irresponsibility," Chrysler Corporation (1943), box 35, Hutchinson Papers, HIA.

49. Jefferys, *Management and Managed,* 97–102.

50. Chrysler Corporation, *Peacetime Enterprise Put to War Work* (Detroit: Chrysler Corporation, 1942); Chrysler Corporation, *Chrysler Division at War* (Detroit: Chrysler Corporation, 1943); and B. E. Hutchinson, "Some Facts about Chrysler Corporation before and

during the War," address before the Society of Security Analysts, New York, 24 October 1945, 10–13, 18–22.

51. *Significant War Scenes by Battlefield Artists* (Detroit: Chrysler Corporation, 1947).

CHAPTER 10

1. Chrysler Corporation, *Annual Report for Year Ended December 31, 1945* and *Annual Report for Year Ended December 31, 1947*; K. T. Keller, "The Automobile Industry in the Postwar World," remarks at the seventh annual business conference of the Graduate School of Business, Stanford University, Stanford, California, 22 July 1948, 32–35, box 34, Hutchinson Papers, HIA.

2. "The Chrysler Operation," *Fortune,* October 1948, 105, 151–53, 154.

3. Ibid., 151, 153.

4. Kimes, "Chrysler from the Airflow," 212–14.

5. Keller, "The Automobile Industry in the Postwar World," 2, 3, 6; and Michael Moritz and Barrett Seaman, *Going for Broke: The Chrysler Story* (Garden City, N.Y.: Doubleday, 1981), 52.

6. Dodge advertising materials for the 1950 model year, DCHC.

7. Harris, *The Right to Manage,* 111–15, 119–27. Harris offers the most comprehensive analysis of the business counteroffensive against labor.

8. "Settlement Deadline Is Tonight," *Detroit News,* 11 May 1948; "Sigler Reminds UAW of Penalties: Union Cuts Pay Demand to 17 Cents," *Detroit Free Press,* 12 May 1948; and "Industrial Peace," *Detroit Free Press,* 29 May 1948.

9. "Facts in Brief about the Current Negotiations between Chrysler Corporation and the UAW-CIO," box "Strikes, 2," 1–10, DCHC.

10. Jefferys, *Management and Managed,* 115–16; and "Chrysler's Real Pension Insurance Benefits Backed by Company's Good Faith and Credit Rejected by UAW for 10c 'Kitty' Fund," *Chrysler Motors Magazine,* January 1950, 4–5. This was a statement issued by Herman L. Weckler, Chrysler general manager, which the company inserted in various newspapers on 26 January 1950.

11. "Chrysler's Hundred Days: Two Bullheaded Strategies Locked Horns and Wouldn't Let Go," *Fortune,* June 1950, 70–71; and "Workers' Courage and Solidarity Win Victory over Chrysler Corporation's Blind Selfishness," full-page advertisement, *Detroit Free Press,* 5 May 1950, 15.

12. "Chrysler Corporation's Statement on the Strike Settlement," 4 May 1950, box "Strikes, 2," DCHC. A listing of all mass mailings made by Chrysler during the strike reveals that most of the 20 letters went out to a mailing list of 125,000 or 130,000 recipients.

13. "Workers' Courage and Solidarity Win Victory," 15; and Lichtenstein, *Walter Reuther: The Most Dangerous Man in Detroit* (Urbana: University of Illinois Press, 1997), 283.

14. "Chrysler's 100 Days," *Fortune,* June 1950, 70–72.

15. "The Treaty of Detroit: G.M. May Have Paid a Billion for Peace. It Got a Bargain," *Fortune,* July 1950, 53–55. General Motors first agreed to automatic pay increases to reflect productivity improvements (the annual improvement factor) and to cost-of-living adjustments (COLAs) in its 1948 contract with the UAW. The details are given in Harry C. Katz, *Shifting Gears: Changing Labor Relations in the U.S. Automobile Industry* (Cambridge, Mass.: MIT Press, 1985), 16.

16. Jefferys, *Management and Managed,* 116–17.

17. The best single treatment of Ford's executives is Ford R. Bryan, *Henry's Lieutenants* (Detroit: Wayne State University Press, 1993). Sloan, *My Years with General Motors,* explains the managerial system developed by Sloan in the 1920s.

18. John A. Byrne, *The Whiz Kids: Ten Founding Fathers of American Business—And the Legacy They Left Us* (New York: Doubleday, 1993), 88.

19. Reginald Stuart, *Bailout: America's Billion Dollar Gamble on the 'New' Chrysler Corporation* (South Bend, Ind.: Reginald Stuart, 1980), 50.

20. Quote from "K. T.," *Time,* 16 October 1939, 87.

21. Text of the citation for the Medal of Merit in folder "Miscellaneous," box "Keller 1," DCHC; "Ordnance Department Distinguished Service Certificate," awarded August 1945, folder 11, box 7, K. T. Keller Papers; "Guests Invited to Attend Presentation of Medal Of Merit to Mr. K. T. Keller, Washington, October 17, 1946," folder 17, box 9, K. T. Keller Papers, NAHC; and "Facts about the Making of M-G-M's Remarkable Motion Picture *The Beginning or the End,*" folder 7, box 11, K. T. Keller Papers, NAHC.

22. Stuart, *Bailout,* 52; Moritz and Seaman, *Going for Broke,* 51–52; and Jones, "The Key To Chrysler's Return to Prosperity," 59.

23. Carl Breer, "Zeder-Skelton-Breer History," 443–47, box "ZSB 2," DCHC.

24. Bob Finlay, "Men of Achievement: K. T. Keller," *Forbes,* 15 June 1948, 18–19.

25. "The Chrysler Operation," 154; Jefferys, *Management and Managed,* 107–8.

Chapter 11

1. "Chrysler Thinks Its Troubles Can Be Solved," *Business Week,* 27 March 1954, 42–44, 46, 48–49; William B. Harris, "Chrysler Takes the Bumps," *Fortune,* April 1954, 128, 131, 220, 223, 226; "Chrysler in the Clutch," *Forbes,* 15 December 1954, 15,17; and Vance Johnson, "Chrysler at the Crossroads," *Colliers,* 24 December 1954, 104.

2. "A Rebuilt Chrysler Corp. Gets Back in the Fight," *Business Week,* 30 April 1960, 128–29, 131–32, 134, 137.

3. Memorandum, L. L. Colbert to James W. Lee II, Chrysler Corporation Public Relations Department, 21 February 1946, folder "Biographical Information," box "Colbert 2," DCHC; Arthur W. Baum, "Chrysler Comes Back," *Saturday Evening Post,* 4 February 1956, 96; "External Combustion," *Time,* 29 January 1951, 92; and "Chrysler's New Prexy," *Forbes,* 15 February 1951, 14–15.

4. Baum, "Chrysler Comes Back," 96; "External Combustion," 92, 94; and "Chrysler's New Prexy," 15.

5. "Chrysler's New Prexy," 16; "Chrysler's New Moves Click—Just in Time," *Business Week,* 14 May 1955, 81; "Colbert Is Named Chief Executive," *Automotive News,* 7 May 1956, 1; and folder "Chrysler Corporation Press Information Service, 7/28/1961, Biographical Material on Lester L. Colbert," box "Colbert 2," DCHC.

6. Moritz and Seaman, *Going for Broke:* 55–56; and Stuart, *Bailout,* 61–62.

7. "Some Facts about Chrysler Corporation," 18 November 1954, 3, typescript, box "Chrysler History 2," DCHC.

8. "Briggs' Bodies," *Forbes,* August 1953, 12, 17; and "What Chrysler Bought from Briggs Mfg.," *Automobile Topics,* February 1954, 7.

9. "Proxy Statement, Briggs Manufacturing Company, Annual Report of Shareholders, October 29, 1954," 4, in box "Financial, Miscellaneous," DCHC; "What Chrysler Bought From Briggs Mfg.," 6, 7; and Leonard Westrate, "Implications of Chrysler-Briggs Purchase," *Automotive Industries,* 15 November 1953, 55. The number of Briggs employees transferred to Chrysler is variously listed as 30,000, 35,000, or 40,000. The *Forbes* article on Briggs (August 1953) claimed a total labor force of 46,000, but that figure included the employees who worked on Briggs Beautyware and on defense contracts.

10. "Torture Tests and Speed Trials Color Chrysler Proving Ground Dedication," *Automotive Industries,* 1 July 1954, 35–36; and "Automobile Topics Visits Chrysler's New Proving Grounds," *Automobile Topics,* August 1954, 16–17, 22, 25.

11. Recorded telephone conversation between B. E. Hutchinson and K. T. Keller, 26 July 1950 at 3:00 p.m., found in the folder "Keller," box 29, Hutchinson Papers, HIA. Hutchinson is clearly calling from the company headquarters in Highland Park, Michigan. Keller's location is never clearly stated—he might have been in Washington, D.C., or in California. The quotation is from K. T. Keller's letter, "To the Stockholders of Chrysler Corporation," 27 July 1950, in the "Financial Statement of Chrysler Corporation, June 30, 1950," DCHC.

12. "Defense Historical Summary," box "Defense 1," DCHC.

13. Memorandum on Chrysler Corporation defense work, 12 April 1952, 1–3, box "Defense 4," DCHC; Chrysler Corporation, Evansville plant, *From Evansville to the Sea,* November 1952, Chrysler Corporation press release, box "Evansville plant, DCHC; and "Cross Country Assembly Line," *Inside Michigan,* Michigan AAA, September 1952, 28–29.

14. Memorandum on Chrysler Corporation defense work, 4; and *Special Defense Edition, Chrysler Motors Magazine,* December 1952, 1–21.

15. "New Orleans Engines for Defense: The Story of the Michoud Ordnance Plant, Chrysler Tank Engine Division," box "Defense 1," DCHC; and "V-12 Tank Engine Production," *Automotive Industries,* 15 December 1952, 50.

16. Memorandum on Chrysler Corporation defense work, 4–5; "Huge Crowd on Hand Tuesday as Mighty New Patton Tank Is Unveiled in Newark Ceremony," *Newark (Delaware) Post,* 3 July 1952; "Army Unveils Patton 48, New Medium Tank," *New York Herald-Tribune,* 2 July 1952; and Elie Abel, "Army Ushers in 'Finest Medium Tank,'" *New York Times,* 2 July 1952. These newspaper clippings (and many others), along with the texts of speeches given at the ceremonies of 1 July 1952 are contained in "Official Unveiling of the Patton 48 by the Department of the Army, Chrysler Delaware Tank Plant, July 1, 1952," in folder "Miscellaneous," box "Tank History," DCHC. The innovative metalworking and assembly equipment developed by Chrysler for the Delaware plant is described in Thomas Mac New, "From Open Fields to Tank Production in 18 Months," *Automotive Industries,* 15 December 1952, 34–37, 92. Nonautomotive products are described in "Korean War Period Products, 1950–1954," box "Defense 4," DCHC; and "Some Facts about Chrysler Corporation," 5–6.

17. "Defense Historical Summary," box "Defense 1," DCHC; and "Post–Korean War Products, 1955–1961," box "Defense 4," DCHC.

18. Robert S. Hall, "Keller's Job to Get Missiles into Production as Weapons," *Detroit News,* 27 October 1950; "Guided Missiles Post to Be Held by K. T. Keller," *New York Herald Tribune,* 26 October 1950, 1, 23; "K. T. Keller Heads Guided Missiles; to Help Marshall Coordinate Work," *New York Times,* 26 October 1950; Leo Donovan, "'Push-Button'

War? No, Says Keller," *Detroit Free Press,* 27 October 1950; and Robert S. Ball, "General Due to Aid Keller: Would Help Direct Guided Missile Work," *Detroit News,* 31 October 1950.

19. "Shifting Guided Missiles from Lab to Defense Line," *U.S. News and World Report,* 5 February 1954, 50, 52–53; and letter, K. T. Keller to William J. Coughlin, editor, *Missiles and Rockets Magazine,* 16 May 1961, folder 42, box 1, K. T. Keller Papers, NAHC.

20. "Sterling Heights Assembly Plant, Chrysler Corporation," 3, folder "plant history," box "Sterling Heights 1," DCHC; and Chrysler's Ballistic Missile and Space Activities—First 20 Years, 2–3, box "Defense 4," DCHC.

21. "Chrysler's Ballistic Missile and Space Activities," 1–7; and "Chrysler Sets up Division to Handle Work on Missiles," *Automotive News,* 3 March 1958, 28.

22. Carl Breer, "Zeder-Skelton-Breer History," 448, box "ZSB 2," DCHC.

23. William L. Weertman, "45 Years of Chrysler V-8 Engine Power, 1951–1996," lecture to the W. P. Chrysler Car Club, 17 July 1996, in box "Engines, 1924/1955," DCHC; W. E. Drinkard and M. L. Carpentier, "Development Highlights and Unique Features of the New Chrysler V-8 Engine," *SAE Quarterly Transactions,* July 1951, 346–58; and James C. Zeder, "New Horizons in Engine Development," paper presented at the S.A.E. National Passenger Car, Body, and Materials meeting, Detroit, 4–6 March 1952, in box "Engines, 1924/1955," DCHC; *Annual Report of Chrysler Corporation, Year Ended 31 December 1950,* 6; and brochure, "The Great New Chrysler Fire Power Engine, the Sensation of the Century," box "Engines, 1924/1955."

24. Weertman, "45 Years of Chrysler V-8 Engine Power, 1951–1996,"; Godshall, "DeSoto: Walter Chrysler's Stepchild," 85 and Jeffrey I. Godshall, "Dodge and Then There Were Three," *Automobile Quarterly* 24 (second quarter, 1986): 209.

25. Griff Borgeson, "MT Research Tests the '52 Fire Dome DeSoto," *Motor Trend,* July 1952, 24–26, 44–45.

26. Langworth and Norbye, *The Complete History of Chrysler,* 38, 145; Lamm and Holls, *A Century of Automotive Style,* 160, 162, 165.

27. Virgil Max Exner Jr., interview by David Crippen, 3 August 1989, 64–65, Automotive Design Oral History Project, HFMGV; Lamm and Holls, *A Century of Automotive Style,* 160–62; and Critchlow, *Studebaker,* 124–25.

28. Chrysler Corporation Engineering Division, "Chrysler Corporation Idea Cars and Parade Cars, 1940–1961," 1 November 1961, 1–4, box "Idea Cars 1," DCHC; Ray Thursby, "1955 Chrysler-Ghia Falcon," *Road and Track,* June 1991, 126–27, 130; Lamm and Holls, *A Century of Automotive Style,* 162–64; Jeffrey I. Godshall, "Microphone Taillights and Doughnut Decks: Chrysler Cars of the Exner Era," *Automobile Quarterly* 29 (January 1991): 73; and Virgil Exner, "Styling of 1955 Chrysler Corporation Cars . . . the Forward Look," *Chrysler Magazine,* November 1954, 10.

29. Lamm and Holls, *A Century of Automotive Style,* 165; Virgil M. Exner Jr., interview, 74–75; Johnson, "Chrysler at the Crossroads," 106, 108; and "Organization of Styling Section, Engineering Division, April 1, 1956," box "Styling, 1930's, 1940's, 1950's," DCHC.

30. Johnson, "Chrysler at the Crossroads," 106, 108.

31. "The Forward Look," *Chrysler Magazine,* December 1954, 6.

32. Chrysler product literature (all lines), 1954–62 and Chrysler Corporation annual reports, 1954–62, DCHC; and "Chrysler's New Moves Click—Just in Time," 84.

33. Godshall, "Microphone Taillights and Doughnut Decks," 74; Lamm and Holls, *A Century of Automotive Style,* 166; and James A. Flammang, *Chrysler Chronicle* (Lincolnwood, Ill.: Publications International, 1998), 118–35.

34. Godshall, "Microphone Taillights and Doughnut Decks," 80, 81.

35. Ibid., 81, 83–84; Lamm and Holls, *A Century of Automotive Style,* 166–68.

36. Advertisements for the Chrysler line—1957, DCHC and *Chrysler Corporation Annual Report for the Year Ended December 31, 1957.*

37. Godshall, "Microphone Taillights and Doughnut Decks," 85–86; Kimes, "Chrysler from the Airflow," 215; and Jones, "The Key to Chrysler's Return to Prosperity," 60.

38. Kimes, "Chrysler from the Airflow," 214; Allan Girdler, "The Chrysler Lettercars," *Automobile Quarterly* 13 (fourth quarter 1975): 389; and box "Chrysler 300," DCHC. Beginning with the 1956 model (300-B), the model designation moved to the next letter of the alphabet in subsequent years, except that the 1963 model was designated the 300-J, not the 300-I.

39. Bill Carroll, "The Beautiful Brute," *Car and Driver,* August 1961, 71; and September 1961, 60–62.

40. Carroll, "The Beautiful Brute," 62; Girdler, "The Chrysler Lettercars," 384; and "Chronology of Major Records of Chrysler 300 Engines and Cars," Chrysler Corporation news release, box "Chrysler 300," DCHC.

41. Lamm and Holls, *A Century of Automotive Style,* 168–69; and news release, 8 February 1957, announcing Schmidt's appointment as executive stylist, corporate executive files, folder "William M. Schmidt," DCHC.

42. Lamm and Holls, *A Century of Automotive Style,* 169–70; and Godshall, "Microphone Taillights and Doughnut Decks," 86, 88, 89, 92–95.

43. Jefferys, *Management and Managed,* 7–8, 111.

44. Ibid., 123–25; brochure, "Why Improve Methods of Doing Things on Your Job," folder "Work Standards," in box "Strikes, 5," DCHC; folder "Dodge Strike 1954," in box "Strikes, 5," DCHC; and Johnson, "Chrysler at the Crossroads," 109.

45. Jefferys, *Management and Managed,* 138–45; Lichtenstein, *Walter Reuther: The Most Dangerous Man in Detroit,* 295–96, 513, n. 85; and "Chrysler-UAW Pact Ends Strike at Dodge Main Parts Plant," *Automotive Industries,* 1 January 1959, 12–13.

46. For the Sloan system of product differentiation, see Sloan, *My Years with General Motors,* 149–68. The growth in the size and power of the low-priced models is illustrated in "Autos: On the Slow Road," *Time,* 12 May 1958, 85.

47. "Chrysler in Transition: Ad Strategy in a Boom Market," *Printers' Ink,* 28 October 1955, 38, 40; and "Questions and Answers about the DeSoto Decision," box "End of DeSoto," DCHC.

48. "Ideas Designed to Build Confidence in DeSoto's Future," undated, box "End of DeSoto."

49. Folder "A Program to Discontinue DeSoto," received by H. E. Chesebrough, 2 November 1960; memorandum, W. C. Flaherty to H. E. Chesebrough, manager of the Plymouth-DeSoto-Valiant Division, 11 October 1960; and announcement, Chrysler Corporation Press Information Service, 18 November 1960, all found in box "End of DeSoto."

50. "Summary of Non-Budgeted Costs Due to Discontinuance of DeSoto Passenger Cars," in folder "A Program to Discontinue DeSoto."

51. E. C. Quinn, general manager–Sales Division, Chrysler Motors Corporation to DeSoto owners, 23 November 1960, correspondence file, box "End of DeSoto"; and miscellaneous correspondence between DeSoto owners and Chrysler Corporation, DCHC.

52. Memorandum, James L. Elsman Jr., Chrysler Legal Office, to Sam Petok, 3 May 1963, box "End of DeSoto"; and Godshall, "DeSoto: Walter Chrysler's Stepchild," 91.

53. Rae, *The American Automobile,* 211–12; and John A. Conde, *The American Motors Family Album* (Detroit: American Motors Corporation, 1978), 110–11.

54. A. G. Loofbourrow, V. M. Exner, and R. M. Sinclair, "The Valiant—A New Motoring Concept," paper presented at the Society of Automotive Engineers annual meeting, Detroit, 11–15 January 1960, 1–2, in box "Valiant/Compacts 1," DCHC; Moritz and Seaman, *Going for Broke,* 60; "How the Secret of Midland Avenue Became the Pride of Main Street," Plymouth Division news release (ca. mid-November 1959), 2, folder "Chrysler Small Car Study Program," box "Valiant/Compacts 1"; Product/Volume Planning Department, "Questions concerning the Domestic Small Car Problem," 29 January 1958; and memorandum, E. E. Milliman, Sales Planning, Chrysler Motors, to J. A. Lawson, director of market analysis, Chrysler Motors, 12 March 1958, folder "Chrysler Small Car Study Program."

55. John Guenther, "Why Engineering and Product/Volume Planning Want a Small Car in the 100–106 Inch Wheelbase Range," March 1958; and memorandum, J. A. Lawson, director of market analysis, to H. E. Chesebrough, director of product/volume planning, 13 March 1958, folder "Chrysler Small Car Study Program."

56. "Product Presentation Outline," 5 March 1958 and minutes of meeting number 9 of the Small Car Study Program, 6 May 1958, folder "Chrysler Small Car Study Program."

57. "How the Secret of Midland Avenue Became the Pride of Main Street."

58. Lamm and Holls, *A Century of Automotive Style,* 163; "How the Valiant Got Its Name," Chrysler-Plymouth Division News Bureau press release, box "Valiant/Compacts 1"; and Virgil Max Exner Jr., interview, 91–92.

59. "The Valiant, Chrysler Corporation's New Small Car," *Automotive Industries,* 15 October 1959, 61–63; Ken Fermoyle, "Chrysler's Valiant: Hottest New Compact Car," *Popular Science,* November 1959, 99–103; and "Road Research Report: Valiant," *Sports Cars Illustrated,* April 1960, 64–70, 72, 95.

60. "Road Research Report: Valiant," 65; "New Engineering, Sales Features of the Big Three's Little Three," *Business Week,* 3 October 1959, 108; Byrne, *The Whiz Kids,* 344; John B. Rae, *The American Automobile Industry* (Boston: Twayne, 1984), 124–25; and "Valiant Long-Range Planning," folder "1963 Valiant," box "Valiant 3," DCHC.

61. Chrysler Corporation Public Relations Department news release, 28 April 1960, folder "W. C. Newberg," box "Corporate Executives—N," DCHC.

62. "Newberg Resigns as Chrysler President, Company Cites 'Differences of Opinion,'" *Wall Street Journal,* 1 July 1960; Alfred R. Zipster, "A Chrysler President Is Out in Dispute: New President's Resignation Surprise to Industry," *New York Times,* 1 July 1960; and "Detroiter with Drive: William Charles Newberg," *New York Times,* 1 July 1960.

63. Chrysler Corporation Press Information Service, press release of 21 July 1960 and "Agreement of 21 July 1960 between William C. Newberg, Dorothy B. Newberg, and the Chrysler Corporation," box "Corporate Executives—N."

64. "Newberg's Suit Charges Top-Level Chrysler Plot," *Automotive News,* 23 January 1961, 1, 35, 36, 47; Tom Kleene, "Newberg Asks $5 Million in Damages: Ousted Official Charges

Colbert Plotted Rise, Fall," *Detroit Free Press,* 9 February 1961, 1, 2; Tom Kleene, "Bill Newberg Is Far from Down," *Detroit Free Press,* 22 December 1963; Robert D. Kirk, "Newberg Suit Judge Fires Parting Shot: Delaying Tactics Hit," *Detroit News,* 12 February 1964, 10–A; "Ex-President of Chrysler Tells His Story," *Chicago Daily News,* 26 October 1964; "Chrysler's Ex-Chief Bares Plot," *Detroit Free Press,* 26 October 1964; and Nick Thimmesch, "What's Good for Chrysler Is Good for Lynn Townsend," *Esquire,* March 1969, 26. The lengthy *Automotive News* article includes the full texts of Newberg's bill of complaint and Chrysler's response.

65. "Chrysler Involved in 11 Lawsuits," *Detroit Free Press,* 9 February 1961, 14.

66. Maynard M. Gordon, " 'Outsiders' Map Chrysler Course," *Automotive News,* 24 April 1961.

67. Drew Pearson, "Colbert Explains Bond Holdings," *Detroit Free Press,* 9 February 1961, 9.

CHAPTER 12

1. George S. May, "Lynn Alfred Townsend," in May, *Encyclopedia of American Business History and Biography: The Automobile Industry, 1920–1980,* 451–52; and "The Man on the Cover: Lynn Townsend & Chrysler's Comeback," *Time,* 28 December 1962, 52.

2. Townsend, box 1, biographical files, DCHC; Tom Kleene, "Townsend Named Top Chrysler Aide: VP Moves Up to No. 2 Spot," *Detroit Free Press,* 3 December 1960, 1; and Ralph R. Watts, "Chrysler Shifts VP as No. 2 to Colbert: Townsend in Line for Top Post," *Detroit News,* 3 December 1960, p. 1.

3. Robert Sheehan, "Coal Man at Chrysler," *Fortune,* September 1962, 8; "The Man on the Cover," 52–53; "Townsend, 42, Named Chrysler President to Succeed Colbert," *Automotive Industries,* 15 August 1961, 41; Jones, "The Key to Chrysler's Return to Prosperity," 60; and Thimmesch, "What's Good for Chrysler," 107.

4. Robert Sheehan, "The Price of Success at Chrysler," *Fortune,* November 1965, 141; and Jones, "The Key to Chrysler's Return to Prosperity," 64.

5. "A Revamped Chrysler Tries Fresh Start," *Business Week,* 7 October 1961, 112–14, 116, 118; Sheehan, "Coal Man at Chrysler," 2–10; "The Man on the Cover," 52–53; and Jones, "The Key to Chrysler's Return to Prosperity," 57.

6. "The Man on the Cover," 52.

7. Lamm and Holls, *A Century of Automotive Style,* 169; and Godshall, "Microphone Taillights and Doughnut Decks," 93.

8. Kimes, "Chrysler from the Airflow," 218; Sheehan, "Coal Man at Chrysler," 8; and "The Man on the Cover," 53.

9. Chrysler Corporation annual reports for 1953, 1958; "A Revamped Chrysler Tries Fresh Start," 116; Sheehan, "Coal Man at Chrysler," 9; and Sheehan, "The Price of Success at Chrysler," 141.

10. Elwood Engel, interview by David Crippen, 16 June 1984, Elwood Engel Collection, HFMGV; Lamm and Holls, *A Century of Automotive Design,* 150; and Joseph M. Callahan, "Inside Chrysler Styling," *Automotive News,* 31 December 1962, 9.

11. Lamm and Holls, *A Century of Automotive Style,* 170; Sheehan, "Coal Man at Chrysler," 8; and Callahan, "Inside Chrysler Styling," 17.

12. Sheehan, "The Price of Success at Chrysler," 236.

13. "Biographical Material on Virgil E. Boyd," in box "Love, Boyd, Cafiero," DCHC; and William T. Noble, "Virgil Boyd: Prize Catch for Chrysler 'Headhunters,'" *Detroit News,* pictorial magazine, 13 March 1966, 10.

14. Sheehan, "Coal Man at Chrysler," 9; "The Man on the Cover," 53; Noble, "Virgil Boyd: Prize Catch for Chrysler 'Headhunters,'" 11; Sheehan, "The Price of Success at Chrysler," 142; and "Can Chrysler Make It Stick?," *Forbes,* 15 September 1965, 23.

15. "Corporate Turnaround," *Design Sense,* no. 44 (1965): 4, DCHC; correspondence files, Walter P. Margulies, box "Townsend Office 3,"; Godshall, "Microphone Taillights and Doughnut Decks," 92; and Hugh Quinn, "Chrysler's Image Push Is Tied to Marketing Companywide: Pentastar Replaces Car-Oriented 'Forward Look' Symbol," *Advertising Age,* 1 July 1963, 52.

16. "Corporate Turnaround," 6; "Why Chrysler Changed Its Corporate Identity," *Ward's Quarterly* 1 (winter 1965): 72; "Contact 10," *Detroit News,* 27 February 1973, 6-B; and "A Pentastar Is Born: Consultant Left His Mark by Designing Chrysler's Logo," *Chrysler Times,* 7 June 1996, 4.

17. "Corporate Turnaround," 6; and "Why Chrysler Changed Its Corporate Identity," 72.

18. "Corporate Position on Sanctioned Competitive Events," Chrysler Corporation press release, 26 February 1964, box "Circuit 4," DCHC.

19. Tim Bongard and Bill Coulter, *The Cars of the King: Richard Petty* (Champaign, Ill.: Sports Publishing, 1997), 19–20; Spencer Riggs, "On the Right Track: A Racing Heritage," *Automobile Quarterly* 32 (April 1994): 78; and "Recap of Richard Petty's Racing Career, January 15, 1968," folder "Petty Enterprises," box "Drivers 10," DCHC.

20. Bongard and Coulter, *The Cars of the King,* 38–41, 69–70, 110–15; Riggs, "On the Right Track: A Racing Heritage," 78–79; and Bob Myers, "Officially, Petty's Back in Plymouth," *Charlotte (North Carolina) News,* 17 December 1969, 2C.

21. "Can Chrysler Makes It Stick?," 21; and Sheehan, "The Price of Success at Chrysler," 139.

22. Thimmesch, "What's Good for Chrysler," 105.

23. Jones, "The Key to Chrysler's Return to Prosperity," 62–63.

24. Jones, "The Key to Chrysler's Return to Prosperity," 62; and Sheehan, "The Price of Success at Chrysler," 140, 242.

25. Mira Wilkins and Frank Ernest Hill, *American Business Abroad: Ford on Six Continents* (Detroit: Wayne State University Press, 1964), 18, 47, 50; and Ed Cray, *Chrome Colossus: General Motors and Its Times* (New York: McGraw-Hill, 1980), 234.

26. "A History of Chrysler Canada Ltd.," April 1986, 5–6, box "Chrysler History 5," DCHC; and Chrysler Corporation, "Financial and General Fact Book," July 1968, 19, DCHC.

27. Joseph Geschelin, "Argentina's Automotive Industry, Part VII: Chrysler Argentina S.A.," *Automotive Industries,* 1 June 1965, 47; John Christman, "First All Integrated Car Maker in Mexico," *Ward's Quarterly* 1 (fall 1965): 94; and Chrysler Corporation, "General and Financial Fact Book," July 1968, 20.

28. Moritz and Seaman, *Going for Broke,* 84, 86.

29. Chrysler Corporation, "General and Financial Fact Book," July 1968, 22; James M. Laux, *The European Automobile Industry* (New York: Twayne, 1992), 126, 197–98; and Wilkins and Hill, *American Business Abroad,* 395–97.

30. Stephen Young and Neil Hood, *Chrysler U.K.: A Corporation in Transition* (New York: Praeger, 1977), 58–61.

31. Chrysler Corporation annual reports for 1958–61; Lynn Townsend to Henri T. Pigozzi, 16 January 1962, correspondence files, box "Townsend Office 1," DCHC; and letters, John R. Barlow, manager, Product Advertising, to Simca dealers, 16 April, 28 May, and 1 June 1959, folder "Simca-Rootes Division Import Dealers," box "Dealer Correspondence," DCHC.

32. "Chrysler International Today: Five Years of Progress," 1963, 5–7, 16, box "Chrysler Divisional Histories," DCHC.

33. David Thoms and Tom Donnelly, *The Motor Car Industry in Coventry since the 1890s* (New York: St. Martin's Press, 1985), 161; I. J. Minett, "Confidential Memo for the Record," 26 April 1962, "Memorandum pertaining to Proposed Chrysler-Leyland-Standard Association," and I. J. Minett to L. A. Townsend and F. W. Misch, 8 May 1962, folder "International," box "Townsend Office 3," DCHC.

34. Thoms and Donnelly, *The Motor Car Industry in Coventry,* 164; and Peter King, *The Motor Men: Pioneers of the British Car Industry* (London: Quiller Press, 1989), 128–29.

35. Young and Hood, *Chrysler U.K.,* 78–80; "Chrysler Gets Aboard British Auto Boom," *Business Week,* 13 June 1964, 54; and Robert Heller, "Why Rootes Made the Chrysler Match," *Observer,* 7 June 1964.

36. Young and Hood, *Chrysler U.K.,* 82–85, 138, 164, 217–46, passim.; Chrysler Corporation, "General and Financial Fact Book," July 1968, 20–21; Roy Church, *The Rise and Decline of the British Motor Industry* (Cambridge: Cambridge University Press, 1994), 95; and Rootes Motors, *Annual Report 1969,* box "Chrysler International 3," DCHC.

37. Chrysler Corporation, "General and Financial Fact Book," July 1968, 21–22; Moritz and Seaman, *Going for Broke,* 87–88; and Young and Hood, *Chrysler U.K.,* 63–64.

38. Chrysler Corporation, "General and Financial Fact Book," July 1968, 20.

39. Chrysler Corporation annual reports for 1969, 1975; and James C. Jones, "Ten Years of Investment Pay Off for Chrysler Overseas," *Ward's Auto World,* 1 November 1969, 22.

40. Chrysler Corporation, annual reports for 1963, 1965, and 1968; Joseph Geschelin, "Chrysler's New Huber Foundry," *Automotive Industries,* 1 January 1967, 69–72; and Jeremy Main, "Chrysler's Well-Ordered Comeback—By the Numbers," *Fortune,* November 1968, 172.

41. Chrysler Corporation annual reports for 1960–75; and Chrysler Corporation Defense Group, "Fact Sheet, January, 1977," DCHC.

42. "Background," box "Defense Operations History, 1954–1964," DCHC, 6–8; and Chrysler Corporation news release no. 34879, August 1979, "Chrysler Tank Related Production, 1941–79," box "Defense Operations History, 1954–1964," DCHC.

43. Chrysler Corporation, Space Division, "This Is **Your** Chrysler Saturn Story," March 1965, 22 and "Chrysler's Ballistic Missile and Space Activities: The First 20 Years," May 1971, 9–10, both in box "Defense 4," DCHC.

44. Chrysler Corporation, "Chrysler's Ballistic Missile and Space Activities: The First 20 Years," May 1973, 10–13.

45. James C. Jones, "Comeback in Detroit," *Saturday Evening Post,* 25 May 1963, 75; Jones, "The Key to Chrysler's Return to Prosperity," 65; and Roger Huntington, "The Gas Turbine Takes to the Road," *Ward's Quarterly* 1 (winter 1965): 86–87. The best brief introduction to Chrysler's work on the turbine car is Hans-Loachim Braun, "The Chrysler Automotive Gas Turbine Engine, 1950–80," *Social Studies of Science* 22 (1992): 339–51.

46. Louis C. Hunter, *A History of Industrial Power in the United States, 1780–1930,* vol. 1,

Waterpower in the Century of the Steam Engine (Charlottesville: University Press of Virginia, 1979), 292–342; and Huntington, "The Gas Turbine Takes to the Road," 85.

47. Chrysler Corporation, Engineering Office, "History of Chrysler Corporation's Gas Turbine Vehicles," July 1974, 2, box "Turbine 3," DCHC.

48. Chrysler Corporation, Engineering Division, "Chrysler Corporation's Experimental Gas Turbine Engine," December 1955, 15–16, box "Turbine 3," DCHC; and Huntington, "The Gas Turbine Takes to the Road," 86.

49. Chrysler Engineering Office, "History of Chrysler Corporation Gas Turbine Vehicles," July 1974, 3–5.

50. Chrysler Corporation press release no. 39958, "Turbine Progress Report," 11 January 1959, 1–4.

51. Chrysler Engineering Office, "History of Chrysler Corporation's Gas Turbine Vehicles," 1979, 11–13, 17–18.

52. Chrysler Engineering Office, "History of Chrysler Corporation Gas Turbine Vehicles," 1979, 14, 20–22.

53. Chrysler Engineering Office, "History of Chrysler Corporation Gas Turbine Vehicles," July 1974, 20–21, 25–27.

54. "Summary of Chrysler Corporation Turbine Consumer Delivery Program, October 29, 1963–January 28, 1966," box "Turbine 2," DCHC; and "Users' Evaluation of the Turbine Car," remarks by Dr. David R. Miller, manager of marketing and consumer research, Chrysler Corporation, at a meeting in Detroit with representatives of the press, radio, and television on 12 April 1966, box "Turbine 3," DCHC. All interviews with turbine users were tape-recorded, but this researcher has been uable to locate the tapes.

55. Huntington, "The Gas Turbine Takes to the Road," 83–85; and Jones, "The Key to Chrysler's Return to Prosperity," 57.

56. Chrysler Engineering Office, "History of Chrysler Corporation Gas Turbine Vehicles," July 1974, 39–42.

Chapter 13

1. Main, "Chrysler's Well-Ordered Comeback," 164–65, 167, 172, 174; "What's Wrong at Chrysler: Its Conservatism Helped a While Back—but Not Now," *Business Week,* 5 July 1969, 46–48; Arthur M. Louis, "Chrysler's Private Hard Times," *Fortune,* April 1970, 102–5, 146, 151–52; "Chrysler Tries without a Mini," *Business Week,* 5 September 1970, 58–59; "How Chrysler Fights a Skid," *Business Week,* 17 April 1971, 72–73, 76; and "What's Wrong at Chrysler?" *Forbes,* 1 December 1973, 28, 30–33.

2. "The Auto Executive: He Has to Run Faster Just to Keep Up" (story on Robert Anderson), *Business Week,* 12 March 1966, 95–100; Robert P. Edney, "Man on the Move" (Riccardo), *Signature: The Diners Club Magazine,* November 1968, 53; and "What's Wrong at Chrysler," *Business Week,* 47.

3. "Boyd Elected as Chrysler President; Townsend Now Chief Executive Officer," *Michigan Manufacturer and Financial Record,* January 1967, 7; and Louis, "Chrysler's Private Hard Times," 103.

4. Louis, "Chrysler's Private Hard Times," 146, 151; and George Cantor, "To Chrysler's John Riccardo, It's All Numbers (But Then Why Is He Called the 'Flame Thrower'?)," *Detroit Free Press Magazine,* 22 August 1971, 16–18.

5. "Total Corporation Capital Expenditure, 1964–1978 Calender Years," box "Financial 15," DCHC.

6. Moritz and Seaman, *Going for Broke,* 126–27; Main, "Chrysler's Well-Ordered Comeback," 172; and Lee Iacocca and William Novak, *Iacocca: An Autobiography* (New York: Bantam Books, 1984), 155.

7. Lamm and Holls, *A Century of Automotive Style,* 171; and Joseph Geschelin, "Engineering Highlights of Chrysler Corporation's 1965 Cars," *Automotive Industries,* 15 August 1964, 58.

8. Elwood P. Engel, "Team Styling at Chrysler," *Automotive Industries,* 1 November 1969, 90; Charles K. Hyde, report on the Chrysler Center, buildings 411 and 412, for the Historic American Engineering Record, May 1997; and "Remarks by Lynn A. Townsend at the Dedication of the Walter P. Chrysler Building, Highland Park, Michigan, 2 August 1972, "Speeches," vol. 5, box 1, Lynn A. Townsend Papers, BHL.

9. Louis, "Chrysler's Private Hard Times," 146.

10. Robert Irvin, "Chrysler's Cocky Cafiero Battles Production Bugs," *Ward's Auto World,* August–September 1970, 43–44; "Chrysler Tries without a Mini," 59; advertisement, "Extra Care . . . in Customer Care: Your Chrysler Man in Detroit Really Cares What You Think. Chrysler Corporation Cares, Too. Write Byron Nichols," file "Byron J. Nichols," box "Corporate Executives—N," DCHC; and "History of Chrysler Corporation Passenger Car Warranty, January 1980," box "Warranty," DCHC.

11. "What's Wrong at Chrysler," *Business Week,* 46–47; and Louis, "Chrysler's Private Hard Times," 105, 151–52.

12. What's Wrong at Chrysler?" *Forbes,* 28, 30.

13. Moritz and Seaman, *Going for Broke,* 114.

14. Ibid., 28, 32. Production figures by model are from Flammang, *Chrysler Chronicle,* 183–72, passim.

15. One of the best treatments of Chrysler's muscle cars is Nicky Wright, *50 Years of Chrysler's Hottest Cars* (New York: Gramercy Books, 1999).

16. Memorandum, H. E. Weiss to F. Walter, "Sporty Appeal," 29 March 1963 and H. E. Weiss, "The Origin of the Barracuda," 9 May 1966, folder "1964 Barracuda," box "Barracuda/Charger," DCHC.

17. Production statistics are from James T. Lenzke, ed., *Standard Catalog of Chrysler, 1914–2000,* 2d ed. (Iola, Wis.: Krause, 2000), 444–68; and Jeffrey I. Godshall, "Barracuda: Braving Turbulent Waters," *Automobile Quarterly* 25, no. 4 (1987): 424–45.

18. C. Van Tune, "Dodge Charger, 1966–1973," *Motor Trend,* February 1994, 102, 104–5; Patrick Bedard, "1969 Dodge Charger Daytona," *Car and Driver,* December 1988, 123–29; Daniel Charles Ross, "'69 Dodge Charger Daytona: The Hemi-Powered Flying Wing," *Motor Trend,* July 1990, 112–14; and "Warner Brothers Finds Homes for Dukes of Hazzard Cars & Parts," *Mopar Collector's Guide,* February 1993, 26–29. Production figures are from Lenzke, *Standard Catalog of Chrysler, 1914–2000,* 235–74.

19. John Sloan, "Birth of the Road Runner, Part 1: The Incredible Inside Story of Plymouth's More Popular Musclecar," *High Performance MOPAR,* May 1991, 48–50.

20. Ibid., 50; letters, C. B. Hanson, product planning manager, to J. J. Cordier, Chrysler International S.A., 10 May 1967; and Sam Clark, merchandising manager, Warner Bros.–Seven Arts Pictures, to Gordon C. Cherry, Belvedere Product Planning, 3 October 1967, all found in folder "Road Runner 1968, 2 Dr H. T.," box "Muscle," DCHC.

21. Sloan, "Birth of the Road Runner, Part 1," 51; "Birth of the Road Runner, Part 2: Bringing the Bird to Market," *High Performance MOPAR,* July 1991, 20; and "Horn History," folder "Road Runner Product Development," box "Muscle."

22. "Motor Trend's 1969 Car of the Year—Road Runner," *Motor Trend,* February 1969, 32–34; and Gary Blonston, *Plymouth: Its First 50 Years,* 2d ed. (Detroit: Chrysler-Plymouth Division, Chrysler Corporation, 1978), 53–54. Production statistics are from Lenzke, *Standard Catalog of Chrysler, 1914–2000,* 240–46, 453–70.

23. Lenzke, *Standard Catalog of Chrysler, 1914–2000,* 457–58.

24. Ibid., 457–70.

25. Engel, "Team Styling at Chrysler," 56–57.

26. Jeffrey Godshall, "Barracuda: Braving Turbulent Waters," 445.

27. Lamm and Holls, *A Century of Automotive Style,* 170–71, 286–89.

28. James J. Flink, *The Automobile Age* (Cambridge, Mass.: MIT Press, 1988), 386–87; and B. Bruce-Briggs, *The War against the Automobile* (New York: E. P. Dutton, 1977), 85.

29. Moritz and Seaman, *Going for Broke,* 144–46; and Flink, *The Automobile Age,* 387.

30. Chrysler Corporation annual report, 1969, 8; Chrysler executives, "Charles Heinen," DCHC; and Zachare Ball, "Female Auto Engineer Was a Pioneer," *Detroit Free Press,* 22 November 1986, 8-D.

31. National Academy of Engineering, *The Competitive Status of the U.S. Auto Industry: A Study of the Influences of Technology in Determining International Industrial Competitive Advantage* (Washington, D.C.: National Academy Press, 1982), 81, 84; Flink, *The Automobile Age,* 388; and Robert B. Reich and John D. Donahue, *New Deals: The Chrysler Revival and the American System* (New York: Times Books, 1985), 28.

32. Flink, *The Automobile Age,* 384–85.

33. Moritz and Seaman, *Going for Broke,* 158–59.

34. Edney, "Man on the Move," 53; and Cantor, "To Chrysler's John Riccardo, It's All Numbers," 15.

35. Cantor, "To Chrysler's John Riccardo, It's All Numbers," 15.

36. Ibid., 15–16; and Reich and Donahue, *New Deals,* 24.

37. Chrysler Corporation news release, "Biographical Material on Eugene A. Cafiero," 1 October 1975; and Walter Mossberg, "Gene Cafiero Labors to Enhance the Quality Of Assembly-Line Work," *Wall Street Journal,* 7 December 1972, 22.

38. Irvin, "Chrysler's Cocky Cafiero Battles Production Bugs," 43–35; and "The Comer at Chrysler Tries a New Road," *Business Week,* 13 July 1974, 76–78, 80, 82.

39. Moritz and Seaman, *Going for Broke,* 76–77; Main, "Chrysler's Well-Ordered Comeback," 172; Eleanore Carruth, "Look Who's Rushing into Real Estate?" *Fortune,* October 1968, 160–63, 168, 172, 174; and Chrysler Realty Corporation annual reports, 1968–76, box "Chrysler Divisional Histories 1," DCHC.

40. Louis, "Chrysler's Private Hard Times," 105; and "The Auto Slump Spreads," *Business Week,* 14 December 1974, 59.

41. Moritz and Seaman, *Going for Broke,* 104–9; and Reich and Donahue, *New Deals,* 21–22.

42. "The Auto Slump Spreads," 59, 64.

43. Greg Conderacci, "Chrysler to Trim Some Effective Prices $200 to $400 in Steepest Such Retreat by Auto Industry Thus Far," *Wall Street Journal,* 7 January 1975, 3; "Don't Dilly Dally or Delay, Today Is Opening Day," advertisement announcing "Chrysler Corporation's Car Clearance Carnival," DCHC; Chrysler Corporation press release, 7 March

1975, research subjects, folder "Cash-Back Customer Rebate, 1975," box "Rebates," DCHC; "Chrysler Ties Rebates to Dealer Program," *New York Times,* 1 May 1975, 59; "Chrysler Motors Corporation Rebate Program, Official Program Rules, April 30, 1975 through May 31, 1975" and "Chrysler Motors Corporation, Cash-Back Customer Rebate Program for Participating Dealers, Official Program Rules, June 27, 1975 through November 30, 1975," folder "Chrysler Motors Corporation Rebate Program, 1975," box "Rebates."

44. Walter B. Smith, "Chrysler to Recover? 'Significant Improvement' for Second Quarter," *Detroit News,* 9 July 1975, 7-C; and "Out, but Not Down, Lynn Townsend Tells How He Built Chrysler and Why He Left It," *Detroit Free Press,* 10 August 1975, Detroit section, pp. 13–16.

45. Peter J. Schuyten, "Chrysler Goes for Broke," *Fortune,* 19 June 1978, 54–56, 58.

46. Flammang, *Chrysler Chronicle,* 270, 277, 281, 285.

47. Lenzke, *Standard Catalog of Chrysler, 1914–2000,* 264–68, 474–76; and Plymouth Division print advertising literature, 1976 and 1977 models, DCHC.

48. Moritz and Seaman, *Going for Broke,* 15–16; Reich and Donahue, *New Deals,* 38–39, 44; Ralph Nader and Clarence Ditlow, *The Lemon Book,* 3d ed. (Mount Kisko, N.Y.: Moyel Bell , 1980), 203; and "Volare-Aspen Rust Fix to Total $45 Million," *Automotive News,* 14 April 1980, 1.

49. The production figures are from Flammang, *Chrysler Chronicle.*

50. Clark Hallas, "The 'L-Car,'" *Detroit News Magazine,* 2 April, 1978, 24–25, 40.

51. For a selection of the reviews, see Marshall Spiegel, "Omni-Horizon: Chrysler's First Subcompacts," *Auto Reports,* January 1978, 36; Bob Tripolsky, "We Test Chrysler's New Mini," *Mechanix Illustrated,* January 1978, 27; and John Dinkel, "Chrysler's Plymouth Horizon & Dodge Omni: One of Detroit's Most Significant Designs—Ever," *Road and Track,* January 1978, 52.

52. "Driving the Car of the Year: Omni/Horizon-Another 'First' for Chrysler," *Motor Trend,* February 1978, 29–30.

53. "Chrysler's Big Mistake: The Dodge Omni/Plymouth Horizon Is Judged Not Acceptable," *Consumer Reports,* July 1978, 376–77, 381–83.

54. "Public Relations Response to the Condemnation of a Product, a Report on Chrysler Corporation's Emergency Public Relations Program in Response to Consumers Union Designation of the Plymouth Horizon and Dodge Omni as 'Unacceptable'" and Chrysler Corporation statement 18578, released on 14 June 1978, box "L-Body," DCHC.

55. Clark Hallas, "Horizons, Omnis Spur Bitter Fight," *Detroit News,* 15 June 1978, 1-A, 12-A; William Mitchell, "Consumer Reports' Lowest Rating," and Gregory Skwira, "Chrysler's Vigorous Objections," side-by-side parts of "A Dispute over Omnis and Horizons," *Detroit Free Press,* 18 June 1978, 1-A, 10-A; "Owners Support Chrysler's 'Twins,'" *Detroit News,* 17 June 1978, 1-A, 4-A; Gregory Skwira, "Chrysler Safety Flap: How Bad? Industry Takes Issue with Testing Methods," *Detroit Free Press,* 19 June 1978, 1-A, 13-A; John E. Peterson, "Omni/Horizon Test Validity Questioned," *Detroit News,* 20 June 1978, 1-C; Ted Kade, "Car Magazine Rips Media on Omni Test; Free Press, NBC Accused of 'Distortion,'" *Detroit News,* 22 June 1978, 12-D; "Omni, Horizon Cars Test Safe," Transport Canada, public relations release no. 155/78, 28 June 1978; "No Problem Found in Chrysler Omni/Horizon Handling," NHTSA news release 74–78, 7 July 1978; and "Third Party Opinions: U.S. and Canadian Governments and the City of Seattle," all found in folder "Public Relations Response to the Condemnation of a Product," box "L-Body," DCHC.

56. Transcript of news conference by John Riccardo and Eugene A. Cafiero, Highland Park, Michigan, 26 April 1978, in box "Riccardo 1," DCHC; Clarke Hallas, "Safety Agency Backs Omni," *Detroit News,* 8 July 1978, 1-A; Ted Kade, "Big Three's Small Cars Score Big Sales Revival: Pinto, Chevette, Omni/Horizon in Sales Comeback," *Detroit News* 24 August 1978, 1-A, 8-A; and Moritz and Seaman, *Going for Broke,* 5.

57. Moritz and Seaman, *Going for Broke,* 16–17, 235–36.

58. Chrysler Corporation annual report, 1976, 8 and annual report, 1982, 19; Chrysler Corporation news release, 28 February 1980; "Chrysler Tank Production," January 1981; and "XM1 Lima Army Tank Plant," all found in folder "Tank History," box "Defense 6," DCHC.

59. Richard Mendel, "The First Chrysler Bail-Out: The M-1 Tank," *Washington Monthly,* February 1987, 17–23.

60. Chrysler Corporation annual reports, 1960–82; Moritz and Seaman, *Going for Broke,* 119; Reich and Donahue, *New Deals,* 21, 25–26, 31, 45; and Jack Egan, "Chrysler: Auto Maker Again in Midst of Choppy Financial Waters," *Washington Post,* 12 March 1978, 1, 6.

61. Moritz and Seaman, *Going for Broke,* 121; Chrysler Corporation annual report, 1976, 20; "Chrysler Sells Airtemp Assets to Fedders Corp.: Firm Receives $585 Million in Cash, Notes and Stock for Money-Losing Unit," *Wall Street Journal,* 24 February 1976, 1; and "Agreement to Purchase Airtemp," box "Airtemp 2," DCHC.

62. Moritz and Seaman, *Going for Broke,* 79; and Chrysler Corporation annual report, 1979, 5,6.

63. Chrysler Corporation, "International Fact Book," 1975, box "Chrysler Divisional Histories," DCHC.

64. Steven Ludwig, "Chrysler Builds a European Structure," *International Management,* October 1971, 18–19.

65. Moritz and Seaman, *Going for Broke,* 187–89. Excellent analyses of the negotiations and the rescue package can be found in Young and Hood, *Chrysler U.K.,* 217–335; Stephen Wilks, *Industrial Policy and the Motor Industry* (Manchester: Manchester University Press, 1984), 118–205; and Edmund Dell, "The Chrysler UK Rescue," *Contemporary Record* 9 (1992): 1–44.

66. Moritz and Seaman, *Going for Broke,* 191–92, 311–12; and Leonard Apcar and Felix Kessler, "Chrysler Plans to Sell All European Units to Peugeot for $426 Million Cash, Stock in Major Retrenchment," *Wall Street Journal* 11 August 1978, 3.

67. Chrysler Corporation annual report, 1979, 27; and "Supply Agreement Dated as of the 31st Day of January, 1978 for G54B Gasoline Engines between Chrysler Corporation and Mitsubishi Motors Corporation," folder, "M. M. C. Engines," box "International 4," DCHC.

68. Flink, *The Automobile Age,* 388–89; and Moritz and Seaman, *Going for Broke,* 164.

69. Moritz and Seaman, *Going for Broke,* 170–71.

70. Ibid., 181, 184.

71. Moritz and Seaman, *Going for Broke,* 8–11, 217–19; and Reich and Donahue, *New Deals,* 45.

CHAPTER 14

1. Stuart, *Bailout;* Moritz and Seaman, *Going for Broke;* and Reich and Donahue, *New Deals.*

2. Chrysler Corporation, "Financial and General Fact Book," 1986, F-1, O-3; and Chrysler Corporation annual report, 1982, 1.

3. "Transcript of News Conference Conducted by John Riccardo, Chairman and Chief Executive Officer, Chrysler Corporation, and Eugene A. Cafiero, President, at Highland Park, Michigan, on Friday, July 28, 1978," folder "John J. Riccardo Transcripts, 1978, 1979," box "Riccardo 1," DCHC.

4. "Transcripts of News Conferences Conducted by John Riccardo, Chairman and Chief Executive Officer, Chrysler Corporation, and Lee A. Iacocca, President, at Highland Park, Michigan, on Thursday, November 2, 1978 and on Monday February 26, 1979," folder "John J. Riccardo Transcripts, 1978, 1979."

5. Kirk Cheyfitz and J. Patrick Wright, "The Rise and Fall and Rise of Lee Iacocca," *Monthly Detroit,* February 1979, 51–52; Iacocca and Novak, *Iacocca,* 16, 18; Moritz and Seaman, *Going for Broke,* 202–3; and entry for Lido Anthony Iacocca, *Comus,* Allentown High School yearbook, 1942, 96, loose in box "Iacocca 1," DCHC.

6. Iacocca and Novak, *Iacocca,* 22–26. He claimed he switched his major to industrial engineering, but *The 1945 Epitome,* Lehigh University's senior class yearbook, listed his degree as "mechanical engineering" (22).

7. Iacocca and Novak, *Iacocca,* 30–31, 40, 44–46; and Moritz and Seaman, *Going for Broke,* 204–7.

8. Iacocca and Novak, *Iacocca,* 63–74; "Ford's Lee Iacocca," *Time,* 17 April 1964, 92, 99–102; and "The Mustang—A New Breed out of Detroit," *Newsweek,* 20 April 1964, 97–101.

9. Iacocca and Novak, *Iacocca,* 78–84; and Moritz and Seaman, *Going for Broke,* 208–11.

10. Iacocca and Novak, *Iacocca,* 98–132; and Cheyfitz and Wright, "The Rise and Fall and Rise of Lee Iacocca," 47–50.

11. Iacocca and Novak, *Iacocca,* 141–47; and Moritz and Seaman, *Going for Broke,* 211–18.

12. "Iacocca to the Rescue," *Newsweek,* 13 November 1978, 99, 101; and "It Won't Be Easy," *Forbes,* 27 November 1978, 130.

13. Moritz and Seaman, *Going for Broke,* 223–25; and Iacocca and Novak, *Iacocca,* 152–53, 154.

14. Maynard M. Gordon, *The Iacocca Management Technique* (New York: Ballantine Books, 1985), 13–17; Iacocca and Novak, *Iacocca,* 47–49, 167; and Moritz and Seaman, *Going for Broke,* 242.

15. Leonard M. Apcar, "Chrysler President Lee Iacocca Promotes Harold Sperlich, a Former Ford Official," *Wall Street Journal,* 22 November 1978, 5; Tom Kleene, "Iacocca Shakes Up Chrysler's Top Brass," *Detroit Free Press,* 22 November 1978, 8A; David C. Smith, "Iacocca at Chrysler: Pizzazz at the Top," *Ward's Auto World,* December 1978, 89; Lamm and Holls, *A Century of Automotive Style,* 255; and Iacocca and Novak, *Iacocca,* 122–23.

16. Ford Motor Company news release, 11 March 1976, announcing Bergmoser's retirement, Bergmoser biography file, NAHC; and Moritz and Seaman, *Going for Broke,* 227.

17. Iacocca and Novak, *Iacocca,* 168–70; and Moritz and Seaman, *Going for Broke,* 228–29, 239–40.

18. "Chrysler," *Ward's Auto World,* November 1979, 32–33; and Chrysler Corporation news release, 9 April 1981 (retirement of E. F. Laux).

19. Iacocca and Novak, *Iacocca,* 174–76; Moritz and Seaman, *Going for Broke,* 226–27, 231–35, 338; and Richard E. Dauch and Dr. Jack Troyanovich, *Passion for Manufacturing* (Dearborn, Mich.: Society of Manufacturing Engineers, 1993), 14–15, 18.

20. Iacocca and Novak, *Iacocca,* 178–81; Moritz and Seaman, *Going for Broke,* 243–44; Ralph Gray, "No Backseat Role for K & E: Laux," *Advertising Age,* 26 March 1979, 2, 83; and

Stuart Elliott, "Doing Business Like Detroit Never Did It Before: How Kenyon & Eckhardt Is Selling Mr. Iacocca's Cars," *Detroit Free Press,* 16 March 1980, Detroit section, pp. 8–10.

21. Elliott, "Doing Business Like Detroit Never Did It Before," 8–10; Iacocca and Novak, *Iacocca,* 179–80; and Gray, "No Backseat Role for K & E: Laux," 2, 83.

22. Elliott, "Doing Business Like Detroit Never Did It Before," 11–12; Iacocca and Novak, *Iacocca,* 267–70; Sonja K. Foss, "Retooling an Image: Chrysler Corporation's Rhetoric of Redemption," *Western Journal of Speech Communication* 48 (winter 1984): 83; Ralph Gray, "Star Power for Chrysler," *Advertising Age,* 7 September 1981, 2, 71; and "Lee Iacocca of Chrysler: Crisis Plans Paying Off," *Advertising Age,* 2 January 1984, 1. The best description of Iacocca's camera shyness and his initial unwillingness to do TV ads is found in Peter Wyden, *The Unknown Iacocca* (New York: William Morrow, 1987), 169–80.

23. "Remarks by John Riccardo, Chairman of the Board, Chrysler Corporation, at the Annual Convention of the Automotive Organization Team, Las Vegas, Nevada, Sunday, February 11, 1979" and "Transcript of News Conference Conducted by John Riccardo, Chairman of the Board, Chrysler Corporation, and Lee A. Iacocca, President, at Highland Park, Michigan, on Tuesday, July 31, 1979," folder "John J. Riccardo Transcripts, 1978, 1979," box "Riccardo 1," DCHC.

24. Reich and Donahue, *New Deals,* 101, 104, 106, 114–15.

25. Edward Foldessy, "Chrysler Could Default on Its Bank Loans unless It Gets Financial Aid of Some Sort," *Wall Street Journal,* 8 August 1979, 1; and Donald Woutat, "GM Will Lend to Chrysler: $230 Million Offered; Finance Subsidiary Will Help Dealers Buy New Cars and Trucks," *Detroit Free Press,* 15 August 1979, 1A, 19A.

26. Andy Pasztor and Robert S. Greenberger, "Miller Rejects Chrysler's Aid Plan; Lack of Other Help Pledges Is Cited," *Wall Street Journal,* 17 September 1979, 1; Leonard M. Apcar, "Chrysler's Riccardo to Quit This Week; Decision Stuns Automotive Community," *Wall Street Journal,* 18 September 1979, 3, 16; and Chrysler Corporation press release, 17 September 1979," folder "John J. Riccardo Transcripts."

27. Edward Lapham, Keith E. Crain, and Robert M. Lienert, "Volkswagen AG Plans to Purchase Chrysler, Create New Global Automotive Superpower," *Automotive News,* 25 June 1979, 1, 6; Iacocca and Novak, *Iacocca,* 192–94; Moritz and Seaman, *Going for Broke,* 258–60; and Robert W. Irwin and Keith E. Crain, "Schmuecker: No VW Help for Chrysler Corp.," *Automotive News,* 8 October 1979, 2, 49.

28. Marjorie Sorge, "UAW Asks U.S. to Buy an Interest in Chrysler Corp.," *Automotive News,* 23 July 1979, p. 1; Marjorie Sorge, "Fraser Prices Chrysler Aid," *Automotive News,* 30 July 1979, 1; and Robert L. Simison, "UAW Locals Torn by Chrysler's Need, Loyalty to Workers: Officers Meeting Today Hoping to Resolve Dilemma and Solidify Bargaining Stance," *Wall Street Journal,* 9 August 1979, 1.

29. Reich and Donahue, *New Deals,* 57–58, 103; Moritz and Seaman, *Going for Broke,* 279–80; and Iacocca and Novak, *Iacocca,* 209–10, 217.

30. Charles B. Camp, "No. 3 Auto Firm's Plea for Federal Aid Shakes Industry, Washington: Concern Is Relying on Help; Uncertainty Upsets Many of Its Workers, Suppliers," *Wall Street Journal,* 3 August 1979, 1, 14; Paul Lienert and Louis B. Heldman, "At Chrysler Corp., It Was a Horrible Week," *Detroit Free Press,* 5 August 1979, 13D, 18D; "Loan Guarantees for Chrysler Ranging Up to $750 Million May Be Proposed by the Administration, Sent to Congress; but Carter Rejects Concern's Request for $1 Billion Advance

against Taxes," *Wall Street Journal*, 10 August 1979, 1; and Reich and Donahue, *New Deals*, 97–98, 103–6.

31. Reich and Donahue, *New Deals*, 61–71; and Iacocca and Novak, *Iacocca*, 219–20.

32. Pasztor and Greenberger, "Miller Rejects Chrysler's Aid Plan," 1.

33. Andy Pasztor, "Bailout Lobby: How Chrysler Corp. Mobilizes Support of Bid for Federal Aid," *Wall Street Journal*, 6 September 1979, 1, 16.

34. Iacocca and Novak, *Iacocca*, 222–24.

35. "Testimony by Lee A. Iacocca, Chairman, Chrysler Corporation, before the Subcommittee on Economic Stabilization of the Committee on Banking, Finance and Urban Affairs, United States House of Representatives, Washington, D.C., October 18, 1979" and Statement by Lee A. Iacocca, Chairman of the Board, Chrysler Corporation, before the U.S. Senate Committee on Banking, Housing and Urban Affairs, November 15, 1979," box "Loan Guarantee 1," DCHC.

36. "Carter Plan to Aid Chrysler Urges U.S. Loan Guarantee of $1.5 Billion; but Firm Would Be Obliged to Raise Equal Amount, Meet Other Conditions," *Wall Street Journal*, 2 November 1979, 1.

37. For detailed accounts of the passage of the act, see Reich and Donahue, *New Deals*, 118–59; and Moritz and Seaman, *Going for Broke*, 276–90.

38. Iacocca and Novak, *Iacocca*, 187; and letter, Thomas Miner, director of labor relations, Chrysler Corporation, to Marc Stepp, director, Chrysler Department, UAW, 20 October 1980, folder "Appraisals and Personnel," box "Bergmoser 3," DCHC.

39. Reich and Donahue, *New Deals*, 161–63.

40. Ibid., 124–26; Moritz and Seaman, *Going for Broke*, 284; "Plan to Elect UAW's Chief to Chrysler's Board Raises Issues," *Wall Street Journal*, 26 October 1979, 1; "Doug Fraser Press Conference, Rockford, Illinois, May 13, 1980," folder "Doug Fraser Press Conference," box "Financial 18," DCHC; and "1980 Meeting of Stockholders, Tally Sheet," folder "1980 Shareholders Meeting, May 13, 1980," box "Financial 18," DCHC. In *Iacocca* (236), the Chrysler chairman claimed he asked Fraser to become a director before the first round of UAW concessions, mainly because of Fraser's intelligence and political savvy and *not* as a condition for the concessions.

41. A. H. Raskin, "The Labor Leader as Company Director," *New York Times*, 27 April 1980, F-1, F-14, F-15.

42. Reich and Donahue, *New Deals*, 164–67.

43. Ibid., 164; Moritz and Seaman, *Going for Broke*, 302, 311; and "Chrysler Adds $450 Rebates in Sales Push; Step Applies to Some Mid-Size Cars, Vans," *Wall Street Journal*, 5 March 1980, 1.

44. "Chrysler to Lay Off 20% of Its Salaried, Other Staff to Save $200 Million a Year," *Wall Street Journal*, 23 April 1980, 2, 33; John E. Peterson, "Canadians Clear Way for Guarantee," *Detroit Free Press*, 11 May 1980, 1A; and "Chrysler's 9-Month Scramble for Help," *Detroit Free Press*, 11 May 1980, 1A, 7A.

45. Reich and Donahue, *New Deals*, 169, 173–74, 185, 191–93. The detailed story of the negotiations with the banks is told in Reich and Donahue, *New Deals* and in Moritz and Seaman, *Going for Broke*, 298–317.

46. Reich and Donahue, *New Deals*, 202–5 and Iacocca and Novak, *Iacocca*, 250.

47. Reich and Donahue, *New Deals*, 158, 194–95; Moritz and Seaman, *Going for Broke*, 326–27; and Iacocca and Novak, *Iacocca*, 257–58.

48. Leo-Arthur Kelmenson to Lee A. Iacocca, 19 June 1980, folder "Kenyon & Eckhardt," box Bergmoser 7, DCHC; and James A. Benson and Judith M. Thorpe, "Chrysler's Success Story: Advertising as Anecdotes," *Journal of Popular Culture* 25 (winter 1991): 130.

49. Iacocca and Novak, *Iacocca,* 251–52; Moritz and Seaman, *Going for Broke,* 242; and Reich and Donahue, *New Deals,* 40.

50. Robert W. Irvin, "Chrysler to Build New Compacts at Jefferson Ave.," *Automotive News,* 11 June 1979; "$100-Million Revamp for Chrysler 'K' Plant," *Automotive News,* 17 March 1980; Jenny King, "Changing Chrysler Plant to K-Car a Big Job," *Automotive News,* 31 March 1980; and Reich and Donahue, *New Deals,* 208.

51. Francis J. Gawronski, "Chrysler K-Car to Stress Ease of Diagnosis, Repair," *Automotive News,* 16 June 1980, 17.

52. News releases from Richard A. Vining and from the UAW, 27 June 1980, folder "Labor-UAW," box "Bergmoser 8," DCHC; Moritz and Seaman, *Going for Broke,* 323; and Dauch and Troyanovich, *Passion for Manufacturing,* 17–19.

53. Press packets for K-car launches at Jefferson assembly plant, Detroit, 6 August 1980 and at Newark, Delaware, assembly plant, 3 September 1980, box "K-Cars 1," DCHC; Moritz and Seaman, *Going for Broke,* 323–24; and Reich and Donahue, *New Deals,* 208. The enthusiasm of fleet owners for the K-cars can be seen in "Aries & Reliant to Pave Way for Chrysler's Comeback: Lessors Favorably Impressed by the Company's Front-Drive Compacts," *Automotive Fleet,* June 1980, 18–23.

54. Iacocca and Novak, *Iacocca,* 255; Moritz and Seaman, *Going for Broke,* 357, n. 4; and Gordon, *The Iacocca Management Technique,* 163–64.

55. Moritz and Seaman, *Going for Broke,* 328–29; and Reich and Donahue, *New Deals,* 216–17. H. E. Weiss (conversation with the author on 31 July 2000) recalled that in the early shipments to dealers, half the K-cars had sticker prices of $10,000 + .

56. Memorandum, John B. Naughton, senior executive vice president, sales and marketing, to J. B. Bergmoser, president, "1981 'K' Body $5,880 Product Program," 18 November 1980 and memorandum, Joseph A. Campana, director of marketing plans and programs, to John B. Naughton Sr., 26 November 1980, materials courtesy of W. E. Weiss.

57. Moritz and Seaman, *Going for Broke,* 324, 327, 330; and Iacocca and Novak, *Iacocca,* 255.

58. "1981 Car of the Year: Winner, Chrysler K-Car," *Motor Trend,* February 1981, 76; and "1981 Car of the Year: Testing," *Motor Trend,* February 1981, 71. The quotation from *Popular Science* is from Moritz and Seaman, *Going for Broke,* 328.

59. Moritz and Seaman, *Going for Broke,* 329; and Gawronski, "Chrysler K-Car to Stress Ease of Diagnosis, Repair," 20.

60. Chrysler Corporation press releases, Windsor, Ontario, 11 August 1980; Moritz and Seaman, *Going for Broke,* 329; and Flammang, *Chrysler Chronicle,* 307, 315, 321.

61. Moritz and Seaman, *Going for Broke,* 331; and Reich and Donahue, *New Deals,* 217, 221.

62. Reich and Donahue, *New Deals,* 218–23, 237.

63. Ibid., 219–21, 226–34.

64. Moritz and Seaman, *Going for Broke,* 334–35.

65. Reich and Donahue, *New Deals,* 238–40; and Iacocca and Novak, *Iacocca,* 258–61.

66. Reich and Donahue, *New Deals,* 240–41.

67. *Detroit Free Press,* 3 March 1982, 4C; and *Detroit Free Press,* 12 March 1982, 8C.

68. *Detroit Free Press,* 21 July 1982, 7C; Reich and Donahue, *New Deals,* 246; and Chrysler Corporation, *Report to Shareholders for the Year Ended December 31, 1982,* 31.

69. Reich and Donahue, *New Deals,* 246, 248–52.

70. "Chrysler Plans Entirely New Model Line—Up by 1985: Compact K-Cars First of New Generation That Will See Even Omni/Horizon Replaced," *Automotive Fleet,* June 1980, 24–26.

71. Lenzke, *Standard Catalog of Chrysler, 1914–2000* 264–65, 286–87.

72. Moritz and Seaman, *Going for Broke,* 338; Alexander L. Taylor III, "Iacocca's Tightrope Act," *Time,* 21 March 1983, 58, 60; and Lenzke, *Standard Catalog of Chrysler, 1914–2000,* 118, 315, 501. Chrysler assembled these rear-wheel drive cars (the M-body) at Windsor, Ontario, through June 1983, then at the St. Louis assembly plant no. 2 from September 1983 through November 1986, and finally at the Kenosha, Wisconsin, plant.

73. Iacocca and Novak, *Iacocca,* 279; and "Summary, Government Guaranteed Loans," folder "Chrysler Survival," box "Loan Guarantee 1," DCHC.

74. Reich and Donahue, *New Deals,* 254–57; Iacocca and Novak, *Iacocca,* 279, 283–85; and "Summary, Government Guaranteed Loans," folder "Chrysler Survival."

75. Reich and Donahue, *New Deals,* 257–61.

76. Iacocca and Novak, *Iacocca,* 286; Reich and Donahue, *New Deals,* 261–62; and Dorin P. Levin, *Behind the Wheel at Chrysler: The Iacocca Legacy* (New York: Harcourt Brace, 1995), 80.

77. "Iacocca Remuneration since November 2, 1978," box "Iacocca 1," DCHC; Chrysler Corporation, "Notice of Annual Meeting of Stockholders and Proxy Statement," 7 June 1984, 17 May 1985, and 14 May 1986; and Gordon, *The Iacocca Management Technique,* 180–81.

78. Reich and Donahue, *New Deals,* 261–62; and Douglas Fraser, interview by author, 29 August 2000, transcript at WRL.

79. Reich and Donahue, *New Deals,* 259–60. All of the employment figures come from Chrysler Corporation, "Financial and General Fact Book," 1986, O-3.

80. Reich and Donahue, *New Deals,* 207.

81. Chrysler Corporation annual report, 1976, inside back cover; "Chrysler Corporation Facilities Fact Book," August 1979, box "Facilities, General 1," DCHC; and Reich and Donahue, *New Deals,* 209.

82. Reich and Donahue, *New Deals,* 247, for the Sperlich statement. Iacocca's comments are found in "Transcript of L. A. Iacocca's Remarks to Security Analysts, Detroit, December 1, 1983," folder "Speeches, 1983," box "Iacocca Speeches 1," DCHC.

83. "Corporate Car: Reliability History & Targets," 24 September 1979, folder "G. Butts," box "Bergmoser 2," DCHC; and conversation with H. E. Weiss, 25 July 2000.

84. Memorandum, E. W. Gaynor to J. K. Givens and J. H. Pyle, 12 October 1979; note, J. K. Givens to Gar Laux, 22 October 1979; and memorandum, J. Paul Bergmoser, president, to George F. Butts, vice president of quality, safety, and manufacturing engineering, 31 October 1979, folder "G. Butts."

85. Memorandum, J. Paul Bergmoser to George Butts, 5 November 1980, folder "G. Butts"; memorandum, "'K' Body Power Brake Improvement Changes," Stephan Sharf to H. K. Sperlich, 13 February 1981 and memorandum, "'K' Body Product/Quality Improvement Status," S. Sharf to J. Paul Bergmoser, 27 February 1981, folder "S. Sharf," box "Bergmoser 17," DCHC.

86. Andy Pasztor and Alan Bayless, "Chrysler Raises Estimate of 1980 Deficit, Discloses Waiver of Some Pollution Rules," *Wall Street Journal,* 18 March 1980; Moritz and Seaman,

Going for Broke, 97, 324–25; Chrysler Corporation, *Report to Shareholders for the Year Ended December 31, 1982,* 9; and Chrysler Corporation, "General and Financial Fact Book," January 1988, M-1.

87. Reich and Donahue, *New Deals,* 243–45.

CHAPTER 15

1. Chrysler Corporation, *Report to Shareholders,* 1982, 1983, 1983, and 1984; Bunn, *Dodge Trucks,* 270.
2. David C. Smith and Daniel F. McCosh, "Chrysler's '84 Minivan: From Inception to Expectations," *Ward's Auto World,* March 1983, 36, 40; and Brock Yates, "A Van for All Seasons: Wherein the Chrysler Corporation Reinvents Space on Wheels," *Car and Driver,* May 1983, 39–41.
3. Alexander L. Taylor III, "Iacocca's Minivan: How Chrysler Succeeded in Creating One of the Most Profitable Products of the Decade," *Fortune,* 30 May 1994, 58–59; and Iacocca and Novak, *Iacocca,* 281–82.
4. Smith and McCosh, "Chrysler's '84 Minivan 40–41, 43; Taylor, "Iacocca's Minivan," 59, 62; and "Ten Years of Leadership, 1984–1994," box "Minivan," DCHC.
5. Smith and McCosh, "Chrysler's '84 Minivan," 36, 98; Taylor, "Iacocca's Minivan," 62; and Yates, "A Van for All Seasons," 40.
6. Yates, "A Van for All Seasons," 39 and John McElroy, "1984 Chryslers: An Analysis of Success," *Road and Track,* September 1983, 97.
7. Folder "St. Louis Assembly II, Fifth Avenue," box "St. Louis II (3)," DCHC; "Chrysler, Plymouth & Dodge Minivans: 10 Years of Leadership, 1984–1994," box "Minivan" Bunn, *Dodge Trucks,* 271, 275, 179; and Flammang, *Chrysler Chronicle,* 347–99, passim.
8. Rogers National Research, *1979 National Survey of Early Model New Car Buyers,* March, 4:H-2, H-3, *1984 National Survey of Early Model New Car Buyers,* 4:H-2, H-3, and *1989 National Survey of Early Model New Car Buyers,* 3:H-2, H-3.
9. Rogers National Research, *1979 National Survey of Second Quarter New Car Buyers,* August, 4:E-5 and *1984 National Survey of Second Quarter New Car Buyers,* August, 1:B-6, B-9; Maritz Marketing Research, *1989 National Survey of Early Model New Car Buyers,* 4:B-5 and *1989 National Survey of Early Model New Truck Buyers,* 1:B-8, B-9.
10. "Ten Years of Leadership, 1984–1994"; memorandum, "Integral Child Safety Seat Research—LH Research Clinic," C. D. Hudson, manager of product research, to 68 recipients, 25 January 1989, folder "Ten Years of Leadership, 1984–1994"; and *1992 Chrysler Corporation Report to Shareholders,* 15.
11. Folder "St. Louis Assembly Plant 1, News Release, August 15, 1983," box "St. Louis II," DCHC; and Flammang, *Chrysler Chronicle,* 329, 335, 341, 347, 399.
12. "A Car Is Born," July 1985, box "LAI Press 21," DCHC; and Flammang, *Chrysler Chronicle,* 338, 341, 347, 357.
13. Flammang, *Chrysler Chronicle,* 347, 357, 364, 372, 380, 388, 399, 407.
14. Bunn, *Dodge Trucks,* 279, 282, 283.
15. Ibid., 350, 357, 364, 372, 380, 388, 399.
16. Ibid., 364, 372, 380, 388, 399, 407, 411.
17. Levin, *Behind the Wheel at Chrysler,* 234, 241–44.

18. Ibid., 315–99, passim.

19. Ibid., 88, 111, 241–42; Christopher A. Sawyer, "Marriage, Italian Style," *Autoweek,* 11 April 1988, 33, 38; and Flammang, *Chrysler Chronicle,* 364, 372, 380.

20. Lindsay Brooke, "Question Marque: Is Chrysler in over Its Head with the TC by Maserati?" *Automotive Industries,* April 1988, 34–36; Daniel Charles Ross, "Chrysler's TC by Maserati: A One-Egg Omelette," *Motor Trend,* June 1988, 60, 62; Jan A. Zverina, "Sporty TC Is No Vintage Roadster: Chrysler-Maserati Model Suffers an Identity Crisis," *Detroit News,* 5 April 1989, 1G; and "Chrysler's TC by Maserati: One Man's Diamond Is Another Man's Lump of Compressed Coal," *Road and Track,* June 1989, 101–3.

21. Levin, *Behind the Wheel at Chrysler,* 76.

22. Ibid., 91; Chrysler Corporation news release, 19 June 1985, folder "Chrysler Technologies," box "Chrysler Divisional Histories," DCHC; and Chrysler Corporation, *1986 Report to Shareholders,* 22.

23. Chrysler Corporation, *1985 Report to Shareholders,* 20–21, 40.

24. Chrysler Corporation news releases, 19 June 1987 and 20 August 1987, folder "Electrospace," box "Gulfstream 1," DCHC and *1987 Report to Shareholders,* 12, 39.

25. Lamm and Holls, *A Century of Automotive Style,* 290.

26. Chrysler Corporation, *1983 Report to Shareholders,* 6 and press releases, 16 April 1984 and 22 January 1986, box "PG, AZ 2," DCHC; and "Remarks by L. Donald Geschwind, Vice President of Program Management at Chrysler Motors, at the National Press Preview for Dodge Shadow and Plymouth Sundance, Wittmann, Arizona, January 23, 1986," box "PG, AZ 2."

27. Albert Lee, *Call Me Roger* (New York: Contemporary Books, 1988), 113–14, 242. The most complete history of Saturn is Joe Sherman, *In the Rings of Saturn* (New York: Oxford University Press, 1994).

28. "Transcript of Remarks of Lee A. Iacocca, Chairman of the Board, Chrysler Corporation, at a Meeting of the Security Analysts, Detroit, March 11, 1985," folder "Security Analysts Dinner, Detroit, Michigan, 3/11/1985," box "LAI Speeches 2, 1984–1985," DCHC; and Chrysler Corporation, *1985 Report to Shareholders,* 17.

29. Brock Yates, *The Critical Path: Inventing an Automobile and Reinventing a Corporation* (New York: Little, Brown, 1996), 63.

30. Chrysler Corporation, *1985 Report to Shareholders,* 4–5, 33; and Ernest J. Yanarella and William C. Green, eds., *The Politics of Industrial Recruitment: Japanese Automobile Investment and Economic Development in the American States* (New York: Greenwood Press, 1990), 103–16.

31. Flammang, *Chrysler Chronicle,* 372–73; "Announcement of MMC/CC Joint Venture, October 7, 1985," box "Diamond-Star 1," DCHC; joint press conference held by Lee Iacocca and Toyoo Tate, president of Mitsubishi Motors Corporation, "Announcement of the Chrysler/MMC Joint Venture, October 7, 1985," box "LAI Speeches 4, 1985," DCHC; and "Groundbreaking, April 18, 1986," box "Diamond-Star 4," DCHC.

32. Press release, "Chrysler to Concentrate on Core Business," 6 December 1989 and press release, "Chrysler Corporation Sells Gulfstream Aerospace," 13 February 1990, both in folder "Chrysler Technologies," box "Divisional Histories," DCHC.

33. Chrysler Corporation, *1990 Report to Shareholders,* 16, *1991 Report to Shareholders,* 17, and press release, "Chrysler, Mitsubishi Motors Agree to Major Restructuring of Diamond-Star Joint Venture," 29 October 1991, folder "Diamond-Star Press Information," box "Diamond-Star 1."

34. Chrysler Corporation, *1989 Report to Shareholders,* 5 and *1990 Report to Shareholders,* 1.

35. Chrysler Corporation, *Teaming Up to Be the Best! The History behind the Chrysler/American Motors Merger* (Detroit: Chrysler Motors Corporation, 1987), 20–23, 29–37.

36. George S. May, "American Motors Corporation," in May, *Encyclopedia of American Business History and Biography: The Automobile Industry, 1920–1980,* 6–8; Rae, *The American Automobile,* 211–12; Conde, *The American Motors Family Album,* 110–11; Ann M. Job, Helen Fogel, and Tim Kiska, "Chrysler May Buy Big Part of AMC," *Detroit Free Press,* 6 November 1986, 15A; Ann M. Job, "Inside the Chrysler-Renault-AMC Talks," *Detroit Free Press,* 21 November 1986, 14C; and James V. Higgins and Eric Starkman, "Proposed Chrysler-AMC Merger: End of Era?" *Detroit News,* 10 March 1987, 9A.

37. Chrysler Corporation, *1986 Report to Shareholders,* 10; Marjorie Sorge, "Kenosha Eyed for New Jeeps: Decision Could Hurt AMC's Toledo Plant," *Detroit News,* 7 January 1987, 7C; and "Wisconsin Employment Statistics," 23 January 1987, box "Chrysler/AMC 1," DCHC.

38. Jim Mateja, "UAW Concessions Sought by AMC in Chrysler Deal," *Chicago Tribune,* 11 December 1986, section 3, p. 4; letter, Richard A. Calmes, vice president of personnel and industrial relations, to Marc Stepp, director of American Motors Department, UAW, 26 December 1986, box "Chrysler/AMC 1," DCHC; and "Chrysler L-Body Contract Assembly Proposal," 9 January 1987, box "Chrysler/AMC 1."

39. Chrysler Corporation, *1986 Report to Shareholders,* 25; Levin, *Behind the Wheel at Chrysler,* 101–3; Marjorie Sorge, "Chrysler-AMC Discuss New Venture," *Detroit News,* 7 November 1986, 2E; John Bussey, "Chrysler's Miller and Bidwell Kept 'Titan' Bid for AMC from Sinking," *Wall Street Journal,* 13 March 1987, 1; Kathleen Hamilton, "Warranty: Chrysler Goes to 7/70 to Top GM, Ford," *Automotive News,* 9 February 1987, 98; William Hampton and John Rossant, "Now, for Chrysler's Next Trick . . . It Needs Strong Car Sales and a Sharp Knife to Make the AMC Deal Pay," *Business Week,* 23 March 1987, 33; and letter, Bennett E. Bidwell, vice chairman, Chrysler Corporation, to Joseph E. Cappy, president and chief executive officer, American Motors Corporation, 9 March 1987, box, "AMC/Chrysler 1."

40. Ann M. Job, "Inside the Chrysler-Renault-AMC Talks," *Detroit Free Press,* 21 November 1986, 14C; Edward Miller, "Chrysler's Deal Hailed: Talks on Deal Got Serious in Summer," *Detroit News,* 10 March 1987, 9A; Brian Gruley, "Chrysler Deal Hailed: $1 Billion Bid for AMC Is a Smart Move, Analysts Say," *Detroit News,* 10 March 1987, 6A; and Bussey, "Chrysler's Miller and Bidwell Kept 'Titan' Bid For AMC From Sinking," 1.

41. Letter of intent, Chrysler Corporation to Regie Nationale des Usines Renault, 9 March 1987, box "AMC/Chrysler 1," DCHC; Jacob M. Schlesinger and Amal Kumar Naj, "Chrysler to Buy Renault's Stake in AMC; Seeks Rest of Company," *Wall Street Journal,* 10 March 1987, 1; and Jon Lowell, "AMC Deal Shocks Execs with Decisiveness: Chrysler Comeback Enters New Phase: Merging, Marketing, Models and Mega-management," *Ward's Auto World,* April 1987, 35.

42. Letter, R. D. Headman, assistant general counsel, American Motors Corporation, to Thomas McGovern, listing representative, New York Stock Exchange, 23 March 1987; "Confidential American Motors Corporate Calendar," 18 March 1987; American Motors Corporation, proxy statement for stockholders, 2 July 1987, all found in box "Chrysler/AMC 1"; and "Presentation to the Board of Directors, American Motors Corporation, by Shearson Lehman Brothers, Inc., May 19, 1987," box "Chrysler/AMC 3," DCHC.

43. Edward Miller and Marjorie Sorge, "Chrysler, AMC Workers Feel Ax: Firings Could Grow to 4,500; Amdec Staff Is Hardest Hit," *Detroit News,* 31 October 1987, 1A, 8A; and Warren Brown, "Buyout Brings Pain to AMC: Merger with Chrysler Means Job Losses, Reassignments," *Washington Post,* 22 November 1987, 1.

44. Marjorie Sorge, "Chrysler to Lay Off 400 in Kenosha: Changes Start Next Week," *Detroit News,* 30 October 1987, 2E; Edward Miller, "5,500 Lose Jobs in Chrysler Closing," *Detroit News,* 28 January 1988, 1A, 12A; Marjorie Sorge, "Aged Facility Earns Place in Industrial History," *Detroit News,* 28 January 1988, 1F; and Marjorie Sorge, "Officials Accuse Chrysler of Breaking Word," *Detroit News,* 28 January 1988, 1F, 3F.

45. David Sedgwick and Helen Fogel, "Kenosha Deal May Give Workers Up to $10,000 Each,"*Detroit News,* 3 May 1988, 1A, 9A.

46. Chrysler Corporation, *Report to Shareholders 1987,* 24 and *1992 Chrysler Corporation Report to Shareholders,* 52–53; Bunn, *Dodge Trucks,* 262, 271, 279, 302; and Flammang, *Chrysler Chronicle,* 356.

47. Yates, *The Critical Path,* 58–61. This book considers in detail the development of the Chrysler Corporation's all-new 1996 model minivans.

48. Ibid., 36–37, 44–45, 69; and Levin, *Behind the Wheel at Chrysler,* 238.

49. Quoted in Yates, *The Critical Path,* 75.

50. Levin, *Behind the Wheel at Chrysler,* 201–3; and Yates, *The Critical Path,* 42–44.

51. Levin, *Behind the Wheel at Chrysler,* 195–203; and Yates, *The Critical Path,* 44–53.

52. Lamm and Holls, *A Century of Automotive Style,* 294; Levin, *Behind the Wheel at Chrysler,* 292; and Yates, *The Critical Path,* 67.

53. Robert A. Lutz, *Guts: The Seven Laws of Business That Made Chrysler the World's Hottest Car Company* (New York: John Wiley & Sons, 1998), 24–25; Yates, *The Critical Path,* 66; Levin, *Behind the Wheel at Chrysler,* 236–40; and Jack A. Seamonds, "Chrysler Aligns Engineering by Platform Group," *Detroit Free Press,* 6 February 1989, 3C.

54. Levin, *Behind the Wheel at Chrysler,* 254–61; and Yates, *The Critical Path,* 67–69. Dauch had earned the praise of industry observers in the mid- and late 1980s. See Darienne L. Dennis, "Lee Iacocca's Production Whiz," *Fortune,* 22 June 1987, 36–38, 42, 44.

55. "Chrysler Forms Teams in Effort to Aid Efficiency," *Detroit Free Press,* 14 January 1991, 4F; Janet Braunstein, "Chrysler Corp. Reorganizes Management Team: Developing New Vehicles Faster Is Goal," *Detroit Free Press,* 15 January 1991, 1E; "Chrysler Revamp Aimed at Product Development," *Chicago Sun-Times,* 15 January 1991, 38; and Yates, *The Critical Path,* 75–77.

56. Yates, *The Critical Path,* 77; and Levin, *Behind the Wheel at Chrysler,* 256, 275–76.

57. Levin, *Behind the Wheel at Chrysler,* 217–19; and Flammang, *Chrysler Chronicle,* 399, 415.

58. *Chrysler Corporation Report to Shareholders, 1990,* 6–15; and Flammang, *Chrysler Chronicle,* 399, 407, 411.

59. Levin, *Behind the Wheel at Chrysler,* 89–91; Yates, *The Critical Path,* 143; and Bunn, *Dodge Trucks,* 308–9. The advantages of the platform team system versus the "smokestack" system are clearly laid out in Lutz, *Guts,* 27–41.

60. Lamm and Holls, *A Century of Automotive Style,* 296–97; and Levin, *Behind the Wheel at Chrysler,* 256–57.

61. Robert E. Roach, "Chrysler Denies Shift to Suburb," *Detroit News,* 26 January 1986, 1A; Ann M. Job and Gregory Huskisson, "Chrysler to Move 5,000:; City Is Anxious," *Detroit*

Free Press, 24 October 1986, 3A; Edward Miller, "Chrysler Eyes Job Shifts: Transfers Considered to Aid Highland Park," *Detroit News,* 31 October 1986, C1; and Earle Eldridge, "Chrysler's Offer Accepted," *Detroit News,* 15 April 1987, B1.

62. Levin, *Behind the Wheel at Chrysler,* 210–11, 291–92.

63. Chrysler Corporation, *Report to Shareholders, 1988,* 6; *Report to Shareholders, 1989,* 18; *Report to Shareholders, 1990,* 19; *Report to Shareholders, 1991,* 4; *Report to Shareholders, 1992,* 3; and "Chrysler Technology Center, Auburn Hills, Michigan, Masterplan Summary," ca. 1988, box "CTC," DCHC.

64. Memorandum, Michael K. Morrison to Thomas G. Denomme, LAI Technical Center, 3 January 1989 and Memorandum, M. K. Morrison to L. A. Iacocca, Chrysler Technologies Center, 11 January 1991, box "CTC."

65. Levin, *Behind the Wheel at Chrysler,* 310–12; and "Trade with Japan and U.S. Economic Policy, Remarks by Lee A. Iacocca, Chairman of the Board, Chrysler Corporation, to the Economic Club of Detroit, January 10, 1992," box "LAI Speeches 22, 1991/1992," DCHC.

66. Barnaby J. Feder, "Blunt Talk by Iacocca, Just Back from Japan," *New York Times,* 11 January 1992, L-33, L-44; Greg Gardner, "Chrysler's Chief Blasts Japanese," *Detroit News,* 11 January 1992, 1A, 5A; "The Excuse Maker," *New York Times,* 14 January 1992, A-22; Clay Chandler, "Iacocca's Claim on Jeep Sales Questioned: More Than Japanese Red Tape Is to Blame for High Price," *Wall Street Journal,* 14 January 1992, A10; and Levin, *Behind the Wheel at Chrysler,* 308–9.

67. News release, U.S. Department of Justice, U.S. Attorney, Eastern District of Missouri, 24 June 1987, folder "Odometer Mess—1990," box "St. Louis 4," DCHC.

68. John E. Peterson, "U.S. Charges Chrysler, 2 Execs," *Detroit News,* 25 June 1987, 1A, 4A; Edward Miller, "Nader Denounced Odometer Tampering: Compensate Buyers, Chrysler Urged," *Detroit News,* 26 June 1987, 1A, 4A; Bryan Gruley, "2 Chrysler Execs Plead Innocent to Odometer Fraud," *Detroit News,* 27 June 1986, 1C; and Thomas G. Donlan, "Still a Lousy Idea: The Odometer Imbroglio Haunts Chrysler," *Barrons,* 6 March 1989, 24.

69. Chrysler Corporation press release, 24 June 1987, folder "Odometer Mess—1990"; letters, Lee A. Iacocca to Chrysler Motors vehicle owner, 1 July 1987, folder, "Odometer Mess—1990"; and "Prepared Remarks by L. A. Iacocca, Chairman of the Board, Chrysler Corporation, at a Press Conference, Highland Park, MI, July 1, 1987," box "LAI Speeches 1987," DCHC.

70. "Chrysler Settles Odometer Case," *Detroit News,* 15 December 1987, 1C; and Ron Stodghill II, "Judge Fines Chrysler on Sales Fraud: Company to Pay $7.6 million for Offering Used Cars as New," *Detroit News,* 11 August 1990, 1A.

71. Taylor, "Iacocca's Minivan," 66; Yates, *The Critical Path,* 72–74; and Paul Ingrassia and Joseph B. White, *Comeback: The Fall and Rise of the American Automobile Industry* (New York: Simon & Schuster, 1994), 201–2; and *Consumer Reports,* February 1991, 23.

72. Melinda Grenier Guiles, "Chrysler Corp. Facing Rough Stretch Again, Struggles to Cut Costs: In an Ever-Tougher Market, Firm Lacks Diversification and Rivals' Deep Pockets," *Wall Street Journal,* 29 November 1989, 1; and Alex Taylor III, "After the Departure at Chrysler . . . Gerald Greenwald Plays Down Chrysler's Problems: Impartial Observers Think He Quit at the Right Time," *Fortune,* 2 July 1990, 55.

73. Levin, *Behind the Wheel at Chrysler,* 234–35.

74. Ibid., 114–17, 120, 123–27.

75. Ibid., 212–13; Edward Miller, "Chrysler President Resigns: Wizard behind Mini-Van," *Detroit News,* 22 January 1988, 1A, 5A; Bill Vlasic, "Sperlich Put His Imprint on Auto Industry: Outspoken, Innovative Style Left Some Impressed, Others Infuriated," *Detroit News,* 22 February 1988, 1E, 2E; John Lippert, "Sperlich to Leave Chrysler Motors," *Detroit Free Press,* 22 January 1988, 12C; and Al Rothenberg, "Sperlich Speaks Out," *Ward's Auto World,* August 1989, 39, 43.

76. Wendy Zellner, "Chrysler's Next Generation: An Heir Apparent and New, Upscale Cars," *Business Week,* 19 December 1988, 52–55; and Levin, *Behind the Wheel at Chrysler,* 129, 132.

77. Levin, *Behind the Wheel at Chrysler,* 132–33, 136–37; Gregg Gardner, Janet Braunstein, and Ron Stodghill II, "Iacocca's Successor Quits: Gerald Greenwald to Join Airline: No Replacement Named," *Detroit Free Press,* 31 May 1990, 1A, 13A; "Greenwald's New Contract Reportedly Pays $9 Million," *Detroit Free Press,* 9 June 1990, 9A; and Julianne Slovak, "'The United Job Is History-Making,' Gerald Greenwald Talks about Why He Left Chrysler, the Challenge ahead at United Airlines, the Charge That He's an 'Excitement Junkie,' and the Difficulties in Saying Goodbye to Lee," *Fortune,* 2 July 1990, 53–54.

78. Levin, *Behind the Wheel at Chrysler,* 135–37.

79. Ibid., 103, 271–72, 282–85, 315–16.

80. Doron P. Levin, "Chrysler's Heirs Are More Apparent," *New York Times,* 15 January 1991, C4; and Levin, *Behind the Wheel at Chrysler,* 272, 282, 298–99, 303–6, 314.

81. Levin, *Behind the Wheel at Chrysler,* 109–0, 112–13, 273–77, 294–95.

82. Ibid., 271–72, 282–86, 296–98.

83. Ibid., 297, 300–304, 314.

84. Ibid., 315–19.

85. Keith Naughton, "Disappointed Dealers Call Lutz 'Cornerstone' of Chrysler Progress," *Detroit News,* 18 March 1992, 1E; Bradley A. Stertz and Paul Ingrassia, "How a Deadlock Led Chrysler to Go Outside for Its New Chairman: Board Turned to GM's Eaton, Rejecting Bid of Iacocca, Who Vows to Fade Away," *Wall Street Journal,* 17 March 1992, A1, A6; and Amanada Bennett and Joann S. Lublin, "Predecessor's Presence Clouds Power Transfer," *Wall Street Journal,* 17 March 1992, B1, B5.

86. Wilton Woods, "Iacocca's Last Stand at Chrysler," *Fortune,* 20 April 1992, 63–64, 68, 70, 72–73; John Templeman, "Life after Lee at Chrysler: Eaton's Cost-Cutting Skill Will Come in Handy, but Infighting May Be Fierce," *Business Week,* 30 March 1992, 24; Keith Naughton and Bradley A. Stertz, "Iacocca Quits as Chrysler Director," *Detroit News,* 3 September 1993, 1A 10A; and Joanne Miller, "Iacocca Quits Board after 'Fantastic Ride:' Free Trade Agreement May Be on His New List of Things to Do," *Detroit Free Press,* 3 September 1993, 1A, 12A.

87. Lee Iacocca and Sonny Kleinfield, *Talking Straight* (New York: Bantam Books, 1988), 54; Jay Stuller, "Lee Iacocca and an America That's Back on Its Feet," *Saturday Evening Post,* October 1984, 46–47, 105, 106, 110; and "A Spunky Tycoon Turned Superstar: Straight-Talking Lee Iacocca Becomes America's Hottest New Folk Hero," *Time,* 1 April 1985, 30–35, 38–39.

88. Lee Iacocca to Elizabeth H. Dole, secretary of transportation, U.S. Department of Transportation, 22 July 1985, box "LAI Speeches 4, 1985," DCHC.

89. "A Spunky Tycoon Turned Superstar," 35; and Iacocca, *Talking Straight,* 3–14, 169–70, 246–47.

90. "Iacocca: The Lion in Winter Talks to *Fortune*," *Fortune*, 29 August 1988, 43; "Iacocca, Lee's Parting Shots," *Fortune*, 7 September 1992, 58; and David Sedgwick, "Iacocca Goes Out in Style at Chrysler, Last Hurrah: Total 1992 Compensation Was $14.5 Million," *Detroit News*, 26 March 1993, 1A, 6A.

Chapter 16

1. Ingrassia and White, *Comeback*, 434–36.
2. Ibid., 436, 440–41.
3. Ibid., 443–46.
4. Ibid., 447–49.
5. Ibid., 450–51; and Flammang, *Chrysler Chronicle*, 407, 411, 415, 418.
6. Yates, *The Critical Path*, 71–74, 227; and Flammang, *Chrysler Chronicle*, 380, 388, 399, 407.
7. Yates, *The Critical Path*, 58, 80–87.
8. Memorandum, D. F. MacRae, manager of business planning and product research, to 38 recipients, 12 November 1991, "Driver's Side Rear Door Research," folder "Ten Years of Leadership, 1984–1994," box "Minivan," DCHC; and Yates, *The Critical Path*, 84–85, 125–26, 285–86.
9. Yates, *The Critical Path*, 96, 120–21, 134–35, 139.
10. Ibid., 199, 210–11.
11. Ibid., 221–23, 246–50, 274–76, 291; and Flammang, *Chrysler Chronicle*, 407, 411, 415.
12. Lutz, *Guts*, 49–53.
13. Ibid., 53–56.
14. Ibid., 58–60; Levin, *Behind the Wheel at Chrysler*, 110–11, 273–74; and Flammang, *Chrysler Chronicle*, 388, 399, 407, 411, 415, 418.
15. Lutz, *Guts*, 83–84; Flammang, *Chrysler Chronicle*, 418; and Bill Vlasic and Bradley A. Stertz, *Taken for a Ride: How Daimler-Benz Drove Off with Chrysler* (New York: William Morrow, 2000), 152.
16. Vlasic and Stertz, *Taken for a Ride*, 27–29; and Stephen Kindel, "Sweet Chariots: How Chrysler, Said to Be at Death's Door Just Two Years Ago, Became Detroit's Profit Leader," *Financial World*, January 18, 1994, 49.
17. Vlasic and Stertz, *Taken for a Ride*, 34–36; and Levin, *Behind the Wheel at Chrysler*, 321–23.
18. Vlasic and Stertz, *Taken for a Ride*, 71–73, 166, 182–84.
19. Ibid., 74–75, 153–54.
20. Ibid., 151, 164–65, 182–83.
21. Michelle Maynard, "Lutz: Chrysler Move Was a Last-Minute Decision," *Detroit News*, 18 September 1992, E-1; and Valerie Basheda, "Chrysler's Highland Park Offer: $90 Million," *Detroit News*, 21 November 1993, A-1, A-12.
22. Yates, *The Critical Path*, 100–102; Kindel, "Sweet Chariots," 52–53; and Chrysler Corporation, *1996 Report to Shareholders*, 8–9.
23. Yates, *The Critical Path*, 235–39, 258, 261–63, 282–83.
24. "Chrysler Board Cool to Kerkorian's Offer," *Detroit News*, 13 April 1995, 1A.
25. Vlasic and Stertz, *Taken for a Ride*, 49–50.
26. Levin, *Behind the Wheel at Chrysler*, 281, 322, 326.

27. Ibid., 227–28.

28. Vlasic and Stertz, *Taken for a Ride,* 1–16, passim.

29. Ibid., 52–58, 70.

30. Ibid., 80–85, 106–8, 199–22.

31. Ibid., 21–23, 36–40, 62–64, 95–102.

32. Ibid., 168–76.

33. Ibid., 185–94, 197–207, 219, 231–32, 238–39, 245.

34. Ibid., 270–71; and Dave Phillips, "Chrysler Board Quietly Says Goodbye," *Detroit News,* 22 May 1998, 1A, 6A.

35. Vlasic and Stertz, *Taken for a Ride,* 202, 271, 280, 338; and Rachel Konrad, "Good-Bye, Chrysler," *Detroit Free Press,* 12 November 1998, 1A, 11A.

36. Edmund L. Andrews and Keith Bradsher, "This 1998 Model is Looking More Like a Lemon," *New York Times,* 26 November 2000, BU-1, BU-11.

37. *DaimlerChrysler Annual Report, 1998,* 31–32; *DaimlerChrysler Annual Report, 1999,* 35, 37; *DaimlerChrysler Interim Report, Quarter 3, 2000,* 7, 38, 40, all found in the DCHC; Jeffrey McCracken, "A Screeching Halt: DC Slams on Brakes after Strong 5-year Run," *Detroit Free Press,* 30 January 2001, 3A; and Susan Carney, "Chrysler Reports $111 Million Profit in First Quarter," *Detroit News,* 26 April 2002, 1G.

38. Daniel Howes, "How Chrysler Lost American Leaders: Holden Ouster Shows DCX Woes are More Serious Than Thought," *Detroit News,* 15 November 2000, 1A, 5A; Andrews and Bradsher, "This 1998 Model is Looking More Like a Lemon," *New York Times,* 26 November 2000, BU-11.

39. Vlasic and Stertz, *Taken For a Ride,* 299–303, 308–9 discuss the contrasting management styles of the Germans and Americans.

40. Ibid., 277, 308–9.

41. Ibid., 182–83, 275–76, 317, 330–39.

42. Bill Vlasic and Mark Truby, "Eaton 'Did Not Have to be King,'" *Detroit News,* 27 January 2000, 9A; Andrews and Bradsher, "This 1998 Model is Looking More Like a Lemon," *New York Times,* 26 November 2000, BU-11.

43. Daniel Howes, "How Chrysler Lost American Leaders: Holden Ouster Shows DCX Woes Are More Serious Than Thought," 1A, 5A; and Susan Carnbey and Daniel Howes, "Exodus Reshapes Chrysler," *Detroit News,* 18 March 2001, 1A, 8A.

44. Bill Vlasic and Bradley A. Stertz, "Kerkorian Sues DCX for $9B," *Detroit News,* 28 November 2000, 1A, 7A and Daniel Howes and Bill Vlasic, "DCX's Legal Woes Intensify," *Detroit News,* 29 November 2000, 1B, 3B.

45. Mark Truby and Daniel Howes, "What's Next? Zetsche: 'Today is Our Turning Point,'" *Detroit News,* 30 January 2001, 1A, 8A; Daniel Howes, "Miscalculations Sowed Seeds of Today's Crisis," *Detroit News,* 30 January 2001, 4A; and Bill Vlasic and Daniel Howes, "DCX Minivan Strategy Backfired: Dealers Overloaded With Older Models," *Detroit News,* 10 December 2000, 1A, 8A.

46. Susan Carney, "Chrysler Reports $111 Million Profit in First Quarter," *Detroit News,* 25 April 2002, 1G.

Gray Motor Company, 21
The Great Detective, 147
Great Engines and Great Planes, 147
Greenwald, Gerald, 238, 246, 247, 249, 252, 265, 290, 291; leaves Chrysler, 289
Greenway, C. M., 12
Grisinger, Buzz, 120
Grumman Albatross air-sea rescue plane, 167
guaranteed loans. *See* Chrysler Loan Guarantee Act
Gulfstream Aerospace, 273, 275

Hamilton Standard propellers, 168
Hanks, Sam, 167
Harbridge House. *See Corporate Strategies of the Automotive Manufacturers*
Harris, Steve, 311
Haskell, J. Emory, 11
Haynes, Frederick J., 49, 50, 61, 62, 64, 66
H-body cars, 269. *See also* Chrysler model cars, LeBaron GTS (Grand Touring Sedan); Dodge model cars, Lancer
Heinen, Charles, 217
"hemi-head" engine, 170
Herlitz, John, 216, 312
Highland Park, Mich., 125, 284, 285, 304, 305
Hillman car, 199
Holden, James, 303, 304, 310, 312, 313
Honda Motor Company, 280
Honda Study Team, 280
Horvath, Karl, 185
House Banking Committee, 244
Household Finance Corporation, 241
Hubbert, Jurgen, 308
Hudson, Joseph L., 19
Hudson Motor Car Company, 19, 275; Detroit plant, 276; nameplate, 276
Hughes Aircraft Corporation, 273
Humber Company, 199; car, 199
Hutchinson, B. (Bernard) E. (Edwin), 25, 79, 101, 102, 103, 104, 106, 112, 130, 154, 159, 167

Iacocca: An Autobiography, 292
Iacocca, Antoinette, 235
Iacocca, Lee, foundation, 293
Iacocca, Lido (Lee) Anthony: 216, 218, 219, 233, 234, 241, 246, 247, 251, 256, 258, 261, 274, 281, 282, 301; and automotive style, 264, 272; and American Motors Corporation purchase, 277, 278; and the Chrysler Technology Center (CTC), 284–85; compensation, 236, 243, 257, 293; early life, 235; early reforms at Chrysler, 237–40; and federal loan guarantees for Chrysler, 242–44, 252, 253, 255; at Ford Motor Company, 235–36, 266; "Japan-bashing," 286, 287; and the K-cars, 248–50; and Kirkorian, Kirk, 305, 306, 307, 308; and the Loan Guarantee Board, 252, 253; and management turnover at Chrysler, 265, 288–90; and odometer scandal, 187–88; and platform teams, 297, 298; retirement, 290–91; Statue of Liberty-Ellis Island Foundation, 293
Iacocca, Mary, 257, 293
Iacocca, Nicola, 235
Iacocca Institute (Lehigh University), 293
"if you can find a better car—buy it" tag line, 240
Indiana, state of, 246
Indianapolis 500: 1926, 40; 1941, 121. *See also* racing
Industrial Designers' Institute, Gold Medal Award, 175
International Business Machines (IBM), 305
"Iron Eagle" team, 281
Irving National Bank, 35

Jackson, Roscoe, 19
Jeep CJ, 277. *See also* Jeep Grand Cherokee
Jeep Grand Cherokee, 265, 281, 282, 283, 284, 285, 317
Jeffery, Thomas B., 278
Jeffery Company, 8
Jenks, C. C., 25
Jupiter missile, 169

Kahn, Albert, 48, 136, 141
Kaiser Jeep Corporation, 275, 276
Kaiser Willys Corporation, 275
K-car: (Dodge Aries, Plymouth Reliant), 248–51, 225, 254, 255, 260, 281, 292; clones, 290, 293; "K-car" moniker, 248; platform, 254, 255, 271
Keller, Kaufman Thuma (K. T.): 79, 101, 102, 103, 106, 112, 116, 118, 119, 122, 130, 135, 147,

GREAT LAKES BOOKS

Waiting for the News, by Leo Litwak, 1990 (reprint)

Detroit Perspectives, edited by Wilma Wood Henrickson, 1991

Life on the Great Lakes: A Wheelsman's Story, by Fred W. Dutton, edited by William Donohue Ellis, 1991

Copper Country Journal: The Diary of Schoolmaster Henry Hobart, 1863–1864, by Henry Hobart, edited by Philip P. Mason, 1991

John Jacob Astor: Business and Finance in the Early Republic, by John Denis Haeger, 1991

Survival and Regeneration: Detroit's American Indian Community, by Edmund J. Danziger, Jr., 1991

Steamboats and Sailors of the Great Lakes, by Mark L. Thompson, 1991

Cobb Would Have Caught It: The Golden Age of Baseball in Detroit, by Richard Bak, 1991

Michigan in Literature, by Clarence Andrews, 1992

Under the Influence of Water: Poems, Essays, and Stories, by Michael Delp, 1992

The Country Kitchen, by Della T. Lutes, 1992 (reprint)

The Making of a Mining District: Keweenaw Native Copper 1500–1870, by David J. Krause, 1992

Kids Catalog of Michigan Adventures, by Ellyce Field, 1993

Henry's Lieutenants, by Ford R. Bryan, 1993

Historic Highway Bridges of Michigan, by Charles K. Hyde, 1993

Lake Erie and Lake St. Clair Handbook, by Stanley J. Bolsenga and Charles E. Herndendorf, 1993

Queen of the Lakes, by Mark Thompson, 1994

Iron Fleet: The Great Lakes in World War II, by George J. Joachim, 1994

Turkey Stearnes and the Detroit Stars: The Negro Leagues in Detroit, 1919–1933, by Richard Bak, 1994

Pontiac and the Indian Uprising, by Howard H. Peckham, 1994 (reprint)

Charting the Inland Seas: A History of the U.S. Lake Survey, by Arthur M. Woodford, 1994 (reprint)

Ojibwa Narratives of Charles and Charlotte Kawbawgam and Jacques LePique, 1893–1895. Recorded with Notes by Homer H. Kidder, edited by Arthur P. Bourgeois, 1994, co-published with the Marquette County Historical Society

Strangers and Sojourners: A History of Michigan's Keweenaw Peninsula, by Arthur W. Thurner, 1994

Win Some, Lose Some: G. Mennen Williams and the New Democrats, by Helen Washburn Berthelot, 1995

Sarkis, by Gordon and Elizabeth Orear, 1995

The Northern Lights: Lighthouses of the Upper Great Lakes, by Charles K. Hyde, 1995 (reprint)

Kids Catalog of Michigan Adventures, second edition, by Ellyce Field, 1995

Rumrunning and the Roaring Twenties: Prohibition on the Michigan-Ontario Waterway, by Philip P. Mason, 1995

In the Wilderness with the Red Indians, by E. R. Baierlein, translated by Anita Z. Boldt, edited by Harold W. Moll, 1996

Elmwood Endures: History of a Detroit Cemetery, by Michael Franck, 1996

Master of Precision: Henry M. Leland, by Mrs. Wilfred C. Leland with Minnie Dubbs Millbrook, 1996 (reprint)

Haul-Out: New and Selected Poems, by Stephen Tudor, 1996

Kids Catalog of Michigan Adventures, third edition, by Ellyce Field, 1997

Beyond the Model T: The Other Ventures of Henry Ford, revised edition, by Ford R. Bryan, 1997

Young Henry Ford: A Picture History of the First Forty Years, by Sidney Olson, 1997 (reprint)

The Coast of Nowhere: Meditations on Rivers, Lakes and Streams, by Michael Delp, 1997

From Saginaw Valley to Tin Pan Alley: Saginaw's Contribution to American Popular Music, 1890–1955, by R. Grant Smith, 1998

The Long Winter Ends, by Newton G. Thomas, 1998 (reprint)

Bridging the River of Hatred: The Pioneering Efforts of Detroit Police Commissioner George Edwards, by Mary M. Stolberg, 1998

Toast of the Town: The Life and Times of Sunnie Wilson, by Sunnie Wilson with John Cohassey, 1998

These Men Have Seen Hard Service: The First Michigan Sharpshooters in the Civil War, by Raymond J. Herek, 1998

A Place for Summer: One Hundred Years at Michigan and Trumbull, by Richard Bak, 1998

Early Midwestern Travel Narratives: An Annotated Bibliography, 1634–1850, by Robert R. Hubach, 1998 (reprint)

All-American Anarchist: Joseph A. Labadie and the Labor Movement, by Carlotta R. Anderson, 1998

Michigan in the Novel, 1816–1996: An Annotated Bibliography, by Robert Beasecker, 1998

"Time by Moments Steals Away": The 1848 Journal of Ruth Douglass, by Robert L. Root, Jr., 1998

The Detroit Tigers: A Pictorial Celebration of the Greatest Players and Moments in Tigers' History, updated edition, by William M. Anderson, 1999

Father Abraham's Children: Michigan Episodes in the Civil War, by Frank B. Woodford, 1999 (reprint)

Letter from Washington, 1863–1865, by Lois Bryan Adams, edited and with an introduction by Evelyn Leasher, 1999

Wonderful Power: The Story of Ancient Copper Working in the Lake Superior Basin, by Susan R. Martin, 1999

A Sailor's Logbook: A Season aboard Great Lakes Freighters, by Mark L. Thompson, 1999

Huron: The Seasons of a Great Lake, by Napier Shelton, 1999

Tin Stackers: The History of the Pittsburgh Steamship Company, by Al Miller, 1999

Art in Detroit Public Places, revised edition, text by Dennis Nawrocki, photographs by David Clements, 1999

Brewed in Detroit: Breweries and Beers Since 1830, by Peter H. Blum, 1999

Detroit Kids Catalog: A Family Guide for the 21st Century, by Ellyce Field, 2000

"Expanding the Frontiers of Civil Rights": Michigan, 1948–1968, by Sidney Fine, 2000

Graveyard of the Lakes, by Mark L. Thompson, 2000

Enterprising Images: The Goodridge Brothers, African American Photographers, 1847–1922, by John Vincent Jezierski, 2000

New Poems from the Third Coast: Contemporary Michigan Poetry, edited by Michael Delp, Conrad Hilberry, and Josie Kearns, 2000

Arab Detroit: From Margin to Mainstream, edited by Nabeel Abraham and Andrew Shryock, 2000

The Sandstone Architecture of the Lake Superior Region, by Kathryn Bishop Eckert, 2000

Looking Beyond Race: The Life of Otis Milton Smith, by Otis Milton Smith and Mary M. Stolberg, 2000

Mail by the Pail, by Colin Bergel, illustrated by Mark Koenig, 2000

Great Lakes Journey: A New Look at America's Freshwater Coast, by William Ashworth, 2000

A Life in the Balance: The Memoirs of Stanley J. Winkelman, by Stanley J. Winkelman, 2000

Schooner Passage: Sailing Ships and the Lake Michigan Frontier, by Theodore J. Karamanski, 2000

The Outdoor Museum: The Magic of Michigan's Marshall M. Fredericks, by Marcy Heller Fisher, illustrated by Christine Collins Woomer, 2001

Detroit in Its World Setting: A Three Hundred Year Chronology, 1701–2001, edited by David Lee Poremba, 2001

Frontier Metropolis: Picturing Early Detroit, 1701–1838, by Brian Leigh Dunnigan, 2001

Michigan Remembered: Photographs from the Farm Security Administration and the Office of War Information, 1936–1943, edited by Constance B. Schulz, with Introductory Essays by Constance B. Schulz and William H. Mulligan, Jr., 2001

This Is Detroit, 1701–2001, by Arthur M. Woodford, 2001

History of the Finns in Michigan, by Armas K. E. Holmio, translated by Ellen M. Ryynanen, 2001

Angels in the Architecture: A Photographic Elegy to an American Asylum, by Heidi Johnson, 2001

Uppermost Canada: The Western District and the Detroit Frontier, 1800–1850, by R. Alan Douglas, 2001

Windjammers: Songs of the Great Lakes Sailors, by Ivan H. Walton with Joe Grimm, 2002

Detroit Tigers Lists and More: Runs, Hits, and Eras, by Mark Pattison and David Raglin, 2002

The Iron Hunter, by Chase S. Osborn, 2002

Independent Man: The Life of Senator James Couzens, by Harry Barnard, 2002

Riding the Roller Coaster: A History of the Chrysler Corporation, by Charles K. Hyde, 2003

For an updated listing of books in this series, please visit our Web site at http://wsupress.wayne.edu